INVENTORS OF IDEAS

AN INTRODUCTION TO WESTERN POLITICAL PHILOSOPHY

Second Edition

DONALD G. TANNENBAUM
Gettysburg College

DAVID SCHULTZ
Hamline University

THOMSON
WADSWORTH

Australia · Canada · Mexico · Singapore · Spain · United Kingdom · United States

Executive Editor, Political Science: David Tatom

Assistant Editor: Heather Hogan

Editorial Assistant: Dianna Long

Technology Project Manager: Melinda Newfarmer

Marketing Manager: Janise Fry

Marketing Assistant: Mary Ho

Project Manager, Editorial Production: Emily Smith

Print/Media Buyer: Karen Hunt

Permissions Editor: Sarah Harkrader

Production Service and Compositor: Stratford
Publishing Services

Copy Editor: Leslie Connor

Cover Designer: Brian Salisbury

Text and Cover Printer: Transcontinental Printing/
Louiseville

Printed in Canada
1 2 3 4 5 6 7 07 06 05 04 03

For more information about our products, contact us at:
Thomson Learning Academic Resource Center
1-800-423-0563
For permission to use material from this text,
contact us by: Phone: 1-800-730-2214
Fax: 1-800-730-2215
Web: http://www.thomsonrights.com

Wadsworth/Thomson Learning
10 Davis Drive
Belmont, CA 94002-3098
USA

Asia
Thomson Learning
5 Shenton Way #01-01
UIC Building
Singapore 068808

Australia/New Zealand
Thomson Learning
102 Dodds Street
Southbank, Victoria 3006
Australia

Canada
Nelson
1120 Birchmount Road
Toronto, Ontario M1K 5G4
Canada

Europe/Middle East/Africa
Thomson Learning
High Holborn House
50/51 Bedford Row
London WC1R 4LR
United Kingdom

Latin America
Thomson Learning
Seneca, 53
Colonia Polanco
11560 Mexico D.F.
Mexico

Spain/Portugal
Paraninfo
Calle/Magallanes, 25
28015 Madrid, Spain

Library of Congress Control Number: 2002117467

ISBN 0-534-61263-6

To **Ellyn** *(and foo Allney),*
always in my heart —D.G.T.

and

To **Jim Young,**
my first political-theory teacher
and mentor —D.A.S.

BRIEF CONTENTS

Part Four POSTMODERN POLITICAL THOUGHT
AND BEYOND

CONTENTS

Part Two MEDIEVAL POLITICAL THOUGHT

PREFACE

You say you want a revolution. . . . / You say you'll change the
Constitution. . . .

—The Beatles, "Revolution," 1968

Two things fill the mind with ever-increasing wonder and awe, the
more often and the more intensely the mind of thought is drawn to
them: the starry heavens above me and the moral law within me.

—Immanuel Kant, *The Critique of Pure Reason*, 1781

The Beatles' words invoked the spirit of their time. It was a period of
change and rebellion, when young people questioned social and political
norms. Some two centuries earlier, Kant had questioned the spirit and
assumptions of his time. Kant was responding to the fundamental question
of how individuals can understand their place as human beings in an awe-
inspiring universe they did not create, and his answers provoked an upheaval
arguably as significant in the long run as those stemming from the English,
the American, or the French revolutions (see Chapters 13, 14, 16, and 18).
The quotations from the Beatles as well as Kant demonstrate that the fundamental questions of politics continue to address some of the most important
aspects of human existence.

Inventors of Ideas was written to help students see how political philosophy connects diverse aspects of human life in ways most people do not realize. It is designed for those enrolled in first courses in political philosophy and
for the professors who teach them. It can be used in conjunction with primary
sources; but it can also stand on its own as an introduction to political philosophy, as a component of an introduction to the study of political science, or
as part of a course examining the scope and methods of the discipline. Whatever the specific course content, the text is intended to be a user-friendly introduction to the subject.

The overall aim of the book is to discuss concisely the views of over thirty
major Western political thinkers in order to demonstrate how their views

about politics and society are critical to understanding the politics of our own time. It should enable students to develop a solid appreciation of how important political philosophy is, whether they want a revolution, wish to change the Constitution, or just understand the stars above and the moral law within them.

A political philosophy textbook need not be merely a channel for transmitting information from book to reader. A text can promote active learning that excites and engages students, and fosters pleasure in philosophical inquiry. It can demonstrate that philosophical study is not a hindrance to understanding or pursuing practical politics. On the contrary, for any well-educated politician or political scientist, philosophy and politics must unite, as Aristotle (Chapter 4) observed many centuries ago.

As both specialists and teachers, we are sensitive to the tension between the importance of a scholarly presentation of the subject and the needs of beginning students. Accordingly, we have written at a reading level that respects the "inventors of ideas" but makes them accessible to a wide range of intellects. Although we assume no previous background in political philosophy, we have tried to avoid oversimplification of critical ideas and issues by employing challenging terms and quotations that scholars would recommend to anyone seeking to understand the fundamentals of the field. Names, terms, and concepts that are likely to be unfamiliar to the novice are regularly identified in the text.

There are a number of strategies we have employed to foster critical thinking throughout *Inventors of Ideas*.

BROAD RANGE OF THINKERS

There will always be more philosophers than any political philosophy text can cover, but our aim is to present as broad a range of thinkers as possible, from the Greek playwrights and Plato, to Rousseau and Mary Wollstonecraft, to Karl Marx and Sigmund Freud. We hope that students will begin to appreciate the depth and breadth of the field, and that the range of thinkers will allow them not only to learn about each philosopher and his or her ideas but to explore the tensions between faith, reason, science, and skepticism that have persisted throughout the history of political thought.

KEY THEMES AND ACTIVE LEARNING STRATEGIES

Inventors of Ideas is organized around several key themes that are designed to provoke student inquiry. For instance, instructors might ask students to compare how each writer handles the ever-present, unresolved tension between valuing the individual versus supporting the collective and the way each answer influences periodic shifts in how people define the public interest. Another theme considers the difference it makes, practically as well as theoretically, whether a philosopher holds, say, a postmodern rather than a medieval view of such key values as equality and the role of government. A third theme might examine how the evolution of science has affected the power of faith to influence political affairs. And how have perceptions of women, family, and citizenship evolved over the centuries?

We address newer issues as well as many of the traditional themes taught in standard introductory courses. Gender issues, for example, are a relatively recent theme in secondary literature. Our treatment of this theme is consistent with our goal of discussing the implications of political theories for all groups of people who have received separate treatment by philosophers over the centuries. There is no anachronistic attempt to read into philosophers' motives, merely consideration of the ideas the writers themselves have introduced. By covering the same themes again and again, we challenge students to actively participate in the subject matter.

In each chapter, questions are raised that have no single answer. They are posed to invite critical thinking by the reader and perhaps serve as the basis for class discussion. Depending on each teacher's objectives, consideration of the answers may be limited to the philosopher under consideration, expanded to a comparison between several philosophers, and even discussed in light of contemporary issues and problems.

OBJECTIVITY VERSUS SUBJECTIVITY

We present each philosopher as objectively as possible, but in such limited space we cannot discuss the many alternative interpretations offered by scholars. Of course we had to make a number of subjective choices in selecting interpretations to include in the text, but the student who would transcend such subjectivity can refer to the Notes and Additional Readings at the end of each chapter, especially those references, marked with an asterisk, that present interpretations alternative to ours. Rather than being confused or put off by conflicting interpretations, students who examine one or more of them can analyze the reasons for such differences and the consequences of various interpretations for the understanding of citizenship and government as well as any particular philosopher. By so doing, they can see for themselves what a vibrant and open-ended field of study political philosophy truly is.

NEW FEATURES

It is in this spirit that we are pleased to offer this second edition. We believe the book's success is due to professors who have adopted it not only accepting its concepts and contents as a useful basis for discussing the thoughts of our inventors of ideas but also because of its approach. This approach, described more fully in Chapter 1, presents a parallel framework used by the great political philosophers through time. It shows what the "greats" have in common, and distinguishes the approaches of the ancient, medieval, modern, neomodern, and postmodern schools. This is done in a way which is both comprehensible to beginning students and which gives them a basis for a deeper understanding of the unique contributions of each philosopher. It is accomplished, not by forcing the ideas of each thinker into a straitjacket, but by showing how his or her ideas fit into what we detect and describe as a "common approach."

We have also added a new Chapter 20, which sets forth the continuing challenge of political philosophy for the future.

Inventors of Ideas **Online.** We recognize that critical thinking can be advanced by reading original philosophical works. Both the text and the quotations from primary sources therein can give students the necessary tools and confidence to tackle the originals. Our hope is that this book makes students aware of the substantial value of reading primary works and that they not only better understand them but derive substantial pleasure and benefit from so doing.

From http://politicalscience.wadsworth.com/tannenbaum2 students can access the URL Web links cited in each chapter that will take them to sites which feature these original works. This site also contains the following diagrams and charts that illustrate important concepts described in the text.

- Plato's Line: his stages of knowledge (Chapter 3)
- Aristotle: the relationship between natural political economy and communities (Chapter 4)
- Aristotle's classification of forms of government (Chapter 4)
- Hobbes's political contract (Chapter 12)
- Locke's social contract and comparison with Hobbes's political contract (Chapter 13)
- Rousseau's social contract and comparison with Locke's social contract and Hobbes's political contract (Chapter 14)
- Two voting schemes for legislative bodies: single member district and proportional representation (Chapter 17)
- Marx's stages of history (Chapter 18)

ACKNOWLEDGMENTS

A large number of people contributed to the strengths of this book. There are the many authors we have read whose insights helped us to understand more fully the ideas of the masters; many of them are cited in the references. Over the years, our students, through their questions and comments, have provoked us to rethink many points and have motivated us to write the best possible work for their successors.

The following have read all or part of the manuscript and have offered valuable advice for improving it: William Everdell, St. Ann's School, Brooklyn, N.Y.; Sugwon Kang, Hartwick College; Gary Johnson, Lake Superior State University; Christopher Kelly, Boston College; Harold Levy, University of Maryland, Baltimore County; W. Wesley McDonald, Elizabethtown College; George Menake, Montclair State University; Ellyn Schumacher; Peter Stillman, Vassar College; James Stoner, Louisiana State University, Baton Rouge; Dale Tahtinen, Michigan Technological University; and Amie Godman Tannenbaum, Gettysburg College.

We thank the following reviewers at Wadsworth Press for their comments and suggestions: Peter Lawler, Berry College; John Pottenger, University of Alabama, Huntsville; Jack Waskey, Dalton State College; and Ruth Ann Watry, Northern Michigan University. Also to those who reviewed the original edition for St. Martin's Press: Andrew Aoki, Augsburg College; Andrea Ciliotta-Rubery, State University of New York, The College at Brockport; David Freeman, Washburn University; John Gunnell, SUNY Albany; Thomas J. Hoffman, St. Mary's University; Michael Hoover, Seminole Community College; Barbara Knight, George Mason University; Bradley Macdonald, Colorado State University; Richard K. Matthews, Lehigh University; Chris McDonald, University of Georgia; Kenneth Peter, San Jose State University; John Young, Andrews University; and Edward Younkins, Wheeling Jesuit University.

Thanks also for support to Bruce Auerbach, Albright College; Susan Behuniak, LeMoyne College; Jane Bennett, Goucher College; Aryeh Botwinick, Temple University; Marla Brettschneider, University of New Hampshire; Ron Christenson, Gustavus Adolphus College; Lisa Disch, University of Minnesota; Kate Forhan, Siena College; Barbara Koziak, St. Johns University; Alan Levine, American University; Joseph Losco, Ball State University; Francis Moran III, Jersey City State College; Nancy Love, Pennsylvania State University; Lori Marso, Union College; Wilson Carey McWilliams, Rutgers University, New Brunswick; Peter O'Brien, Trinity University; Kent Rissmiller, Worcester Polytechnical Institute; Steven Salkever, Bryn Mawr College; Gordon Schochet, Rutgers University, New Brunswick; Mary Segers, Rutgers University, Newark; Sussan Siavoshi, Trinity University; Paul Stern, Ursinus College; James Ward, University of Massachusetts, Boston; and Kerry Whiteside, Franklin and Marshall College. Special thanks from D.G.T. to H. Mark Roelofs, New York University, for his counsel and understanding over the years.

We are fortunate to have two very supportive editorial folk at Wadsworth Press: our editor, David Tatom, and Heather Hogan, assistant editor. Without them, this book simply would not be.

Our collaboration has been a very positive and satisfying one. If one of the advantages of coauthorship is that each of us can contribute to strengthening the arguments of the other, then shouldn't another be that each can claim that any remaining errors or omissions must be attributable to the other's failure to point them out and suggest alternatives? To be intellectually honest, the answer must be no. We are jointly responsible for any strengths this book has but individually responsible for any shortcomings remaining in it. Finally, we welcome comments from both those who find this book a work of value and those who would suggest improvements.

ABOUT THE AUTHORS

Donald G. Tannenbaum teaches political philosophy at Gettysburg College. He is the Founding Editor of *Commonwealth: A Journal of Political Science,* has written widely for scholarly books, journals, and symposia, served as consultant to the Jacob K. Javits Fellowship Program Review Board of the U.S. Department of Education and to a number of political science departments, and been President of the Northeastern Political Science Association (1993–1994) and the Pennsylvania Political Science Association (1988–1990). Professor Tannenbaum received his Ph.D. in politics from New York University, which named him a University Honors Scholar. In 2002 he was honored with an American Political Science Association/Pi Sigma Alpha citation recognizing him for a campuswide teaching award, which he attributes, in part, to his use of this text in several of his classes.

David Schultz is professor in the Graduate School of Public Administration and Management at Hamline University, and he holds appointments as an adjunct professor of law at Hamline University, the University of Minnesota, and the University of St. Thomas. He has a Ph.D. in political science and a J.D. from the University of Minnesota. Professor Schultz is the author or editor of sixteen books and over forty articles. His most recent publications include *Leveraging the Law: Using the Courts to Achieve Social Change* (1998); *The Politics of Civil Service Reform* (1998); *It's Show Time! Media, Politics, and Popular Culture* (2000); *Encyclopedia of American Law* (2002); *Social Capital: Critical Perspectives on Community and "Bowling Alone"* (2002); and *Money, Politics, and Campaign Finance Reform Law in the States* (2002).

1

POLITICAL PHILOSOPHY: INTRODUCING THE CHALLENGE

INTRODUCTION

Suppose the government threatened to execute you if you wouldn't report your parents' religious activities. What would you do?

If one of your best friends was executed by the government for treason when you knew the friend was innocent, what would you think about the kind of justice your government offered? What might you do about it?

Imagine your government wanted everyone to conform to the same religion or economic theory simply because the leader favored it, even though this stand was not only objectionable to you but threatened a destructive civil war. What convincing arguments might you use to try to prevent that war, or to justify taking one side or the other?

What if you were fired from a high-level but nonpartisan government job after many years' service simply because a new political party came to power. What could, or would, you do to get your old job back?

Or suppose the government passed a law that you thought was immoral. Do you always have an obligation to obey the law? If you could break a law without getting caught, would you do so?

Questions such as these inspired great political philosophers from Plato to Machiavelli, Hobbes, and Locke to write. Similar questions are faced by people throughout the world today, and may well touch you personally at some point in your life.[1]

On the other hand, you may tend to think about less personal questions. Does history, the record of human life, as wretched and full of suffering as it may be for many people, have any meaning? On what basis? What is the best regime or government imaginable? Should people have absolute and total liberty to question such a government or its associated economic system? Why? What is human nature, and how do various answers to this question relate to ideas about government and the public interest?

It is good for you to think about such matters, for youth is the inheritor of the past as well as the legator of the future. This viewpoint implies a double obligation: to know the past, and to create the future. Both duties require an awareness of heritage and a source of inspiration in the present. This book provides a perspective for understanding the best the past has created and what might be done now to help secure a better future.

ORIGINS OF WESTERN POLITICAL THOUGHT

The origins of Western political thought began with Plato, who asks,

> Do you agree, then, that when we speak of a man as having a passion for a certain kind of thing, we mean that he has an appetite for everything of that kind without discrimination? . . .
> So the philosopher, with his passion for wisdom, will be one who desires all wisdom, not only some part of it.[2]

Aristotle tells us that the search for wisdom, the wellspring of philosophy, begins with wonder.[3] Historical evidence indicates that organized political societies, a sense of wonder, and the search for wisdom existed before there were philosophers.[4] Long ago people held beliefs about such things as authority, justice, and obedience. Evidence of these beliefs is found in a number of written and oral sources that constitute the traditions of ancient peoples: myths, sagas, and folklore, from the Old Testament and Viking legends to Greek poets and playwrights.

Recorded, systematic philosophy by individual thinkers, however, appears to have begun in the West with the ancient Greeks. Someone, probably Socrates (c. 469–399 B.C.E.), originated the philosophic idea of the psyche, or soul.[5] This idea implies that humans have a higher purpose in life than mere existence or the satisfaction of physical (bodily) appetites. The most basic questions of philosophy from then until now have been, what is this higher purpose, and how can it be achieved? The basic question of political philosophy stems from these queries: What should the role of government be in helping humans achieve their higher purpose? In answering this and related questions,[6] political philosophers make qualitative distinctions between good governments (those that help) and bad governments.[7]

Political philosophy is not simply an abstract exercise. Ideas do matter. They serve as weapons to question, to probe, to challenge, and even to justify authority. Throughout history, political philosophers such as Socrates, Martin Luther, and John Locke have been persecuted, even executed, by political authorities for the ideas they espoused. Their ideas were a threat because political philosophies represent alternative ways of understanding the world, describing relations between people, governments, religions, families, and members of society. Thus political philosophy is a living tapestry of hope, loss, and struggle over ideas and their political consequences.

This is not to say we can fully know the consequences of following any set of coherent ideas, any more than we can necessarily know the results of a political action. For example, laws to reduce poverty can result in a more impoverished population. Actions taken to stop terrorism have led to increased terrorist activity. However, we can reasonably anticipate some results of political ideas. For example, if only dictators are praised, how can we expect democracy to result? If we do not challenge oppression, how can freedom flourish? But if the values of democracy and freedom are available, they become possible options.

COMMON TREATMENT, DIVERSE RESULTS

Although they write independently of each other, political philosophers are usually familiar with the work of their predecessors. This familiarity results in treatment of common major themes. The commonality among philosophers is reflected in several key areas, and this book examines several of them.

First, philosophers consider the political *crisis,* or set of problems in their own time that motivated them to write. The crisis may represent a challenge to the current political order from a foreign or domestic force, a decline seen in society, or even an intellectual threat from a detested set of religious, political, or economic ideas. In response to each crisis they offer philosophical answers, asking, in effect, what should I (or we) do, and why?

Second, philosophers each present a personal *methodology,* or method of thinking about politics. Methodology includes a view of reality, a set of assumptions about society, and a definition of the world that is, to each philosopher, both reasonable and universal in that it applies to all people, everywhere, despite the fact that the methodology differs among writers. Moreover, each philosopher asks how we can justify political solutions. Can political truth be demonstrated rationally, or must truths be accepted on faith? Are there really any truths upon which all of us can agree? In short, philosophers wonder how to approach each problem they would help resolve and how to justify their solution.

Third, they present their individual views of *human nature,* or what are people really like? Here they typically go beyond the question of whether human nature is simply "good" or "bad" to a more complex analysis that involves discussion of a higher purpose. For example, definitions of human nature can lead to valuing the individual over the collective, or vice versa, or into questions of whether humans are naturally peaceful but have been corrupted by society. Questions about human nature can consider whether we are essentially rational or motivated primarily by passions, and what difference it makes if either is true. They even include whether there is in fact a human nature that is constant and predictable. Furthermore, is the nature of men and women the same, and if not, how does this belief influence their ideas about social order? Perhaps the "best" should rule and the rest should obey, in which case philosophers then ask who are the "best" and what counts in measuring that quality.

Finally, philosophers present a version of the proper role of government in dealing with the crisis or set of problems they have identified. What is in the public interest in this case? What sort of response is best for people faced with such critical issues? Views of the public interest are based on each writer's methodology and theory about human nature, including, of course, discussion about the forms, organization, structure, and offices of government. This theme also involves the relationship of government to things that may be considered nongovernmental, such as economics, religion, education, social class, the family, and sometimes even the proper geographic setting for government.

But if their work reflects a fairly common treatment of certain issues, philosophers neither emphasize those issues equally, nor in the same detail, nor do they reach like conclusions. If their results were even close to each other's, there would be little point in studying so many philosophies. In fact, what makes them so interesting, and ultimately useful, is the diversity of their approaches and conclusions.

We can appreciate the value of such diversity when we reflect that we are all born into a culture that gives us an official version of reality. It takes a long time for most people to discover that we have absorbed but one possible version, and that our version cannot be fully examined, much less changed, unless we have alternative visions or ideas. So, beyond any intrinsic interest humans might have in solving puzzles, by contemplating and comparing diverse ideas, the study of political philosophy can offer several visions for our consideration and action.

On one level, philosophers tell us something about their culture, the problems they faced, and the immediate solutions they offered. But on another level, they may make observations that transcend their particular situation, addressing problems that persist even today. Sophocles' play *Antigone*, for example, speaks to the problem of reconciling conflicting duties to family, religion, and political society. St. Thomas Aquinas and St. Augustine write about church–state issues, or the proper relation between religion and government. Plato and Aristotle address the questions of who is the most fit to rule and what is the best way to order society. John of Salisbury and John Locke write on such issues as the limits of political power and how much control a government should have. And Aristophanes' play *Lysistrata*, Mary Wollstonecraft, Friedrich Nietzsche, and John Stuart Mill break new ground in addressing the role that women should have in society.

By answering these broad questions, any philosopher's work can serve as a key to revealing your own values and beliefs. As you read this book, ask yourself which ideas you find really interesting and true, and why. What relevant experiences do you know for yourself? What, in fact, are your political experiences? However unimportant those experiences may seem at first, they help form the basis of your own political philosophy. And forging your ideas on the philosophers' anvil enables you to make the fullest use of them, particularly when you and your society face a political crisis.

COMPARING POLITICAL PHILOSOPHERS

Once we understand the views of the individual philosophers in the context of their times, we are ready to compare different philosophers' ideas. We can do so by examining similarities and differences in concepts, or what each means by the terms *human nature, justice, equality,* and so forth. But beyond philosopher-by-philosopher comparisons, the views of groups of philosophers may be summed up by categorizing them according to consistent patterns found in Western political philosophy. Philosophers are often characterized by whether they are "ancient," "medieval," "modern," or "postmodern."[8] These labels can be used in a number of ways, one of which is related to a major theme of this book: the roles of reason and science in political philosophy. A few examples illustrate differing perspectives on this theme.

> For you have been told that the highest object of knowledge is the essential nature of the Good, from which everything that is good and right derives its value for us. . . . So the order of our commonwealth will be perfectly regulated only when it is watched over by a Guardian who does possess this knowledge. (Plato, an ancient philosopher)[9]

> The City of God of which we are treating is vouched for by those Scriptures whose supremacy over every product of human genius does not depend on the chance impulses of the minds of men. (St. Augustine, a medieval thinker)[10]

> Human knowledge and power meet in one. (Francis Bacon, very much a modern)[11]

> Since Copernicus, man seems to have got himself on an inclined plane—now he is slipping faster and faster away from the center into—what? into nothingness? (Nietzsche, a postmodern)[12]

More specifically, this book looks at the roles that science and reason, as well as faith and other forms of knowing, play in defining and justifying political knowledge. Central concerns are: What arguments and evidence do thinkers offer to support their political philosophy? Does political truth exist, and if so, how do we know it? If there is no truth, or if we cannot know it, does that mean there is no right or wrong? These questions are critical to all political philosophers.

If faith and belief have often been invoked to support political claims, so too have science and reason. The earliest development of science stemmed from observations of the heavens by peoples in prehistoric times and in the ancient Near East, Egypt, and Mesopotamia. But it was the advance of science in the Greek world that coincided with the development of philosophy.[13]

Science may be defined as systematized knowledge of the physical world that is gained through the process of observation (or, more recently, experimentation). In ancient Athens, early scientific thinkers rejected mythological explanations of physical events involving the personal intervention of gods in human affairs. Instead they preferred accounts that focused on natural causes and reasons, leading Democritus to develop his atomic theory and Hippocrates of Cos to the origins of medicine.

Scientific discoveries led some thinkers to conclude that they could improve their lives by applying their natural reasoning powers to dealing with human problems, including those involving political matters. They used both reason and science to ask penetrating questions about metaphysics (what is real?), epistemology (how do we know what we know?), ethics (how should we act?), and methodology (what is the best method for answering these questions?). The specific responses of individual philosophers to these questions are treated in later chapters, but methodology, or a philosopher's method of thinking about political questions, can illustrate how different writers apply reason, science, and faith to reach conclusions about political problems, and how these writers can then be labeled and compared.

The method of many of the *ancient* political philosophers from Plato to Cicero can be described as idealism. Idealism means that high ideals, or what we would call abstract principles, such as justice, truth, virtue, and reason, are regarded as real entities. To say they are real means that they are more important than, and take priority over, objectives regarded as of lesser value, such as wealth, power, or getting popular support. For Plato and other ancient, or classical, writers, reason can be used to discover certain real truths or ideas that serve as the basis for political knowledge.

From St. Augustine on through the Middle Ages, most Christian writers reflected a *medieval* outlook, believing that religious faith and the Bible were the sources of all important knowledge. These writers can be described as theo-idealists, as they reconciled ancient pagan idealism with medieval Christian belief by placing idealism in the service of faith rather than reason. To them, God in heaven is both real and the embodiment of all other ideal values. Accordingly, the highest human objective for theo-idealists is heavenly salvation, and even in the political arena this objective takes precedence over lesser and apparently more practical earthly objectives, such as wealth, political influence, physical strength, and even secular wisdom. The theo-idealist orientation influenced such early modern thinkers as Luther and Calvin.

The moderns are a diverse group ranging from early modern through neo-modern to late modern philosophers. The *early moderns,* from Machiavelli on, are materialists and oftentimes empiricists or rationalists. To them, material values take precedence over any interest in ideals or salvation, and these values become apparent either through our senses by way of empirical knowledge, or through our mind and rational analysis. For moderns, "otherworldly" objectives are seen as inferior, if not completely without merit. For Machiavelli, questions of ethics are severed from political considerations, and the active replaces the contemplative. On the other hand, early moderns embrace certain values that had previously been subordinated or rejected by both ancient and medieval political philosophers. Such values as political power, wealth, physical pleasure, progress through scientific and technological discovery, and earthly contentment are considered the highest goals people can seek. The method of early moderns, including Hobbes, Locke, Bacon, and Descartes, links material priorities to goals by appealing to a more practical reason, a more empirical analysis, than the ancients would approve of. These writers then create artificial political entities, or governments, that enable them to gain their material objectives.[14]

Later critics of these modern materialists include Hume and Kant, Burke and Rousseau, and Hegel and Marx. They challenge many prior assumptions about knowledge and truth, suggesting that they are neither as certain nor as exact as the moderns think. To these *neomodern* critics, modern materialism is a necessary but temporary objective which must be replaced as a method and goal if we are to realize our true humanity.[15] The neomodern method represents a return to a form of the idealism of the ancients, but it is based on human passion rather than reason. It is this combination of idealism and emotionalism that marks their special outlook, not just their criticism of the early moderns.

Late moderns, such as Jeremy Bentham and John Stuart Mill, return to the reason of the early moderns, but their outlook is tempered by such critics as Hume and Kant. Reacting to that criticism, they alter modern thought by attempting to reconcile materialism with other human values. In so doing, they reject certain earlier rigidities, such as natural law, natural rights, and contract theories.

The final group of thinkers we consider includes the *postmodern* philosophers, beginning with Nietzsche. The method of the postmoderns is essentially skeptical and critical toward reason, taking the stance that none of the methodological or other certainties of any of their predecessors, from Plato onward, fits the world as it is today. They refute the idea that there has been any forward movement or progress throughout human history, much less in the ideas presented by political philosophers. Consequently, they urge us to criticize and even reject everything that we have received from the past, and to replace it with an ever-changing, ever-evolving approach that is fragmented, inconclusive, playful, without any sense of seriousness, and that ultimately transposes our current philosophical exhaustion of (and with) ideas "into a heterogeneity of local impulses."[16] In some ways, postmodern methodology represents a return to Socrates of ancient Athens, who questions everything and requires that people defend their beliefs against his inquiries as the only means to genuine knowledge of the truth, which may only turn out to be that we know nothing with any certainty. But it also reminds us of the supreme value of reason, of the importance of thinking as well and as carefully as possible when formulating political goals.

As you read about the different philosophers, ask how they justify arguments. Ask also what sources they appeal to when defending their claims, and what goals and assumptions their political philosophies adopt. Note that in each era certain approaches and assumptions seem dominant, tying the different philosophers of each period together, and contrasting them with those of earlier or later traditions of political thought.

THE INDIVIDUAL AND THE COLLECTIVE

In his tribute to modern liberty, John Stuart Mill said,

Mankind can hardly be too often reminded that there was once a man called Socrates, between whom and the legal authorities and public opinion of his time there took place a memorable collision. . . . This acknowledged master of all the eminent thinkers who have since lived . . . was put to death by his countrymen, after a judicial conviction, for impiety and immorality.[17]

This is but one poignant illustration of a basic problem that the human condition imposes on us, one with important political consequences. All great Western political philosophers recognize a conflict between the claims of two demanding entities: the individual and the collective.[18] Some philosophers have given prominence to the importance of individual interests, and others have emphasized the collective good, providing us with two useful comparative labels: individualist and collectivist.

The conflict between the individual and the collective has also been termed the problem of the one and the many. Others speak of the Judeo-Christian dilemma of "I" and "thou," the existential conflict between the "self" and the "other," or the civil war in the human spirit between anarchy and conformity.[19]

Whatever it is called, this conflict is central to the Western political tradition, and no great philosopher favors just one side. The question is, which is more important to produce the best results for both sides? To date no thinker has resolved this to the satisfaction, and exclusion, of all other contenders.

Putting the individualist or collectivist label on the major writings of philosophers may distort the uniqueness of their total perspective, since the great philosophers do to some extent take into account the claims of both sides. They may express in their writings certain concepts that contradict the overall label given to them. Thus calling certain writers individualists should be seen as a statement that the major emphasis of their works makes this a useful label for comparing them with others, not that they necessarily express only individualist thoughts in all aspects of their philosophies.

Those philosophers who favor the dominance of the collective typically depict society as an organism. In an organic society, the individual is related to the collective as the organs (e.g., the heart or liver) are related to the body. They are organically interdependent, and it is as foolish to talk of personal happiness or individual rights against the collective as it is to consider the rights of the liver against the body. Thus, they believe that the public interest is to be found in an *organic politics* that puts the welfare of the whole above its parts.

On the other hand, writers who support the priority of the individual over the collective see society as an aggregation, or sum of its diverse parts. For them, the public interest is the outcome of *aggregate politics*, in which summing individual choices produces a majority position that determines who leads the government and which policies are worth implementing.

FAMILY AND GENDER ROLES

One criticism leveled against studying many of the great political philosophers is that they often ignore or pointedly exclude women, various racial and ethnic minorities, and (usually lower) social classes from the political process. This book examines the basis for such criticism as it applies to one or more categories of people within the context of each philosopher's views, such as Aristotle's treatment of slavery, and Marx's ideas on the role of class. For now, three examples of writings on the nature and roles of men and women can suffice to introduce the basis for such criticism.

> It is thus clear that while moral goodness is a quality of all persons . . . temperance—and similarly fortitude and justice—are not . . . the same in a woman as they are in a man. [These qualities of a man are shown in commanding, of a woman in obeying] (Aristotle)[20]

> Wives, be subject to your husbands, as to the Lord. For the husband is the head of the wife as Christ is the head of the church, his body, and is himself its savior. As the church is subject to Christ, so let wives also be subject in everything to their husbands. (New Testament)[21]

> Man's happiness is, I will. Woman's happiness is, He will. (Nietzsche)[22]

Comparison of Roles and Natures of Men and Women. If one dualism that marks out Western political thought is individual and collective, another with clear political significance is male and female. The roles of men and women, and collaterally of the family, are a direct concern of many contributors to political theory, and implied in the thought of the others. In the societies of most of the philosophers, men effectively dominated the political process, just as the rich often controlled the poor and masters ruled slaves. Even though the great philosophers questioned some central assumptions of their societies, they accepted others. Most of these writers are male, and the relationship they define between the sexes is often hierarchical, either reflecting their explicit position or implying that it is proper for men to dominate women. For many ancient and medieval writers, especially, the idea of the feminine is used as a principle that assigns women a subordinate political role and sees them as objects created to satisfy masculine needs. For a number of moderns, the feminine principle is negative, symbolically representing the softer province of ancient philosophy; in practice it serves as a basis for excluding women from politics.

As one perceptive writer has suggested, masculine domination may be indicated in several ways.[23] It might be explicit, wherein because of her assumed feminine nature, female is subjected to male. Women in this case are given an important role in society, but one judged fitting their special, and different, nature. They are considered weak, pliant, emotional, and born for tasks associated with domestic and reproductive activities. Men, on the other hand, are naturally rational, tough, and best fit for tasks in the larger society and government. They are the ones born to be decision makers, politicians, and warriors. The status of women is subordinate, but it is natural that they occupy such a position and therefore it should not be considered in any way cruel or despotic. Indeed it is beneficial for both women and society that they occupy such a position. Such explicit domination of women by men is championed by writers from Aristotle onward, although there are notable exceptions and challenges to this view throughout history.

Advocacy of sexual domination may also be implied from the remarks of philosophers perhaps not directly intended to address gender issues but nevertheless having political consequences that are different for men and women. Hobbes, for example, might hold that his remarks on marriage and the family neither have nor intend any gender bias. He might even argue that he has no need to address gender issues because gender seems unrelated to his central concerns. But since he makes remarks that do have gender-related political significance, for both his time and ours, that significance and its consequences deserve discussion as much as any other key aspect of his political philosophy.

In addition, implicit support for sexual domination may even be found among writers who seem to advocate explicitly the reverse. Thus a group of political philosophers, beginning with Plato, propose gender equality; but if their proposals are examined closely, it becomes apparent that many of them imply such equality only for women who exhibit qualities associated with maleness. Those women who are to enjoy equal status with men are expected to subordinate any tendencies associated with feminine behavior, from emotion to reproduction, in favor of such male characteristics as toughness and self-denial.

As current debates over gender equality and roles make us aware, some people believe that ideas supporting masculine domination represent obvious truth and others vehemently disagree. But even for those who dissent, there is still value in reading such philosophies, namely that they are important in defining Western intellectual tradition. Even if one rejects some ideas as biased and outmoded, it is important to know what these ideas are because they are so important in delineating many issues crucial to feminist thought today (if only by negative example).

In sum, the interplay between the masculine and the feminine influences the roles assigned to men and women in each thinker's overall philosophy. And these perceived differences affect the relationship between family and government the philosophers prescribe.

Role of the Family in Political Thinking. Yet another dualism in Western political thought is that of public and private. These concepts have a number of meanings and implications, but for our purposes, the private domain means family and kinship relations, while the public domain is political society.[24] The central issue is how the public and private interrelate and reinforce one another, specifically, how the structure of the family provides an example of the way political society should be organized. For example, some political thinkers justify a political monarchy by arguing that if a man is the head of the family, then one person should be the head of the government.

Throughout Western political thought, the concept of the family has been critical to political philosophy.[25] At times, it has been described as the first political society and the basis of politics; in other cases, as a realm of domesticity that stands in opposition to the political sphere. Notice as you read how the family is defined and invoked to serve political goals, as well as whether the family is viewed as natural, what roles men and women have in the family, and what roles men and women have in politics. Ask yourself how important the family is to each political philosophy, how persuasive the case is for the roles of men and women in the family, and in what ways those roles are an example of how we define political authority.

DEVELOPMENT OF POLITICAL PHILOSOPHY OVER TIME

Political philosophy presents and judges beliefs or values; it gives reasons for accepting some and rejecting others. In most societies, prevailing beliefs often remain unchallenged for long periods of time. Although the aim of any official version of reality is to stabilize a society, this is especially true in traditional cultures, where the folkways of the social group (e.g., a clan, tribe, or village) are considered "right" without any need for justification. They are immune from questioning in part because the ideas are protected by sanctioned guardians such as high priests or witch doctors. A need for justification usually arises when some crisis or other event provokes questions about beliefs previously taken for granted. If such questioning gives rise to new values that clash with old, accepted traditions, a political crisis emerges. Societies have faced such crises time and again, particularly when undergoing change. An example is socioeconomic change, as when the gap widens between the rich and the poor. Or it may be military, as when a political entity gains or loses an empire. On rare occasions, a single event triggers a philosopher's rejection of an entire society, as when Socrates' trial and execution led Plato to question the whole moral order of the Athenian democracy of his day, especially its notion of justice. Similarly, in the case of Sigmund Freud, the coming of the Nazis in the 1930s prompted him to argue that civilization and culture threatened human existence.

Repeated crises can even lead to an almost total shift in perspective. As new beliefs arise that conflict with old ones, philosophers try to reconcile them. If this is not possible one option is to reject the old beliefs as outdated and useless and wholeheartedly embrace the new. This is, for example, what Plato did to Athenian democracy and what the moderns did to the medieval perspective.

Another approach, however, rejects new values as too threatening to a way of life that is held dear. The old beliefs, and the government based on them, become sacred cows that must not be challenged or even closely examined. This was the response of the Athenians to Socrates' inquiries. A third approach attempts to reconcile the old and the new so that they are philosophically compatible with one another. This is, in part, how Aristotle responded to Plato's ideas, and Locke to Hobbes. Thus by selectively reconciling different approaches, one can agree with some values advanced by philosophers without necessarily accepting their every idea.

TECHNIQUES FOR RECONCILING CONFLICT BETWEEN BELIEFS

Efforts to reconcile philosophical conflicts seek to clarify, to bring out the underlying meaning of values or beliefs and determine how and where they clash. First, note that political philosophers can write on at least two distinct levels: the philosophical and the institutional. These should not be confused. On the philosophical level, writers deal with abstract ideas about human nature; the purpose of government; the roles of society, religion, and the family; and values such as power, justice, and freedom. These ideas are important to an overall definition of society, and they influence the institutional recommendations a philosopher makes. But at the institutional level, political philosophers discuss more concrete matters, such as the political process (e.g., who should pick political leaders and how, and the way in which legitimate decisions should be made), geographic concerns (optimum size or population of the polity), relationships between the territorial parts (unitary, federal), and specific individual rights. Some writers recommend a rather limited set of specific institutions (e.g., Plato in *The Republic*), while others offer a number of alternatives (such as Aristotle's detailing a variety of forms of government).

Descriptive and Prescriptive Statements. On the philosophical level, we need to distinguish between descriptive and prescriptive statements about the political world. Generally speaking, descriptive statements tell us what "is," while prescriptive statements tell us what "should be." Sometimes, however, it is not so easy to distinguish between the two kinds of statements because the sentence structure of both can be the same.[26]

Take, for example, the statement, "All men are created equal." In grammatical form it resembles the descriptive statement, "All men in this room are over sixteen years of age." But to treat the former as a descriptive statement can lead (and has led) to a great deal of confusion and wasted energy. A popular criticism of the writings of political philosophers is that they make many vague, subjective statements from which we can derive no specific conclusions—or from which we can infer almost anything. Such criticism is voiced rather stridently by those who treat such statements as "All men are created equal" as descriptive. They become angry and frustrated, asking how can we in fact find out, or measure, whether the statement is true without a more precise definition of *equal*.

Such a view assumes that confirmation can be based on determining whether *equal* refers to intelligence, wealth, occupation, gender, race, religion, some other criterion, or combination of criteria; and that this will enable an observer to scientifically verify or reject the statement. But when applied to the writings of political philosophers, this assumption is irrelevant, for their writings make clear that when they assert "men are . . ." (or perhaps more appropriately, "humans are"), they are positing something about human nature. Thus, like other philosophical statements about human nature, "All men are created equal" is not a descriptive statement. It cannot be treated as a scientific proposition and then "proven" right or wrong by defining *equal* and then observing people or collecting facts. Rather, it is prescriptive.[27] It is a value statement or moral recommendation answering such philosophical questions as what our primary goal should be, how we should be treated, and how society should be organized to enable us to reach that goal. In other words, the statement is a kind of shorthand that ought to be translated as a moral prescription: All humans should be treated as if they are equal so that they may reach their goals in life. Or, alternatively, to help your fellows gain their true ends, treat them as if they are equal, despite apparent differences, and organize political and other relevant institutions (i.e., social, economic) on that basis.[28] Understanding the prescriptive purpose of philosophical statements can lead us to recognize that each writer asks readers to view or understand reality in one particular way and to act on this vision— but without denying the realities of our senses or science.

Concept Clarification. The next step in reconciling philosophical conflicts is to expose their underlying meaning through concept clarification. This exercise must be done by remaining as objective and unbiased as possible, always trying to view the issues through the mind of the philosopher. Concept clarification requires that we look at ideas such as justice or equality in their abstract or general form. "All men are created equal" is a moral prescription, as we have seen, but depending on who recommends it, the statement may apply to a vague sort of equal opportunity, to political equality (one person, one vote), or even to some kind of social or economic equality (among other things). Concept clarification removes the recommendation from the realm of mere rhetoric, which may make people feel good but means little.

Another example pointing to the need for concept clarification is the term *democracy*. One generally accepted meaning of *democracy* is a state in which rulers are chosen by popular election. But how do we understand a philosopher who recommends a system we call a dictatorship—where no rulers are chosen by popular election—and claims that his government is a "people's democracy"? We need to inquire about what he means, whether his recommendation is truly democratic, and ultimately what *democracy* means.

Concept clarification also requires looking at ideas as they relate to their historical context, or the times in which they were written, since philosophers wrote to influence their contemporaries. Context includes the lives of the philosophers as well as the economics, politics, society, and institutions of their age. For example, had Plato never personally known Socrates, he still might have written a profound work of political philosophy, but one that would have been vastly different from the *Republic*. However, understanding philosophers within the context of their times does not mean their ideas are not relevant to our times; this is confusing biographical motivation with philosophical recommendation. So, although we can trace Plato's great concern for justice back to Socrates' fate and thereby understand its source more fully, this is a different matter from what Plato meant by justice. Plato, and his successors, did write about their personal experiences in order to influence their contemporaries, but the larger questions they tackled and the recommendations they made are of perennial and universal value. The one does not preclude the other.

CONCLUSION

With his usual discernment, American writer Henry David Thoreau identifies several of the central issues of political philosophy:

> Unjust laws exist: shall we be content to obey them, or shall we endeavor to amend them, and obey them until we have succeeded, or shall we transgress them at once? . . . Why does [government] always crucify Christ, and excommunicate Copernicus and Luther, and pronounce Washington and Franklin rebels?[29]

Political philosophers respond to questions about actual human problems or conflicts in their societies that they view as related to government. The long tradition of Western political philosophy emerges from their examination of these political problems and their need to react to and even displace old, established theories.

By creating new theories, political philosophers present a fresh set of recommendations to guide peoples' political behavior, prescriptions based on beliefs that are as explicit and coherent as possible. Speaking in inherited language, they develop and expand that language, inventing the vocabulary we use to organize our political life and recommending that we follow the values they favor. Thus the tradition of Western political philosophy represents the continuing effort to change human thought about the political world in order to lead people to a better society.

The philosophers discussed in this book move beyond the narrow or specific problems facing their own societies to generalize about broad issues with relevance for a universal audience. Challenging both their society and ours, they transcend time. Whatever the content of the message, each provides a comprehensive vision, a new perspective for dealing with problems in a changing world. Every one may be regarded as a genuine revolutionary with a pen, speaking with greater force, clarity, wisdom, and comprehensiveness than most of us can muster. In so doing, they often "converse" with each other as well as with us.

The level of abstraction at which philosophers write, although sometimes difficult for the beginner to understand, is important for promoting such conversations; without it they might simply remain time-bound popularizers of narrow problems and solutions for their contemporaries. This, they most assuredly are not. The ideas they originally developed to meet the problems of their time can be applied, within limits, to situations they could never have anticipated. For example, the ideas of nineteenth-century writer Karl Marx have been adapted to a number of different twentieth-century situations and societies. Despite the collapse of several regimes established by the former Soviet Union and based (some would argue improperly) on Marx's ideas, there are those who believe his writings are still relevant for our world. The same might well be said of any of the great political philosophers.

Because political philosophy develops through the interaction of conflicting beliefs, the style of writing is often argumentative. We may, for example, see Rousseau conversing with but opposed to Locke, or moderns rejecting ancients. However, such opposition is not the reader's only possible perspective. Another might be found in the ancient Indian tale of the blind men and the elephant (which is in its way another commentary on human nature). The story has many versions, but one is that a wealthy lord recruits a number of blind people and asks each to describe an elephant, using only their sense of touch. One man feels the trunk and says the elephant is like a snake. Another touches its tail and describes the animal as a rope. A third paws its side and proclaims that an elephant is like a wall. Of course an elephant is each of these, and more. Thus we might view each philosopher as adding a valuable new perspective to our understanding of the complex thing called human progress.[30]

The category of human progress has numerous subcategories, one of which is political progress. Progress may be said to occur to the extent that the many are freed from the arbitrary, irrational, tyrannical control of the few. In the case of Western political philosophy, this change comes about when people act on ideas which lead to the replacement of political (and economic) power of the stronger by controls on such elites. This in turn opens up the creative potential of many more people in ways that promote greater individual and social happiness.

Another aspect of political progress emerged with the rise of democratic governments. Philosophers since Plato have recognized the need to protect the liberty of the few individuals and minority groups that dissent from majority opinion but are then threatened by power-hungry mobs seeking to directly suppress the peaceful expression of that dissent, or have government do so.[31]

Political progress does not always move forward in an inevitable direction, but follows an uneven, uncertain, at times reversible path. From this perspective, the twentieth century may, on balance, appear to reflect backsliding rather than progress.[32] Today it often seems that political power works for the forceful few, who leash the many to destructive forces, some threatening elimination of the human race as a whole. In the past, new political philosophers have emerged to help redirect human progress forward before humankind has been extinguished. Will it happen again? To recognize what is new, when and if it appears, requires first being aware of what is old.

What follows is designed to introduce you to the old, and thus help you see how far we have come and prepare you for the new. As you read about each philosopher, consider which ideas resonate best for you as an individual, and how you might interrelate them to form the basis of your own political philosophy. Ask: In what ways does that philosophy use and improve on the views of past thinkers? Of the major problems we face today, which are (or are not) addressed by such a philosophy?

Notes

1. See the latest annual reports of such independent groups as Freedom House or Amnesty International.

2. Plato, *The Republic of Plato,* trans. F. M. Cornford (London: Oxford University Press, 1972), 475b.

3. Aristotle, *Metaphysics,* ed. J. Warrington (London: J. M. Dent, 1956), A. c. 2, 982 b 17.

4. See Elman Service, *The Origins of the State and Civilization* (London: Methuen, 1975); and Nicholas Postgate, *The First Empires* (Oxford: Elsevier, 1977).

5. W. K. C. Guthrie, *Socrates* (New York: Cambridge University Press, 1971); see also Alfred Taylor, *Socrates: The Man and His Thought* (Garden City, N.Y.: Doubleday, 1953). A prephilosophical concept of the soul was advanced in ancient Egypt.

6. Related questions include: Why do people enter society? What makes authority legitimate? How should government be organized? And how can we define or discover the public interest, which is the source of public policy, or the laws, actions, and decisions of government?

7. Political philosophy is a subfield of the larger field of political science. The other subfields, such as comparative politics and international relations, study what actual governments do, and using the insights of political philosophy, determine whether what governments do is good or bad (or somewhere in between) and how we can improve bad governments (or aspects of them) and maintain good ones.

8. For a work treating aspects of this subject with considerable depth and subtlety at a more advanced level, see Stanley Rosen, *The Ancients and the Moderns: Rethinking Modernity* (New Haven, Conn.: Yale University Press, 1989).

9. *Republic,* 505a, 506b.

10. St. Augustine, *City of God* (New York: Penguin, 1972), 429.

11. Francis Bacon, *Novum Organum,* Aphorism III.

12. Friedrich Nietzsche, *Genealogy of Morals* (New York: Vintage, 1967), 155.

13. On early science, see Patricia Phillips, *The Prehistory of Europe* (Bloomington: University of Indiana Press, 1980); and George Sarton, *Ancient Science and Modern Civilization* (Lincoln: University of Nebraska Press, 1964).

14. For an excellent study of the interplay between the development of modern science and social reform movements in the seventeenth and eighteenth centuries, see Geoffrey V. Sutton, *Science for a Polite Society: Gender, Culture, and the Demonstration of Enlightenment* (Boulder, Colo.: Westview, 1995).

15. Chapter 18 shows how Marx's and Engels's "materialist" methodology serves the cause of idealism.

16. Jeffrey C. Isaac, "On Rebellion and Revolution," *Dissent* (Summer 1989): 383.

17. John Stuart Mill, "On Liberty," in *Utilitarianism, Liberty and Representative Government* (London: J. M. Dent, 1910), ch. II.

18. For some writers the collective refers to the state, or to its government. The state is a political community with full independence and a definable geographic territory in which an organized government is located. Other writers identify the collective with a society, which includes its class, economic, social, cultural, religious, and educational aspects, and may either include or exclude state and government as legitimate sources of authority. For a fuller discussion on the state, see A. P. D'Entrèves, *The Notion of the State* (Oxford: Clarendon, 1967).

19. See, for example, Cyril E. Robinson, *Hellas: A Short History of Ancient Greece* (Boston: Beacon, 1955); Martin Buber, *I and Thou,* rev. ed. (New York: Scribner's, 1984). On existentialism, see Jean-Paul Sartre, *Being and Nothingness* (New York: Philosophical Library, 1943); or a collection of excerpts from some of Sartre's works that is more accessible to the beginning student, *Existentialism and Human Emotions* (New York: Wisdom Library, 1957).

20. Aristotle, *The Politics of Aristotle,* trans. E. Barker (New York: Oxford, 1952), I, 1260a.

21. Ephesians 5:22–24.

22. Friedrich Nietzsche, *Thus Spoke Zarathustra,* trans. W. Kaufmann (New York: Viking, 1966), 67.

23. Diana H. Coole, *Women in Political Theory* (Boulder, Colo.: Lynne Rienner, 1988).

24. Jean Bethke Elshtain, *Public Man, Private Woman* (Princeton, N.J.: Princeton University Press, 1981).

25. Carole Pateman, *The Sexual Contract* (Palo Alto, Calif.: Stanford University Press, 1988).

26. In addition, Thomas A. Spragens reminds us that "even the simplest statement of fact" contains some prescription, and that by shaping our ideas political philosophers "will shape our political actions (or what 'is') as well." *Understanding Political Theory* (New York: St. Martins, 1976), 103–4.

27. The formal term for this is *normative*. A normative statement presents a subjective value judgment, in contrast to an empirical statement, which can be tested and verified.

28. The opposite view, that people should be treated as if they are unequal, despite any apparent similarities, and the political system organized accordingly, has been held by a number of writers, beginning with Plato.

29. Henry David Thoreau, "Civil Disobedience," in *Walden and Civil Disobedience,* ed. O. Thomas (New York: Norton, 1966), 231. In a note the editor points out that Copernicus was not actually excommunicated, but that his writings on the solar system were banned by the Roman Catholic Church.

30. Describing the development of political philosophy through the ages as progressive is the expression of a personal outlook based on its evolution from the ancients through medieval and modern writers. This is a view rejected by some postmodern thinkers, who do not regard new as necessarily better.

31. In Chapter 17 we discuss John Stuart Mill's examination of this two-sided dilemma. Recognizing the need to protect individual liberty against politically powerful individuals and collectives, governmental and social, he opposes both tyranny practiced by government and what he calls "tyranny of the majority." Mill's predecessors implicitly weigh in on this two-sided threat to political progress when they discuss the relationship between the individual and the collective.

32. Note, for example, the rise of Nazism and the communism of the Soviet Union, as well as mass murder in World War II and the political violence since then around the world, ranging from September 11, 2001, in the United States to massacres in Bosnia, Rwanda, East Timor, the Sudan, and so many other troubled areas. On the other hand, note the demise of Nazism, the Soviet Union, and apartheid in South Africa. As Robert A. Dahl summarizes the status of democracy at the end of the twentieth century in *On Democracy* (New Haven, Conn.: Yale University Press, 1998), 145: "The twentieth century was a time of frequent democratic failure. On more than seventy occasions democracy collapsed and gave way to an authoritarian regime. Yet it was also a time of extraordinary democratic success [which] made that century far and away the most flourishing period for democracy in human history."

Additional Readings

(* indicates alternative interpretation)

Dahl, Robert A. *On Democracy.* New Haven, Conn.: Yale University Press, 1998.

D'Entrèves, A. P. *The Notion of the State.* Oxford: Clarendon, 1967.

Rosen, Stanley. *The Ancients and the Moderns: Rethinking Modernity.* New Haven, Conn.: Yale University Press, 1989.

*Strauss, Leo. *Natural Right and History.* Chicago: University of Chicago Press, 1953.

The following works are listed here only, but are relevant to a number of chapters.

Coole, Diana H. *Women in Political Theory.* Boulder, Colo.: Lynne Rienner, 1988, 1993.

Elshtain, Jean Bethke. *Public Man, Private Woman.* Princeton, N.J.: Princeton University Press, 1981, 1991.

Okin, Susan Moller. *Women in Western Political Thought.* Princeton, N.J.: Princeton University Press, 1979, 1992.

Pateman, Carole. *The Sexual Contract.* Palo Alto, Calif.: Stanford University Press, 1988.

Saxonhouse, Arlene W. *Women in the History of Political Thought: Ancient Greece to Machiavelli.* New York: Praeger, 1985.

Spelman, Elizabeth V. *Inessential Women: Problems of Exclusion in Feminist Thought.* Boston: Beacon, 1988, 1990.

Wolin, Sheldon S. *Politics and Vision: Continuity and Innovation in Western Political Thought.* Boston: Little, Brown, 1960.

Inventors of Ideas Online

Visit http://politicalscience.wadsworth.com/tannenbaum2 for links related to material in this chapter, including an online encyclopedia of all things philosophical kept current by experts in the field.

2

The Playwrights of Athens: Sophocles and Aristophanes

INTRODUCTION

The ancient Greek world centered on the political community of the *polis,* or city-state. The Greek polis was one of the earliest forms of political organization in the West, and it stands in contrast to the modern nation state.[1] Modern Western societies take it as given that individuals have distinct political rights to protect themselves from their governments. There is also a value placed on individuality and the individual moral conscience that makes each person worthy of respect and dignity. The worlds of politics and the family are generally distinct, carrying with them unique loyalties and duties that are not often thought of as overlapping. Consequently, modern Western political societies are diverse, often involving many distinct groups distinguished by such factors as religion, ethnicity, and kinship. Yet these factors, along with gender, are not supposed to be criteria influencing who has political power.

In the ancient Greek world, however, many of these assumptions were not generally accepted. Early Greek society was characterized by a sense of unity that did not usually distinguish among political, theological, or family loyalties, or see them as conflicting with one another.[2] Rather, they blurred together and overlapped in the sense that religious, familial, and political norms mutually defined and reinforced the specific roles and obligations individuals held. Obedience to parents was supported by religious commands, and obedience to the king was demanded much in the same way one was supposed to obey a father.

In addition, there was no recognition of individuality in the modern understanding of the term.[3] Obligations to the state, to the gods, and to the family were perceived to be in harmony, and they were unquestioned, accepted as part of a tradition guiding and binding one's duties. In a funeral oration for slain warriors of Athens, Pericles (a famous general) expresses this sense of obligation and respect for tradition when he states,

> but all this ease in our private relations does not make us lawless as citizens. Against this fear is our chief safeguard, teaching us to obey the magistrates and the laws . . . whether they are actually on the statute book, or belong

to that code which, although unwritten, yet cannot be broken without acknowledged disgrace.[4]

The unquestioned respect for tradition and traditional values compelled individual deference to, not disagreement with, authority or else serious problems were thought to ensue. This respect for tradition also shaped an approach to knowledge, science, and the world in ancient Greek culture that differed from ours. Modern Western society is scientifically oriented. Most of us generally believe that there are knowable causes for most visible events in the world, rather than accept the view that events happen by chance, or that explanations are a mystery. We also do not accept laws or rules unless there is some good, rational reason to support them. For the ancient Greeks of the sixth century before the Common Era, this was not always true. Their world was more traditional than ours. It was a prescientific, prerational world; reason and basic scientific thinking were not used to explain the world. Generally, rational explanations were neither expected nor offered to support rules or laws of society, both because no one questioned them and because these rules were based on traditions that were accepted by all.

Ancient Greece was a world of myth, not science, constituting a personal "I–thou" relationship with the world.[5] The world, indeed the universe, was seen as alive, and the Greeks' relationship to it as personal. Gods and traditions were used to explain things, fate or chance was seen as a goddess, and basic changes in the world were initially explained as acts of intervention by supernatural personal forces, not as the result of natural forces we now describe in a scientific and rational fashion.

In the fifth century B.C.E., this traditional and myth-oriented perspective started to change. Efforts to understand the world became more rationalistic, and this gave birth to philosophy.[6] In *Metaphysics,* Aristotle, an important ancient Greek philosopher, argues that "all men by nature desire to know" and,

> owing to their wonder men both now begin and at first began to philosophize; they wondered originally at the obvious difficulties, then advanced little by little and stated difficulties about the great matters, e.g., about the phenomena of the moon and those of the sun and of the stars, and about the genesis of the universe.[7]

It is this spirit of wonder, or the desire to know, that first led the Greeks to seek to explain, understand, and question not just the physical world around them, but also their society, community, and politics.

Many early philosophers known as the Presocratics (philosophers in Greece before Socrates) sought to explain the universe. Socrates is often considered the first philosopher to question the moral and political world of ancient Greece,[8] but a number of poets and playwrights of his time also raised important questions about politics and society. Many of the Greek stories, including Homer's *Iliad and Odyssey,* Hesiod's *Theogony,* Thucydides' *Peloponnesian War,* and Herodotus' *Histories,* were not simply tales of the great deeds of men. Such poems, plays, and stories were efforts to use rhetorical or theatrical situations to raise and highlight numerous political questions and conflicts viewed as threatening to unity.

Two playwrights engaged in questioning the changes and events they perceived in their world were Sophocles (496–406 B.C.E.) and Aristophanes (447–385 B.C.E.). In Sophocles' *Antigone* and Aristophanes' *Lysistrata*, the lead characters question the political unity of the Greek world and the reasons for or causes of that unity. In both plays, as in many of the tragedies of that time, the questioning is assigned to women who, because of their sheltered or outsider status in society, are able to represent a unique perspective and challenge to the polis.[9] And both plays, whether comedy or tragedy, are the product of wonder and speculation, since they confront many political questions later found in Socrates, Plato, and Aristotle as well as throughout Western political philosophy.

These two plays appeared at a time when many of the accepted values of the Greek world were undergoing change. The plays question emerging values that clash with the traditional ones, even as they embody a move away from myth and tradition and toward reason to explain the changes. More specifically, by questioning the unity of the Greek world, of political obligation and its relation to familial and religious duties, the plays examine our obligation to law and government by inquiring into its basis and limits, as well as grounds for civil disobedience. In addition to many political issues, both plays address important questions about the family, gender roles, and the differences between men and women. The social conflicts revealed in these two plays foreshadow important themes both in ancient Greek philosophy and in Western political thought for the next 2,500 years.

ANTIGONE

Antigone is a classic Greek tragedy, often read as a literary work, involving a confrontation between an individual and a king. Yet the multiple conflicts described in this play are tremendously political. The story of *Antigone* has attracted significant attention throughout history because its conflicts raise many questions about politics, law, religion, and the family.[10] In addition to the dispute between Antigone and Creon, several other important political issues in this drama are repeated throughout Western political thought.

The play was written with war and rebellion as a background framing the events of the script. It opens following a civil war in Thebes over the succession to the throne. One of Antigone's two brothers, Eteocles, refuses to honor an agreement to rule alternatively with their other brother, Polynices. When both die in battle, their uncle, King Creon, orders that Polynices' body not be buried but left to be feasted upon by vultures. Left unburied, the Greeks thought, the soul would forever wander the earth, unable to go to Hades. Antigone decides to bury her brother Polynices, in accordance with the ancient burial traditions of the Greeks but in defiance of Creon. For this, she is captured and sentenced to be buried alive. Upon hearing of Creon's order,

Haemon protests his father's sentence on his fiancée. Unbeknownst to Creon, Haemon eventually commits suicide. Eurydice, Creon's wife, sorrowful over her son's death, also commits suicide. At the end of the play, Creon realizes that he has been mistaken to defy tradition and seeks to free Antigone, but it is too late. She, his son, and his wife are all dead.

Antigone is an inherently political play that raises fundamental questions about the nature of law, politics, and political obligation. It questions the assumption that religious, familial, and political duties are mutually reinforcing, and adds yet another dimension by raising issues of gender.

The matter of political obligation versus conscience first surfaces when Antigone says that she will challenge Creon's order and bury her brother. Why does she do this? The answer is given in an exchange between the strong-willed Antigone and her more traditional sister Ismene, who ultimately refuses to help:

> ANTIGONE: Will you lift up his body with these bare hands and lower it with me?
>
> ISMENE: What? You'd bury him—when a law forbids the city?
>
> ANTIGONE: Yes! He is my brother and—deny it as you will—your brother too. No one will ever convict me for a traitor.
>
> ISMENE: So desperate, and Creon has expressly—
>
> ANTIGONE: No, he has no right to keep me from my own.[11]

Thus familial obligation to her brother is one defense appearing to outweigh political duties; and so is obligation to the gods and tradition:

> CREON: You, tell me briefly, no long speeches—were you aware a decree had forbid this?
>
> ANTIGONE: Well aware. How could I avoid it? It was public.
>
> CREON: And still you had the gall to break the law?
>
> ANTIGONE: Of course I did. It wasn't Zeus, not in the least, who made this proclamation—not to me. Nor did that Justice, dwelling with the gods beneath the earth, ordain such laws for men.[12]

More specifically, when Creon questions Antigone about her obligation to him and why she has disobeyed the law, Antigone states that she has an obligation to higher laws:

> Nor did I think your edict had such force that you, a mere mortal, could override the gods, the great unwritten, unshakable traditions. They are alive, not just today or yesterday: they live forever, from the first of time, and no one knows when they first saw the light.[13]

Antigone's response here is suggestive on several important fronts. First, there is the recognition of a higher law that commands individuals, one no earthly law or command of a king can supersede. This implies a difference between earthly and divine law. A further implication is that earthly law must conform with this higher law of the gods and eternal tradition. Only when earthly and higher law are in conformity does an individual have an obligation to obey the former. When in conflict, the primary obligation is to the higher law.

That passage in *Antigone* foreshadows what later becomes the natural law tradition in Western thought. This tradition emphasizes that there is an ultimate sense of justice, rules, or standards by which to judge right and wrong in the world, and that to be considered just, human laws must conform to these eternal, natural laws. For many political thinkers, belief in the existence of an eternal and unchanging standard of justice is important to defining and judging the moral or political rectitude of human institutions, as well as guiding how individuals ought to act. If there is in fact some ultimate concept of justice, and if we can know it, then we can also know how to organize society and how to act correctly.

Antigone's appeal to a higher law also raises the important questions of political obligation and civil disobedience. Under what conditions are individuals compelled to obey the laws of the state? Also, when and for what reasons are individuals permitted to disobey these laws, if at all? For Creon, obedience to his laws is absolute and unquestioning:

> But whoever steps out of line, violates the laws or presumes to hand out orders to his superiors, he'll win no praise from me. But that man the city places in authority, his orders must be obeyed, large and small, right and wrong. Anarchy—show me a greater crime in all the earth! She, she destroys cities, rips up houses, breaks the ranks of spearmen into the headlong rout. But the ones who last it out, the great mass of them owe their lives to discipline. Therefore we must defend the men who live by law.[14]

Thus, for Creon, one has an absolute duty to obey the law. To break it invites anarchy and disorder. If one person is allowed to disobey, it might lead to mass disobedience, resulting in civil discord and war. The only way to prevent political anarchy is to command all to obey the law, regardless of personal reasons, and to punish those who disobey.

Yet Antigone does disobey, and Sophocles appears to argue that she is justified. Antigone's defense of her actions raises four sets of conflicts or overlapping loyalties. First, there is the question of conscience; second, of religion; third, of family; and fourth, of gender. Sophocles' world is that of moral harmony with eternal moral laws. Disobedience of these laws breaks that harmony, with dire repercussions.[15] The consequences of breaking the moral harmony become clear to Creon once he recognizes what justice is, and he then changes his mind about Antigone's sentence:

> Now—I'm on my way! Come, each of you, take up axes, make for the high ground, over there, quickly! I and my better judgment have come round to this—I shackled her, I'll set her free myself. I am afraid . . . it's best to keep the established laws to the very day we die.[16]

When Creon realizes that Antigone, Haemon, and Eurydice are all dead, he must recognize his responsibility:

So senseless, so insane . . . my crimes, my stubborn, deadly—Look at us, the killer, the killed, father and son, the same blood—the misery! My plans, my mad fanatic heart, my son, cut off so young! Ai, dead, lost to the world, not through your stupidity, no, my own.[17]

Thus order and tradition must be upheld for Sophocles;[18] any abrupt challenges are dangerous. Antigone questions the basic order and harmony in the universe that unite the family, state, and religion. The play questions the political cosmology that holds the Greek world together. This cosmology makes the laws and structure of the polis an extension of the imperatives of the gods, the heavens, the universe, such that down to the level of the individual there is a sense of order that defines a place for each person.

Yet who really challenges this harmony? Is it Antigone, in her disobedience to Creon, or is it Creon, when he first issues the decree preventing burial of the dead? Creon's own admissions suggest that the tragedy which unfolds is due to his failure to recognize the eternal laws of the gods. He has struck a blow against nature with his orders.

Yet, in another way, Antigone's actions also challenge the moral universe of the ancient Greeks. By challenging the law of Creon, she presents a distinction between legitimate and illegitimate rule, which suggests that some rulers are not so much rulers as tyrants. In several places Sophocles notes distinctions that Plato and other future political philosophers make when he claims that kings seek the public good, or the good of their subjects, while tyrants are unjust, acting out of self-interest in a way that treats the state as a private domain:

ANTIGONE: Lucky tyrants—the perquisites of power! Ruthless power to do and say whatever pleases them.[19]

CREON: Am I to rule this land for others—or myself?

HAEMON: It's no city at all, owned by one man alone.

CREON: What? The city is the king's—that's the law!

HAEMON: What a splendid king you'd make of a desert island—you and you alone.[20]

TIRESIAS: And the whole race of tyrants lusts for filthy gain.[21]

Thus Antigone's challenge is to the abuse of power by a tyrant, a decision to defy human law to defend higher values, and not simply an act of civil disobedience. It is the appeal to conscience to do what is correct. Antigone's defiance of Creon is a defense of the individual over the state, an appeal for morality over legality, and a statement that an individual has a right to question authority and power. So Antigone's act of defiance is also a statement about individualism, individual rights, and the right of conscience that can, on occasion, stand in opposition to what the majority, law, or ruler demands. It is a statement that the individual has the right, and perhaps the duty, to use her own judgment to decide what is right and wrong. It is a rejection of the claim that political obligations are absolute duties based on unchallenged assumptions, and that power alone compels obedience to the law.

The second conflict that emerges in *Antigone* is that between religion and the state.[22] Antigone's defense of her actions by appealing to a higher religious morality[23] suggests that the gods have instructed her on what is right and wrong. Her religious views are important to her judgment of Creon's edict and motivate her pointing out that Creon's orders go against the gods. In other words, Antigone's religious views pit the state against religion,[24] with the apparent result that religious loyalties and duties take precedence over those to the state. Antigone's decision to obey the gods over Creon makes her a religious martyr, much like Socrates is in his refusal to back down from his search for truth, as commanded by the gods. She is also much like Jesus and other Christian saints, who died to uphold religious values over mandates of the state.

The third level of conflict in the play is that between the family and the state. Antigone's duty to her brother, to bury him,[25] makes personal familial loyalties seem more important than her obligations to the state.

Sophocles' *Antigone* thus poses the dilemma that our duties to family, religion, and politics may not always mutually support one another. Antigone demonstrates the need for harmony among these three sets of duties by revealing their potential to clash, possibly with disastrous results. But Sophocles' play also proposes that duties to religion and tradition come first, followed by those to the family. Justice, then, is doing what the gods command, which in this case is to respect familial duties. These obligations may be superior to those to the state; and the state has an obligation not to violate such traditions. *Antigone* suggests that the universe represents a seamless harmony of duties and obligations, but that human motives can disturb this unity and precipitate "a fall from grace" (as it is later described in the Christian tradition). Human behavior—here Creon's violation of tradition and the gods—precipitates a breakup of the unified moral universe into the distinct spheres and duties of the family, religion, and politics, forcing conflicted individuals to make choices between their several obligations.

Yet if *Antigone* implies that our obligations to politics, religion, and the family can conflict, it also suggests the possibility that such conflicts can be resolved into some type of harmony if we respect that harmony. Political philosophy is a questioning process, a search for answers, an attempt to find another way to imagine or visualize the world and how it is organized. Political questioning may be subversive, and it may be a threat to established order, but such questioning is critical to securing freedom, political knowledge, and justice. *Antigone* probes the naturalness of the status quo, suggesting another way to look at the world, but at the same time implying that this questioning does not come without danger.

The fourth conflict *Antigone* raises is that between men and women. When Creon first learns that someone has buried Polynices against his orders, he assumes a man has done it:

SENTRY: All right, here it comes. The body—someone's just buried it, then run off . . . sprinkled some dry dust on the flesh, given it proper rights.

CREON: What? What man alive would dare—[26]

CREON: I swear to Zeus as I still believe in Zeus, if you don't find the man who buried that corpse, the very man, and produce him before my eyes, simple death won't be enough for you.[27]

Once the sentry discovers that a woman, Antigone, has defied the law, the nature of the disobedience against Creon takes on a different dimension: It is now also a matter of a woman defying a man. As a result, Antigone's actions threaten the male-dominated order of society and must be punished for that reason:

CREON: Go down below and love, if love you must—love the dead! While I'm alive, no woman is going to lord over me.[28]

CREON: Stop wasting time. Take them in. From now on they'll act like women. Tie them up, no more running loose; even the bravest will cut and run, once they see Death coming for their lives.[29]

CREON: Therefore we must defend the men who live by law, never let some women triumph over us. Better to fall from power, if fall we must, at the hands of a man—never be rated inferior to a woman, never.[30]

In other words, men are rulers, women subjects, and better for a state to fall to other men than for women to take power. The cosmology or harmony that Sophocles proposes is one where the roles of men and women are defined by the logic of the universe. Men are the natural rulers of the household and therefore should also be rulers of the state. Creon, in lashing out at Haemon for his inability to control his fiancée, Antigone, states, "Show me the man who rules the household well: I'll show you someone fit to rule the state."[31] Impugning Haemon's masculinity and criticizing his lack of control over Antigone leads then to questioning his fitness for political rule. Also, by comparing the state to the household, the play implies the naturalness of male political and familial authority, and that father, husband, and king mutually reinforce one another.

Antigone's disobedience of Creon, then, is not simply an act of political rebellion. On the one hand, it is a defense of traditional gender roles in that the duties and positions of men and women in the universe are natural, and that a woman challenging male authority leads to tragic results.

On the other hand, the play questions traditional gender roles and assumptions. It indicates that women are capable of political action, including defiance, and that political authority is not exclusively a male domain. In effect, it says that men may be wrong in how they run the state, and that women may do a better job. Sophocles' *Antigone* suggests that politics would be different if women ruled.

LYSISTRATA

An even more direct questioning of the male-dominated world of ancient Greece is found in *Lysistrata*. *Lysistrata* was written in 411 B.C.E. It takes place against the backdrop of the Peloponnesian War, when Athens was locked in a major conflict with the city-state of Sparta.

In the play, the war is dragging on, and fearing that the Athenian people might act rashly to end it, the "Committee of Ten for the Safety of the State" takes command of the government and continues the war. *Lysistrata* pokes fun at this committee's decisions to keep Athens in a state of war. The play is a plea for peace, but not a call for Athens to surrender. It is a call for both sides to negotiate a mutually satisfactory truce.

Aristophanes uses Lysistrata, the female lead, as a voice to question the ability of the committee to make decisions. The perspectives of women are also enrolled to demonstrate the results of the sacrifices of war upon Athens. Lysistrata says at one point that the women have been asked to make a double sacrifice: first, producing sons, and then sending them off to fight.[32] The play opens with Lysistrata asking women of both Athens and Sparta: who is tired of this war? All of the women admit that they are. Lysistrata announces to the assembled women that she has a plan to end it:

> Then I will tell you my plan: there is no need to keep it back. Ladies, if we want to force our husbands to make peace, we must give up sex.[33]

Lysistrata proposes that the women withhold sex from their husbands, and moreover, under the pretext of making religious sacrifices, that Athenian women take over the temple on the Acropolis, where the money for prosecuting the war is stored. No one is to submit or surrender until the men agree to make peace. Initially the Athenian women object to sexual abstinence as a bargaining tool, but they finally agree to it once the Spartan women consent to join the protest by extending the sexual ban to their own city-state.

When the men return from battle and are denied marital relations, they are unnerved. To counter the women's rebellion, they make efforts to burn the women out of the Acropolis.[34] They also try to lure the women out by appealing to their maternal duty to care for their children.[35] Neither tactic succeeds. Eventually, the sexual desires and needs of the men in both Athens and Sparta are too great, which drives them to the bargaining table to negotiate peace. In the end, their desire for war and aggression is overcome by their sexual needs.

In this play, too, numerous suggestions about politics, war, men, and women are made, and these comments are highly political. First, there is the description by the local magistrate of women as temptresses who are conniving, plotting, and irrational:

> I hear it's the same old thing again—the unbridled nature of the female sex coming out. . . . Look at the way we pander to the women's vices—we positively teach them to be wicked.[36]

In addition, they are described as lesser creatures that men cannot give in to:

> Our noble magistrate, why waste your words on these subhuman crea-
> tures? Know you not how we were given a bath when fully clothed, and
> that without the benefit of soap?
>   Now question here, and test her out, and never own she's right: It's
> shameful to surrender to a girl without a fight.[37]

The men are initially depicted as leaders who are rational, aggressive, warlike, and sexually demanding. However, the men and women soon seem
to reverse roles. As they act to secure the war's end, the women appear rational and aggressive, while the men are depicted as weak, falling prey to their
passions.

A second element in the play is the recognition of the division of labor
between the sexes. In several passages, it describes statecraft, war, and politics
as the duties of men, suggesting that these activities are essentially masculine
and not suitable to women's talents. For example, at one point, when the
women suggest that they should take over management of the state's finances,
the magistrate responds that "it's against nature" for women to do that.[38]
Activities such as child rearing and domestic care, however, are women's
duties because these are what they are best suited for.

This passage and others signal early in the Western tradition that many
of the gender stereotypes persisting to this day had their roots early in
Greece, or at least in Athens. Moreover, the play also defines a distinction
between politics and the household, that the two are different, that men are
the head of both, and that women be excluded from politics and confined to
the household.

Use of the familial metaphor for politics and political authority is found in
both *Lysistrata* and *Antigone,* with duty and justification for obeying the king
and obedience to one's father and husband given parallel emphasis. Both
plays enlist the bond of love and obligation to parents or children for political
purposes (views that are carried forward in the works of many later thinkers).
They generalize the strength and power of family bonds, as well as the familial metaphor, to serve as justification for political rule. If the state is like a
large family, then the political bond that holds people together is some type of
love or affection for the state and its rulers.

Yet Aristophanes also constructs scenarios where he questions the traditional distinctions of politics versus the household and the duties of men versus those of women. In several circumstances, *Lysistrata* implies that the skills
of the household are not distinct from those of the state. Instead, they are the
essence of what the state is about. For example, one passage suggests that
women can control and manage public finances because they have been managing households and their finances for quite some time:

> MAGISTRATE: Well, the first thing I want to know is—what in Zeus's name do
> you mean by shutting and barring the gates of our own Acropolis against us?
>
> LYSISTRATA: We want to keep the money safe and stop you from waging war.

MAGISTRATE: The war has nothing to do with money.

LYSISTRATA: Hasn't it? Why are Peisander and the other office-seekers always stirring things up? Isn't it so they can take a few more dips in the public purse? Well, as far as we're concerned they can do what they like; only they're not going to lay their hands on the money in there.

MAGISTRATE: Why, what are you going to do?

LYSISTRATA: Do? Why, we'll be in charge of it.

MAGISTRATE: You in charge of our finances?

LYSISTRATA: Well, what's so strange about that? We've been in charge of all your housekeeping finances for years.[39]

Claiming that women routinely clean up after their husbands in the house, Lysistrata also says that the women should take over politics from the men and clean up the mess the latter have made.[40] War, instead of being the duty of men, is actually like housework and thus should be in the care of women.[41]

But *Lysistrata* makes its most direct statement that women are fit to rule because of their household experience in the passage where governance is compared to making yarn and knitting:

MAGISTRATE: But the international situation at present is in a hopeless muddle. How do you propose to unravel it?

LYSISTRATA: Oh, it's dead easy.

MAGISTRATE: Would you explain?

LYSISTRATA: Well, take a tangled skein of wool, for example. We take it so, put it to the spindle, unwind it this way, now that way. That's how we'll unravel this war, if you'll let us. Send ambassadors first to Sparta, this way, then to Thebes, that way—

MAGISTRATE: Are you such idiots as to think that you can solve serious problems with spindles and bits of wool?

LYSISTRATA: As a matter of fact, it might not be so idiotic as you think to run the whole City entirely on the model we deal with wool.

MAGISTRATE: How d'you work that out?

LYSISTRATA: The first thing you do with the wool is wash the grease out; you can do the same with the City. Then you stretch out the citizen body on a bench and pick out the burrs—that is, the parasites. After that you prise apart the club members who form themselves into knots and clots to get into power, and when you've separated them, pick them out one by one. Then you're ready for the carding: they can all go into the basket of Civic Goodwill—including the resident aliens and any foreigners who are your friends—yes, and even those who are in debt to the Treasury! Not only that. Athens has many colonies. At the moment they are lying around all over the place, like stray bits and pieces of the fleece. You should pick them up and bring them here, put them altogether, and then out of all this make an enormous great ball of wool—and from that you can make the People a coat.[42]

Thus the metaphor of making yarn and knitting, duties performed by women, is used to justify why women have the skills to enter politics and run the state. Politics, like war, is not simply something men can perform; women, too, are fit to engage in it because of their household experiences. By describing statecraft as like woolwork, the women offer the argument that masculinity may not be a qualification for politics. Women may in fact be more fit than men because they, not men, have the skills necessary to run the polis and bring about harmony.[43] Not surprisingly, the men do not willingly accept this assault on them and the state by the women. The women's action is described as a political conspiracy;[44] and if left unchecked, women will "be adept at every manly art."[45] The men see the action by the women not just as a political threat, but as an assault on the traditional roles of men and women, as well as the right and pride men take in ruling over women. The battle of the sexes is emphasized when the men say that they cannot be worsted by women because it is "shameful to surrender to a girl without a fight."[46]

Here the play joins gender roles to political power, suggesting that what the women are attacking is the political power of men over women and men's ability to define what roles and rights women can have. The political role of men over women, described as patriarchialism, uses the metaphor of the father as the head of the family over his wife as a basis for giving men political power in the state.[47]

But is politics an essentially male or masculine activity? Would politics change if women ran the world? Would politics be different? These are questions that *Lysistrata* implicitly asks, and answers. Aristophanes carries these questions over into another play, *The Ecclesiazusae* (*The Assemblywomen*). Here, women disguise themselves as men and vote to turn political power in Athens over to themselves. As in *Lysistrata*, the skills women acquire tending to the family are described as appropriate for managing the state: "I propose that we hand over the running of Athens to the women. They are, after all, the people to whom we look for the efficient management of our homes."[48] What happens when women rule? They make "all land, all money, and private possessions" common property,[49] and traditional families are abandoned so that the "whole city will be just one big communal residence."[50] These egalitarian and communal social policies adopted by the women are sharply at odds with those articulated by men. Although the play is a comedy—a farce—it raises questions about how men and women view the world, how they act, and how politics might be different if men and women were to change roles.

Both *Lysistrata* and *The Ecclesiazusae* suggest that politics is not something uniquely male. Women and men do have different experiences and perspectives, which indicates that politics might be different if governed by women. Women, as mothers and wives, would bring a maternal, caring, and less conflict-ridden approach to politics, in contrast to the more aggressive and warlike traits of politics organized by men. *Lysistrata*, by suggesting these differences between men and women, anticipates similar claims made recently by cognitive and developmental psychologists.[51] Hence the play asks whether biology and hormones are the source of the different approaches of men and women to politics, or whether different life experiences explain the way men and women see things. Is the fact that women give birth, nurse, and so forth important in molding different images or visions of politics? Given their different experiences, can men really understand women, and vice versa?

By the time *Lysistrata* ends, sharp differences between the men and women seem to have faded. Both are depicted as creatures of their passions and as equally capable of using sex to secure their goals. When the women organize to bring peace, the men feel threatened by them, and this threat seems to be both sexual and political. However, the play leaves open the question of whether the women win because of their political power or because of male, or human, weakness. At the end of the play the women do not seem to have achieved a lasting victory that changes their gender roles. They appear, instead, to have used their sexuality to achieve a short-term end to the war, later resulting in the return to traditional sex roles.[52]

CONCLUSION

Antigone and *Lysistrata* can be read on several levels. They first articulate issues of politics and political conflict that dominate ancient Greek political theory, reappearing later in the writings of Plato and Aristotle. Concern with the nature of political obligation and justice; the problem of reconciling the demands of the state, family, and society; as well as the relationship between the individual and the state are discussed in these two plays (and others written in ancient Athens).

Second, beyond providing scenarios that dramatize these issues, both *Antigone* and *Lysistrata* use female leads to introduce questions about gender roles, the nature of female subordination, and the use of family structure to define and justify political organization. These plays address ideas that have been repeatedly investigated throughout the West over the last 2,500 years, and anticipate many themes of current political interest.

Finally, both plays can be read as speaking to broader social issues or metaphors for other conflicts individuals face in their lives. For example, Creon can be seen as a modern day business leader and Antigone an employee faced with the moral dilemma of what to do when her own values and the law conflict with the demands of the workplace. Similarly, *Lysistrata* is not simply a humorous battle of the sexes; it suggests deeper questions about the ability of men and women to get along, how to foster social or political change within organizations, and the efficacy of appealing to reason or the passions when seeking to persuade others. In short, both plays probe the psychology of power—be it political, economic, or familial—and the dynamics of challenging it, asking whether and how the powerless can confront the powerful, and how the world might be different if women had a voice.

Notes

1. Further discussion of the political organization of the polis is found in Chapter 3.
2. Michael Grant, *The Rise of the Greeks* (New York: Scribner's, 1987), 39.
3. Arlene W. Saxonhouse, *Fear of Diversity: The Birth of Political Science in Ancient Greek Thought* (Chicago: University of Chicago Press, 1992), 1–2.
4. Thucydides, *The Peloponnesian War,* trans. R. Crawley (New York: Everyman's Library, 1968), 93.
5. Henri Frankfort, *Before Philosophy* (New York: Penguin, 1966).
6. Sheldon S. Wolin, *Politics and Vision: Continuity and Innovation in Western Political Thought* (Boston: Little, Brown, 1960), 28–30.
7. Aristotle, *Metaphysics,* in *The Basic Works of Aristotle,* ed. Richard McKeon (New York: Random House, 1941), 692.
8. W. K. C. Guthrie, *Socrates* (New York: Cambridge University Press, 1984), 110.
9. *Fear of Diversity,* 51–52, 76.
10. George Steiner, *Antigones: How the Antigone Legend Has Endured in Western Literature, Art, and Thought* (New York: Oxford University Press, 1986).
11. Sophocles, *Antigone,* in *The Three Theban Plays,* trans. R. Fagles (New York: Penguin, 1982), 61.
12. *Antigone,* 81–82.
13. *Antigone,* 82.
14. *Antigone,* 94.
15. H. D. F. Kitto, *Greek Tragedy* (London: Metheun, 1966), 148.
16. *Antigone,* 117.
17. *Antigone,* 124.
18. Edith Hamilton, *The Greek Way* (New York: Avon Books, 1973), 190.
19. *Antigone,* 84.
20. *Antigone,* 97.
21. *Antigone,* 114.
22. *Antigones,* 104, notes how Hegel saw Antigone as embodying both the clash of legality and morality and religion and civil conflict.
23. *Antigone,* 106.
24. *Antigone,* 77, 98.
25. *Antigone,* 60.
26. *Antigone,* 71.
27. *Antigone,* 74.
28. *Antigone,* 86.
29. *Antigone,* 90.
30. *Antigone,* 94.
31. *Antigone,* 94.
32. Aristophanes, *Lysistrata,* in *Lysistrata: The Acharnians, the Clouds,* trans. A. H. Sommerstein (New York: Penguin, 1983), 204.
33. *Lysistrata,* 184.
34. *Lysistrata,* 192.
35. *Lysistrata,* 215–17.
36. *Lysistrata,* 196–97.
37. *Lysistrata,* 199.
38. *Lysistrata,* 200.
39. *Lysistrata,* 199–200.
40. *Lysistrata,* 201.
41. *Lysistrata,* 202.
42. *Lysistrata,* 203–4.
43. Plato, "The Statesman," in *Plato: The Collected Dialogues,* eds. E. Hamilton and H. Cairns (Princeton, N.J.: Princeton University Press, 1961), 1048–50, standard passages

281e–283c. The metaphor of statecraft and wool craft is later used by Plato in his dialogue "The Statesman," where the art of wool working is appealed to as the skill necessary for a lawmaker to bring unity to the community.

44. *Lysistrata*, 206.

45. *Lysistrata*, 208.

46. *Lysistrata*, 198–99.

47. Carole Pateman, *The Sexual Contract* (Palo Alto, Calif.: Stanford University Press, 1988), 23.

48. Aristophanes, "The Assemblywomen" in *The Knights, Peace, The Birds, The Assemblywomen, Wealth*, trans. David Barrett (New York: Penguin, 1978), p. 229.

49. "The Assemblywomen," p. 242.

50. "The Assemblywomen," p. 245.

51. Carol Gilligan, *In a Different Voice* (Cambridge, Mass.: Harvard University Press, 1982).

52. *Fear of Diversity*, 5.

Additional Readings

Barker, Sir Ernest. *The Political Thought of Plato and Aristotle*. New York: Dover, 1959.

Finley, M. I. *Ancient History, Evidence and Models*. New York: Viking, 1986.

Hamilton, Edith. *The Greek Way*. New York: Avon Books, 1973.

Saxonhouse, Arlene W. *Fear of Diversity: The Birth of Political Science in Ancient Greek Thought*. Chicago: University of Chicago Press, 1992.

Saxonhouse, Arlene W. *Women in the History of Political Thought: Ancient Greece to Machiavelli*. Westport, Conn.: Praeger, 1985.

Steiner, George. *Antigones: How the Antigone Legend Has Endured in Western Literature, Art, and Thought*. New York: Oxford University Press, 1986.

Inventors of Ideas Online

Visit http://politicalscience.wadsworth.com/tannenbaum2 for links related to material in this chapter, including sites containing the full texts of *Antigone, Lysistrata*, and *The Ecclesiazusae*.

3

PLATO: ADVOCATING JUSTICE

INTRODUCTION

If all of philosophy is but a footnote to Plato, what would philosophy be like if he had chosen another career? Plato (c. 427–347 B.C.E.) was born into an important family of Athens, one that traced its heritage back to a great statesman, Solon. A number of his relatives were active in politics, mostly on the antidemocratic side.[1] Plato took a different path, that of the philosopher, to redress the injustice that politicians had visited on his revered teacher and friend, Socrates. The philosopher Socrates was executed for the crimes of impiety to the gods and corrupting the youth of Athens because he asked embarrassing questions about those in power. The death of Socrates set Plato on the road to build a shrine of dialogues to the man he thought should have been the ruler of Athens, rather than its victim.[2]

Plato's *Republic* is regarded as a central classic of Western political thought. It is both Plato's most idealistic work on political philosophy and in many ways his most influential. It argues for the importance of Socratic knowledge, of philosophy, and of education, and asserts that the pursuit of material wealth and power politics is meaningless. It serves as both an answer to Socrates' accusers and a defense of Socrates' position by one who obviously loved him as well as his ideas.[3]

Most of the Platonic dialogues were originally written for oral delivery to an interested audience and their tone is dramatic. For example, the *Apology* gives Socrates' replies to the jury concerning the charges brought against him at his trial. The *Crito* discusses an attempt by a friend to convince Socrates to run away in order to evade the death sentence imposed on him, and Socrates' reasons for refusing to flee. But what is really important about these and the other dialogues is that, in addition to narrating events, they contain many reflections about critical themes that Plato also discusses in the *Republic*. Among these are the origin and meaning of the universe and human life; the method for acquiring genuine knowledge; and the importance of education, art, and love.

The *Republic* begins as a dialogue, or discussion, between Socrates and several questioners at the home of Cephalus, a wealthy retired merchant. The central question they pursue, in one form or another, throughout the entire work is, what is justice? The discussion is leisurely, relatively calm, and (especially for Socrates) so reasoned that, on the surface at least, it is not obvious that the dialogue takes place at a time of severe crisis in the polis of Athens. Recent political and economic developments had widened the gap between rich and poor, and the increasing inequality between the several classes raised the question of justice.

More immediately, just before Socrates' execution, Athens had been decisively beaten by its enemy, the Greek city-state of Sparta, in the Peloponnesian War, which lasted from 431 to 404 B.C.E. Due to this defeat, many Athenians had lost faith in the traditional beliefs they had inherited from their tribal ancestors. For them, finding justice was no longer a matter of following the old customs based on the will of the gods. They were confused and sought new directions.

The confusion, and the resulting moral crisis, which spread through the polis, is reflected in the widely different definitions Plato's companions give to justice. Cephalus, the most traditional member of the gathering, says justice lies in being honest and giving both men and the gods what is due them. Cephalus' son, Polemarchus, claims that justice consists in helping one's friends and hurting enemies. And Thrasymachus, supported in part by Plato's two older brothers, Glaucon and Adeimantus, sees justice as whatever is in the interest of the stronger. Together, they represent the range of thinkers who, along with Socrates, tried to resolve Athens' moral crisis by raising some fundamental questions.[4]

The questions they raise are simultaneously profoundly complex and simple: Why do things change, or at least why do things such as the old tribal ways appear to change? Are there any constants, any things that do not change? Is anything of value permanent or lasting? And what is the place of humans in all this: how should we properly relate to the social order of things and, ultimately, to the universe? The answers they give are based on a new way of thinking, one that rejects traditional mythical explanations for events. Instead, they seek natural causes, which implies that humans can control their own lives and futures if they can but understand nature.

There are two groups among these new philosophers. One, the *relativists*, claim that no truth is certain or permanent. Rather, all truth is relative to the particular situation and based on nothing more than local practice, whatever that might be. Public opinion can serve as the basis for truth as well as tribal custom. And even if tribal custom is taken by a relativist as the source of truth, custom does so as a shifting, ever-changing base, and not the sure, permanent guide it had provided the traditionalists and their followers in precrisis times.

The other group, the *absolutists*, believes there is, and always has been, a real truth that exists independently of our changing desires or customs or public opinion. It is there whether we wish it or not, and our obligation is to search it out and to live according to it.

The relativist position can be exemplified by one of its major representative groups, the Sophists. In the *Republic*, Thrasymachus serves as their chief spokesman. To a Sophist, reality is found in the doctrine of constant change. Our senses, which make us aware of the world around us, tell us that nothing is fixed or lasting, and that material objects, opinions, and people are constantly undergoing change. Everywhere, different individuals sense matter and change from different perspectives and in different locales. All political beliefs and practices are merely customary, based on the continually changing history, traditions, and opinions of each society. This is why people live under different kinds of governments, with different political rules and institutions.

Justice, then, is neither natural nor the same thing to people everywhere, nor does it mean the same thing in all societies. Rather, it is conventional and varies from place to place, depending on whatever is defined as just by public opinion in a society at any moment in time. This opinion, Thrasymachus tells Socrates, constantly shifts to follow the interest of the powerful, who are known by their ability to sway public sentiment. The strong control society for their own selfish purposes, reflecting a basic human urge that only a few can carry off. Everyone else must follow the stronger, or they will be crushed. Great ideals of philosophy or the public good do not guide political action. What counts are power and its tangible rewards, such as wealth and prestige.

In keeping with their practical view of politics, the Sophists hired themselves out as political advisers, pollsters, and lawyers. They trained Athenian citizens in the techniques of persuading others to give them votes and political support. They also advised litigants in courts, where verdicts were based on swaying a majority of large juries.

Against the Sophists, the absolutist position was exemplified by Plato, speaking through Socrates. Platonic dialogues, such as the *Republic,* illustrate the use of a dialectic method of seeking truth through reasoned debate. The idea of the dialectic is for each side to press the logical implications of asserted statements and their opposites until only the clear, unvarnished truth remains. Of course, this is not quite what happens in the *Republic.* The narrative is a setup for the sharp-minded Socrates to repeatedly demonstrate the false logic of the Sophist position. The views of Socrates' opponents are not given full consideration, and indeed as the work moves on they receive less and less attention until all we are left with is one side of the debate. Behind the apparent openness of the dialogue, which portrays Socrates as a questioner and searcher after truth, and one who says nobody (including him) truly knows justice, is a fundamental assumption about the nature of the universe that leads directly to absolutist conclusions.

PLATO'S METHOD

An exchange between Glaucon and Socrates introduces Plato's method of thinking about political issues.

GLAUCON: And whom do you mean by the genuine philosophers?

SOCRATES: Those whose passion it is to see the truth.

GLAUCON: That must be so; but will you explain?

SOCRATES: It would not be easy to explain to everyone; but you, I believe, will grant my premise.

GLAUCON: Which is—?

SOCRATES: That since beauty and ugliness are opposite, they are two things; and consequently each of them is one. The same holds of justice and injustice, good and bad, and all the essential Forms: each in itself is one; but they manifest themselves in a great variety of combinations, with actions, with material things, and with one another, and so each seems to be many.[5]

Plato's method begins with the assumption that the one explanation for why things change is found in the doctrine of the forms. This doctrine partly agrees with the relativist view that all matter is constantly undergoing change and decay. However, Plato goes further: Behind changing material objects, and the institutions and opinions based on them, is a reality that is constant. It consists of a number of eternal forms which never change and endure forever. These invisible forms exist, independently of the material world of the senses, in heaven. Each form is a universal idea, a divine value known only to the intellect, and superior to any earthly, material, or conventional goal.

For example, when we call someone a "person," we mean that this individual has certain traits in common with all other members of the category called persons. When we designate an object as a desk, we are saying that it has the necessary attributes of "deskness." To Plato, it is the forms that are truly real; all physical objects are merely the appearances the forms emit. Furthermore, all matter has an ideal form—humans, city-states, even justice. To Plato, only philosophers can know the forms, being the only ones capable of discovering them because of their refined ability to reason. Thus the sense experiences on which the relativists rely to try to define and apply values like justice can only provide a distorted and corrupt view of reality. Follow them and, driven by irrational desires, one bounces from one opinion to another, ending up skeptical of all political values and practices.

Those who know the forms, however, perceive the true nature, the essence, the ideal shape or natural pattern of physical objects and events. That which is natural is the basis of reality, and it can be known by the application of reason. The capacity to reason lies in the immortal soul, which lives on after the body dies. It guides the philosophers to a higher purpose, directing them to the difference between good and evil and to an absolute and completely knowable standard of the "good," or ideal justice.

Justice is the highest goal of political life because it enables everyone to fully realize themselves, to fulfill their true natures. In our deepest being, all of us have the urge to search for justice, and we are obligated to seek it insofar as our individual intellects or natures allow. This obligation requires that individuals be led by reason, and that societies be ruled by those who have the fullest capacity for rational thought. Thus those who fully know and understand the form of true justice—the wise philosophers—should be elevated to political leadership in the ideal state. Only this arrangement can serve as the correct foundation for the *Republic*.

KNOWLEDGE AND JUSTICE

Knowledge of the forms begins with the senses, but ends in concepts independent of the senses. To explain this, Plato uses the image of a vertical line divided into two levels. Each level is subdivided into two, producing four parts or stages. The lower level represents the physical world of matter and appearance. At its first sublevel, the bottom stage, people see only the shadows of things, the images of objects. The meanest animals, as well as ordinary unthinking folk, can detect this world of mere existence. At the second stage, objects themselves appear, which leads those who function at this level, such as the Sophists, to express beliefs and opinions.

The higher level is the world of the mind and the soul. The third stage is that of abstraction. This is the realm of those who fully understand theoretical matters—the mathematician, the scientist, the student of logic. The fourth and highest stage of cognition or knowing is one that only a few can reach, only those who are naturally qualified by superior intellect and considerable education. This stage is reality, or true knowledge, and only philosophers can reach it.[6]

Further, of all the forms, the highest one at the highest stage "is the essential nature of the good, from which everything that is good and right derives its value for us."[7] All other forms refer back to this idea of the good. It is the absolute standard for evaluating everything, and dependent on nothing else; it is the original cause in the universe. As such, it unifies all material things in the universe, and applies to both individuals and governments.

HUMAN NATURE

Plato believes that all things can and must be judged as good or bad, whether a desk, a person, or a political regime, depending on how well each fulfills its nature or essence. The form of the good is the basis for such judgments. It is *ethical*, since it establishes the standard for judging imperfect, actual humans and governments. But it is also *political*, because it can serve as the solid foundation for the government (or state) established according to true human nature. Only by fully serving people's true natures can any state be judged as good. Thus realizing the good in the state and its citizens is the foundation of justice.

Recall that the *Republic* is a philosophical discussion between Socrates and his companions on the nature of justice. He rejects the several partial definitions offered by his fellows: that it is moral (Cephalus), ethical (Polemarchus), political (Thrasymachus), or social (Glaucon and Adeimantus). His rejection is based on his absolutist perspective, an idea of natural justice that unites all their partial views into one scheme. Justice, he says, is a quality, an idea of the good, that makes humans at once moral and ethical and social-political. In this way, he links justice in the polis with justice in the individual, absorbing the private into the public. Only in the just state can individuals fully realize their true nature as both good people and good citizens; without such political order they are in chaos.

All of these aspects of justice are united by Plato's idea that all people are by nature *rational,* in that they all have some capacity for reason, but that they are also naturally unequal, in that some have more of this capacity than others. In each soul, reason should rule appetite, and in the just, or ideal state, those with greater reason should rule those with less.

THE IDEAL STATE

The state originates in the fact that isolated individuals are not self-sufficient. Rather, they are social (i.e., political) animals united by certain basic needs. These are, first, the material needs of economic self-sufficiency and security, but at a higher level they are social needs such as friendship. Plato says that to treat humans justly, all must regard others as citizens first, and that the just state must be organized on that basis.

The Need for Specialization

You remember how, when we first began to establish our commonwealth and several times since, we have laid down, as a universal principle, that everyone ought to perform the one function in the community for which his nature best suited him. Well, I believe that that principle, or some form of it, is justice.[8]

For each individual, what is just varies with one's abilities; justice requires that one does what he or she is by nature best fit to do. Plato assumes that there is one, and only one, proper role for each person. Some are born to be rulers, others to labor. The just state is based on this principle of specialization, this economic division of labor. Thus citizens must subordinate their personal wishes to a higher reason and do what they are told for the public good. The result is a twofold order, social and psychological, produced by the harmony among all members of society and the peace within each soul. The just state unites their true economic needs and sociopolitical natures.

This picture contrasts sharply with the unjust state, which is in utter chaos. Here people's economic and social needs compete with each other due to the rule of appetite over reason. Those in power elevate their individual desires over the collective good. The never-ending desire for more control and luxuries leads to internal instability, war, and continual social upheaval. The growth of individuals is curbed, as is the proper growth of society as a whole, for people are unable to satisfy their deepest needs. In the disordered state, which to Plato means those that fall short of the ideal, true philosophers seem useless to the majority of citizens because they don't know how much they need them. The majority are like the patient who is ill but regards the physician who would help (i.e., the philosopher) as a dreamer who talks a strange language. Furthermore, the opinion of the majority seduces many potential philosophers into becoming Sophists who give the public what it wants. This can be changed, but only by uniting the separate activities of philosopher and legitimate ruler into the role of philosopher-king.

Plato imagines how to effect this union in the "Allegory of the Cave." The cave is like a democracy, which Plato detested as a regime encouraging the excesses and injustices of appetite and public opinion. Residents of the cave live at the lower level of cognition, seeing only the shadows of objects, just as in a democracy most people live in a dream world of pseudoknowledge. They have beliefs about specific things, and can perhaps recognize a beautiful piece of art or a just law, but their standards for judging these material things are superficial and ever-changing.

By contrast, the philosopher is like the one who goes outside the cave and sees the real world in full sunlight. In other words, he has reached the fourth stage of cognition and knows the form of the good. But he is ridiculed when he returns to the cave and tells the others what he saw. Believing that they already see, the majority are sure of themselves, since public opinion is on their side.

However, with the help of patient reason and education, true philosophers can help everyone to participate in the good in accordance with their nature. The philosopher's duty is to return to the cave and lead the majority to see for themselves, as Socrates had tried to do. Ultimately, a state becomes just when philosophers are given the authority to rule. They do not seek power for its own sake, as do the pseudophilosophers, the Sophists. Rather, they rule because they realize that if they do not, they are governed by inferiors and a just state cannot be established.

Class Structure and Functions

So if a state is constituted on natural principles, the wisdom it possesses as a whole will be due to the knowledge residing in the smallest part, the one which takes the lead and governs the rest. Such knowledge is the only kind that deserves the name of wisdom, and it appears to be ordained by nature that the class privileged to possess it should be the smallest of all. . . .

That illustrates the result we were doing our best to achieve when we were choosing our fighting men and training their minds and bodies . . . so that, in virtue of having both the right temperament and the right education, their convictions about what ought to be feared and on all other subjects might be indelibly fixed. . . . Such a power of constantly preserving, in accordance with our institutions, the right conviction about the things which ought, or ought not, to be feared, is what I call courage. . . .

[I]t appears now that these protectors of our state will have a life better and more honourable than . . . the life of a shoemaker or other artisan or of a farmer.[9]

Plato provides some detail on the structure of the just state, which he calls the Republic. He divides members into three classes: the rulers; the auxiliaries (to the rulers); and the workers, who are politically unequal. The auxiliaries and the workers are subject classes and do not participate in governmental decision making; they merely carry out the directives of the rulers.[10]

But each class plays a necessary part in this organic, or interrelated, polis. Each carries out a key function that is its contribution to the whole. Each has characteristic traits that define the obligations and rewards that guide its actions. The traits specify the place of every individual in the society. Class lines are clearly drawn, and each class is limited to one function.

The workers constitute the largest, and politically lowest, class. Their trait is appetitive. They seek wealth and other material things to gratify their physical wants and needs. Unlike the other two classes, they are permitted to own private property, marry, and live in nuclear family units. At the same time, however, they have sufficient reason, developed through limited education, to recognize the right of the wise to rule. Thus they temper their appetites and willingly allow their wealth to be restricted by the rulers to promote social justice and harmony. This means that there are no extremes of wealth and poverty among the workers. Economically, the workers' function is to provide for the material needs of the Republic. Its members are engaged in all those tasks of agriculture and craftsmanship necessary for economic well-being, from farmer to shoemaker to carpenter.[11]

The two higher classes, the rulers and the auxiliaries, are called guardians. They are the governors, and both are composed of men and women who are equal to one another based on their class traits.

The auxiliaries are spirited and courageous, and have been trained to love honor. They are kind to their friends, the obedient fellow citizens, but ruthless toward enemies. And, "like watchdogs obeying the shepherds of the commonwealth," their function is to execute the rulers' decisions.[12] They form the bureaucracy of the Republic, including the police and the army, which are needed to control signs of greed among the workers.

The key trait of the few rulers, the philosopher-kings and philosopher-queens, is their reason, and their function is that of decision making. They are a highly trained administrative and political class that directs the entire Republic, including the educational process and the placement of all individuals in their proper class and function. They are the source of all law and directives, which are grounded in their sense of equity or fairness and based on a reason only they possess.

The legitimate right of rulers to political power is absolute. The justification for this lies in both their natural talents and their education. They "know themselves," that is, they know the difference between good and evil, and can apply this knowledge to their decision making. They can do so because they have come rationally to know the good, which enables them to control their appetites and govern justly.

Both classes of guardians are selfless, disciplined, and dedicated to duty. They have no expectation of either personal happiness or economic gain from their service. To them, government simply represents the most important and fitting job for people who combine the highest levels of knowledge and virtue. But to prevent private or class interests from conflicting with their political obligations, Plato places two restrictions on them that do not apply to the workers. First, guardians may not have nuclear families. Husbands and wives

are shared by all, as are children. To prevent an unjust caste system from arising, offspring may not inherit class membership from their parents. Instead,
when they mature, all children are placed in the class that their individual
traits qualify them for. Second, guardians may not own private property.
Under a system of communism, or joint ownership, all their goods are held in
common and distributed only on the basis of fundamental needs.[13] They are
to enjoy no luxuries, live in common barracks, and eat their meals in a common dining hall. Guardians accept these restrictions because they care more
for the good of the state than themselves or their children. They know that
the values of service and justice are more important than wealth, power, or
family.

Education and Censorship. Plato believes that civic virtue, or good citizenship, can be taught. His scheme of education is designed as an alternative
to laws. It teaches each class its obligations and encourages the classes to regulate themselves as much as possible. Given this mission, education is totally
in the hands of public authorities.

It is the job of each generation of rulers to oversee the recruitment and
training of the next, for the rulers are also philosopher-educators. The purpose of education is to train children from an early age to adopt the norms
of society so they might become sociable and happy citizens. It is open to
all at the beginning, but it is basically an elitist scheme in which only a few
individuals receive further training if their aptitude and the needs of society
allow it.[14]

The education of the workers teaches them to obey their superiors and
control any excessive materialistic desires. The auxiliaries learn to accept and
follow their rulers' every command, and are trained to be courageous in protecting the state. Plato's educational scheme produces a few rulers who possess wisdom. While only rulers can be educated to know the good, all others
can participate in the rulers' goodness after learning the special kind of virtue
befitting their class. That special virtue makes all subjects into good individuals who are qualified to live in a well-ordered Republic.

All education is designed to serve the state—to unify the classes and to
strengthen the commanding role of the rulers. Such subjects as music, literature, and the arts are taught more for their higher moral and political value
than for their own sake. This purpose justifies censorship of all new musical
forms and any passages in poetry that present bad examples and undermine
people's faith in the gods. It also sanctions myths, "noble" lies that are taught
for valid, state-approved reasons. The "Allegory of the Metals," for example,
supports the class structure:

> [W]e shall tell our people in this fable, that all of you in this land are broth-
> ers; but the god who fashioned you mixed gold in the composition of those
> among you who are fit to rule, so that they are of the most precious quality;
> and he put silver in the Auxiliaries, and iron and brass in the farmers and
> craftsmen.[15]

Such myths, though not completely rational, are to be taught and accepted as truth by all, even the rulers. Plato differentiates them from harmful lies such as the opinions of the Sophists, which could divide the Republic and pit antagonistic classes against each other to benefit a few politicians.

The Role of Women. Plato breaks sharply with some traditional ancient Greek views of women's place in society.[16] Recall that his guardian classes are composed of women and men, who are equal, and that neither lives in a nuclear family. Plato did this because of his denial of any private role for the guardians, which led him to radically question every politically relevant difference between the sexes.[17] As a result, Plato has been called a revolutionary and a feminist, and was thought to hold that biology is not destiny and that women's intellect can contribute positively to government.[18] But how radical is he really?

In the Republic, a few women are guardians and thus decision makers. But Plato establishes a fundamentally elitist society in which the many, both men and women, are permanent subjects. In addition, the women who are granted equality with men have no access to the private realm of the family. They lose that which, to some feminist critics, is most important—their feminine side—which is not compensated for by developing their rational side or enjoying equality with a few men. Nevertheless, Plato establishes the principle that political discrimination between the sexes requires proof that the discrimination can be justified.

INEVITABLE DECLINE OF THE IDEAL STATE

Plato's vision has a tragic side: Even if the ideal state can be established, it cannot last. His world is ruled by a cycle of creation, decay, and dissolution that can only rarely be escaped, and then only for a brief time. He sees the Republic being replaced one day by another form of government, which he calls a *timocracy*. The auxiliaries, who emphasize courage, honor, and war, take over from the philosophers.

But this form does not last either. Over time, courage fades, and the timocracy is followed in a later generation by an oligarchy, or rule of the wealthy. They are motivated by greed and fear of losing what they have. They control the government so as to protect and enlarge their wealth. After a time, the poor masses demand liberty and a democracy, wherein all have a share in governing and the needs of the many poor come first. Near anarchy inevitably follows, according to Plato. So someone calls out for a strongman to restore order. The strongman starts out by ruling as a benevolent dictator, but soon shows himself as a tyrant. Reflecting the values advanced by Thrasymachus, he is the exact opposite of the philosopher, an educated but twisted genius who brings the state to its lowest level. Under tyranny, wherein the ruler cares only for satisfying personal desires, soul is sacrificed for appetite and virtue for evil. It is the worst form of government Plato can imagine.

CONCLUSION

In some ways, our disordered times are like those of Plato, and the certainty he often expresses may be as hard to understand now as it was then. We question his proposals for the Republic, echoing Adeimantus's judgment that the rulers will not be happy. To this Socrates replies that they may not be happy as individuals, but that the aim of the Republic is not to make any one individual or class happy. It is to secure the greatest possible happiness for the state as a whole. The result is a harmonious society in which all are organically interrelated. Plato's premise is that the state is simply the individual writ large. As the traits of reason, spirit, and appetite are organically interdependent in the just individual, with reason ruling the other two, so it is in the just state. Rulers depend on workers for their material needs, and workers depend on rulers for guidance. If each class has its own trait and function, there is no class warfare, or even discord, for all classes have what they economically need to do their job and live well. In the *Republic,* ideas of rich and poor have no meaning.

One of Plato's central ideas, which is so familiar today that we almost take it for granted, is that for a government to be just it must serve the public interest, for the benefit of all who live under it. To Plato, this means that the good state is obliged to provide all its citizens with justice, or the opportunity to participate according to their basic individual natures.

He argues that we are born with unequal traits, abilities, and talents, and that government must be directed by those who are capable of organizing a just society. His choice reflects a second original notion: that political authority must be given to the persons who can unite wisdom and power, who can give the state the unity necessary to be a good state for all its people.

Whether one agrees with the specifics, the *Republic* is important because it was the first major work of political philosophy in the West. Plato's vision is comprehensive, an integrated package based on a view of truth superior to that found in any existing regime, "one that set forth forever the stamp of his genius on . . . political philosophy."[19] It represents the earliest effort to systematically distinguish between the essentials (the right or just) and the accidents of life (the socially acceptable or expedient). This original work reminds us of the obligation to question the society in which we live, rather than accept it as the only possibility available. As the unexamined life is not worth living, so the unexamined state may not be worth living in.

Plato was not scientific in the modern sense of the word. But his attitude, together with those of other philosophers of his era, both relativist and absolutist, contribute to the early scientific view that political and social issues are open to rational analysis, and that reason can be used to temper politics and people.[20]

Certainly, those who have asserted that all political thought (indeed, all Western philosophy) is but a footnote to Plato have a point. Whether rejecting his conclusions or agreeing with them, all subsequent writers have had to come to terms with his sweeping vision.

The *Republic* argues for the superiority of the collective over the individual. Plato has a sincere concern for the collective (government and society) and for individuals as well. His conclusion is that the welfare of these entities can best be promoted through a political system that does not so much establish a hierarchy of state over society, or collective over individual, as refuse to distinguish between them.[21] We can trace the reasons for this to Plato's position that reality is an ideal found in forms, which are knowable only to the true philosopher. He then recognizes the superior reason of philosophers as the legitimate source of just government, which places long-range duties above immediate desires and is most beneficial to the individual as well as the community.

It is evident that the community Plato had in mind is geographically similar to a polis. Whatever the capacity of rulers for wisdom, Plato likely thought that a larger state would make it more difficult for rulers to fully know each other and their subjects, and to control society as completely as his scheme requires for justice.

Some interpreters of Plato's *Republic* claim that he wrote it because he believed it could be realized in practice. They usually dismiss the political conclusions of the book as the product of a utopian dreamer.[22] To others, who focus on Plato's tragic vision of the inevitable decay of a supposedly ideal polis, his work is not a blueprint for an actual society. Rather, they see it as setting a standard by which actual governments may be evaluated, and setting the stage for narrowing "the gap between the possibilities grasped through political imagination and the actualities of political existence."[23] They cite Plato's myths and allegories as illustrations of how difficult, even impossible, it would be to establish and maintain a Republic, since how could we expect rational philosophers to believe in them? As Socrates asks later in the dialogue, "Is it not in the nature of things that action should come less close to truth than thought?"[24]

This viewpoint suggests that although the theory may never be fully realized in practice, it can be useful for framing questions about governments. From this perspective, the *Republic* does not provide us so much with answers as, in true Socratic fashion, it leads us to a recognition of the problems people face in seeking justice. If we do not use the comprehensive perspectives of political philosophers to judge and renew troubled governments, what more valid criteria can we apply? Thus the *Republic* is not only Plato's response to the Sophists, but the ultimate political question for all time.

Notes

1. For more on Plato's life and family, see A. E. Taylor, *Plato: The Man and His Work* (Cleveland: World, 1966).

2. Plato wrote a total of some twenty-seven dialogues, or conversations about philosophical topics, as well as a number of epistles, or letters. Seven are considered major political works: in addition to the *Republic*, these are *Gorgias*, on the role of education in politics; *Apology,*

Crito, and *Phaedo,* on Socrates' trial, imprisonment, and execution; and *Statesman* and *Laws,* late works that are less utopian and more practical in their discussion of politics.

3. Plato's *Seventh Epistle* indicates the influence of Socrates' views on justice, human nature, and government.

4. Pre-Socratic philosophers deserve credit for being the first "political thinkers," for they were the earliest ones to identify politics as a distinct field of inquiry. Sheldon S. Wolin, *Politics and Vision: Continuity and Innovation in Western Political Thought* (Boston: Little, Brown, 1960), 29–32.

5. Plato, *The Republic of Plato,* [sec.] 475d–476a. Quotations are from the trans. by F. M. Cornford (London: Oxford University Press, 1972), praised as "indispensable" by Reginald Allen in his *Greek Philosophy: Thales to Aristotle,* 2d ed. (New York: Free Press, 1985), 435. References are to standard section numbers found in most editions of the Republic.

6. See http://politicalscience.wadsworth.com/tannenbaum2 for a link to an illustration of Plato's stages of knowledge.

7. *Republic,* 505a.

8. *Republic,* 433a.

9. *Republic,* 428e–29a, 429e–30b, 466a–b.

10. *Republic,* 440d.

11. See, for example, *Republic,* 547d and 598b–c.

12. *Republic,* 440d.

13. Plato's communism is a far cry from the kind developed many centuries later by Karl Marx. Plato's applied only to a minority of the people, Marx's to the entire population. Plato's originated from class cooperation, Marx's from class warfare.

14. See Robin Barrow, *Plato, Utilitarianism, and Education* (London: Routledge, 1975); and Irving M. Zeitlin, *Plato's Vision: The Classical Origins of Social and Political Thought* (Englewood Cliffs, N.J.: Prentice Hall, 1993).

15. *Republic,* 415a.

16. On the traditional Greek view of women, see especially Arlene W. Saxonhouse, *Women in the History of Political Thought: Ancient Greece to Machiavelli* (New York: Praeger, 1985), ch. 2; and Diana Coole, *Women in Political Theory: From Ancient Misogyny to Contemporary Feminism* (Boulder, Colo.: Lynne Rienner, 1988), ch. 1.

17. Susan Moller Okin, *Women in Western Political Thought* (Princeton, N.J.: Princeton University Press, 1979), ch. 2. In fact, Plato excised all irrelevant consideration not only of sex but of age, class, family, race, tradition, and history; see Jean Bethke Elshtain, *Public Man, Private Woman: Women in Social and Political Thought* (Princeton, N.J.: Princeton University Press, 1981), ch. 1.

18. Elizabeth V. Spelman, *Inessential Woman: Problems of Exclusion in Feminist Thought* (Boston: Beacon, 1988), ch. 1.

19. *Politics and Vision,* 31.

20. Beginning with Book 8, Plato initiates his classification of forms of government, which he develops in the later dialogues, *Statesman* and *Laws.* Aristotle uses them as the basis for one of the major systematic planks in his development of political science.

21. For a view of Plato as an enemy of the individual and an originator of totalitarianism, see Karl Popper, *The Open Society and Its Enemies,* vol. I: *The Spell of Plato,* 5th ed. (Princeton, N.J.: Princeton University Press, 1966).

22. See, for example, Dale Hall, "The Republic and the 'Limits of Politics,'" *Political Theory* 5:3 (1977): 293–313.

23. *Politics and Vision,* 20. See also Leo Strauss, *The City of Man* (Chicago: University of Chicago Press, 1964); Allan Bloom, "Response to Hall," *Political Theory* 5:3 (1977): 315–20; and Darryl Dobbs, "Choosing Justice: Socrates' Model City and the Practice of the Dialectic," *American Political Science Review* 88:2 (June 1994): 263–77. Plato's use of myths and allegories to undergird the *Republic* also shows how difficult it would be to establish one, since there is a contradiction between the need for rational philosophers to rule and the need for them to believe such myths.

24. *Republic*, 473a. A recent work which uses considerable originality and subtlety to take a stand between the two positions is Adi Ophir, *Plato's Invisible Cities: Discourse and Power in the Republic* (New York: Barnes & Noble, 1991).

Additional Readings

(* indicates alternative interpretation)

Dobbs, Darryl. "Choosing Justice: Socrates' Model City and the Practice of the Dialectic." *American Political Science Review* 88:2 (June 1994): 263–77.

Guthrie, W. K. C. *Socrates*. Cambridge: Cambridge University Press, 1971.

*Hall, Dale. "The Republic and the 'Limits of Politics.'" *Political Theory* 5:3 (1977): 293–313.

Monoson, S. Sara. *Plato's Democratic Entanglements: Athenian Politics and the Practice of Philosophy*. Princeton, N.J.: Princeton University Press, 2000.

Ophir, Adi. *Plato's Invisible Cities: Discourse and Power in the Republic*. New York: Barnes & Noble, 1991.

*Popper, Karl. *The Open Society and Its Enemies*. Vol. I. *The Spell of Plato*. 5th ed. Princeton, N.J.: Princeton University Press, 1966.

Taylor, Alfred. Socrates: *The Man and His Thought*. Garden City, N.Y.: Doubleday, 1953.

Zeitlin, Irving M. *Plato's Vision: The Classical Origins of Social and Political Thought*. Englewood Cliffs, N.J.: Prentice Hall, 1993.

Inventors of Ideas Online

Visit http://politicalscience.wadsworth.com/tannenbaum2 for an illustration of Plato's stages of knowledge and links related to material in this chapter, including sites containing a translation of the complete text of Plato's *Republic*, the texts of his political works, *Statesman* and *Laws*, as well as his earlier dialogues.

4

ARISTOTLE: ENDORSING COMMUNITY

INTRODUCTION

Of all the long journeys Aristotle made during his life (384–322 B.C.E.), the most important one of his youth took him from his remote birthplace to the city of Athens. There, the teenager became a student at Plato's Academy when the great master was in his sixties, and the years Aristotle spent with Plato profoundly influenced his thinking.[1]

Aristotle discusses political issues in a number of his works, but the *Politics* is considered the account of his most important political views.[2] If Aristotle disagrees significantly with Plato's *Republic* on a number of points (noted later) he shares with his teacher certain assumptions and conclusions, such as the importance of education and the foolishness of a life devoted to the pursuit of power politics and wealth. Because he was born outside of Athens, Aristotle was ineligible to become an Athenian citizen.[3] Nevertheless, he was a strong admirer of the Athenian polis. This is evident from the first paragraph of the *Politics*. It immediately draws our attention to "the most sovereign of all" associations, which "includes all the rest" and is directed to the pursuit of the highest good for all, human happiness or the good life.[4] The association that makes the good life possible is none other than the polis. Aristotle's central concerns in the *Politics* may be stated quite simply: Why has the Greek polis, specifically the Athenian city-state, declined as a viable form of government, and what should be done about it?[5]

The decline of Athens was accompanied by the rise of the Macedonian army-empire led by Aristotle's former student, Alexander the Great. Aristotle's entire philosophy in the *Politics* rejects the imperial model of Alexander, and in Book II he also sets forth objections to a number of other options. One major target is Plato's *Republic*. Aristotle's disagreement with Plato is twofold. First, he takes issue with Plato's political economy. He disagrees with Plato's communism for the guardian classes, arguing that such a commonality of families and property is contrary to human nature. It destroys two basic needs all men, even the wisest, have. One of these is family love, and Aristotle says one cannot love that which is everyone's as much as what is one's own. He also claims that a modest amount of private property is a natural need for all men, rulers included. It is essential to each person's legitimate economic ends, both to secure the basic necessities of life for oneself and to show kindness to one's fellows through charity. Furthermore, the pleasure one derives from having and using property is harmless as long as it is not excessive or selfish. So, Aristotle concludes, property may be put in private hands, but its use should further the common ends or goals of the community.

A second area of strong disagreement with Plato's ideas centers on Aristotle's opposition to rule by philosopher-kings. Contrary to rulers governing based on their theoretical knowledge of the forms, Aristotle thinks that practical knowledge, arising from experience, is a sounder basis for governing.

ARISTOTLE'S METHOD

The source of Aristotle's disagreement with Plato is their differing views of what is real. Whereas Plato believes that reality consists of the eternal forms found in heaven, Aristotle thinks that the real nature of anything cannot be located outside of the object itself. His method of knowing reality is to focus on the highest end or goal of an object. This principal end, called the *telos*, is what anything becomes when its growth is complete if it is able to develop fully from its inner nature. For example, the telos of an acorn is an oak tree, which does not yet exist but will exist if the acorn develops naturally. For Aristotle, then, one discovers or "sees" reality in objects. Because it stems from the inner telos of the object, reality is not a Platonic form above and outside of it. Aristotle does not so much reject forms as link them to experience, and he thus brings Plato down to earth. In this way, he is more "scientific" than Plato.

Moreover, Aristotle believes it is natural for man to shape objects to fulfill basic (or natural) human needs. Therefore telos can also refer to what a thing, whether a chair or a polis, will become when its shaping is complete. Furthermore, one can know the end of the polis only after the study of many actual city-states. In pursuit of such knowledge, Aristotle and his colleagues studied the constitutions of some 158 Greek city-states, which is the earliest known exploration into comparative political science. Finally, knowledge enables one to exercise the unique human faculty of judgment. For once we know its telos we can judge whether any particular object, be it a tree, chair, man, or polis, is good or bad.

HAPPINESS, VALUES, AND HUMAN NATURE

The soul rules the body with the sort of authority of a master: mind rules the appetite with the sort of authority of a statesman or monarch. In this sphere [i.e., in the sphere of man's inner life] it is clearly natural and beneficial to the body that it should be ruled by the soul, and again it is natural and beneficial to the affective part of the soul that it should be ruled by the mind and the rational part.[6]

To Aristotle, the basis for judging any polis is its telos, which is human happiness or the good life. He agrees with Plato that this telos is an activity of the soul, not the body; in other words, happiness is not the same as physical pleasure. Rather, it involves the search for knowledge that leads to wisdom, and it is wisdom that brings men to self-realization and happiness.

Aristotle's concept of happiness includes a distinction between two kinds of decisions or actions, rational and irrational. Rational acts are based on use of the mind and are exclusively human. Thus Aristotle concludes that human nature is rational. That man, by nature, is a rational animal means that his goal is to exercise his reason to the fullest; only then can he be happy. By virtue of reason man is also a political animal. Only such rational beings can establish a polis based on reason, and they cannot live just lives apart from the polis.

Men as rational and political animals are wholly absorbed within an organic community where the individual and the collective are interdependent. The good polis can never be a place where a mere collection of people pursue private interests in a public arena. When men set themselves apart from the polis by satisfying personal concerns, they harm the community. Aristotle says they are acting irrationally. Leading such a separate life qualifies them as either beast or god, but not human.

Aristotle believes that the emotions which express appetites or desires have an appropriate place in the polis, once they are controlled by reason. Reason exercises this control over appetites when guided by the principle of the golden mean. The golden mean is Aristotle's idea of the best available guide to right conduct. He believes that almost all things have a good (or proper) use and a number of bad (improper) ones. Excess or extremes in either direction can injure things of value. For example, for the body, excess may consist of too much or too little exercise, food, drink, or sleep. Thus that which is good is not some ideal, as Plato thinks, but a golden mean between the extremes of excess and deficiency. And the task of the good polis is to determine the proper mean in those things it must regulate, and to translate that mean into its laws. Good laws, Aristotle believes, present good examples and implant good habits in people, which constitute the foundation of a good polis.

POLITICAL ECONOMY

All articles of property have two possible uses. Both of these uses belong to the article as such, but they do not belong to it in the same manner, or to the same extent. The one use is proper and peculiar to the article concerned; the other is not.[7]

Political economy, or the interrelation of politics and economics, is as important to Aristotle as it is to Plato. Aristotle's treatment of this relationship can also serve to illustrate one way the doctrine of the golden mean works. By its nature, economics is merely instrumental—a tool. Like food or drink, it can be used either rationally or irrationally. It can be a means to the rational end of the polis, which is happiness, or it can bring unhappiness. Although a polis must balance many instrumental values in search of this end, economics is concerned with only a single aspect: the amount of wealth necessary for true happiness. Wealth has a proper limit that the higher end or goal of the polis defines. When subordinated to rational politics, wealth can be put to good use and can help the polis. If unbalanced, or allowed to run to excess, if it appeals to the irrational appetites of citizens in a mad quest for economic superiority, wealth can corrupt the polis to the core. In general these principles lead to the recognition that certain kinds of economic activity are rational, or good, while others are irrational, or bad, for the polis.

The most basic form of good economic activity is directed toward use of a product. Examples include farming, fishing, or making a pair of shoes that its maker will wear. In all cases, human labor is applied to raw materials, and the resulting products directly fill a need of the producer and his or her family. Therefore, this activity is natural; it is not an end in itself, but it has use value.

As a society becomes more complex, trade grows, as does the specialization of labor. People begin to make products that they exchange for goods made by others through a barter system. Thus things take on an exchange value in addition to their use value. Exchange is good as long as the exchange value of a product is incidental to getting a product from maker to user.

Further development of society introduces money to the economy. The role of money is good as long as it is simply a refinement of the barter system, that is, if it serves as a basis for comparing unlike things being exchanged and if the most natural (use) value of the product remains central to the economic process. The role of money is unnatural and harmful to the polis, however, when profit becomes its purpose. The most extreme case is when money is invested in order to make more money, as with payments of interest. In this case, the natural purpose of production and trade, the focus on use value, is lost. The profit motive introduces injustice, and an unlimited desire for wealth replaces natural limits on human needs. The irrational appetites that are unleashed can run wild, and the natural relationship between economics and politics—the golden mean—is destroyed. The polis is doomed.

Clearly, Aristotle believes material goods are necessary; people cannot be economically deprived and still enjoy happiness. But the material means to this higher end must not be allowed to become the ends. Happiness of the soul is vastly superior to wealth on Aristotle's scale of values.[8]

COMMUNITY

A *natural impulse* is thus one reason why men desire to live a social life even when they stand in no need of mutual succor; but they are also drawn together by a *common interest*, in proportion as each attains a share in good life. The good life is the chief end, both for the community as a whole and for each of us individually.[9]

Unlike Plato, whose central concern is justice, Aristotle focuses on community. This does not mean that Aristotle is uninterested in justice; he is. But, paralleling his disagreement with Plato over the nature of reality, Aristotle thinks of justice as something to be found within an actual community, rather than in an earthly representation of a heavenly form.

To be human, Aristotle says, is by definition to be part of a community. All communities originate from the need to preserve human life, but have as their ultimate goal the happiness of their members. The community that follows the golden mean, avoiding extremes, provides the necessary conditions for each person's search for the good life. These conditions include meeting basic material needs as well as friendship and political stability. One can hope to find happiness only when living in a community that provides these conditions.

In Aristotle's scheme, there are three kinds of community, each established for some higher purpose than existence or even material advantage. Ranking them from lowest to highest, they are the household, the village, and the polis.

Household, Wife, Woman, and Slave. The household originates from the biological urges men and women share with all other animals. Thus it is based on natural relationships people enter into impulsively, not just rationally or deliberately. Economically, the household is based on production for use by family members. But it is not established only to satisfy the basic needs of its members, or mere survival. One of its ends is family life, including interdependence between husband and wife, each of whom has a key role in meeting household requirements.

However interdependent, husband and wife are not equal. Because Aristotle judges them naturally superior in reason, men are dominant. This is clear in Aristotle's description of men's three roles in the household: father, husband, and master. As father, he must rule his children so they are prepared for life after they leave his household. Female children must be trained to become wives. Although such training is primarily the task of the mother, a daughter's relationship with her father teaches her the appropriate relationship she is to have later with her husband. Sons, on the other hand, are trained not only to be husbands but also for lives as free men, as citizens.

As husbands, men must rule their wives permanently. Because of their natural superiority due to their reasoning power, they are more fit to command, women to obey. However, women are in no way to be considered slaves, since they are not by nature mere instruments created for men's use. Rather, women are complements to men. Husbands must rule wives "constitutionally," that is, with reason, and not despotically.

As for the man's role of master, Aristotle recognizes two kinds of slave: conventional and natural. A slave by convention is someone who is not by nature fit to be one. Such people have reason and are qualified for citizenship in their own polis. They are usually enslaved following the defeat of their army in warfare, a common practice in Aristotle's time. A natural slave, on the other hand, lacks reason and must be ruled permanently by a master. This arrangement benefits both master and slave. When left to themselves, natural slaves are irrational and unable to manage their own affairs. But when they obey their master's rational orders, they are better off, since by obeying they participate in their master's virtue. Masters, of course, benefit because slaves allow them the leisure time necessary for citizenship.

Aristotle reaches these conclusions about women and slaves because he sees all people as part of a natural order, arranged from top to bottom, based on the ability to reason. As the soul rules the body and reason governs passion, men must rule women and masters their slaves. Those who lack reason live their lives in serving positions, for the mutual benefit of everyone.[10]

Village. The village, or social community, originates from a union of households. Its ends are twofold. The village provides a greater degree of protection and economic self-sufficiency than is possible for any of the single households that constitute it. It permits production for exchange, while a household alone is limited to production for use. The village also facilitates friendship, which Aristotle considers a natural requirement for all humans, and friendship promotes social harmony.

The highest sort of friendship can only be based on equality. This is unattainable in the household, since whether he acts as husband, parent, or master, the man is involved in an unequal relationship which precludes true friendship. The village is the natural setting for fraternity among rational men.

Polis. The heart of the *Politics* is Book III on the polis, which is regarded as the foundation of political science in the West. For Aristotle,

> Hierarchy, like teleology, gives meaning to the world, for it establishes what is highest, what is the best. What is, exists for the sake of the best; without hierarchy, the world would lack meaning and nature would be chaotic.[11]

The polis, the supreme form of community for Aristotle, has the highest purpose of all communities. The end (telos) of the polis is the highest because it both involves the entire population, and enables rational men to participate in the political process to reach a higher degree of happiness and virtue than is possible in any of the smaller communities.

As a union of villages, the polis overcomes the limitations of the household and the single village, making it a more natural and therefore better form of association. However, the polis cannot replace the two lesser forms of community; it requires their continued existence and performance of their natural functions. Subordination for Aristotle does not dictate suppression.

The end of the polis is the good life. This includes economic and social harmony as well as political happiness. In the polis, money is properly used for exchange of goods and services. Economically, it is an autarky. An autarky is a self-sufficient economic unit that requires neither imports nor exports to satisfy the natural needs of all its members. Everything people need can be made in the polis. This, in turn, is based on a specialized division of labor in which each individual finds a natural work task in life. Like Plato, Aristotle believes that only the polis is large enough to permit such occupational specialization. Combined with the capacity for autarky, the economics of specialization of the polis helps promote the development of an ethical, well-rounded self in each member.[12]

Socially, the polis promotes the highest form of friendship—political friendship. The polis also displays a spirit of good will in which all men recognize their mutual interdependence in the service of community goals. This does not require identity of opinion, but a common desire to harmonize individual views and to serve a higher telos.

POLITICAL FORM OF THE POLIS

When discussing the political form or structure of the polis, Aristotle differs sharply from Plato. Plato favors a form of government dominated by permanent rulers who govern without law. Aristotle points to a great danger in such an arrangement. Even if Plato's ruler possesses great virtue and wisdom, he or she is still human, potentially subject to emotional and appetitive passions, and thus corruptible. The rule of one, or even a few, Aristotle believes, is more easily corrupted than the rule of the many.

He also says that giving all free men a role in the state helps to stabilize the regime, since excluding some of those fit to participate may lead them to become enemies of the government. This raises the question of who is best fit to judge whether the results of governmental policy are in the public interest—the rulers or the governed? He concludes that it is better to rely on the many governed than on even the most expert rulers.

However, it is not the emotions or passions of the many that Aristotle relies on, but their collective wisdom. Each citizen brings some bit of personal wisdom, as well as a bit of virtue and experience, to the collective task of governing. Some people see one part of a problem or solution, some another, and together they see the whole picture. In other words, when added together, the collective capacity to build a harmonious polis is superior to that of one or a few wise individuals. All the same, the expertise of the few governors who hold political office at any given time should not be ignored. They too have a role to play. In fact, Aristotle concludes that in most cases a just government is a mixed government, one that takes full advantage of multiple perspectives and assigns a role to each citizen.

Aristotle further thinks wealth and poverty are inevitable in all societies, and that every polis is thus marked by class division between the few rich and the many poor. This is a social reality that cannot be ignored. The result is class conflict and a constant threat of instability, violence, and revolution. However, a mix of citizens' talents can produce a blend of class interests, and all classes can contribute, whether rich, poor, or middle. In this, Aristotle supports political equality side by side with economic inequality.

In addition to favoring mixed government as the most stable form, Aristotle makes a strong case for an important corollary, the rule of law:

Rightly constituted laws should be the final sovereign; and personal rule, whether it be exercised by a single person or a body of persons, should be sovereign only in those matters on which law is unable, owing to the difficulty of framing general rules for all contingencies, to make an exact pronouncement.[13]

The law, "rightly constituted," is Aristotle's legitimate sovereign authority.[14] Since it is not certain that those who rule will always be virtuous and give priority to the public interest, there is risk in giving them complete power. Thus supremacy of the law made by all is better than potentially arbitrary supremacy of the rulers.

In general, Aristotle applies the term *constitution* to any form of government. More specifically, it refers to "an organization of offices in a state, by which the method of their distribution is fixed, the sovereign authority is determined, and the nature of the end to be pursued by the association and all its members is prescribed."[15] In other words, the arrangement of offices or political institutions, the distribution of functions to them through rules and processes, and the determination of the sovereign or ruling part are based on the telos of the polis, the idea of the good a people has of itself. In the best polis, this idea of the good is translated into laws that bind everyone, rulers and ruled alike.

In Book IV, Aristotle generalizes about actual constitutions and their varieties, based on his study of the 158 constitutions of Greek city-states mentioned earlier. He notes that there are many kinds of constitutions, and thus a number of different forms of government, each in accord with the nature of the inhabitants of the particular community. The *Politics* first discusses the many kinds of government, such as five different types of kingship and five of democracy. Then, based on his own preference (for mixed government of all classes that is in the public interest and wherein laws are supreme), Aristotle classifies governments into a typology depending on who rules and he judges whether that rule is true or perverted.[16]

Power to rule may rest with the one, who reserves ultimate decision-making power to himself; the few, who exercise sovereign authority through a council of relative equals; or the many, who legislate through an assembly. All true constitutions have a telos that is just, or in the public interest of all, meaning that there is a mixed government in which a number of classes are represented and law is supreme. A perverted form of government, on the other hand, is one dominated by the private interest of a single ruler or ruling class, wherein the will of the rulers replaces the rule of law. This yields a six-fold typology that is more complex, flexible, and indicative of relative merit (or demerit) than that of Plato's *Republic*, where there is only one true constitution and all others are considered perverted.[17] Despite that Aristotle has his own preferences among these six forms of government, he is willing to allow for some virtue in each of the six. In fact, none of the forms is wholly without some merit and any of them can, with the correct input of education and new laws, develop into a more just form of government.

In a monarchy, or kingship, one virtuous person rules, guided by a law that calls for rotation in office and directs decision making to the public interest. A tyranny is based on the arbitrary rule of a permanent despot who is above the law and rules to suit his own personal interest. Aristotle considers tyranny the worst form of government but thinks tyranny the only form possible for the large states of his time, the huge army-empires that were threatening the independence of the Greek city-states.

An aristocracy is rule by the best few who combine personal merit and wealth with rule in the public interest, while in an oligarchy the few rulers are also wealthy but promote the interest of their own class above all others.

Democracy, to Aristotle, is a negative term for a perverted constitution. It serves the lawless greed of the many poor of free birth who constitute a majority. Although it is in effect mob rule ("mobocracy"), Aristotle considers it the least bad of the three perverted forms of government, as it is in the class interest of a greater number of people than the other two, and thus approximates more closely the interest of the whole people.[18]

Polity, on the other hand, is Aristotle's term for the best possible form of true constitution. It is the most likely of the true forms for a virtuous people to have. It is the best because it reflects reason and moderation, being structured to counteract the potentially destabilizing effects of class antagonism in any society. Polity mixes quality and quantity and merit and wealth with numbers, giving the balance to the many but effective control to a virtuous middle class that exercises sovereign authority in the public interest under law.

A stable polity requires the presence of a large middle class. Aristotle defines the middle class as combining those who compose the poorer segment of the wealthy class with the richer segment of the lower class. Because it is in the middle, this aggregate class is able to blend the perspectives of the rich and the poor to reflect the mean. The size of the middle class must be large enough to enable it to politically dominate the polis so that neither extreme segment, rich or poor, can take control. Aristotle prefers a middle class that is larger than the combined size of the rich and the poor, but at the very least he thinks it should be larger than either of the other two classes. The rich and freeborn poor are included as full citizens who alternate as rulers and subjects.[19]

Whereas Plato says in the *Republic* that participation by the masses should consist of only obedience to authority, Aristotle sees politics as a demanding task involving rotation in political office for virtually all citizens at some time.[20] Such participation benefits the polity, both because legitimate views can be considered and because potential opposition to the government is avoided. The result of mixed, stable government, Aristotle believes, is good law and a law-abiding citizenry that reinforces the stability established by blending class membership. The ultimate test of stability, he says, is not that a majority supports the constitution totally, but that no important faction or class favors violent change.[21]

POLITICAL CHANGE

In Book V, Aristotle examines the reasons for political decline, some of which were mentioned earlier. He says that because all states have weaknesses they are only partially able to reach their highest potential due to such corrupting factors as ignorance, passion, and the absence of sufficient virtue among the populace. But while recognizing that deterioration is inevitable, Aristotle believes that if citizens understand the sources of political weakness they may, within limits, control the pace of decline.

> The conclusion which clearly follows is that any polis which is truly so called, and is not merely one in name, must devote itself to the end of encouraging goodness. Otherwise a political association sinks into a mere alliance, which only differs in space [i.e., in the contiguity of its members] from other forms of alliance where the members live at a distance from one another. Otherwise, too, law becomes a mere covenant—or (in the phrase of the Sophist Lycophron) "a guarantor of men's rights against one another"—instead of being, as it should be, a rule of life such as will make the members of a polis good and just.[22]

One fundamental cause of decline in a good polis, noted as early as Book III, is conflict over justice in any society marked by extremes of wealth. Such conflict both indicates and helps to intensify the loss of the mean, the organic harmony necessary to sustain government. As a result, citizens are excessively concerned with personal well-being rather than with the polis as a whole. Law then merely guarantees rights rather than setting forth mutual obligations. What follows is a sharp division of the polis into opposing economic classes. The rich face the many poor, with the middle class squeezed out. The next likely stages in this decline are violence and then revolution.

Aristotle is aware that even the best of laws, and institutions, and a mixed class system do not ensure a stable polis. Underlying the institutions and practices of the sound state is the spirit of the constitution. If this spirit is permitted to decay, the polis surely degenerates. Prevention of decay requires that citizens always act with the public interest in mind. They must show the greatest respect for the letter and spirit of the law, even in the most trivial matters. Too, government officials must not personally profit from holding office.

Education must support a sound constitutional structure and virtuous behavior. Education has a major role in fostering the potential for virtue citizens are born with, particularly by teaching moderation and willingness to sacrifice for the common good.[23] Beyond what children learn at home, by example from their parents, education is the job of the state. It should prepare men for citizenship, for sharing in political decision making, for ruling and being ruled in turn. In some respects, education is lifelong, as citizens learn from the virtuous example of other citizens and from the laws of the just polis. For a virtuous population, education and good law are more effective teachers than the threat of police power; they are the best defense of a good polis against decline.

Writing as an objective political scientist but with the possible aim of easing the oppression subjects suffer under perverted constitutions, Aristotle even tells rulers of corrupt regimes how they can preserve their power. For example, he anticipates Machiavelli[24] when he advises tyrants, who rule the least stable form of government of all, how to slow the inevitable decline of their regimes. He urges them to divide and conquer their people, create a strong spy system alert to opposition, and neutralize those who threaten their power. Tyrants should also encourage class hatred, even warfare, between rich and poor. Subjects must be kept strangers to one another at all costs. Any association that promotes friendship or community of interests must be suppressed, for if subjects begin to trust each other, they may organize and challenge the tyrant. Aristotle also says that while manipulating the populace behind the scenes, in public as much as possible the tyrant should appear to be a monarch. He should not flaunt his wealth by lavish personal spending, but instead erect great public works for citizens to admire and to provide continuing employment for the poor. He should appear formally religious by openly worshiping the gods and observing conventional rites and practices, for this leads the general public to think he is not unjust, whatever his regime's oppressive actions. Aristotle reveals purposes for giving such advice that go beyond the purely scientific study of all sorts of constitutions. He concludes that if tyrants try hard enough to appear as monarchs, they will not only rule longer but also develop practices that ease their people's burdens.

CONCLUSION

Aristotle, like Plato, emphasizes the superior role of the collective and the relatively inferior position of the individual. But both philosophers are less concerned with hierarchically ordering individual and collective than they are with integrating these elements into a seamless whole. Both focus on an organic community in which politics pervades all individual and social activities. They share a vision of a universal order "which dictates the place of each virtue in a totally harmonious scheme of human life."[25] Justice, true freedom, and happiness can be realized through participation in the good polis.

By favoring such goals, and their means for getting there, Aristotle as well as Plato reflect a temperament that is conservative, elitist, and characteristically ancient. Aristotle is conservative in his great concern for preserving the stability of the polis. Like Plato, he recognizes that change is perhaps inevitable and there is always potential for revolution. He wants to delay these as long as possible, opposed as he is to violence and supportive as he is of education, in order to maintain political stability and effect gradual change. And both are elitist, agreeing that some people are by nature superior to others, even if the two philosophers disagree on who those superior beings are.

Aristotle and Plato also share an ancient perspective, their understanding of reality being similar, that leads to parallel views on the relationship between the individual and the collective. Both are committed to the view that ideals are real and more important than material things. Both believe that reason is the "engine" propelling us to judge any polis, and providing people with the necessary criteria for making political judgments.

At the same time, Aristotle and Plato differ on whether ideals are located in heaven or in objects, which leads to disagreement on a number of specifics. In a relative sense, Aristotle's position on several key issues is more moderate than Plato's. Aristotle insists that the telos of any object must be found in the object itself, not, as Plato would have it, outside it. Aristotle shows this more "down-to-earth" perspective in his advocacy of the golden mean, a position falling between extremes, rather than Plato's utopian ideal, which is an extreme. Aristotle simply mistrusts excess in any form.

Thus he does not advocate starting from scratch to secure a better (much less a perfect) polis, as Plato arguably does. He favors working with existing laws, customs, habits, and the very nature of the populace—its constitution writ large. Unwilling to completely condemn all but one form of government, Aristotle's *Politics* allows for a number of ways to reach a just polis.

Aristotle has a theoretical ideal, but he is willing to settle for a form of government that is the product of practical reason. His more moderate and practical perspective leads him to defend the rule of the many as the most feasible form of government, rather than support a regime with just a few wise rulers. He separates the task of philosophy from that of governing, and advocates rule of law (a mean) over the edicts of an all-wise ruler. But while he rejects the elitism of the philosopher-king, he also rejects Plato's sexual and communistic egalitarianism within the ruling class, replacing it with a male-dominated constitution where economic differences are taken for granted, as are inferior positions for women and "natural" slaves.[26]

Finally, while Aristotle sees the politics of the polis as organic, and the polis itself as an organic unity, this unity is not total. Rather, he thinks of the polis as composed of many parts. If most of life's highest goods are to be realized in the community, a few, such as the search for wisdom, may be conducted by individuals in private. Self-fulfillment, even a degree of self-love, compatible with the ends of the polis may be permitted, as long as it is not excessive, that is, it does not threaten the basic unity of the polis.

So, in many ways, Aristotle rejects a number of the major ideas his teacher, Plato, advances in the *Republic*. He refutes them by establishing new, less idealistic, basis for political thought. However, Aristotle does not replace Plato's contribution. Instead, Plato serves Aristotle as a base, a source of ideas that he modifies to present a different perspective. Had Plato not written the *Republic*, Aristotle's *Politics* would surely have been different. And both strongly influenced later political philosophers.[27] It is therefore worth asking of these successor philosophers, what in their thought reflects Platonic influences? What indicates the power of Aristotle's ideas?

Notes

1. Two accounts that discuss Aristotle's life and work are Jonathan Barnes, *Aristotle* (New York: Oxford University Press, 1992), and the classic by A. E. Taylor, *Aristotle* (New York: Dover, 1955).

2. Other works of Aristotle dealing with subjects related to the *Politics* include discussions on ethics, metaphysics, logic, rhetoric, psychology, zoology, and physics, the most important of which are titled *Nichomachean Ethics, On the Generation of Animals* (natural history), and *On the Soul* (psychology).

3. For studies of citizenship in Athens, see Philip B. Manville. *The Origins of Citizenship in Ancient Athens* (Princeton, N.J.: Princeton University Press, 1990) and W. G. Forrest, *The Emergence of Greek Politics* (London: Weidenfield & Nicholson, 1966).

4. Aristotle, *The Politics of Aristotle*, I, 1252a. Quotations are from the translation by Ernest Barker (New York: Oxford University Press, 1952), cited below as *Politics*. References are to the standard citation found in many editions of this work: book and section.

5. Among the factors involved in this decline were "war, colonization, monetary changes, technological innovation, economic depression, class dislocation, and the unsettling effects of contacts with different cultures. . . ." Sheldon S. Wolin, *Politics and Vision: Continuity and Innovation in Western Political Thought* (Boston: Little, Brown, 1960), 65.

6. *Politics*, I, 1254b.

7. *Politics*, I, 1257a.

8. For a work that discusses the contemporary relevance of Aristotle's mean, see Stephen G. Salkever, *Finding the Mean: Theory and Practice in Aristotelian Political Philosophy* (Princeton, N.J.: Princeton University Press, 1990).

9. *Politics,* III, 1278b.

10. However, Aristotle confesses that rule over the household is exercised in the interest of the husband and master. For an insightful discussion of his views on women and slaves, see Susan Moller Okin, *Women in Western Political Thought* (Princeton, N.J.: Princeton University Press, 1979), ch. 4. Elizabeth Spelman, *Inessential Woman: Problems of Exclusion in Feminist Thought* (Boston: Beacon, 1988), ch. 2, points out the political implications of Aristotle speaking about "women" but failing to distinguish between free women and female (or male) slaves.

11. Arlene Saxonhouse, *Women in the History of Political Thought: Ancient Greece to Machiavelli* (New York: Praeger, 1985), 69.

12. See http://politicalscience.wadsworth.com/tannenbaum2 for a link to a diagram of the relationship between Aristotle's natural political economy and his communities.

13. *Politics*, I, 1252a.

14. *Politics*, III, 1282b. Here he follows Plato's later works, *Statesman* and *Laws,* where the rule of law and mixed-class government are considered more achievable than rule by philosophers.

15. *Politics*, IV, 1289a.

16. See http://politicalscience.wadsworth.com/tannenbaum2 for a link to a chart of Aristotle's forms of government.

17. It follows the scheme in Plato's *Statesman.*

18. In his later works, Plato agrees with Aristotle on the role of law, but not on rule by the many.

19. Aristotle omits another class of people when he assigns roles in the polis: free laborers. They, like women, are neither citizen nor slave. But, unlike his apparent certainty about women, Aristotle is not clear how one can tell whether laborers are "by nature rulers or ruled." *Inessential Woman*, 199, n. 33.

20. Most citizens rule as legislators or members of a court of law; executive roles generally require special expertise (such as military judgment) not possessed by the average citizen. *Politics and Vision*, 57.

21. Mary P. Nichols, *Citizens and Statesmen: A Study of Aristotle's Politics* (Savage, Md.: Rowman & Littlefield, 1992) contains a wide-ranging discussion of Aristotle's polity.

22. *Politics*, III, 1280b.

23. Aristotle's goal in educating citizens resembles Plato's aim in training the Republic's guardians: self-sacrifice for the common good to preserve a well-ordered polis against decline. However, Aristotle's educational scheme omits both censorship and lies, however noble.

24. Barker, in *Politics*, 247, n. 1.

25. Alasdair MacIntyre, *After Virtue: A Study in Moral Theory* (London: Duckworth, 1981), 133.

26. The "good life not only excludes but depends upon the exclusion of a great majority of people, including all women," slaves, and those in the laboring class. They can never hope to achieve the highest virtue. Susan Moller Okin, *Justice, Gender and the Family* (New York: Basic, 1989), 52. Aristotle's model of the good life is in fact based on a masculine and aristocratic ideal. At the same time, he does leave women a role and identity of their own, rather than turn her into a masculine norm, like Plato. She is to be "controlled rather than defeminized. . . ." Diana Coole, *Women in Political Theory: From Ancient Misogyny to Contemporary Feminism* (Boulder, Colo.: Lynne Rienner, 1988), 47–8.

27. For a discussion of some of Aristotle's key ideas and their relation to contemporary political issues, see Bernard Yack, *The Problems of a Political Animal: Community, Justice, and Conflict in Aristotelian Thought* (Berkeley: University of California Press, 1993).

Additional Readings

Barnes, Jonathan. *Aristotle*. New York: Oxford University Press, 1992.

Curren, Randall R. *Aristotle on the Necessity of Public Education*. Savage, Md.: Rowman & Littlefield, 2000.

MacIntyre, Alasdair. *After Virtue: A Study in Moral Theory*. London: Duckworth, 1981.

Manville, Philip B. *The Origins of Citizenship in Ancient Athens*. Princeton, N.J.: Princeton University Press, 1990.

Nichols, Mary P. *Citizens and Statesmen: A Study of Aristotle's Politics*. Savage, Md.: Rowman & Littlefield, 1992.

Salkever, Steven G. *Finding the Mean: Theory and Practice in Aristotelian Political Philosophy*. Princeton, N.J.: Princeton University Press, 1990.

Yack, Bernard. *The Problems of a Political Animal: Community, Justice, and Conflict in Aristotelian Thought*. Berkeley: University of California Press, 1993.

 ## *Inventors of Ideas* Online

Visit http://politicalscience.wadsworth.com/tannenbaum2 for visual representations of some of the key concepts in Aristotle's works and links related to material in this chapter, including sites containing the full text of the *Politics* and other works attributed to Aristotle, including the *Constitution of Athens*, *Metaphysics*, and the *Nicomachean Ethics*.

5

CICERO AND ROMAN POLITICAL THOUGHT: THE TRANSFORMATION OF THE POLITICAL

INTRODUCTION

After Aristotle, political thought underwent a profound change. The Greeks had defined politics, political theory, and citizenship in terms of the polis, or the small, homogeneous, face-to-face democracy. The polis involved active participation, at least by the more affluent male citizens, in the political affairs of the community, emphasizing consensus and shared values.

But numerous historical events made the ideals of Greek political thought irrelevant to the day-to-day politics of the average person. Notably, Aristotle's most famous student, Alexander the Great (356–323 B.C.E.), destroyed the polis. He did so by creating an empire, through conquest, which stretched from the Greek lands to India. The creation of a huge state, which covered thousands of miles and included many different languages, people, and cultures, made the ideals of the polis seem no longer applicable. The political community could no longer really aspire to resting on the values of small, participatory-based politics wherein people shared common values. Thus Alexander created new problems of governance. First, by labeling himself both a king and a god, Alexander created an image of rulership that merged the divine and the secular. This meant that all political power was to be vested in one person, which was difficult to reconcile with participatory and democratic politics. Second, Alexander's large empire forced the need to attach new meanings to citizenship and the duties of the citizen, and created the problem of building political institutions to adequately represent the diverse needs and interests of the various peoples within the state.

More specifically, Alexander's empire challenged existing definitions of political geography and authority.[1] The creation of a large empire freed individuals from the polis and eliminated the basic relationship between the self and the world. But in what community were individuals to be members then? What role should individuals assume in the cosmos? Who would rule, and what would be the justification for political authority? These were the questions that the destruction of the polis prompted. But Alexander's early death and the rapid demise of his empire meant that there was not enough time to redefine lasting political values based on the concept of empire.

STOICISM

One attempt to redefine the relationship of the individual to the community entails recasting the political values of the polis to apply to a large and diverse political community. Stoicism is a philosophy that undertakes this redefinition. Stoicism has its origins in Greek thought, developing at around the time of the decline of the Greek city-states and the rise of Alexander the Great's empire. Stoic philosophy has at least three different movements, of which the third is Roman in origin. It is a philosophy arguing that the proper role for humans in the universe is a life lived according to nature. In addition to stressing this value, Stoicism also emphasizes a universality encompassing a commitment to human equality and membership in a world community that transcends existing political boundaries and borders. For example, Seneca, one of the Roman Stoics, states,

> Let us take hold of the fact that there are two communities—the one, which is great and truly common, embracing gods and men, in which we look neither to this corner nor to that, but measure the boundaries of our state by the sun; the other, the one to which we have been assigned by the accident of our birth.[2]

As a philosophy that has moral, political, and religious overtones, Stoicism redefines citizenship and authority by stressing that all individuals (perhaps including women) are equal members of a world community regulated according to the principle of reason, which is the law of nature.[3]

Marcus Aurelius further draws Stoic reason, law, and the sense of community together when he argues,

> If our intellectual part is common, then reason also, in respect of which we are rational beings, is common; if this is so, common also is the reason which commands us what to do, and what not to do; if this is so, there is a common law also; if this is so, we are fellow-citizens; if this is so, we are members of some political community; if this is so, the world is in a manner a state. For of what other common political community will any one say the whole human race are members?[4]

Marcus Aurelius makes clear the emphasis on law and legality in Stoicism, especially its Roman version.[5] Among the Stoics, the nature humans are expected to live by is a universal law governing all creatures, including the gods. This universal law determines what is just and unjust, as well as what is deemed appropriate in particular situations.

Stoicism is a good philosophy for troubled times. It stresses tranquility, concord, human self-sufficiency, and retreat from politics and worldly affairs. For Stoics, there is a natural harmony among humans and nature; and if one

can live naturally and retreat from human passions, one can find this harmony, achieve happiness, and live in concordance or peace. Thus the heart of
Stoicism is a search for human nature uncorrupted by the state and human
desires. Stoicism, like some other Greek philosophies of the day (e.g., Epi-
cureanism), seeks refuge from the discord of the day in a political community
that seems unaffected by it. It overcomes the difficulties of human diversity by
recognizing equality in a political community that appears to transcend crumbling political institutions. Such an appeal to a larger cosmos represents a
searching for a sense of membership in something at a time of political alienation, disaffection, social destruction, and decline. It is a search for meaning
and perhaps spirituality in a time of crisis.

By granting citizenship in another world, Stoicism also represents an
antipolitics of individualism and community.[6] By itself, Stoicism is incapable
of providing definitions for political structures and institutions. The stress on
an apparent otherworldliness or larger political cosmos diverts political
attention and loyalty from day-to-day politics, placing it at odds with the
needs of the political leaders who wished to build new earthly empires at that
time.

Stoicism's values do leave an important and lasting legacy, evolving in two
directions. One direction is the incorporation of Stoicism into Roman political thought, most especially Roman legal tradition.[7] Here, for example, writers such as Polybius (200?–118 B.C.E.) undertook an examination of Roman
political institutions in light of the Aristotle's classification of governments
based on which social classes ruled—monarchy, aristocracy, and democracy,
and their perversions—as well as a mixed government. Polybius's importance
resided first in developing a theory of governments that depicted the degeneration through various forms that all regimes would face. Second, Polybius
had a significant influence on Cicero and later medieval thinkers, both of
whom would use his classification and degeneration of governments as a
starting point in much of their political analysis.

The other offshoot of Stoicism is toward the religious sphere, providing
guidance for philosophers such as Seneca, as well as eventually being adapted
to help define Christianity. The first direction gives Stoicism an institutional
backing, permitting it to justify the political structures of the Roman Empire.
The more religious focus of Stoicism has an anti-institutional focus, providing
impetus for Christian and philosophical attacks on Roman and other existing
political institutions. In both cases, Stoic philosophy helps prepare the way
for the creation of a new and larger community, be it the diverse Roman
Empire or the Kingdom of God in the Christian tradition.

DIFFERENCES BETWEEN GREEK
AND ROMAN POLITICAL THOUGHT

During the Roman era, there were few original political thinkers of major
significance. The most notable was Marcus Tullius Cicero. Roman political

thought provides institutional context to Stoic ideas, but it also derives from Greek ideas in many ways. Roman thinkers, however, transformed Greek ideas and ideals in many important ways.

Greek politics and political thought are characterized by an inward focus, and Roman thought by its outward turn. In other words, the Greeks see the essence of politics as involving common involvement within the polis. With the Romans, the aim of politics is toward creating and maintaining an empire. Similarly, whereas the Greeks emphasize more the shared communal values of the polis, especially education and political participation (as described in Pericles' funeral oration), the Romans mythologize their leaders and value power and power politics. In many ways, the Romans make cults of personality around their leaders.[8] In Rome, loyalty is not to the polis or political community, but to the caesar or other great leaders, who assumes an almost godlike status. In fact, even more so than the Greeks, the Romans revere leaders, such as Romulus, the founder of Rome, and other great men who perform grand and noble deeds.

In contrast to the Greeks, who abhor self-interest and political factionalism as dangers to politics, the Romans readily recognize that self-interest,[9] power, and party competition are at the heart of politics.[10] Instead of political activity being about virtue or the pursuit of knowledge, it is preeminently about power and self-interest. In fact, from the founding of Rome throughout its history, one of the perennial conflicts and crises was how to confine self-interest and channel it, power, and the abilities of great leaders into supporting rather than destroying the empire.[11]

Overall, the contrast between the Greeks and the Romans lies in how politics is defined. The Greeks stress civic education and participation, commonality, loyalty to the polis, and disdain for self-interest. The Romans seek (much like American founders 2,000 years later, in the *Federalist Papers*) to deal with the problems of self-interest in a large, heterogenous political system, which cannot grant the same level of participation and citizenship duties as in a small, homogeneous political community.

In addition, much of Roman political thought is influenced by its history, which is filled with crises and changes. For example, the early history of Rome was marked by the rule of seven successive kings. After this monarchy, it moved on to a republic, replete with several governing structures. At different times during the republic, there was a senate, composed of the heads of the leading families of Rome; the consuls, who represented the people; and the comitia, composed of several thousand individuals who gathered intermittently to debate and vote on public issues. As Rome expanded to become an empire, it was ruled by nearly all-powerful dictators, including the caesars and Caligula, among others. These changes forced upon Roman political thought political problems and questions that the Greeks never had to confront.

Addressing new problems results in a more practical focus to Roman philosophy and political thought.[12] Instead of engaging in speculative politics, such as the idea of the good as in the case of Plato, Cicero and other Roman thinkers stress the practical and the applied. For example, while Plato argues that the acquisition of knowledge and virtue is its own good, Cicero states that virtue must be applied,[13] and that true knowledge lies in action, speech, and practical affairs.[14]

The Roman treatment of women also represents both continuity with and a break from Greek practices. Under the Romans, women still could not vote or take an active or official role in politics, yet the status of women in the household was far more free than among the Greeks.[15] Within the Greek family, women had lived in relative seclusion, while in Rome women were equal partners with men in the household, often with equal responsibility for religious practices.[16] Moreover, early Roman law made wives totally dependent on their husbands, but subsequent marriage-law reforms gave women more independence. In several situations throughout Roman history, women agitated for political reforms, actions unheard of in Greece (except in Aristophanes' comedies and farces).[17]

Even after reform, however, Roman law still favored men, who could obtain divorces from their wives and retain custody of children more easily. Property laws; laws regulating prostitutes, concubines, and female slaves; and the entire gamut of other Roman laws continued to relegate women to secondary citizens in public life, confining their role to management of the family.[18]

Historians such as Livy also described women's roles. But for Livy, battles over women represent important events in Roman legend and history much in the same way that the battle with the Persians after Paris abducted Helen of Troy was important to the Greeks. Except for such references, Roman political thought generally ignores women, as is the case with Cicero.

CICERO

Marcus Tullius Cicero (106–43 B.C.E.) was an important Roman political thinker, orator, lawyer, and statesman who once served as a Roman consul. His writings best articulate many of the trends in Roman political thought noted above.[19] He wrote in the last century before the birth of Jesus. He is a Stoic and well versed in the writings of the Greeks, including Plato and Sophocles. He had a tremendous influence on other Roman thinkers and Christians, especially St. Augustine. Cicero's works were quoted in the writings of others, making his texts an important channel by which the values of Greeks and, more importantly, the Romans were introduced to Christians.

Cicero's two main political works are *On the Commonwealth* (*De Res Publica* in Latin), which follows both the dialogue format and many of the arguments in Plato's *Republic,* and *On the Laws* (*De Legibus* in Latin), a book about law. *On the Commonwealth* which disappeared after the twelfth century and was not again recovered until the nineteenth, addresses mainly the topic of the best political regime, while *On the Laws* discusses the institutional and legal instruments necessary to maintain and order the ideal republic.[20] In addition, Cicero wrote *On Duties* and *On the Orator*, both of which develop important points about personal virtue and the skills required for political success.

The Commonwealth. The first philosophical topic in *On the Commonwealth* is a discussion of public duty and examples of such duty. Cicero states that defending the commonwealth is the highest obligation individuals have. It is a duty second only to one's duty to the gods, which ranks it as even more important than duty to family or parents. This claim suggests some opposition between private and public lives. In fact, Laelius, one of the characters in *On the Commonwealth*, indicates early on in the dialogue that he is concerned with looking at the relationship between public and private lives, asking if what occurs beyond the home affects one's private life. He raises this question because the initial subject of the dialogue is a rumor about the sighting of two suns. Philus, another character, responds that the home is not just a structure of four walls, but encompasses the entire universe. This point, a nod to Stoic ideas about human membership in a larger, cosmic community, leads to consideration of the many different factors relevant to a discussion of public and private lives as well as the duties in each.

Eventually, discussion of two suns prompts Laelius to state that recent events in Rome appear to have created a divide, practically rendering two senates and two peoples. He asks how can one bring about a union of people and the senate.[21] Scipio, a third character, is then asked to explain the best constitution for a state. He offers a definition of the true commonwealth:

> For what is the commonwealth except the people's affair? Hence, it is a common affair, that is, an affair belonging to a state. And what is a state except a considerable number of men brought together in a certain bond of harmony?[22]

The cause of people coming together is a "social instinct natural to man" with the state, according to Cicero in *On Duties*. The formation of the commonwealth represents the fifth stage of society or union, evolving first out of the man and wife relationship, then parent and child, the household, the city, and finally the state. Hence, as with both Plato and Aristotle, Cicero sees the origin of the state as growing out of the family, with the state and the duties to it being the most important of these relationships.

Scipio proceeds to argue that some type of authority is needed to hold the commonwealth together. Following Plato, he argues that there are three pure types of states, monarchy, aristocracy, and democracy. These rules are characterized by the love of subjects and reason, wisdom, or freedom respectively.[23] Scipio states that although a monarchy is the best of the pure forms of government, he prefers one that mixes all three of the forms, for two reasons.[24]

First, there is a life cycle to pure states, with all three governments eventually degenerating into corrupt forms. But adopting a mixed government can perhaps prevent this corruption from occurring, and thus halt or slow down the life cycle.

Second, a mixed state achieves a balance between the values of a monarchy and those of an aristocracy. Scipio considers the maintenance of equality in a democracy to be impossible or unjust because all are not equal.[25] But a mixed government combines the different virtues of reason, wisdom, and freedom,[26] it does not arouse a wild and untamed spirit in the citizens,[27] and it achieves a balance of rights among the different classes of people in society.[28]

Despite the mixing of different types of governments and their virtues, Scipio prefers that reason and monarchy should rule in the state. If reason is the best part of the soul and should rule the individual, then the same should be true of the state, with a king ruling along with a senate representing the aristocracy.[29]

Thus Cicero, through Scipio, describes the perfect institutions for the state. Not coincidentally, Rome is the embodiment of the perfect state. Its government is superior because it is both the product of many generations of thought[30] and geographically situated in the best place a city can be. It is far enough away from the corrupting influences of the sea, it has hills for defense, and it is near enough to a river to have all its advantages and none of its disadvantages. Cicero's description of Rome and the best political institutions suggests that *On the Commonwealth* is substantially a defense of the political status quo, and that Scipio is simply restating and defending traditional values of Roman political thought.

Law and Justice. The dialogue also addresses some Stoic themes about law and justice, which Cicero elaborates on in more depth in *On the Laws*. A true commonwealth is a government that produces harmony, but harmony is obtained only when the state is a true people's affair, that is, one that binds the people together according to the law. Good laws protect the equal rights of all, although the notion of equality must respect the differences among groups and classes in society.[31] Moreover, a commonwealth seeks concord or balance, much in the same way music requires harmony, and the only time concord can be achieved is when justice is the aim of the laws.[32] Philius, a fourth character, states that the search for justice should pertain only to society and not all of nature. He asks whether justice and customs are not the same thing, to all peoples, suggesting that perhaps justice and law are conventional.[33] This question is similar to one posed in the *Ethics*, when Aristotle asks whether the duties of the good man and good citizen coincide. Philius says,

> If justice were natural, then nature would have laid down our laws; all peoples would be subject to the same laws; and the same people would not be subject to different laws at different times. Now I put the question to you: If it be the duty of a just man and a good citizen to obey the laws, what laws should he obey?[34]

Laelius responds that law is not conventional:

> There is in fact a true law—namely, right reason—which is in accordance with nature, applies to all men, and is unchangeable and eternal. By its commands this law summons men to the performance of their duties; by its

prohibitions it restrains them from doing wrong. Its commands and prohibitions always influence good men, but are without effect upon the bad. To invalidate this law by human legislation is never morally right, nor is it permissible ever to restrict its operation.[35]

In *On the Laws,* Cicero develops in more detail his views on the role of law in a republic. He defines the term as follows:

Law is the highest reason, implanted in Nature, which commands what ought to be done and forbids the opposite. This reason, when firmly fixed and fully developed in the human mind, is Law.[36]

Cicero goes on to expand this definition and clarify its implications. For example, he states that law is a natural force, a command from the gods, coequal with the gods; and that law is the origin of justice, with justice defined as the basic sense of right and wrong in the universe. Justice commands or proscribes forever; it is an eternal standard. For Cicero, even if there were no written law or custom against rape, the rape of Rome would still be wrong.

Cicero also describes the law as "right reason" containing justice.[37] This definition means that all those who have reason have the capacity to know what the law is because it is "universally imprinted on all minds." Because of the similarity of all members of the human race, everyone has the potential to know the law so long as he or she lives in harmony with nature.[38] Law also binds kings and other rulers, such that their earthly laws must conform with the rule or law of right reason, justice, and nature. This means that eternal law is a standard by which we can distinguish between good and bad human laws.[39] Because the purpose of eternal law is justice, the purposes of earthly law are the justice for and safety of a state's citizens.[40]

Thus, through conflicts parallel to those in *Antigone,* Cicero explicitly states that unjust rulers are not true or legitimate rulers; they are tyrants. In an analysis which is later employed by St. Augustine, Cicero states that governments are people united for certain loves, such as greed. Most commonwealths are like the "rule of robbers" or a "pack of thieves." Law is the guiding principle of the true commonwealth, and a true commonwealth, for Cicero, is a group of people united in the love of justice. In a republic, only when the laws mirror true law and serve justice can there be harmony with nature and an internal sense of concord. If it is not so aligned, it is full of discord and conflict.

Overall, a true commonwealth—that is, one that serves the people—has a common bond that holds people together. This common bond is a respect for true justice and the eternal laws of reason and nature. It promotes concord if it brings human law and ideal law together.[41] Such a true commonwealth discourages political strife and people breaking up into political groups or factions.[42]

Public and Private Virtues. Despite that the primary goal of *On the Commonwealth* and *On the Laws* is to describe the perfect commonwealth, Cicero does not ignore the private aspects of life and other competing obligations. For example, the Latin word for republic, *res publica*, means "the public thing," indicating that the government stands in contrast to *res privata*, or "private thing." Throughout Cicero's writings, he recognizes that there is a tension between the public and the private, or the individual and the state, and he seeks ways to accommodate the two.

As discussed earlier, in *On the Commonwealth*, Laelius asks if what happens beyond the home affects private life, and the answer is that the entire universe is the home. This suggests an effort to make everything, from the commonwealth to the cosmos as a whole, relevant to private life. It also appears to render private and public lives indistinguishable from one another. Later on in the dialogue, Cicero considers the opposition between the good man and good citizen, and reconciles the two in creating a commonwealth ruled by true justice. In that case, the virtues required of the good man are the same as that of a good citizen.

On Duties inquires into the responsibility people have for their actions as well as what rules are to guide behavior. Cicero states that the concept of "decorum," or a sense of "fitting," is the way to seek to use the intellect to ensure that the soul is in harmony with nature.[43] If we can achieve harmony with nature in the soul, much like human laws achieve harmony with the true law of reason, then we will be just and virtuous. Here, Cicero's discussion again parallels Plato's discussion of harmony and balance in the soul as corresponding with the harmony of the universe.

Decorum also helps one to understand duties, and what Cicero calls mutual helpfulness, enables one to clarify the relative rankings of different duties.[44] The most important duty is to the gods, followed by the duty to the state, then to one's parents, then children, then other family members, and then friends and other people. Under this hierarchy, both religious and public duties take precedence over private family duties. What Cicero provides here is a way out of the dilemma Antigone faces. For Antigone, the duties to family, state, and religion seem to both clash and be indistinguishable at the same time.

In the writings of Cicero that have not been lost, he states little about family duties or organization. In *On the Commonwealth*, there is one sentence indicating that women should serve their husbands: "Nor indeed should an overseer be put in charge of the women, as is customary among the Greeks, but let there be a censor to teach husbands to govern their wives."[45] Clearly Cicero follows Roman legal custom, which makes men the rulers of the household in the same way that they rule the state. Yet missing from his writings are any references that draw parallels between the family and the state and any similarities in the duties in the two spheres. How Cicero would reconcile a woman's duty to the state versus that to her husband is unclear.

Finally, in addition to the general hierarchy of duties, Cicero states that leaders have a duty to protect the interest of citizens over their personal interest, and give precedence to the majority interests over that of a faction.[46] He also argues that leaders have an obligation to protect property rights, abstain from burdensome taxation, help ensure that all have an abundance of necessities in life, and remain above suspicion and corruption.[47] Cicero praises public service over and above merely giving money for the benefit of the public.[48]

Seeking justice or being virtuous is self-rewarding. While *On Duties* does emphasize that a leader should be virtuous and just, Cicero also states that maintaining a good reputation is important, because wisdom, justice, and honesty are important.[49] Important also is the ability to persuade, and in *On the Orator*, Cicero describes in detail the art of public speaking, the education required, and how important these skills are to be an effective ruler and communicator. The impression given in this book is that Cicero thinks of the orator as the model of what the perfect ruler should be—a person perhaps not too far different from what Cicero himself was.

CONCLUSION

Roman political thought bridges the world and values between the Greeks and the medieval Christian and modern political philosophers. After the demise of the Greek polis, thinkers considered how to give meaning to political authority and citizenship within the context of a larger and more diverse community. Cicero and the Roman legal tradition offer one approach, defining citizenship in a world community of Roman political institutions. Cicero also defines a hierarchy of roles and duties to be assumed by the individual, family, state, religion, and men and women. Although many concepts of community and civic duties are different from those among Greek thinkers, many others, especially with regard to women and the family, remain largely the same.

While Cicero can be described as simply a Roman expositor of Greek political ideas, he is also an important thinker in his own right, serving first as an important bridge that connects these Greek ideas to Stoicism. Secondly, his emphasis on describing a commonwealth and a statesman or leader as serving the people forms the basis of ideas that would eventually be used to advocate popular governments, including both democracies and representative republics. Third, his views on natural law connect Cicero both to Sophocles and to later Christian writers. The significance here is that the appeal to natural law, as seen in *Antigone*, serves as a powerful tool of dissent and criticism of the status quo, supporting theories of civil disobedience as far reaching as found in the writings and deeds of abolitionists, Martin Luther King, Jr., and antiabortion protestors. Thus Cicero, while often read as an apologist for Rome, can also be seen as holding positions that radically challenge the status quo.

Notes

1. Sheldon S. Wolin, *Politics and Vision: Continuity and Innovation in Western Political Thought* (Boston: Little, Brown, 1960), 73.

2. A. A. Long and D. Sedley, eds. and trans., *The Hellenistic Philosophers,* vol. I (Cambridge: Cambridge University Press, 1967), 431.

3. Arlene W. Saxonhouse, *Women in the History of Political Thought: Ancient Greece to Machiavelli* (Westport, Conn.: Praeger, 1985), 104.

4. Marcus Aurelius, *Meditations,* in *Great Political Thinkers: Plato to the Present,* eds., W. Ebenstein and A. O. Ebenstein (Fort Worth, Tex.: Holt, Rinehart & Winston, 1990), 178.

5. Charles Howard McIlwain, *The Growth of Political Thought in the West* (New York: Macmillan, 1932), 116.

6. *Politics and Vision,* 81.

7. *Growth of Political Thought,* 106, 116, 150.

8. R. H. Barrow, *The Romans* (New York: Penguin, 1979), 144; *Politics and Vision, 76–77.*

9. *Politics and Vision,* 86–87.

10. Lily Ross Taylor, *Party Politics in the Age of Caesar* (Berkeley: University of California Press, 1949).

11. Sallust, "Conspiracy of Catiline," in *The Jugurthine War: The Conspiracy of Catiline* (New York: Penguin, 1980), 181.

12. Edith Hamilton, *The Roman Way* (New York: Avon Books, 1973), 163.

13. Marcus Tullius Cicero, *On the Commonwealth,* trans. G. H. Sabine and S. B. Smith (Indianapolis: Bobbs-Merrill, 1976), 105–6.

14. Marcus Tullius Cicero, *On Duties,* trans. H. G. Edinger (Indianapolis: Bobbs-Merrill, 1974), 9, 11.

15. Richard A. Bauman, *Women and Politics in Ancient Rome* (New York: Routledge, 1992), 2.

16. J. P. V. D. Balsdon, *Roman Women: Their History and Habits* (New York: Barnes & Noble, 1962), 45.

17. *Women and Politics,* 2–7.

18. *Roman Women,* 209–30.

19. *Growth of Political Thought,* 107.

20. James E. Holton, "Marcus Tullius Cicero," in *History of Political Philosophy,* ed. L. Strauss and J. Cropsey (Chicago: University of Chicago Press, 1987), 158.

21. *On the Commonwealth,* 126.

22. *On the Commonwealth,* 129–30.

23. *On the Commonwealth,* 131, 140.

24. *On the Commonwealth,* 140, 190.

25. *On the Commonwealth,* 139.

26. *On the Commonwealth,* 151.

27. *On the Commonwealth,* 175.

28. *On the Commonwealth,* 185.

29. *On the Commonwealth,* 144, 173.

30. *On the Commonwealth,* 155–57.

31. *On the Commonwealth,* 136.

32. *On the Commonwealth,* 193–95.

33. *On the Commonwealth,* 205.

34. *On the Commonwealth,* 206.

35. *On the Commonwealth,* 215–16.

36. Marcus Tullius Cicero, *De Legibus,* trans. C. W. Keyes (Cambridge, Mass.: Harvard University Press, 1928), 44.

37. *De Legibus,* 45.

38. *De Legibus,* 45

39. *De Legibus,* 48.

40. *De Legibus,* 51.

41. *On the Commonwealth,* 231.

42. *On the Commonwealth,* 250.

43. *On Duties,* 44–47.

44. *On Duties,* 73.

45. *On the Commonwealth,* 235.
46. *On Duties,* 40.
47. Charles Norris Cochrane, *Christianity and Classical Culture* (New York: Oxford University Press, 1980), 54.
48. *On Duties,* 105–7.
49. *On Duties,* 90.

Additional Readings

Barrow, R. H. *The Romans.* New York: Penguin, 1979.

Bauman, Richard A. *Women and Politics in Ancient Rome.* New York: Routledge, 1992.

Cochrane, Charles Norris. *Christianity and Classical Culture.* New York: Oxford University Press, 1980.

Hamilton, Edith. *The Roman Way.* New York: Avon Books, 1973.

McIlwain, Charles Howard. *The Growth of Political Thought in the West.* New York: Macmillan, 1932.

Saxonhouse, Arlene W. *Women in the History of Political Thought: Ancient Greece to Machiavelli.* Westport, Conn.: Praeger, 1995.

Taylor, Lily Ross. *Party Politics in the Age of Caesar.* Berkeley: University of California Press, 1949.

Wolin, Sheldon S. *Politics and Vision: Continuity and Innovation in Western Political Thought.* Boston: Little, Brown, 1960.

Wood, Neal. *Cicero's Social and Political Thought.* Berkeley: University of California Press, 1980.

 Inventors of Ideas **Online**

Visit http://politicalscience.wadsworth.com/tannenbaum2 for links related to material in this chapter, including online texts of a number of Cicero's major works.

6

PAUL AND AUGUSTINE: EMERGENCE OF THE CHRISTIAN POLITICAL WORLD

INTRODUCTION

Christian political thought was a product of its times. It reflected many of the same forces influencing other political movements of the day. Yet, in many other ways, Christianity was unique and departed from Roman political traditions.

Cicero's political thought addresses the discord and conflict of the times by adapting Stoic assumptions to the legal and institutional traditions in Roman culture. His writings reflect a continuing commitment to reason and rationality inherited from the Greeks, and Cicero's arguments place basic trust in Roman institutions to articulate reason and justice, and to promote order and citizenship within the confines of human political institutions. As it spread through the Roman Empire, Christianity similarly adopted many of the Stoic ideas about community, egalitarianism, and universality.[1] Yet it expresses faith in neither reason nor Roman or other human institutions to attain a meaningful sense of citizenship and justice.

Christianity initially adopted an otherworldliness and a commitment to faith over reason that placed its values in opposition to Roman political institutions. It did so because Christians believed that the Greco-Roman institutions had failed.[2] It was not until St. Augustine (discussed later in this chapter) that the Christian church confronted the problem of institutionalizing and reconciling their doctrines with political authority.[3]

Describing the central political meaning of the teachings of Jesus, Paul, and the Apostles is complicated. The political and theological messages of Christianity are related, and sorting through the various interpretations to ascertain the core of what it represents would be controversial and impossible. But several themes and passages reveal how Jesus and his early followers view political authority and their relationship to it.

One message of Christianity is that it is open to all, regardless of faith, nationality, or gender.[4] According to Paul, "There is neither Jew nor Greek, there is neither bond nor free, there is neither male nor female, for ye are all one in Jesus Christ."[5] Elsewhere, when Jesus is confronted by Pilate, who asks Jesus if he is the king of the Jews, Jesus states, "Mine is not the kingdom of this world; if my kingdom were of this world, my men would have fought to my being surrendered to the Jews. But my kingdom is not of this world."[6] The message of Paul and Jesus is that the community, or commonwealth, that Christians are members of is one that transcends those on earth. Like Cicero, who sees a community as united by love, the Christian community is united by the love of God, and seeks to incorporate all within a universal empire based on a shared faith.

Given this advocacy of an otherworldly community, Christians see themselves in a position that serves as a genuine alternative to Rome,[7] and perhaps creates dual loyalties to church and state.[8] Both Jesus and Paul seek to address the problem of conflicting loyalties. At one point, Jesus reaffirms a duty to political authority, stating, "Render therefore unto Caesar the things which are Caesar's, and unto God the things that are God's."[9] Paul elaborates upon this point:

> Let every person be subject to the governing authorities. For there is not authority except from God, and those that exist have been instituted by God. Therefore he who resists the authorities resists what God has appointed, and those who resist will incur judgment. For rulers are not terror to good conduct, but to bad. . . . Therefore one must be subject, not only to avoid God's wrath, but also for the sake of conscience. For the same reason you also pay taxes, for the authorities are ministers of God.[10]

Both these passages recognize the dual commitments Christians have to church and state. Later on, during the Middle Ages, both passages would become important language justifying the subordination of secular authority to the church.

HUMAN NATURE AND CHRISTIAN EQUALITY

Another political message of Christianity is egalitarianism, or equality. Paul's statement about men, women, and Jews, among others, suggests a basic equality of everyone in the Christian community. In other passages, Jesus proposes a commitment to poverty, pacifism, and helping the poor. The Sermon on the Mount, for example, represents perhaps most powerfully Jesus's theological message about charity, forgiveness, and inclusivity. Yet these same statements have connotations that the political order should try to treat all equally, even if genuine equality and citizenship are not possible except in God's kingdom. The political message of the Sermon on the Mount is a message to all, but especially to the outcast and powerless, offering the comfort that liberation will eventually come in heaven.[11] This political message of salvation may not be a full-fledged opposition to political authority, but it does encourage indifference to it.

Third, while another message of Jesus and early Christians seems to recognize women as equal to men, this message is quickly lost or contradicted. In the life of Jesus, women such as his mother, Mary, and Mary Magdalene occupy important roles, and Jesus seems to speak to both men and women.[12] But Paul retracts many of the original gender-neutral or egalitarian claims, enjoining women to remain subordinate to their husbands:

> Wives, be subject to your husbands, as to the Lord. For the husband is the head of the wife as Christ is the head of the church, his body, and is himself its savior. As the church is subject to Christ, so let wives also be subject in everything to their husbands.[13]

Elsewhere Paul states,

> Let a woman learn in silence with all submissiveness. I permit no woman to teach or have authority over men; she is formed to keep silent. For Adam was formed first, then Eve; and Adam was not deceived, but the woman was deceived and became a transgressor.[14]

Thus Paul relegates women to a secondary political status, invoking the Bible and religious precepts as justification. Religious and paternal metaphors support one another, compromising the gender equality that seems to be part of Jesus's message. Paul preaches this secondary status in marriage, despite that he requires both men and women to recognize one another's conjugal rights.[15] For example, women do not have the option of divorce for mistreatment in marriage; they seem confined to silent acceptance of their lot on earth despite hopes for equality in the new religious community of the Christian faith.

ROME AND CHRISTIANITY

In its first four centuries following Jesus's death, Christianity underwent numerous changes. Perhaps the most important was that Christianity moved away from being a minority, oppositional religion and political movement. In 311 C.E., the Roman Empire declared neutrality toward Christianity and Emperor Constantine proclaimed himself a Christian. Then in 378 C.E., Emperor Theodosius made Christianity the official religion of the Roman Empire.[16] Up to that time, the Romans persecuted Christians, in part because the latter seemed unsupportive of the state and often was viewed as at odds with both the political and theological principles of Rome.[17] As troubles mounted in the first few centuries of the Common Era, including political turmoil and invasions by enemies, many Romans contended that Christianity and Rome's eventual conversion to it were the causes of the empire's problems.

Early Christians did express indifference to Roman authority.[18] Citizenship for Christians resided in membership in the otherworldly empire, their concerns were with salvation and fighting the oppression of Rome. Christianity was a political message aptly suited to the outcasts of Rome.[19] But in receiving official recognition and sanction from Rome, Christianity took its first steps away from an opposition theory of liberation toward a theology that defended the medieval political power of the church.

The roots of that transformation lie in the changing social world and social structure of Christianity in the fourth century C.E. It is at this point that Rome became a Christian government and the church and state merged.[20] Due to that change, the church had to reconcile itself with political power in ways it had not had to confront before. Now, instead of being on the outside, the church was part of the political establishment. What was needed, then, was some way to accommodate church and state authority in a way that recognized the altered social and political context of both. Christianity had to articulate a doctrine defending the need for political authority while at the same time insisting on a true Christian commonwealth transcending any earthly political institution.

ST. AUGUSTINE AND TRANSFORMATION OF CHRISTIAN POLITICS

St. Augustine of Hippo (354–430 C.E.) offers perhaps the most compelling and persuasive picture and explanation of the changing social reality facing the church.[21] He presents a view that accommodates Christianity with political power by positing free will, emphasizing the origin of sin and the naturalness of human wickedness, and claiming a need for a government to become both a preventive and a punishment for human sin as a result of the Fall from grace.[22] Augustine also provides a theological argument questioning the legitimacy of secular political institutions, preparing the way for future church control of secular rulers.

Augustine, relying on personal experiences described in his *Confessions*[23] as well as interpretations of Genesis, reads the Garden of Eden story as the basis for political society.[24] Adam's sin changed the basic structure of the universe. It effected a Fall from Grace with God and commenced a history that will end only with the second coming of Christ.[25] This account of the human condition appears in Augustine's most famous book, *The City of God,* which is over one thousand pages long and took more than twenty years to write. This work represents a systematic rethinking of Christian faith, and in the process, it incorporates and transforms large portions of Greek and Roman philosophy, especially Plato and Cicero, in support of Augustine's arguments.

Augustine began writing the *City of God* in 410 C.E., in the wake of the sack of Rome by non-Christian peoples from the north. He was responding to a charge by a Roman official named Volusianus that the empire fell because Constantine had converted to Christianity and thus Christianity was to blame. Had Rome not converted, had it kept faith in its own gods, Volusianus contended, it would not have faced all the attacks and problems that were occurring. By the time the *City of God* was completed, however, it provided both a theology and a politics to support a church that would come to rule Europe for the next one thousand and more years.

Augustine responds to Volusianus with several claims. First, he contends that Romans were corrupt and deserved to be punished for their vices. Second, if it were not for the love and mercy of Jesus Christ, the sack of Rome would have been worse. Third, Rome had many calamities before it became Christian; hence the conversion was not the cause of its problems. Fourth, if the Roman gods were so good, why did they not protect Rome? Finally, Augustine contends that Rome was not a true republic because it was united by the love of pride.[26] This last point is crucial. Here Augustine turns to Cicero's definition in *On the Commonwealth* of a true commonwealth as an association of individuals united by a common love of right and community interest.[27]

Augustine goes on to ask if Cicero's definition is adequate. Augustine argues no,[28] contending that a true republic is formed only when it is united by the shared love of Christ.[29] No other commonwealth, united for any other type of love, is a real or true commonwealth.

This discussion of pride, and the differences between a true commonwealth and Rome or other earthly republics, produces a distinction that sounds very Platonic. In fact, Augustine asserts that Platonists have positions that are the "closest approximation" to the Christian position.[30] The distinction Augustine is referring to is the one between the ideal and eternal republic and the faint representations found on earth. It emerges in his discussion of the City of God versus the city of man. The true republic is the City or kingdom of God, a commonwealth not found on earth, while the city of man is what has emerged on earth through history, as a result of human sin and the Fall from God's Grace in Eden. The origins of these two cities are critical to understanding Augustine's political theology and visions of the state and human nature.

Adam, Eve, and Human Nature. Augustine turns to the Genesis story of Eden, the state of nature, to develop his arguments about human nature and political society.[31] His account is a theology, but also the basis of a politics that crafts new relationships between the individual and the state and society. Eden represents a prepolitical time, when no state is necessary. Human nature is innocent but possesses the capacity for free will. Individual free will, including the capacity to sin or turn against God, is necessary to give humans dignity and differentiate them from animals.[32] Free will is also necessary to live a good, virtuous, and just life,[33] and when one turns the will toward God, greater glory is achieved. But if one chooses to seek private gain, or avarice,[34] one turns away from God. The decision to seek good or evil is an individual choice, granting everyone personal responsibility over how to conduct their lives.

Humanity's Fall from Grace, which resulted from being tempted by the serpent and eating the apple from the Tree of Knowledge, is an abuse of free will. It is turning love away from the lightness and goodness of God and toward pride and self-love.[35] It is an attempt by humans to try to be the same as God, yet this act of will, the first sin for Augustine, instead subjects "human nature to all the process of decay which we see and feel, and consequently to death also."[36] It is this sin that necessitates a political order after humans are banished from the Garden of Eden:

> God created man aright, for God is the author of natures, though he is certainly not responsible for their defects. But man was willingly perverted and justly condemned, and so begot perverted and condemned offspring. For we were all in that one man, seeing that we all were that one man who fell into sin through the woman who was made before the first sin. We did not yet possess forms individually; but there already existed the seminal nature from which we were to be begotten. And of course, when this was vitiated through sin, and bound with death's fetters in its just condition, man could not be born of man in any other condition. Hence from the misuse of free will there started a chain of disasters; mankind is led from that original perversion, a kind of corruption at the root, right up to the disaster of the second death.[37]

Government and Political Order: Emergence of the Two Cities. Because of the Fall from Grace, humans are not naturally sociable. Rather, they are self-interested and need the state to compel order, obedience, and social cooperation. Without the state, anarchy would result. In other words, Adam and Eve's sin and the Fall from Grace destroyed the cosmic order of the universe, and the original harmony in nature and among humanity. Augustine says, "For the human race is, more than any other species, at once more social by nature and quarrelsome by perversion. And the most salutary warning against this perversion or disharmony is given by the facts of human nature."[38]

From this original sin emerges the creation and separation of two cities, each with its own political and moral values and loves that hold them together:

> Adam was therefore the father of both lines of descent, that is, of the line whose successive members belong to the earthly city, and of the line who are attached to the City in heaven. But after the murder of Abel . . . there were two fathers appointed, one for each of those lines of descent. Those fathers were Cain and Seth; and in their sons, whose names had to be recorded, indications of these cities began to appear with increasing clarity in the race of mortals.[39]

The City of God is united by love of Jesus, while earthly cities, including Rome, are united by lesser loves:[40]

> We see then that the two cities were created by two kinds of love; the earthly city was created by self-love reaching the point of contempt for God, the heavenly City by the love of God carried as far as contempt of self. In fact, the earthly city glories in itself, the Heavenly City glories in the Lord.[41]

According to Augustine, Rome was founded on the sin of self-love, the root of envy, which he considered the worst of all loves:

> The first founder of the earthly city was, as we have seen, a fratricide; for overcome by envy, he slew his own brother, a citizen of the Eternal City, on

pilgrimage in this world. . . . For this is how Rome was founded, when Remus, as Roman history witnesses, was slain by his brother Romulus.[42]

Furthermore, Augustine sees Rome's founding as symbolic of the founding of all earthly cities:

> Thus the quarrel that arose between Remus and Romulus demonstrated the division of the earthly city against itself; while the conflict between Cain and Abel displayed the hostility between the two cities themselves, the City of God and the city of men. Thus the wicked fight among themselves; and likewise the wicked fight against the good and the good against the wicked.[43]

Referring to the story in Genesis, Augustine describes how the two cities emerge after Adam through the lineages of his two sons, Cain and Abel. Each city has unique characteristics, the City of God represented by Jerusalem, and the city of man represented by Babylon and Rome. Thus one important idea arising from Augustine's reading of Genesis is that the state is a product of sin, which produced a disharmony among individuals and renders political organizations imperative.

A second important idea is that the state's origin is located at a certain point in God's plan for the universe. For Augustine, the state emerges in time; that is, time commences with the Fall from Grace.[44] Both the Greeks and Romans see time as a cyclical pattern, but Augustine rejects the cyclical idea. Thus Augustine's Christianity effects a major change in political and historical thinking. He advances the notion that history has a purpose, moving humanity in a direction toward something. The final goal of history is the eventual destruction of the city of man and the triumph of the City of God, and the end of history will occur when Christ returns for the Final Judgment.[45]

Human Nature, History, and the True Republic. Augustine's vision of history draws important parallels between the chronology of creation in Genesis, the human soul, and the life stages of man.[46] The parallels are important because they link together the Bible, history, the political community, and the individual. First, Augustine establishes the Bible as the source of knowledge and truth, describing the plan or providence that God has for humankind and history. Here he suggests that individual harmony is connected to harmony and justice in the universe.

Second, describing history in terms of the stages of human life suggests that history has a sense of growth or development much like humans. Paralleling history to a human life also reveals where Augustine thinks the Roman Empire is located in history, that is, in the old age of human life, or near the end of human history. Locating Rome near the end of history demonstrates that the Christian era is further along or more advanced in history than were previous eras, which places it closer to the realization of God's final purpose for humanity.

Third, human nature and sin are important to history and the state's existence as well. The state and human affairs are located within a historical pattern that is part of a larger order or providence God has for the universe. History is the battle between the values of the two cities, values that emerged with Adam and separated when Cain killed Abel. Battle between the two cities takes place throughout history, with the final resolution occurring when the City of God, the real commonwealth, emerges victorious over earthly republics, like Rome. Thus human history is a movement away from the Garden of Eden, where there was no political discord or state, to a situation where conflict and discord now exist and need control by a government. To Augustine, the true republic, the City of God, is united by love of God:

> It follows that justice is found where God, the one supreme God, rules an obedient City according to his grace, forbidding sacrifice to any being save himself alone; and where in consequence the soul rules the body in all men who belong to this City and obey God, and the reason faithfully rules the vices in a lawful system of subordination; so that just as the individual righteous man lives on the basis of faith. . . . But where this justice does not exist, there is certainly no "association of men united by a common sense of right and by a community of interest." Therefore there is no commonwealth; for where there is no "people," there is no "weal of the people."[47]

The contrast between the City of God and the city of man leads Augustine to rethink Cicero's definition of true commonwealth:

> If, on the other hand, another definition than this is found for a "people," for example, if one should say, "A people is the association of a multitude of rational beings united by a common agreement on the objects of their love," then it follows that to observe the character of a particular people we must examine the objects of its love. . . . And, obviously, the better the objects of this agreement, the better the people; the worse the objects of this love. . . . the worse the people. By this definition of ours, the Roman people is a people and its estate is indubitably a commonwealth. . . . And because God does not rule there the general character of that city is that it is devoid of true justice.[48]

Elsewhere, Augustine further clarifies what a true commonwealth is, noting the importance of justice:

> Remove justice, and what are kingdoms but gangs of criminals on a large scale? What are criminal gangs but petty kingdoms? A gang is a group of men under the command of a leader, bound by a compact of association, in which the plunder is divided according to an agreed convention.[49]

> But true justice is found only in that commonwealth whose founder and ruler is Christ; if we agree to call it a commonwealth, seeing that we cannot deny that it is the "weal of the community."[50]

As for Rome, Augustine asserts that all states are created by divine providence,[51] and that the Roman Empire is "good according the standards of the earthly city."[52] But it was created to serve individual glory and pride, not the glory of God, thus preventing it from being the City of God.[53] Rome's purpose on earth, then, is to "suppress the grievous evils of many nations," reducing all evil and sin to the basic one of pride which can then be destroyed by Jesus.[54]

Implications of the Doctrine of the Two Cities. In the *City of God*, Augustine offers a political theory that places earthly political institutions within the context of Christian theology. The significance of his recasting of Greek and Roman political thought is that it simultaneously delegitimizes secular political institutions, makes them creations of God, and places them subordinate to the demands of the Christian church.

Augustine's theory of history is also important, on several counts. First, it explains human nature as wicked and fallen, necessitating both religious institutions, to tend to the soul, and political institutions, to address the anti-social behavior of individuals. Second, it makes human existence purposive, in that salvation and eventual membership in the City of God are the goals. Third, by defining what a true republic is, Augustine provides a standard of justice by which human law and institutions can be measured. Laws that fail to conform to the higher standards of justice are not real laws. This appeal to a higher standard is similar to natural law in Cicero's thought, the theory of the good in Plato's philosophy, and perhaps even the standards invoked by Antigone.

Augustine never stated that the City of God was the Christian church. But later in the Middle Ages, he was read as saying exactly that. The result was that Augustine's idea of the two cities was used to justify the subordination of the individual to the state and the church, and secular authority to religious authority, making the church an important political institution. In fact, with the gradual disappearance of the Western Roman Empire and the demise of secular political institutions in Europe, the church came to be the dominant political institution for the next one thousand years.

Reinterpreting history in terms of Christian theology also resulted in the collapse of political language into religious rhetoric. With the cessation of secular learning after the Fall of Rome, many of the writings of Plato, Aristotle, and other political thinkers were lost to Christian Europe until 1200 C.E. or later. The void was filled by Augustine and other religious thinkers, who described politics solely in terms of a Christian theology. This paved the way for subsequent Christians to endow the church with political power, and throughout the Middle Ages to contemplate the issue of how to use that power to secure Christian ends.

FAITH VERSUS REASON

Christianity and Augustine's questioning of Roman authority, as well as his reinterpretation of history, were successful because of crises and turmoil that were already gripping an empire in decline. Institutional and political crises led to loss of confidence in reason and rationality to address social problems and understand human affairs, providing the basis for political obligation grounded in faith.[55] For Augustine, the collapse of Roman institutions is not simply a failure of a pagan theology, but of the ideology of reason and rationality found in Greek and Roman philosophy that built and sustained those institutions. The demise of Roman institutions shook the "confidence in man's ability to understand this world by reason," continuing the decline in more classical methods to apprehend and order the world.[56]

Stoics responded to the crises of political order and institutions by redefining political citizenship and membership in otherworldly institutions. Early Christians, especially Augustine, respond by questioning the classical ideology itself, turning toward faith as an alternative source of knowledge and means to organize one's life.[57] They argue against reason as self-structuring in its capacity to solve social problems and bring about order.[58] Augustine places authority in Christian faith, especially the Scriptures, as the source of knowledge that gives human existence and history its meaning.[59]

Augustine contends that there is a plan for the universe which is laid out in the Scriptures.[60] God's plan is revealed in history, through the unfolding of human events. The plan, as revealed in the mystery of the Trinity, tells of human salvation, the importance of Jesus, and the location of human history and political institutions, such as Rome, in God's plan. Augustine's questioning of the classical ideology of the Romans involves a rejection of their explanations of history, historical change, and the role of humans in both. He transfers the source of knowledge to the Bible. Proof that what the Scriptures say is true must ultimately rest on faith and not reason, with Christians admonished to accept Christian dogma as the final arbiter of justice and veracity.[61]

Augustine's appeal to faith is a suitable and viable answer to the questioning of classical ideology and reason that was taking place. In the midst of disorder, Augustine is able to appeal to a religion that offered explanations for what was happening in the world. Christianity responded to the breakdown in order and authority by providing a new paradigm, or set of values, to structure the world. The new ideology offered hope to those who were looking for answers, and it provided those answers by appealing to the mystery of God and his revealed word in the Scriptures.

WOMEN, FAMILY, AND SEXUAL DESIRE

Women occupy an ambiguous status in Augustine's political thought. This ambiguity reflects the contrasting treatment of women by Jesus and Paul. On the one hand, women are viewed as equal to men, on the other, as subservient and as the object and cause of sexual desires. Augustine sees women as both equal members in the City of God and of secondary status in the city of man. In part, this dual status reflects Augustine's distinction of all humans into the rational soul and the carnal body, with the former partaking of the divine, and the latter the baseness of human desire and lust:

So when man lives by the standard of truth he lives not by his own standard, but by God's. . . . By contrast, when he lives by his own standard, that is by man's and not by God's standard, then inevitably he lives by the standard of falsehood. . . . Therefore, to behave according to human standards is the same as to be "of the flesh," because by "the flesh," a part of man, man himself is meant.[62]

Although Augustine divides humans into the soul and the flesh, he does not mean that the body is the source of sin. Instead, a sinful soul willfully corrupts the body and turns it toward lust and evil.[63] It is the Fall from Grace that disengages the body and desires, including sexual desires, from reason, making it possible for bodily desires to turn one from God.

Augustine's views on women are tied to his disdain for sexual desires and the flesh as well as by Adam and Eve's relationship in the Garden of Eden. According to Genesis, woman's body was originally created from man's: "So Yahweh God made the man fall into a deep sleep. And while he slept, he took one of his ribs and enclosed it in flesh. Yahweh God built the rib he had taken from man into a woman, and he brought her to the man."[64] But though Eve's body comes from man, her soul comes directly from God; Augustine states that on Judgment Day, the souls of men and women will equally rise to heaven.[65] Thus, in the spiritual sense men and women are the same, but on earth their bodily differences matter, and women are placed in an inferior position.

Augustine's autobiography, *The Confessions,* is further indication that he sees men and women as spiritually equal. Here Augustine reiterates Paul's statement that in spirit there is neither male nor female, Jew, nor Greek, free nor slave.[66] And in the *City of God,* he states that, upon resurrection, women will keep their sexual organs and female form, but that "female organs will not subserve their former use; they will be part of a new beauty, which will not excite the lust of the beholder."[67] For Augustine, in heaven there is no marriage. Men and women are spiritually equal, living like the angels. Bodily differences, marriage, and lust do not exist in the City of God; they are part of the punishments and requirements of the city of man.

Before the Fall from Grace, human anatomy does not seem to be important. Augustine describes Adam and Eve in the Garden of Eden as originally living in a state of both innocence and equality:

The pair lived in a partnership of unalloyed felicity; their love for God and one another was undisturbed. There was a serene avoidance of sin; and as long as this continued, there was no encroachment of any kind of evil.[68]

Between man and wife there was a faithful partnership based on love and mutual respect; there was a harmony and a liveliness of mind and body.[69]

In the Garden of Eden marriage exists, yet it appears to be a marriage of equals. Within this marriage, sex also exists, but Augustine describes it as a sex without lust, undertaken in innocence and without shame. However, when Eve eats from the Tree of Knowledge and tempts Adam, Eve is tempting him sexually, arousing a sexual lust that forces him to sin also. The result is that innocence is lost, sex produces shame, and women are rendered sub-servient to men because of their sinning. Thus lust is a product of the Fall from Grace,[70] making sex something no longer innocent but shameful, even in the context of marriage and for the purpose of producing children. Proof of this shameful nature, for Augustine, is that sex is done in private, away from the eyes of others.[71]

Augustine's interpretation of the Garden of Eden story renders sexual desire as something dangerous, sinful, and shameful. His accounts of his own sexual desires and corruption in the *Confessions* reveal that he fears the sexual drive and bodily temptation he sees women as causing. Because he connects sexual desire to women, he views them as the cause of man's downfall and for human mortality, and the reason for the need for political institutions.

Because of her sins, God relegates Eve and all subsequent women to serving men. "To the woman he said: 'I will multiply your pains in childbearing, you shall give birth to your children in pain. Your yearning shall be for your husband, yet he will lord over you.'"[72] Women's status in the city of man, one of marriage and service to men, is sanctioned by both the sinful nature of Eve and women, and fiat of God. Religious injunctions thus demarcate and justify family and gender roles for Augustine, as well as render sexual desire shameful and sinful. In Augustine's account, the two are linked, placing women in the role of the evil seductress for which they are condemned to an inferior position in the city of man.

CONCLUSION

St. Augustine's contribution to political thought was a new orientation for political theory that would leave a legacy enduring even to the present time. Augustine succeeded in making Christian theology the final arbiter of truth and political legitimacy, forcing thought and discussion of politics, visions of the family, and male and female relations, into a frame of reference to a Christian God and religion. His reformulation of many traditional political concepts into religious issues moved politics away from the values of the Greeks and Romans, and into a discourse that would empower the Christian church with tremendous political authority and control over secular rulers. Politics lost its own unique vocabulary and justifications, and combined the secular and spiritual in an ambiguous synthesis.[73] The new role of politics was based on individual subordination to the state directed by the Christian church. However, although the individual was subordinated to a new religious order, the Christian emphasis on free will and the personal choice to seek salvation also created a sense of individualism not found in earlier political theories.

St. Augustine provided an important set of political and theological arguments to pave the way for Christianity to become a governing religion, and not simply an opposition force within the Roman Empire. But would

Christianity change as it grew more powerful? How would religious leaders justify their newfound political power? Would it change them? Would the merging of political power with religious doctrine taint the latter, or force compromises, or would the two cities doctrine undermine earthly institutions? Interpreters of Augustine's arguments would have to sort out the relative relationships among the individual, church, and state, and between the sacred and the political.

Notes

1. Peter Brown, *The World of Late Antiquity: A.D. 150–750* (London: Harcourt Brace Jovanovich, 1971), 67.

2. R. H. Barrow, *The Romans* (New York: Pelican, 1979), 202.

3. Elaine Pagels, *Adam, Eve, and the Serpent* (New York: Random House, 1988).

4. Arlene Saxonhouse, *Women in the History of Political Thought: Ancient Greece to Machiavelli* (Westport, Conn.: Praeger, 1985), 128.

5. Galatians 3:28.

6. John 18:36.

7. Sheldon S. Wolin, *Politics and Vision: Continuity and Innovation in Western Political Thought* (Boston: Little, Brown, 1960), 102.

8. *The Romans*, 178.

9. Matthew 22:21.

10. Romans 13:1–6.

11. *The World of Late Antiquity*, 67.

12. *Women in the History of Political Thought*, 125.

13. Ephesians, 5:22–24.

14. 1 Timothy 2:11–14.

15. 1 Corinthians 7:3–4.

16. *The Romans*, 182–84.

17. *The Romans*, 178.

18. *The Romans*, 179.

19. *The World of Late Antiquity*, 67.

20. Charles Howard McIlwain, *The Growth of Political Thought in the West* (New York: Macmillan, 1932), 146.

21. Peter Brown, "Saint Augustine," in *Trends in Medieval Political Thought*, ed. B. Smalley (Oxford: Basil Blackwell, 1965), 9.

22. Ernest L. Fortin, "St. Augustine," in *History of Political Philosophy*, eds. L. Strauss and J. Cropsey (Chicago: University of Chicago Press, 1987), 176.

23. "Saint Augustine," 3.

24. *Adam, Eve, and the Serpent*, 144.

25. St. Augustine, *Concerning the City of God against the Pagans*, trans. H. Bottenson (New York: Penguin, 1977), 594.

26. *City of God*, 71.

27. *City of God*, 75.

28. *City of God*, 75.

29. *City of God*, 556–57, 626.

30. *City of God*, 311.

31. *City of God*, 568.

32. *City of God*, 190–95, 503.

33. St. Augustine, *On the Free Choice of the Will*, trans. A. S. Benjamin (Indianapolis: Bobbs-Merrill, 1977), 36, 79.

34. *On the Free Choice of the Will*, 83–84, 125–26.

35. *On the Free Choice of the Will,* 147.
36. *City of God,* 571.
37. *City of God,* 523.
38. *City of God,* 508.
39. *City of God,* 626.
40. *City of God,* 556.
41. *City of God,* 593.
42. *City of God,* 600.
43. *City of God,* 601.
44. *City of God,* 432.
45. *City of God,* 852.
46. Peter Dennis Bathory, *Political Theory as Public Confession: The Social and Political Thought of St. Augustine of Hippo* (New Brunswick, N.J.: Transaction, 1981).
47. *City of God,* 890.
48. *City of God,* 890–91.
49. *City of God,* 139.
50. *City of God,* 75.
51. *City of God,* 179.
52. *City of God,* 213.
53. *City of God,* 197, 204, 477.
54. *City of God,* 201, 599.
55. "Saint Augustine," 4–15.
56. G. L. Keyes, *Christian Faith and the Interpretation of History* (Lincoln: University of Nebraska Press, 1966), 14.
57. Charles Norris Cochrane, *Christianity and Classical Culture* (New York: Oxford University Press, 1980), 411.
58. *Christianity and Classical Culture,* 419.
59. *City of God,* 39, 429.
60. *City of God,* 39; R. L. P. Milburn, *Early Christian Interpretations of History* (London: Adam & Charles Black, 1954), 74.
61. *City of God,* 431, 487–94; St. Augustine, *The Confessions of St. Augustine* (New York: Image Books, 1960), 138–40.
62. *City of God,* 553.
63. *City of God,* 551.
64. Genesis 2:22–23.
65. *City of God,* 1027–29; *Women in the History of Political Thought,* 137.
66. *Confessions,* 356.
67. *City of God,* 1057.
68. *City of God,* 567.
69. *City of God,* 591.
70. *City of God,* 580.
71. *City of God,* 577–80.
72. Genesis 3:16–17; *Confessions,* 383, n. 7.
73. "Saint Augustine," 18.

Additional Readings

Bathory, Peter Dennis. *Political Theory as Public Confession: The Social and Political Thought of St. Augustine of Hippo.* New Brunswick, N.J.: Transaction, 1981.

Brown, Peter. *The World of Late Antiquity: A.D. 150–750.* London: Harcourt Brace Jovanovich, 1971.

Connolly, William E. *The Augustian Imperative: A Reflection on the Politics of Morality.* Newbury Park, Calif.: Sage, 1993.

Figgis, John Neville. *The Political Aspect of St. Augustine's "City of God."* Gloucester, Mass.: P. Smith, 1963.

Keyes, G. L. *Christian Faith and the Interpretation of History.* Lincoln: University of Nebraska Press, 1966.

Pagels, Elaine. *Adam, Eve, and the Serpent.* New York: Random House, 1988.

Saxonhouse, Arlene. *Women in the History of Political Thought: Ancient Greece to Machiavelli.* Westport, Conn.: Praeger, 1985.

Inventors of Ideas Online

Visit http://politicalscience.wadsworth.com/tannenbaum2 for links related to material in this chapter, including the full text of Augustine's *The City of God* and *Confessions* and additional resources, commentaries, and images.

7

THE CONTRIBUTION OF ISLAM: JOHN OF SALISBURY, THOMAS AQUINAS, AND THE RISE OF THE MEDIEVAL POLITICAL WORLD

INTRODUCTION

The collapse of the Roman Empire, the rise of Christianity, and Augustine's rethinking of the relationship between political power and religious faith in the *City of God* left several important legacies that dominated medieval political thought. Not the least was creation of the politics of the sacred, whereby all political issues were discussed in terms of Christianity. Another legacy, left by subsequent interpretations of St. Augustine, was creation of a basic unity in the Middle Ages that made the church the dominant political institution defining the system or values that held Christian Europe together.[1]

With the division of the Roman Empire into eastern and western parts, and the decline of the western empire in the fourth and fifth centuries, there were arguably no major secular institutions until the Carolinian kings of ninth-century France. This meant that the church was the only major institution with any political power in western Europe. By default it became the ruling force of Europe, merging political and religious values.[2] This combination of secular power with Christian doctrine was the context for much political debate during that time.

Several factors made possible and defined the reconciliation of political and religious power. *The City of God* was misinterpreted to equate the City of God with the church, and the city of man with secular institutions. This contributed to the belief among Christian writers that St. Augustine was defending church rule against a purely secular government, with the pope as the secular head of the City of God. In addition, the distinction between the two cities led to a questioning of the importance of secular institutions.

Despite Jesus's plea to "Render unto Caesar that which is Caesar's," loyalty to the church undermined that which was due to Caesar. Finally, Paul's claims that secular rule received its authority directly from God also contributed to the belief that secular institutions were subordinate to the church.

Another factor encouraging subordination of secular institutions to the church was known as the Donation of Constantine. That was a claim that Emperor Constantine had deeded the Roman Empire over to St. Silvester and the church. As a result, secular rulers subsequently obtained their authority to rule from the Pope, thus giving him tremendous power to excommunicate kings in Christian Europe if they strayed from Christian doctrine or his desires. The myth of the donation remained a powerful force legitimizing church authority until the fifteenth century, when it was finally proven false.

With the demise of old secular institutions, what emerged were two political systems competing for allegiance.[3] Determining the relationship or allocation of political power and space between the Pope and local monarchs, and deciding which should hold one's primary loyalty were major problems. There was thus some confusion in keeping the peace between them. Among the questions raised by political thinkers was how local priests were related to rulers. What should one do if secular rule appeared not to serve Christian purposes? What traits should rulers have? Did one have to obey an unjust ruler? What limits should or could be placed on rulers, both secular and religious? What role did the individual occupy in the political and religious communities?

One suggestion for resolving some of these questions, called the Two Swords Doctrine, was offered by Pope Gelasius near the end of the fifth century. Drawing upon Luke 22:7, wherein Peter says to Jesus, "Lo, here are two swords," Gelasius contended that the two swords referred to temporal and spiritual power. Thus, for Gelasius, there were two swords, or authorities, that govern humankind: the church and the emperor of the eastern Roman Empire; and both need the other. The Two Swords Doctrine also stated that all power (both swords) came from God, and that while the church held one sword, it gave the other to kings to rule. Hence kings not only must serve the church but derive their power from them, which gave the pope and local bishops significant power.[4]

The Two Swords Doctrine placed secular rule in a precarious position relative to the church. It suggested that perhaps individuals did not have to obey kings who were tyrants or otherwise abused their authority.[5] Although Augustine seemed to imply that commonwealths that did not serve God were unjust and did not need to be followed, he argued that they nonetheless must be obeyed. Other Christian leaders, including St. Gregory I (540–604), continued to support the duty to obey. Gregory's claim was that the unjust ruler must be obeyed, in both body and mind, because the ruler's actions were in some way justified by God or sin. Subsequent political thinkers in the Middle Ages also addressed the issue of tyranny, offering other solutions to reconcile the dilemma. Among other claims, they argued that secular institutions commanded obedience if they served Christian goals. But the Two Swords Doctrine made it unclear how much control secular rulers had, even over their own subordinates.[6] In any case, the limits were not set by the citizens of the political community, but by the duties the rulers owed to God.

Another factor contributing to the terms of political debate in the Middle Ages was the emergence of a Christian cosmology. This vision of the universe grew out of both Augustine's city of man/City of God distinction and Plato's views of the world. Instead of the Platonic vision that forms are the basis of reality, however, Christians argued that there was a basic unity to the universe, at the center of which was God, and from God there came the pope and the church. As God's representative on earth, the pope was presumed to be infallible and omnipotent. From the church the center of the medieval political world hung, and from God to the church and pope the new political cosmology was structured. In effect, the Christian cosmology assumed a hierarchy, with authority passing from God to the pope, then to the church, down through men, to women, and eventually to the Devil. This same hierarchy also provided justification for a hierarchal political order and rule, much in the same way Plato's vision of the universe provided a blueprint for how to order the ideal republic. The Christian cosmology continued earlier assumptions regarding the family and the inferiority and subordination of women to men; only now, the hierarchical structure of the universe was also used to support women's secondary status.[7]

ARISTOTLE AND THE ARABIC WORLD

The medieval Christian world was not the first to face the challenge of reconciling religion with philosophy. The Arab Islamic world of the twelfth and thirteenth centuries faced similar problems.[8] Efforts to reconcile Islamic divine law with human law, or seeking to locate a place for politics within theology, were issues that also dominated theologians and philosophers across the entire Islamic and Arab worlds. One school of Islam, located in Alexandria, Egypt, was particularly interested in these issues and its scholars increasingly turned to reading numerous classical texts besides the Koran for inspiration and answers, and they also developed extensive commentaries on these books. Among the works that they commented on were those by Plato, Aristotle, and the Neoplatonists, important thinkers from the ancient Greek and Roman philosophical traditions.

Many of the writings of the Greeks and Romans, including Plato and especially Aristotle, had disappeared from the Christian medieval world from the fifth century until the thirteenth century. The loss of these writings, which described secular visions of politics as distinct from Christianity, led to the result that Christian writers such as Augustine dominated political discourse for over eight hundred years. It meant that there were no contrasting visions of the state, political obligation, or church–state relations. Discussions of political power and the goals of politics were thus undertaken and debated by searching for biblical passages and scriptural interpretations to support specific positions and arguments. Hence only the Bible framed the terms of political debate in Europe.

During the time when Europe had no access to the classical writers, however, the Arab world had an important and lively intellectual culture, of which Aristotle and Plato were a part. In fact, Arab thinkers such as Alfarabi, Averroës, and Avicenna studied the classics in detail, and it was from the Arab world, through Moorish Spain, that Aristotle was reintroduced to Christian thinkers in the thirteenth century. Moreover, many of the changes that the Christian West would undergo as a result of the rediscovery of the classical writers was both anticipated and made possible by the Islamic world's importation of Aristotle and Plato into the latter's theological tradition.

Abū-Nasr Muhammad al-Fārābī (873–950), better known as Alfarabi in the Christian West, was a Turkish philosopher who blended Aristotle with Islam. His most important political works include *The Virtuous City* and *The Political Regime,* which advocate creating an ideal city or republic similar to that in Plato's *Republic.* His trilogy of works known as the *Philosophy of Plato and Aristotle* were also an important contribution to the revival of these two thinkers in Islamic and subsequently Christian theology and philosophy.[9]

In discussing governments or constitutions, Alfarabi follows the classical sixfold distinction to describe the virtuous and debased forms of rule by one, the few, and the many. He also draws upon Platonic notions of a philosopher-king who has special knowledge of both divine and human affairs. But Alfarabi also describes a prophet-ruler as one who can command, again much like Plato's legislator as described in the *Statesman.* The prophet-ruler has special imaginative knowledge that is distinct from the philosopher-king. The philosopher-king is not necessarily inferior to the prophet-king in terms of fitness to rule; instead Alfarabi seeks to combine the two as the ideal ruler. However, unlike Plato, Alfarabi seems to endorse both the monarchy and democracy as good regimes, the latter of which seems to well suit the diverse needs of the subjects.

In terms of Alfarabi's Aristotelian roots, he draws upon the latter's metaphysics, especially as mediated or understood through Neoplatonism. Here he takes Aristotle's notions of final causes and levels of being and merges them with Islamic philosophy to produce a theory of the world based on a hierarchy emanating from God. In doing that, he creates a theological metaphysics that is similar to many syntheses found in later Christian medieval thought.

Averroës, or Ibn-Rushd (1126–1198), was an influential Islamic philosopher who lived in Seville, Spain, at the time it was under the control of the Moors. He wrote extensively about Aristotle, and his commentaries were eventually translated into Latin. Averroës draws heavily upon Aristotle's metaphysics to create a hierarchy of reality and knowledge. In his *On God's Knowledge,* he attempts to reconcile a dynamic and changing universe with God's knowledge, in the process distinguishing between eternal knowledge about the cause of things and a more temporal knowledge. This dualism surrounding contrasting types of knowledge would later materialize into a crisis in Christianity as writers sought both to uphold revelation and Aristotelian rationalism as ways to understand and explain the universe.

Avicenna (980–1037) was a Persian who also drew upon the classics, as understood through the Neoplatonists, as well as upon the work of Alfarabi. Avicenna is perhaps the most comprehensive and influential of the Islamic philosophers. His *Canon of Medicine* and, more importantly, his encyclopedia of philosophy entitled *The Healing* were translated into Latin. Avicenna used Aristotelian concepts to construct a cosmology that made God the cause from which the rest of the universe flows. Thus, much like Thomas Aquinas would later write, God serves as the first and final cause of creation, with the temporal world a lesser form of reality as compared to God and the heavens. Classical philosophy thus formed the rational framework upon which Islamic theology could be placed.

Although Alfarabi, Averroës, and Avicenna can be described as significant philosophers on their own merits, both the Jewish and Christian worlds are indebted to them and other Arab and Islamic thinkers who kept alive classical learning and transferred it to them. In the Jewish world, Moses Maimonides' (1135–1204) *Treatise on the Art of Logic* and his *Guide for the Perplexed* sought to reconcile Judaism with Aristotle, producing arguments similar to those found in the works of many of the Islamic writers. But the resulting clash between Christian and Greek political assumptions, starting around 1200, was even more powerful, as it forced significant political debate and a rethinking of political and religious issues. More specifically, thinkers made an effort to reconcile or synthesize Aristotle and Christianity, and the results produced new and different visions of church versus state and secular versus religious order, as well as redefinitions of the goals and assumptions surrounding human nature, what politics was, and how political authority was supported.[10]

JOHN OF SALISBURY

John of Salisbury (1115?–1180) wrote *Policraticus,* one of the more significant tracts of political theory in the Middle Ages, in 1159. Much of the other work written during this period concerned proof of God's existence, issues of canon law, and other theological matters. In fact, *Policraticus* is the only sustained book on political theory written before the rediscovery of Aristotle. Its ideas are not necessarily novel; the book simply sets out to describe what everyone had come to believe about politics, power, and the character of the ruler.

Policraticus is part of the "mirror of prince" genre of books, which were written as advice to rulers on how to rule and what their duties are. The main goals of the book are to distinguish between tyrants and princes, and to describe what traits princes should have, what goals they should pursue, and why it pays for a prince to be Christian. John of Salisbury agrees with Cicero concerning the definition of a commonwealth as a society united by common agreement about law and rights, and this definition provides the touchstone for his discussion of kings, tyrants, and the law. He argues that a prince obeys the law and rules the people by the law's dictates. It is only by ruling through the law that a king can obtain his claim to be in the foremost and chief place in the management of the affairs of the commonwealth.

The first question posed in *Policraticus* is what a prince is, and how to distinguish him from a tyrant. According to John of Salisbury, a prince is one "who receives power from God" and "serves the law and is the slave of justice and right":[11]

> There is wholly or mainly this difference between the tyrant and the prince: that the latter is obedient to law, and rules his people by a will that places itself at their service, and administers rewards and burdens within the republic under the guidance of law in a way favorable to the vindication of his eminent post, so that he proceeds before others to the extent that, while individuals merely look after individual affairs, princes are concerned with the burdens of the entire community. Hence, there is deservedly conferred on him the power over all his subjects, in order that he may be sufficient in himself to seek out and bring about the utility of each and all, and that he may arrange the optimal condition of the human republic, so that everyone is a member of the others.[12]

John of Salisbury further states that the "prince is the public power and a certain image on earth of the divine majesty," and that whatever "the prince can do, therefore, is from God."[13] In other passages, he describes a prince as one who does nothing "inconsistent with the equity of justice,"[14] and that the prince is a law unto himself, in that he is above the laws he writes for others, but he is not above God's divine law.[15]

Policraticus invokes the Two Swords Doctrine regarding the prince's relationship to the church:

> This sword is therefore accepted by the prince from the hand of the Church, although it still does not itself possess the bloody sword entirely. For while it has this sword, yet it is used by the hand of the prince, upon whom is conferred the power of bodily coercion, reserving spiritual authority for the papacy. The prince is therefore a sort of minister of the priests and one who exercises those features of the sacred duties that seem an indignity in the hands of priests.[16]

Thus the prince receives his authority indirectly, through the church, which hands him the duty of enforcing Christian laws through the infliction of physical coercion and punishment.

Finally, a prince does not prefer or let his private affairs get in the way of the duties of others.[17] The prince serves God and the people; that is, he follows an implicit pact that binds him to God and then to the people, and the latter are obligated to obey him because he serves God and justice.

In contrast, John of Salisbury describes a tyrant as one who "usurps power, suppresses justice, and places the law beneath his will."[18] Tyranny is a public crime, it oppresses people,[19] and its origin is in iniquity; it involves placement of the interest of the self ahead of others.[20] Despite this description, John of Salisbury also states,

> Yet I do not deny that tyrants are ministers of God, who by His just judgment has willed them to be preeminent over both soul and body. By means of tyrants the evil are punished and the good corrected and trained.[21]

Given that tyrants are ministers of God, it might appear that citizens have a duty to obey them. However, John of Salisbury sends conflicting messages on this point. Because tyranny is a public crime, or a form of treason,[22] he argues that it is honorable to kill tyrants "if they could not otherwise be restrained."[23] On the other hand, one cannot kill a tyrant if some sacred oath binds one to obeying him.[24] Yet there may be times when it is necessary to remove a tyrant, if he is a particularly unjust one and if there is no other option to correct his behavior. Short of this circumstance, however, citizens are bound to obey him, as he is sent by God to correct them.

On the face of it, John of Salisbury describes a king who can easily become an absolute ruler, greatly tempted to abuse his power. However, numerous factors restrain him, forcing him to follow God's laws and preventing him from becoming a tyrant. Tyrants can be killed, as mentioned earlier, and tyrants always reach a miserable end.[25] By contrast, princes are enriched by being just and receive benefits.[26] They can pass the throne on to a son,[27] and those who serve God go to heaven and live in eternal bliss. None of these benefits is open to the tyrant. Thus rulers have a personal interest in not abusing their power.

Overall, John of Salisbury makes several important points about politics in *Policraticus*. He argues, first, that the good prince is also a Christian prince, thus equating political virtue and power with Christianity. Second, addressing the problem of how to limit political power and the excesses of kings, he says it is God and the threat of violent death that limits them. This is clearly a very unstable solution, but until the notion of constitutionalism evolves later in history, it is the only solution available. Third, he defines the relative power of church and state, that is, that the latter receives its legitimacy from the former so that it is able to use force to compel Christian obedience.

ARISTOTLE AND THE LATE MIDDLE AGES

By the twelfth and thirteenth centuries, conditions in Europe were considerably different than they had been several hundred years earlier. Rulers and secular governments were growing in strength, had a stronger following, and were in a better position to challenge religious institutions. Growing awareness of the church's abuses of political power, resentment of its authority, and the development of local secular empires all led to an emerging crisis on how to reconcile church and state power.

It is at this point that Aristotle was reintroduced to Christian Europe. His works, long preserved in the Arab world, started appearing in the twelfth century through translations by Bishop Raymond of Toledo and William of Moerbeke. Aristotle's vision of human nature, views on government and the polis, and claims about nature contrasted sharply and squarely with Augustinian notions of sin, the Fall from Grace, and political society.[28] His ideas forced political thinkers to address this collision, while also providing some defenders of secular rule an angle from which to challenge the pope's authority and the unity of the medieval world.[29]

The reintroduction of Aristotle to Christian Europe did not change the status of women, however. Thomas Aquinas, for example, adopted Aristotle's assumptions about the family and women's diminished capacity to reason, using them to further justify the status quo.[30] Aristotle's writings also offered a return to the notion of the family as the support and base upon which the state is constructed.

THOMAS AQUINAS

St. Thomas Aquinas (1225–1274), a Christian theologian, wrote a synthesis of Aristotelian and Christian ideas that eventually became official church canon. It provided a new grounding for Christian faith, and it offered a redefinition of Christian political thought to allow for independent authority of secular governments.

In addition to Aristotle, Aquinas also read Cicero, the Roman jurists, and a number of Christian writers. As a result, Aquinas's political theory incorporates Aristotle's idea of telos, the commitment to human reason, and various writers' distinctions among different types of governments. His writings address human nature, the nature of human versus natural law, justice, the goals of commonwealth, types of governments and the nature of ruling, limits on power and its abuses, and the issue of tolerance. The relationships between the individual and the political were already important in the Middle Ages, and would become even more so into the modern era.

Human Nature and Society. One of the clearest contrasts between Aquinas and Augustine lies in their views on the nature of political society and humankind.[31] Unlike Augustine, who sees political society as a remedy for and a consequence of humanity's fallen nature, Aquinas depicts people as rational and social, and political society as natural:

> Man is by nature, however, a social and political animal, living amid a multitude of his kind; more so, indeed, than is the case with all other animals, which natural necessity itself makes clear. . . . For man, however, none of these were provided by nature, but instead of all of these, reason was given to him. . . . It is, therefore, natural for man that he live in the companionship of his kind.[32]

Borrowing from Aristotle, Aquinas argues that man's rational and social capacity, not human sin or his practical inability to live alone, necessitates a political government.[33] Moreover, some goals, purpose, or telos must guide and direct this government. Appealing to Aristotle again, Aquinas argues that in the same way that every ship has a leader, so every state must have one.[34] This also means that there ought to be a ruling principle to help guide the state:

> It is, therefore, necessary for man to live in society with his fellows, so that one may be aided by another and that different persons may be engaged in making different discoveries through their respective powers of reason. . . . If it is natural that man live in society with his fellows, it is necessary that there be some power in men by which that group be ruled. . . . Therefore, in all things which are ordered to one goal, there is to be found some ruling principle.[35]

To Aquinas, one principle that ought to rule a government is reason. But to follow justice and serve his people, a ruler is also required to follow God's natural law as a guiding principle in the commonwealth.

Overall, the political thought of Aquinas no longer depicts the state in negative terms, as a product of human sin. Instead, his adoption of Aristotelian ideas gives the government the important and positive purposes of securing both Christian and secular goals. Politics is not something to be shunned, as it was for St. Augustine. Rather, it is important to individual and collective moral growth and well-being.

Types of Law. Law is critical to defining the connections among the individual, the polity, and God. Aquinas combines Aristotle's views on reason and telos, Cicero's views on natural law, and Christian notions of God to construct a theory of law that guides human affairs. Aquinas distinguishes among four types of laws. First is the eternal law. This is the unchanging reason of God. It is God's plan for the universe, affecting everything, including irrational creatures. Second, there is divine law. Divine law applies mostly to religion and church issues and is apprehended through revelation.

Third, there is natural law. This is the eternal law that is etched upon the human mind; it is found only in humankind. It determines one's telos and helps one seek his or her essential human purposes. There are two types of natural law: speculative reason, which applies to spheres such as mathematics; and practical reason, which contains rules to guide human actions through general principles of justice, including the mandates to seek good, to preserve the self, and to procreate. According to Aquinas, natural law is the "rule and measure" of our actions, directing how one rules and how one is ruled.

Natural law can operate in two ways. In particular actions, it serves as a guide for personal behavior. By appealing to one's reason, one can know and understand what is correct in a particular situation. The other, and far more important, way that natural law works is through human law. For Aquinas, human law must emulate natural law, seeking to promote justice and the will of God. Human law is necessary to help individuals when their own reason fails, and it is important to guiding a community to serve justice and the common purposes of all its members. For human law to be true law, it must follow natural law; it cannot depart from it. Its purpose is to help one fulfill his or her telos, to fulfill one's function as a rational creature, and to seek out the vision of God.

Human law obligates through conscience so long as it emulates natural law; if not, it is not binding. For Aquinas, then, law can be described as an ordinance of reason, promulgated for the common good, by he who has the care of the community. According to Aquinas, "Every human law has just so much of the nature of law as it is derived from the law of nature. But if in any point it departs from the law of nature, it is no longer a law but a perversion of law."[36]

If an unjust law is no law at all, then an unjust ruler appears to be no ruler at all. What this means is that human law has a telos, a goal in furthering an end. It is a religious telos, and the purpose of the state and duty of the magistrate is to further that end. If not, the king is acting contrary to natural law, and he is a tyrant.

Kingship, Tyranny, and the Family. Political authority and human law must obey God and natural law. God and natural law place one set of external restrictions on a ruler, commanding him to act according to the precepts of justice and reason. This bond to serve God is not given to the ruler directly, but it still seems to come more directly from God than earlier Christian writers argued. According to Aquinas, "Human government is derived from the divine government and should imitate it."[37] Paralleling the classical organization of constitutions or regimes into monarchies, aristocracies, and democracies, as well as their perversions or degenerate forms, Aquinas reviews the merits of the rule of one, the few, and the many, eventually drawing upon Christian teaching to support kingship. Given that the divine government, or heaven, is ruled by one entity, God, the same plan should be followed in earthly kingdoms. Thus Aquinas prefers a rule of one for a community,[38] although like Aristotle, he views a mixed government as a way to embody the best of all three types of government:

> Accordingly, the best form of government is in a political community or kingdom where one is given the power to preside over all according to his virtue while under him are others having governing powers according to their virtue, and yet a government of this kind is shared by all, both because all are eligible to govern, and because the rulers are chosen by all. For this is the best form of polity, being partly kingdom since there is one at the head of all, partly aristocracy insofar as a number of persons are set in authority, partly democracy, i.e., government by the people, insofar as the rulers can be chosen from the people, and the people have the right to choose their leaders.[39]

Aquinas's claims about political authority are significant for several reasons. First, they seem to invest secular governments with some direct divine authority, not indirect authority through the church. In other words, secular authority is offered some independent justification; it is not totally dependent on receiving one of its "swords" from the church. Second, governments are necessary because of human sociability, not because of sin. Third, one entrusted to rule must do so for the common good, not to serve personal desires or interests.

On this third point, Aquinas returns to the traditional distinctions between a tyrant and a legitimate ruler, claiming that a tyrant is one who is unjust and seeks his own advantage, while a king is just and seeks the advantage of all.[40] Here there is no difference among Aquinas, Aristotle, and John of Salisbury. Yet, like John of Salisbury, Aquinas fears that a king can abuse his power and become a tyrant, so he sees the need to construct a remedy to deal with tyranny. Aquinas is attentive to the needs for limiting power and structuring authority to ensure that it serves the public good.[41]

On the one hand, Aquinas indicates that God may act to address tyranny. If God does not act, mild tyrannies should be endured[42] because many other fates are worse than some tyrannies, including the threat of an even worse leader. However, some public action may be necessary to address excessive tyranny,[43] including killing the tyrant if God does not act.[44] Thus Aquinas relies on both external checks—God and the king's adherence to natural law—and internal checks—the threat of death—to ensure that secular authority stays in line.

In his discussion of kings and the authority to rule, Aquinas also draws upon some of Aristotle's distinctions between the family and the polity. Just as Aquinas draws a parallel between the king and God to justify monarchy, he makes similar parallels among the family, father, and ruler:

> Therefore, he who rules a complete community, that is, a city or a province, is justly termed king; he who rules a household is called father of the family, but not king. A father has a certain likeness to a king, because of which kings are sometimes called the fathers of peoples.[45]

Elsewhere, Aquinas states that the "individual good, the good of the family, and the good of the political community and the kingdom are different ends," necessitating different rules or types of prudence to govern each.[46] He invokes the paternal metaphor to justify both political rule and the structure of the family, but in his efforts to distinguish among the different types of goods is recognition that politics and political rule are somehow different from the others.[47] This difference opens a distinct space for secular rulers and secular goals, independent of the church. But it also hints at a redefinition of political authority among the self, family, church, and state that has not been noted since Cicero.[48] This distinction would become important to future political thinkers seeking to create a political theory premised on the separation of church and state, and the protection of individual liberty and the family from the state.

Church–State Relations and Tolerance. Although Aquinas hints at a separation of the church from the polity, it is not as complete as it seems. The church still holds authority over the king, reinforcing the church–state order that came to predominate in the Middle Ages:

> The secular power is subject to the spiritual power as the body is subject to the soul. Therefore the power to judge is not usurped if a spiritual authority

enters into temporal affairs in matters in which the secular power is subject to it or which have been given it by the secular power.[49]

Even with a sort of separation of church and state, Aquinas still places the latter subordinate to the former. In other passages, Aquinas draws distinctions between the two, placing limits on the church's intrusion into a state's secular affairs:

> The spiritual and the secular power alike derive from divine power, and that, as a result, secular power is subject to spiritual power insofar as God so disposes, i.e., in those things pertaining to the salvation of souls. In such matters, one should obey the spiritual rather than the secular power. But in those things which pertain to civic welfare, one should obey the secular rather than the spiritual power: "Render to Caesar the things that are Caesar's."[50]

These arguments both retain the traditional Christian assumption that secular governments are subordinate to the church, and at the same time offer independent, divine justification for political rule, complete with an attempt to define the line between the church and the state. Clearly, a secular ruler must be a Christian and serve Christian purposes, but the state is not a mere extension of the church. Aquinas describes lines of power that distinguish between the two, but these are not clear, thus presenting even more potential for conflict.

The synthesis of Aristotle and Christianity that Aquinas produced concerns for tolerance. Although he indicates that Christians are obligated to obey secular power,[51] he specifies different rules for different types of individuals regarding the use of secular power to enforce the Christian faith. Those who have not received and accepted the Christian faith should not be forced to obey, but those who have accepted the faith may be compelled to do so.[52] Nonbelievers cannot rule over the faithful;[53] rulers must be Christian and Christlike in their behavior. And though Christian heretics need not be tolerated, Aquinas argues the Jews deserve tolerance, though they cannot rule over Christians.[54] In sum, the state must serve the church and Christian purposes, including seeking to convert others to Christianity, but there are limits to how far that authority can be extended to non-Christians who are members of the commonwealth. For Aquinas to describe a state containing, and tolerating, some non-Christians was a long step from Augustine, but it represents another one of the changes occurring as a result of Aristotle's influence.

CONCLUSION

The reintroduction of Aristotle and classical thinking into the Christian medieval world via Arab and Islamic thinkers such as Alfarabi, Averroës, and Avicenna had a profound effect. First, it presented Christian thinkers with a challenge: how to accommodate their theology to a set of political assumptions and arguments that were secular, and how to reconcile these two bodies of ways of viewing the world. In terms of the latter, Islamic philosophers provided Christians with an example of how it was possible to reconcile God and religion with Aristotle by making God the first and final cause within an Aristotelian-Christian metaphysics. Reorientating Christianity into a more rational-based theology would be one of the major contributions of Thomas Aquinas, and it would eventually have a dramatic impact on the medieval world. One impact would be that the classical writings would provide political institutions with an independent and emerging secular justification for their existence, eventually allowing them to develop their own distinct legitimacy and space. The result? Over time a gradual separation of church and political institutions became a hallmark of modern Western liberal thought. Aristotle's reappearance into Europe via the Arabic world and his impact on Islam, Christianity, and Judaism invite questions regarding how different these religions may be, and what common roots or assumptions they might share.

John of Salisbury and Thomas Aquinas demonstrate themes common to medieval Christian political thinking. Both address the problems of politics in terms of a Christian discourse and a Christian set of assumptions, and they often reach very similar conclusions about the nature of kingship and political power. But the influence of Aristotle on Aquinas resulted in subtle, unique, and important redefinitions in political thinking. His adoption of some of Aristotle's ideas reintroduced a relatively benign and social vision of human nature into politics, in contrast with the debased depiction of man found in Augustine and John of Salisbury.

Did this reintroduction of classical thinking and the merger of Christianity with Aristotle set the stage for the demise of the medieval world? Reason might be able to place Christianity upon firmer or new foundations, but could not the tools of reason also be turned against religion and religious institutions? Would not a rethinking of human nature also suggest the possibility of a creation of secular politics and political institutions, a new vision of the individual and the community, and a political vocabulary? And what of those Christians who remained wedded to the older Augustinian views? Would they go along quietly with the changes in Christianity, or would they reject these new writings and keep their faith? All these would be significant, emerging issues that the Christian world would need to confront.

Notes

1. Alexander Passerin D'Entreves, *The Medieval Contribution to Political Thought: Thomas Aquinas, Marsilius of Padua, Richard Hooker* (Oxford: Oxford University Press, 1939), 6–9.

2. Sir Ernest Barker, *Essays on Government* (Oxford: Clarendon, 1945), 251.

3. Brian Tierney, *The Crisis of Church and State: 1050–1300* (Englewood Cliffs, N.J.: Prentice Hall, 1964), 1–2.

4. Charles Howard McIlwain, *The Growth of Political Thought in the West* (New York: Macmillan, 1932), 165; Frederick C. Copleston, *Medieval Philosophy* (New York: Harper & Brothers, 1961), 173; R. W. Carlyle and A. J. Carlyle, *A History of Mediaeval Political Theory in the West*, vol. IV (London: Blackwell, 1962), 330.

5. *Medieval Philosophy*, 175–78.

6. *Growth of Political Thought*, 204.

7. Arlene Saxonhouse, *Women in the History of Political Thought: Ancient Greece to Machiavelli* (Westport, Conn.: Praeger, 1985), 140–45.

8. Muhsin S. Mahdi, *Alfarabi and the Foundations of Islamic Political Philosophy* (Chicago: University of Chicago Press, 2001), 29–33.

9. *Alfarabi*, 196.

10. *Crisis of Church and State*, 1–2.

11. John of Salisbury, *Policraticus*, ed. and trans. C. J. Nederman (New York: Cambridge University Press, 1990), 25.

12. *Policraticus*, 28.

13. *Policraticus*, 28.

14. *Policraticus*, 29.

15. *Policraticus*, 30, 35.

16. *Policraticus*, 32.

17. *Policraticus*, 49.

18. *Policraticus*, 25.

19. *Policraticus*, 190.

20. *Policraticus*, 190–91.

21. *Policraticus*, 201.

22. *Policraticus*, 25.

23. *Policraticus*, 206.

24. *Policraticus*, 209.

25. *Policraticus*, 210.

26. *Policraticus*, 55.

27. *Policraticus*, 57.

28. Quentin Skinner, *The Foundations of Modern Political Thought*, vol. 1: *The Renaissance* (New York: Cambridge University Press, 1978), 50.

29. *Medieval Contribution*, 35.

30. *Women in the History of Political Thought*, 147.

31. *Medieval Philosophy*, 167.

32. Thomas Aquinas, "Tolerance and Church-State Relations," in *On Law, Morality, and Politics*, ed. W. P. Baumgarth and R. J. Regan, S.J. (Indianapolis: Hackett, 1988), 263–64.

33. *Medieval Contribution*, 31; *Medieval Philosophy*, 169.

34. "Tolerance," 264.

35. "Tolerance," 264–65.

36. "Tolerance," 59.

37. "Tolerance," 254.

38. "Tolerance," 267.

39. "Tolerance," 116.

40. "Tolerance," 266

41. "Tolerance," 267.

42. "Tolerance," 267; *Medieval Contribution*, 35.

43. "Tolerance," 269.

44. "Tolerance," 270.

45. "Tolerance," 266–67.

46. "Tolerance," 272.

47. "Tolerance," 274.

48. *Medieval Philosophy*, 169.

49. "Tolerance," 259.

50. "Tolerance," 259–60.

51. "Tolerance," 245.

52. "Tolerance," 250.

53. "Tolerance," 252.

54. "Tolerance," 255–56.

Additional Readings

Alfarabi, *Alfarabi the Political Writings: Selected Aphorisms and Other Texts,* trans. Charles E.Butterworth. Ithaca, N.Y.: Cornell University Press, 2001).

Barker, Sir Ernest. *Essays on Government.* Oxford: Clarendon, 1945.

Carlyle, R. W., and Carlyle, A. J. *A History of Mediaeval Political Theory in the West,* vol. IV. London: Blackwell, 1962.

Davidson, Herbert A., *Alfarabi, Avicenna, and Averroes on Intellect: Their Cosmologies, Theories of the Active Intellect, and Theories of Human Intellect.* New York : Oxford University Press, 1992.

D'Entreves, Alexander Passerin. *The Medieval Contribution to Political Thought: Thomas Aquinas, Marsilius of Padua, Richard Hooker.* Oxford: Oxford University Press, 1939.

Mahdi, Muhsin S. *Alfarabi and the Foundations of Islamic Political Philosophy.* Chicago: University of Chicago Press, 2001.

Saxonhouse, Arlene. *Women in the History of Political Thought: Ancient Greece to Machiavelli.* Westport, Conn.: Praeger, 1985.

Skinner, Quentin. *The Foundations of Modern Political Thought,* vol. 1: *The Renaissance.* New York: Cambridge University Press, 1978.

Webb, Clement J. *John of Salisbury.* London: Metheun, 1932.

Inventors of Ideas Online

Visit http://politicalscience.wadsworth.com/tannenbaum2 for links related to material in this chapter, including selections from John of Salisbury's *Policraticus* and the major works of Thomas Aquinas.

8

DANTE AND MARSILIUS: THE END OF MEDIEVAL POLITICAL UNITY

INTRODUCTION

The incorporation of secular, Aristotelian views into the political writings of St. Thomas Aquinas was similarly occurring in other political works in the thirteenth through sixteenth centuries. While Aquinas preserved church domination over secular rule, however, others, who were critics of the church, would not continue that domination in their writings. Dante and Marsilius of Padua used Aristotle to strike a new balance between church and state authority, thus challenging the order and unity that had held Christian Europe together for over a thousand years. The results paved the way for a more secular political community that would free the individual from control by the pope, and led to a new bond between citizen and temporal ruler.

DANTE

Dante Alighieri (1265–1321) is best known as the author of the *Divine Comedy,* an epic poem about his love Beatrice; political intrigue in Florence, Italy; and a journey through hell, purgatory, and heaven. In addition to the *Divine Comedy,* Dante wrote *De Monarchia,* or *On World-Government,* a political tract, around 1310 to 1313. It is a defense of the power of the Holy Roman Empire against papal control. It does not deny the power of the church or seek to subordinate it, but instead to carve out an independent place for secular rule.

De Monarchia defends a world empire that did not exist, so it may be construed as the ideal for what the Holy Roman Empire should be. Dante wrote it as a response to a particular political controversy, when King Henry of the Holy Roman Empire moved to challenge the power of the pope, was temporarily excommunicated, and then forced to take communion and again acknowledge papal supremacy.

Throughout *On World-Government,* Dante refers to Aristotle's *Politics, Ethics, Physics, and Metaphysics* to help him make his points. Like Aquinas,

Dante equates Aristotle's notion of the unmoved mover, or the cause of the universe, with the Christian God. Hence, also like Aristotle and Aquinas, Dante sees a hierarchy from God down to man, which he employs along with a Christian cosmology in many of his arguments, to lend a sense of the divine to secular rule.[1]

Dante opens *On World-Government* by defining a temporal government as a single government over all the men in the world.[2] He then poses three questions, which he indicates both Aristotle and the Bible will help him address:

1. Is a world-government necessary? What is its goal?
2. Whether Roman people have a right to assume such an office?
3. Does authority for this government come from God, or through a servant of God?

Human Nature. Referring to Aristotle's *Nicomachean Ethics*, Dante states that the goal, or telos, of humankind is to organize the multitude for intellectual growth.[3] He contends that all individuals have the potential for intellectual growth but cannot secure it themselves. They need help—a political society—to accomplish this goal. Since everyone has the same goal, everyone should therefore have one universal government to rule over them. The best way to achieve this goal is through the tranquility of world peace under one world government:

> Since it appears that the whole of mankind is ordained to one end, as we proved above, it should therefore have a single rule and government, and this power should be called the Monarch or Emperor. And thus it is plain that for the well-being of the world there must be a single world-rule or empire.[4]

Political Society. Dante offers several reasons for the necessity of a single world-government. First, he claims that if humankind has a unified goal, there should also be a unified ruler.[5] Second, because heaven is ruled by a single and unified ruler, God, humankind most resembles God when ordered under a single unified government. Third, a world-government can resolve conflicts, much like a judge. Fourth, justice is better served in a world-government because a world emperor has neither greed nor desire to be unjust. Fifth, only in a world-government does reason rule and humankind serve itself.[6] Sixth, a unified world-government is closer to God in that it most closely approximates the structure or cosmology of the universe with God at its head:

> Human society is a totality in relation to its parts, but is itself a part of another totality. For it is the totality of particular states and peoples, as we have seen, but it is obviously a mere part of the whole universe. Therefore, as through it the lower parts of human society are well-ordered, so it, too, should fit into the order of the universe as a whole. But its parts are well-ordered only on the basis of a single principle, . . . namely, through its governor, God, who is the absolute world-government.[7]

Source of Secular Authority. Dante then asks if the source of the authority of the world-government is an independent power, distinct from the pope. He argues yes, employing the analogy of the relationship between the sun and the moon:

> After these preliminary observations I can return to the criticism of the argument according to which the two luminaries signify two types of government. . . . In its being the moon is no way dependent on the sun, and not even in its power and functioning, strictly speaking, for its movement comes directly from the prime mover, some of whose rays shine on it. For it has little light of its own, as we observe in eclipses, but in order to increase its power and efficacy it gets light from the sun, where it is plentiful. In like manner, I maintain, temporal power receives from spiritual power neither its being, not its power or authority, not even its function, strictly speaking, but what it receives is the light of grace.[8]

Although Dante acknowledges and agrees with Christian beliefs that "governments are remedies for the infirmity of sin,"[9] he rejects the claim that they need the church to function. Civil governments merely need some support, but are in no way dependent upon the church. Dante also rejects the Two Swords Doctrine, contending that both swords were not originally in the hands of the church.[10] And he rejects the Donation of Constantine as justification for papal control over secular rule, arguing that Roman Emperor Constantine did not have the right to give away the empire to the church, even if he did so as claimed by others.[11]

In addition, Dante offers other claims to show why the Roman Empire had its own independent authority, one not dependent on the church. Dante asserts, for example, that the Roman Empire existed by right,[12] that it existed prior to the church and did not need the church to function,[13] that Rome did serve the common good,[14] and that Rome had a right to rule as evidenced by Jesus's submission to Roman law.[15] In sum, like the moon, Rome had its own independent authority to exist, and this power was not based on the church:

> As to the proposition that the Church could give authority to the Roman government, it must have held this power from either God or from itself, or from some emperor, or from the universal consent of all men, or at least of the greater part of them; there is no other possible source for such a power in the Church; but the Church held this power in none of these ways; therefore it did not hold it.[16]

Overall, Dante asserts that humankind has a double purpose, to seek temporal bliss and eternal bliss. These purposes are achieved in different ways, necessitating that the pope and the emperor have different functions, duties, and spheres of influence.[17] He denies that the original two swords statement by Peter in the Bible is even a reference to two governments. The comment has a different meaning, which does not justify granting all power to the church only to have the latter hand some over to secular rulers. To Dante, secular government helps guide people to specific secular goals, and the pope and church have no right to interfere in this. Because *On World-Government* places secular and spiritual authority on equal planes, it is one of the first major challenges to a Christian political order that subordinated the former to the latter.

MARSILIUS OF PADUA

Marsilius of Padua (1275–1343?) wrote *Defensor Pacis,* or *Defender of the Peace,* in 1324. This work is the first major exposition of a political philosophy that subordinates the church to secular power since the beginning of the Christian Era. It reverses the relationship between church and state altogether, without invoking any sense of the divine to support secular rule.[18] Thus it represents the most radical of the medieval political writings developed as a result of Aristotelian influences. But although, like Dante and Aquinas, Marsilius employs Aristotelian assumptions, he reaches conclusions that are clearly different from those of the two other thinkers.

Marsilius wrote his book when the pope was very powerful, when many were questioning the church's abuse of power, and when doctrinal and religious conflicts were on the rise. The event that seems to have inspired this book was a dispute between Pope John XXII and Ludwig of Bavaria. After a long battle with the pope, Ludwig eventually succeeded in becoming emperor of the Holy Roman Empire. Once he published *Defender of the Peace,* Marsilius obtained protection from Ludwig, staying with him for the rest of his life.

Structure and Laws of the State. Marsilius employs Aristotle's *Politics* to describe the nature, function, and organization of the state. He describes the origin of the state as an outgrowth or union of many households. The impetus for many households to come together to form a political community is that no household alone can be self-sufficient. Thus creating a state ensures that all can secure their goal of living well. And as the state is the union of many different parts, it is the task of the legislator, ruler, or king to bring the different parts together.

To regulate the affairs of the state, Marsilius knows some standard is necessary, and for him, that standard is law. But in a major break with the natural law tradition of Cicero and Aquinas, Marsilius offers a very modern and secular definition of law:

> Law, then, is a "discourse" or statement "emerging from prudence" and "political understanding," that is, it is an ordinance made by political prudence, concerning matters of justice and benefit and their opposites, and have "coercive force," that is, concerning who observance there is given a command which one is compelled to observe, or which is made by way of such a command.[19]

Thus laws are limited to those made by the human mind, not by the church or God; law is simply the product of the legislator.[20] Unlike the views of Cicero, Augustine, or Aquinas, neither natural justice nor the edicts of God are important in the theory of law to Marsilius. The essence of human law is not its conformity to higher mandates. Rather, coercion is at the center of his view of the law, and its purpose is to secure the goals of the commonwealth and the legislator. For Marsilius, it is the legislator, and the legislator alone, who makes the law and holds the coercive force that stands behind it. Neither God nor natural law seems to place an external limit upon the power of a ruler to act. His vision of secular power appears to justify absolute power, then, granting the legislator the authority to do almost anything, without limit or control.

More importantly, Marsilius proposes a major change in political theory by arguing that legislators should be elected:

> Let us say, then, in accordance with the truth and the counsel of Aristotle in the *Politics*, Book III, Chapter 6, that the legislator, or the primary and efficient cause of the law, is the people or of the whole body of the citizens, or the weightier part thereof, through its election or will expressed by words in the general assembly of the citizens, commanding or determining that something be done or omitted with regard to civil acts, under a temporal pain or punishment. By the "weightier part" I mean to take into consideration the quantity and the quality of the persons in that community over which the law is made.[21]

Thus a legislator, elected by some group, is solely entrusted to make law and to use coercion to enforce it. Such an election process to pick a legislator to rule over people and to make laws for the common benefit may sound like the basis of popular sovereignty or majority-rule representation and authority, where legitimacy and limits on power come from within the state rather than outside.[22] However, although Marsilius is attentive to the problem of limiting power by the creation of internal checks upon it, his election process should not be equated with contemporary election by simple majority rule.[23] His notion of who is the "weightier part" includes consideration of factors such as wealth and group membership, as well as numbers. Yet it is still significant that Marsilius redefines the bond that holds a government together and the limits placed on its political power. The critical political bonds are no longer between the church and the ruler, but between the ruler and the people over whom he presides.

Church–State Conflict. After a discussion of the Bible, Cicero, Plato, and Aristotle's *Politics*, Marsilius seeks the greatest good of the state. He concludes that peace, or the search for tranquility, is that goal, or telos. However, recent strife, discord, and conflict were upsetting this goal, so Marsilius looks for the cause of this strife.[24] His conclusion: that the pope's intervention into the affairs of the state threatens the legal order of the commonwealth, and anarchy.[25] More specifically, discord chiefly occurs when the Bishop of Rome seeks to usurp secular political power and control secular offices, and demands highest allegiance:

> In all the seizures of secular power and rulership which the Roman bishops have perpetrated in the past, and which, as everyone can plainly see, they

are still striving with all their might, although wrongly, to perpetuate, no small role has been played in the past, and will be played in the future, by that sophistical line of argument whereby these bishops ascribe to themselves the title of "plentitude of power."[26]

According to Marsilius, the pope's assertion of this plentitude of power grows out of his false claims that the Scriptures and his duty to tend to souls also grants him control of secular power.[27] In particular, the Two Swords Doctrine is one basis for the pope's claims, but like Dante, Marsilius indicates that this passage has been misread; it does not support giving the church the power it claims. The pope does not have the authority to appoint or control a ruler. A ruler is appointed by the people and does not owe his power to the pope. Like Dante, Marsilius also claims that the Donation of Constantine is illegitimate because Emperor Constantine had no right to give away the empire, even if he did do so. Marsilius thus argues that the pope and the church have no authority to interfere in the affairs of the state, including in the selection of the rulers who are chosen by the people.

But unlike Dante, Marsilius contends that strife in a community divided by the power of the emperor and the pope cannot be eliminated unless the church is subordinate to the state in which it is located. For Marsilius, this means that the ruler controls all secular and religious offices and may remove bishops at will. He also contends that the pope is merely the Bishop of Rome, not the top or most important bishop in the church. All are equal. Furthermore, no church official can control secular power, the legislator has the authority to decide the meaning of Scriptures, and no religious person can excommunicate; only the legislator or people can do so.

Overall, Marsilius questions the religious hierarchy that upheld the church's political control over secular governments. He places political power in the hands of people to select a legislator to make law for the community. This process of selection appears to be an early form of what we now call majority rule. Church power is subject to control by the ruler. The result is a new political order between the individual and the state that is not mediated directly by God or religion.

Marsilius's arguments regarding the subordination of the church to the state anticipate later thinkers in questioning the pope's power and seeking to deal with the problem of church–state conflict. The French political thinker Jean Bodin, for example, would propose in the seventeenth century that the only way to deal with this problem is to separate church and state completely so that the state can regulate neither church beliefs nor most religious practices.

CONCLUSION

Along with John of Salisbury and Thomas Aquinas, Dante and Marsilius paint a picture of the rise and fall of medieval political assumptions and ideas. By the thirteenth century, the church's political authority was starting to disintegrate, and it was further challenged by the emergence of strong secular governments. Rulers in these governments were seeking ways to justify their political authority, and independently of the pope.

Initially, the language of Christianity dominated political discourse, forcing thinkers to engage in political debates by reference to the Scriptures. The reintroduction of Aristotle, however, challenged the Christian political discourse, providing the opportunity for secular redefinitions and descriptions of human nature, society, and political power. In some cases, secular authority was enhanced by bestowing upon it an element of the divine. But in other cases, its power was augmented by moving away from purely sacred claims and instead invoking the secular language of Aristotelian politics.[28]

Major thinkers during this period also revealed a concern with problems that would become major issues in modern political thought. Specifically, what are the proper boundaries between church and state, and how should one define the limits and checks on political power? If rulers do get their authority from God, can we ever challenge them? Is political disagreement tantamount to heresy and sin?

In attempting to prevent tyranny, or in redefining the major political bond as being between ruler and people, late medieval thinkers were implicitly concerned with the ideas of constitutionalism and the crafting of clear boundaries of political authority beyond which a government could not go. The solutions proposed by John of Salisbury, Aquinas, Dante, and Marsilius, though perhaps unsatisfactory by contemporary standards, were nonetheless significant efforts in making such issues central to political inquiry.

Notes

1. Majorie Reeves, "Marsilio of Padua and Dante Alighieri," in *Trends in Medieval Political Thought,* ed. B. Smalley (Oxford: Basil Blackwell, 1965), 91.

2. Dante, *On World-Government,* trans. H. W. Schneiden (Indianapolis: Bobbs-Merrill, 1978), 4.

3. *On World-Government,* 6.

4. *On World-Government,* 8–9.

5. *On World-Government,* 9.

6. *On World-Government,* 12–14.

7. *On World-Government,* 10.

8. *On World-Government,* 59–60.

9. *On World-Government,* 59.

10. *On World-Government,* 65.

11. *On World-Government,* 68.

12. *On World-Government,* 25.

13. *On World-Government,* 73.

14. *On World-Government,* 33.

15. *On World-Government,* 49.

16. *On World-Government,* 75.

17. *On World-Government,* 73, 78.

18. Alexander Passerin D'Entreves, *The Medieval Contribution to Political Thought: Thomas Aquinas, Marsilius of Padua, Richard Hooker* (Oxford: Oxford University Press, 1939), 46, 73.

19. Marsilius of Padua, *Defensor Pacis* (Toronto: University of Toronto Press, 1980), 607.

20. *Defensor Pacis,* 36.

21. *Defensor Pacis,* 44.

22. *Defensor Pacis,* 45.

23. *Medieval Contribution,* 74.

24. Frederick C. Copleston, *Medieval Philosophy* (New York: Harper & Brothers, 1961), 182.

25. Leo Strauss, "Marsilius of Padua," in *History of Political Philosophy,* eds. L. Strauss and J. Cropsey (Chicago: University of Chicago Press, 1987), 279.

26. *Defensor Pacis,* 313.

27. *Defensor Pacis,* 316.

28. Brian Tierney, *The Crisis of Church and State: 1050–1300* (Englewood Cliffs, N.J.: Prentice Hall, 1964), 2.

Additional Readings

D'Entreves, Alexander Passerin. *Dante as Political Thinker.* Oxford: Oxford University Press, 1952.

D'Entreves, Alexander Passerin. *The Medieval Contribution to Political Thought: Thomas Aquinas, Marsilius of Padua, Richard Hooker.* Oxford: Oxford University Press, 1939.

Nederman, Cary J. *Community and Consent: The Secular Political Theory of Marsilio of Padua's Defensor Pacis.* Lanham, Md.: Rowman & Littlefield, 1995.

Scott, John A. *Dante's Political Purgatory.* Philadelphia: University of Pennnsylvania Press, 1996.

Tierney, Brian. *The Crisis of Church and State: 1050–1300.* Englewood Cliffs, N.J.: Prentice Hall, 1964.

 Inventors of Ideas Online

Visit http://politicalscience.wadsworth.com/tannenbaum2 for links related to material in this chapter, including the text of Marsilius's *Defensor Pacis* and Dante's major works.

9

MACHIAVELLI:
ESCAPING ANARCHY

INTRODUCTION

If any one political philosopher personifies the transformation from the medieval to the modern era it is the Italian Niccolò Machiavelli (1469–1527). He lived during the Renaissance, an era marked by rejection of some key ideas and institutions of the Middle Ages.[1] The Thomistic synthesis[2] of faith and reason that directed attention to religious concerns was replaced by a modern philosophical outlook orienting people toward secular matters. This shift in focus resulted in the philosophical release of the individual from external restraints. No longer bound to great ideals or the past, to inherited status or medieval relationships, people were emancipated from the claims of community, both secular and religious. Individuals were free to set whatever goals they wished, to achieve whatever they could.

Modern ideas also contributed to, and drew support from, the growing importance of the physical sciences. Scientific observation and experimentation, accompanied by new techniques and instruments of measurement, pointed up earlier limitations imposed by the dictates of political and religious authority. The treatment of the scientific findings of the astronomer Copernicus is but one powerful example.[3] Based on his study of the heavens, he questioned the accepted view (based solely on religious revelation) that the Earth was the center of the universe. Copernicus argued instead that the sun was at the center, and that all the planets, including the Earth, revolved around it. His findings were denounced by church leaders, who sought to prevent the spread of such unorthodox ideas. By imposing the dictates of revelation, however, the authorities were regarded by some people as trying to prevent them from benefiting from useful knowledge. These people also agreed with the scientists that what one senses is more real than, and thus takes priority over, what political or theological authorities dictate one should see and conclude.

The new science moved from investigation of the heavens to the scrutiny of human institutions, including the Roman Catholic Church, the dominant religious body in the West. A revolt against traditional constraints subjected the church to an examination of what it did, not merely what it preached, in effect, bringing it to earth.

Such analysis came at a time when the moral position of the church was eroding due to the divided responsibilities of the popes. While medieval popes exercised religious functions as designated leaders of the church, they also had clearly secular interests as rulers of geographical realms. Their loyalties were split between the responsibility to save souls and the desire to operate their landholdings in a profitable manner, even if the latter contradicted both the teachings of the New Testament and the church's own moral principles. In other words, the personification of the church, the pope, had long preached one thing while he and his subordinates practiced another. The resulting decline in the moral stature of the papacy was hastened by the actions of some Renaissance church leaders whose all-too-human behavior outran their spiritual commitment. Thus Pope Sixtus IV gave aid to members of his family who were involved in the murder of several leaders of the city-state of Florence. Even more outrageous was the secular activity of Pope Alexander VI of the Borgia family. Not only did he use his wealth and political influence to buy the papacy, but he sired illegitimate children, aiding and abetting one of them, Cesare (a professional soldier), in his quest to improve the family's personal fortune through conquest, cruelty, and murder.

Other medieval institutions were also in flux and open to challenge and change. Throughout the Middle Ages, the respective jurisdiction of each class was marked with relative clarity, and vassals were entitled by tradition to rule their fiefs (landholdings or realms) without challenge or interference from their overlords as long as they fulfilled their part of the (largely implied) medieval contract. Pope Alexander VI helped instigate the breakdown of this relationship when he authorized Cesare Borgia, through a formal papal bull (order), to go to war to rid the papal states of various feudal underlords, many of whose families had held their fiefs for centuries. By seeking to oust these "middlemen," the papal enterprise contributed to the decline of feudal classes and their medieval realms, leading to a shift from rural (medieval) values to more urban (modern) ones.

The breakdown of these customary philosophical and legal relationships also led to a decline in the organic view of class and community, and a reappraisal of the delicate relationship of betters and inferiors. As a rejection of both social unity and the importance of birth and inherited rank, this contributed to the rise of self-reliant individualism.

If the feudal realm was in decline, that modern political institution, the nation-state, was on the rise. The nation-state emerged in Western Europe from roots traceable back to the eleventh century. It had undergone a gradual and uneven development, in places such as England, France, and Spain, which was far from complete when Machiavelli wrote in the early sixteenth century.

The story of how nation-states were first established is reflected in the activities of Cesare Borgia and others discussed by Machiavelli, as well as the historical plays of writers such as Shakespeare. Forceful kings, who were medieval lords, went to war and either subordinated or ousted their former (noble) vassals, at times with the assistance of a rising middle class. In observing them gain superiority over internal medieval rivals (later to include feudal lords of larger territories such as the Roman Catholic Church and the Holy Roman Empire) perceptive observers might well have concluded that it was not God or nature, but humans who create political boundaries and rulers. Geographical entities, whether city-states, realms, or nation-states, have no special warrant for existence or any guarantee of continuity from either nature or heaven. They are artificial, man-made contrivances to satisfy the personal needs and desires of participating individuals.

STYLE, SUBSTANCE, AND GOALS

Machiavelli has been misunderstood by many people, some because they disagree with his conclusions, others because of his style. When he was born in Florence during the Renaissance, Italy was not a nation but a collection of mostly small, independent city-states and other realms in constant conflict with one another. When Machiavelli was in his twenties, Florence, which had been dominated by the Medici family for some sixty years, was invaded by France and a new government was installed. Several years later the young Machiavelli joined the new republican government and began his political career. After fifteen years he was a high-level civil servant in charge of military operations and had seen service in the diplomatic corps as an envoy from Florence to various rulers, including Cesare Borgia.

Following a defeat of the combined forces of French protectors and soldiers of Florence by a Spanish army, the Medici were restored to power and those connected with the old republican government were ousted from office. Machiavelli, then in his forties, was suspected of treason by the new rulers, and imprisoned for a time and tortured. But lacking strong evidence, his jailers then exiled him to his country home outside the city walls. It was there that he wrote *The Prince*, in 1513, reportedly between writing Books One and Two of the *Discourses on the First Ten Books of Titus Livius*.[4]

Since *The Prince* is dedicated to the new Medici ruler, Lorenzo, a number of rather literal interpreters have viewed the work primarily (if not exclusively) as a plea for forgiveness. They have understood Machiavelli as a person anxious to return to political work for whoever was in power, and *The Prince* as one of the lengthier job applications the world has known. As such, it was a singular failure, at least in the short run, since Machiavelli was not offered any government work until just a year before his death.

Had Machiavelli's goal been just to secure another job with the Florentine government, *The Prince* would not have emerged as the book it is—a fascinating, complex, intricate work that has prompted multiple interpretations over the centuries. Thus it is more than just a request for employment, as is apparent when one compares it to Machiavelli's lesser known but philosophically parallel work, the *Discourses*.[5]

Machiavelli had two distinct but interrelated goals. The first, a personal one, was the desire to return to active government service. The second stemmed from rejection of the past in his recognition that the city-states of Italy, including Florence, were often unstable and clearly in decline. As a result, their peoples were constantly subjected to control by outside forces, whether Spain, France, or the papacy. Thus a second, political goal he promoted was stability and freedom from every kind of foreign control, secular or religious, for all of Italy. Consequently, *The Prince* and the *Discourses* often proceed on two tracks in simultaneous overlap. Since Machiavelli did not write in a straightforward manner, his themes can be hard to follow and often seem ambiguous, contradictory, and submerged in historical or mythical detail. This problem is further complicated by his bold new approach to political questions, as well as the understandable desire to avoid offending the ruling powers of Florence while at the same time demonstrating the practical value of his knowledge. He sought to reconcile ideas that the conventional thought of his time (and, frequently, ours) might consider antithetical. As a result, there are at least twenty theories about Machiavelli's "true" aims.

However, his style is in keeping with the project he set for himself, namely to deal with his twofold problem by holding onto, even reconciling, a number of apparently conflicting perspectives while exposing "the uncertainty at the foundation of modern political thought."[6] In order to follow Machiavelli's subtle, often quick transitions, and the ironies and paradoxes he reveals, one has to explore his major themes. In some cases, such as his method of approaching political questions, his views are relatively clear and straightforward, so any misreading would stem from disagreement with his perspective. In other cases, such as Machiavelli's response to the problem of stability, examining the sometimes multiple meanings embedded in his basic concepts, meanings that vary with the conditions faced by key decision makers, is necessary.

MACHIAVELLI'S METHOD

> But my intention being to write something of use to those who understand, it appears to me more proper to go to the real truth of the matter than to its imagination; . . . for how we live is so far removed from how we ought to live, that he who abandons what is done for what ought to be done, will learn to bring about his own ruin than his preservation.[7]

In this regard, Machiavelli has "resolved to open a new route, which has not yet been followed by any one," that is, the road to a new science of politics that will replace all of its idealistic predecessors with a more down-to-earth and practical set of principles.[8] This means he is not concerned with ancient or medieval concepts of good or evil, such as Plato's forms or Aquinas's divine law. To Machiavelli, these irrelevant concepts would assume priority over what is really important: the needs of living beings on earth. Political evaluations should not be based on how philosophers of the past have said people should act, for example, that they should reject their appetites, seek the salvation of their souls, bear the cross, or turn the other cheek. Stable government cannot be founded on imagined human potential, and any government based on these fancies is doomed to quick decline.

The positive side of his realistic position is that people should be treated in a manner based on what they are like in fact, on sensed, observable traits such as their selfish motives. This, to him, is the only way to confront the central problem of politics, the results of which were evident in weak internal governments and foreign domination, in Italy and elsewhere. Only a correct awareness of reality can lead one to strong, stable government. To accomplish this program of renewal, people must recognize that private morality cannot be applied to public affairs. Following Renaissance political thought, public and private became autonomous areas to Machiavelli, each with its own rules and language. What might be considered evil in one (say, the private) might be regarded as good and useful in the other (the public). Politics is to be separate and distinct from ethics, morality, and religion. Machiavelli severed the Aristotelian and Thomistic unity of these spheres.

Furthermore, when engaged in politics, individuals must reject what they might think ought to be for what is, shun ends for means, and avoid the appearance of vice, not vice itself. People should be miserly rather than liberal, feared rather than loved, and faithless and deceptive, even violent, if necessary, to achieve important goals. Talk of pure good and evil is meaningless, for "the evil lies so near the good and is so commingled with it, that it is easy to encounter the one in thinking to take the other." Therefore, individuals must not seek the ideal, but settle for "taking the least harmful as good."[9]

This new science of the present is based on an examination of why certain peoples in the past were successful. But to Machiavelli history is something one is urged to learn from, not simply imitate. It should provide guidance for successful political behavior for those who follow its examples, precepts, and truths, enabling them to reduce the uncertainties in the world even if they cannot wholly eliminate them.

Machiavelli is convinced that if people take a clear, hardheaded, realistic look at history they can set themselves on the path to political success. They must learn from past deeds, not from philosophy or theology, and any example that fits is useful, whether from mythology or the actions of tyrants or republicans. Overall, his examples indicate that Italy must return to the principles originally guiding the Roman Republic if it is to achieve the glory its people enjoyed in the past.

HUMAN NATURE

The question of the fundamental nature of the human animal is central to Machiavelli's thinking, and his conclusions, which stem directly from his method, led him to innovate. He discovered a new world of ideas on which all modern political philosophy is built.[10] It has antecedents in the past, such as the thinking of the Sophists of ancient Athens as well as critics of ancient and medieval idealists; and the examples given in *The Prince* and the *Discourses* to support his conclusions are taken from the classical, pagan past as well as from knowledge of his Renaissance times. But the bold conclusions he drew far outstripped those of his predecessors and laid the foundation for the ultimate triumph of modernity.

The basis for this revolution in thought is found in sharp, direct assertions such as, "The desire to acquire possessions is a very natural and ordinary thing, and when those men do it who can do so successfully, they are always praised and not blamed, but when they cannot and yet want to do so at all costs, they make a mistake deserving of great blame."[11] If selfish acquisition is viewed as "natural," it forms an ineradicable part of human nature, a trait people must work with, accommodate, even indulge, as they seek to construct a stable polity. And it is "ordinary," an everyday, regular occurrence that alerts one to both its normality, and the constant danger of strife and the ever-present possibility of instability in any society based on such a view of human nature.

To claim, as Machiavelli effectively does, that humans are selfish animals is to reject the consensus of ancient and medieval philosophers. To the ancients, the threat of such egotism to stable politics was so great that they urged people to overcome or set aside their appetites through the triumph of reason. Medieval thinkers urged them to supplant selfishness with faith. Machiavelli denies that there is any valid external source, whether forms, telos, or God, that can justify replacing "natural" motivations with what are, in his view, fictitious alternatives. He believes people are not by nature community-oriented, and neither the politics of reason nor the politics of salvation can take precedence over more mundane concerns. So he tells people how to satisfy their appetites and at the same time establish stable government, however tenuous. Living beings take center stage, and the range of their goals is as wide as the human imagination. It clearly includes, for Machiavelli, the acquisition of possessions, although the intensity and breadth of this urge varies among individuals according to their needs, desires, and opportunities.

But he does not totally discard ancient or medieval values. People can also embrace rational politics, even religious salvation, if they deem these goals worthy. His central point is not so much rejection of these goals as that they must stem from personal choices, not the directives of external phantoms or their self-appointed agents. The burden this implies is that each individual is fully responsible for his or her choices and actions, and for judging the consequences. Everyone shares that responsibility both individually and equally, as everyone equally shares a human nature that is selfish.

POWER

Machiavelli is the first political thinker to focus on power as a positive concept. To both ancients, like Plato, and mainstream medieval thinkers, power was a negative value, its quest a sign of undesirable irrationality to the former, and sinfulness to the latter. In keeping with his method—the new science of politics—Machiavelli strips the mask from those illusory notions which kept people from attaining political success while teaching them to use deception to secure their goals.

Using language designed to shock his readers into questioning old, accepted values, he will have no part of the idea that those engaged in politics should only possess philosophical knowledge or claim divine sanction. He scorns those who inherit power but do not know how to use it well. What was considered righteous becomes evil, and vice versa. So, "A man who wishes to make a profession of goodness in everything must necessarily come to grief among so many who are not good. Therefore, it is necessary for a prince, who wishes to maintain himself, to learn how not to be good, and to use this knowledge and not use it, according to the necessity of the case."[12] Thus he urges princes not to help others; to be stingy, cruel, deceptive; and to get others to do the dirty work so that they can escape blame.

However, Machiavelli does not favor evil for its own sake. Not all negative qualities are lauded, only those that are "well permitted" and attain their proper ends. The brutality of Cesare Borgia is a prime example. Borgia personally selected an exceptionally "cruel and able" man, de Orco, to restore order in one province by using considerable violence, and then decided to pacify the people by doing something dramatic to make them "peaceful and obedient to his rule." He distanced himself from de Orco's acts by having his henchman murdered and then cut in half; the pieces were displayed for a time in a public square. The spectacle, worthy of some of the worst tyrants of the past, satisfied the already pacified people, so the people of the province praised Borgia for this cruelty correctly used.[13] Machiavelli follows this story with accounts of others who behaved likewise, such as Agathocles the Sicilian and Oliverotto da Fermo. In this manner, he reveals the importance of violence as a means for attaining individual ends.

Machiavelli condemns those who use violence to destroy governments even as he praises those "founders" who establish strong monarchies and republics. Where government is corrupt and public order in danger of total breakdown, only a founder or strong ruler can reverse the decline. In setting his will on the people, this prince can use whatever means necessary, however cruel or manipulative, so as to "impose a new order of things." Such a founder is deserving of great glory, like past creators of stable, winning governments. Political founders rank second only to "the authors and founders of religions," and are followed in prestige by army commanders and those in the arts and professions. In contrast to his praise of founders, though, Machiavelli reserves his strongest condemnation for those who, through their actions or inaction, destroy religions, governments, and armies. They are "the impious and violent, the ignorant, the idle, the vile and degraded."[14]

It is not always easy to tell whether the actions of Cesare Borgia, Agathocles, or da Fermo were reflections of "those who understand"—of founders worthy of praise—or of destroyers. These men seem to be, in Machiavelli's multiple meanings, both, depending on their actions and the consequences of them, as well as hinging on the nature of the people whom the actions were designed to impress. But it is clear that Machiavelli argues for "an economy of violence," that is, its use by those who know where to draw the line between necessary violence and cruelty, and that which is excessive and demoralizing.[15] Since all political life is a ceaseless struggle between selfish competitors, and may involve some public disorder, even violence and law-lessness, the problem is not how to abolish struggle but how to limit its worst effects.

Machiavelli's resolution of this problem is modern and very political. The primary requirement for selfish individuals seeking personal goals is to enter into reciprocal relationships in which each needs power or influence over the behavior of the others. In entering into such relationships, all are equal in their selfishness, and all are free to seek power. This is not to say people can-not act for a common good; they can, but only when they judge that such actions are also in their private interest. Those who appear good or altruistic to others are either rational actors really motivated by desire for personal advantage, or ruled by laziness and retreating from political responsibility. Thus, although human nature is universally selfish, this nature, when trans-lated into human behavior, results in two different kinds of people, elites and masses, each practicing their own form of selfishness.

ELITES AND MASSES

Machiavelli is dismissive of the idea that legitimate rule is hereditary. His scheme recognizes the right of any elite to govern, whether the prince origi-nally came from ordinary folk or inherited the title. To him, elites are supe-rior, calculating people whose selfishness is rational and active. They are the ones who follow Machiavelli's advice to "depend on yourself alone and your own ability."[16] They may use their reason to fully satisfy their passions, or to partially or wholly sublimate their passions to other goals. But they clearly and consciously choose their goals, and in depending on themselves alone they express their freedom. Elites feel free of all irrational restraints (or phan-toms) in pursuit of their goals. Power-driven, they maximize their rational self-interest by any means, or, as Machiavelli succinctly puts it, "The end jus-tifies the means." Thus anyone who wishes to be a part of the elite must be a selfish power seeker, willing to use violence at any time. He urges his elites to study warfare because "it not only maintains those who are born princes, but often enables men of private fortune [commoners] to attain that rank." Therefore,

> Let a prince . . . aim at conquering and maintaining the state, and the means will always be judged honourable and praised by every one, for the vulgar is always taken in by appearances and the issue of the event; and the world consists only of the vulgar, and the few who are not vulgar are isolated when the many have a rallying point in the prince.[17]

Like the elites, the vulgar masses are selfish, but their selfishness consists of irrational passions aimed at fulfilling short-term appetites. They "are so simple and so ready to obey present necessities, that one who deceives will always find those who allow themselves to be deceived."[18] They are ever ready to enjoy what the imperial Romans called bread and circuses, and they fear power and envy the elite. The only things they seriously care about are their physical security and that of their possessions (including their families), as well as their personal prejudices and opinions. These a wise ruler does not disturb, and indeed protects, unless the opposite is absolutely necessary to promote his other ends. In that case, he uses the most fraudulent means possible.

Politically, the masses are shortsighted, weak, and irresponsible—or what political scientists today term apathetic and alienated. They lack civic concern. They are not able to rule themselves. Too stupid to use liberty well, they live in disorder if they do not have a despotic, even tyrannical, prince to rule them. The presence and extent of governmental tyranny reflects the balance between elites and masses in a society. When a ruler is a tyrant, the masses dominate and the elites who can reason well are a small minority. When the elite consists of the many citizens, tyranny is absent. Thus the term *elite,* as used here, refers not to numbers but to a quality that may be present in a minority or a majority, and determines the form of government.

Tyrants can easily rule the masses by providing a minimal level of stability, which allows the masses to feel relatively secure in their possessions and prejudices. As long as these are provided for, they care little about what else their government might be doing; as long as they are content, the ruler's internal position is relatively secure. Thus Machiavelli recommends that tyrants use cruelty and violence sparingly, "to reassure people and win them over by benefiting them."[19]

FORTUNE AND VIRTUE

In Machiavelli's writings, the concepts of fortune and virtue coexist in an uneasy dialectic, a tension between free will and opportunity wherein fortune sets the conditions for success and virtue realizes them. He writes of how "Fortune Blinds the Minds of Men When She Does Not Wish Them to Oppose Her Designs."[20] Fortune plays a part in everyone's life. Nobody has completely free will; everyone acts in situations that are limited by circumstance. This limit on free will defines the sphere of necessity, of fortune. Machiavelli suggests that a key difference between elites and masses is that the latter are dominated by fortune. Fortune is also known as fate or God's will, the arbitrary working of nature that brings about such disasters as earthquakes and floods. It is an incalculable power beyond the control of humans, but one that controls their destinies. And it is a vibrant, energetic force that endangers the liberty of those it controls. It clearly hobbles the lives of the vulgar, fickle, submissive masses. It is the cause of disastrous wars, which result in death for some and the loss of freedom for others. It may even grip a ruler, leading to a loss of power, as Machiavelli says happened to Cesare Borgia. Governments dominated by fortune destabilize, losing relative strength and independence, threatening total breakdown, and opening themselves to conquest, as so often happened in Renaissance Italy.

"Nevertheless," Machiavelli says, "that our free will may not be altogether extinguished, I think it may be true that fortune is the ruler of half our actions, but that she allows the other half or thereabouts to be governed by us."[21] By gaining knowledge, people can limit the influence of fortune. (That, of course, is one reason Machiavelli wrote.) If fortune provides nothing more than "occasions" for exercising virtue, individuals must learn to be like that impetuous force. That is, one must adapt to circumstances and change, be hesitant and careful, or bold and forceful, as each occasion demands. Knowledge helps people to wrestle with fortune and thus more fully control their destiny through the exercise of virtue.

Machiavelli's use of the term *virtue* sets him apart from his premodern predecessors. It refers to an individualistic and secular excellence rather than the idealistic merit of the ancients or the moral goodness of medieval thinkers. It is a quality of elites, a true selfishness that enables individuals to get what they value, whether power, wealth, fame, or even liberty.

By adapting, adjusting strength and cunning to each occasion, as do the lion and the fox, one can see trouble in the distance and act rather than be taken off-guard. As a political state is passive, it needs constant attention devoted to creating order and avoiding disorder, as was true of the citizens of the ancient Roman Republic. All life, and thus all political life, is an unending struggle by people to express their virtue. Those who get what they seek do so because they have demonstrated their virtue and they are judged, by Machiavelli's criteria, as good.

GENDER

A surface reading of Machiavelli's works leads to the conclusion that men and women are opposites in his thinking, much as are elites and masses, fortune and virtue, freedom and enslavement. Men appear to be the only elites, identified with the values of strength and warfare, freedom and virtue, while women and their natures connote timid masses who follow the path of fortune into willing slavery. Thus, noting that the issue of liberty (or autonomy) is Machiavelli's "central preoccupation," one writer says he gives this a traditionally "misogynistic" twist in that it is identified with masculinity, and that which threatens it is feminine.[22] To another writer, securing liberty requires the masculine attributes of "power, coercion, violence," while women represent "softness, compassion and forgiveness"; thus they are excluded from the public arena of politics and government.[23]

Actually, if at times Machiavelli casts women in traditional, even misogynistic roles, he does not fully define them or their attributes by these roles.

Although some of his language does reflect the sexism of his time, he questions the views of men and women that dominated the ancient and medieval world as part of the new world of ideas that was reexamining all things traditional. In so doing, "he makes the differences between what had been opposites so ambiguous that we can no longer tell good from bad or women from men."[24] Consider Machiavelli's assertion that

> it is better to be impetuous than cautious, for fortune is a woman, and it is necessary, if you wish to master her, to conquer her by force; and it can be seen that she lets herself be overcome by the bold rather than those who proceed coldly. And therefore, like a woman, she is always a friend to the young, because they are less cautious, fiercer, and master her with greater audacity.[25]

There is a "peculiar shift" here: friendship comes from violence, and a bold act "creates an order otherwise unattainable."[26] But is it only men who can conquer femininelike fortune? When discussing "How States are Ruined on Account of Women,"[27] Machiavelli makes it clear that the cause is in fact internal misrule and factional divisions between classes, and that the woman involved in his example was merely an incidental actor. It is class conflict that leads to the city losing its freedom. Here, as elsewhere, women are but an indicator of the human diversity that produces political divisions, which must be healed if any populace is to secure liberty. The divisions include the sexes, to be sure, but also factions, classes, princes, and ordinary people.

In sum, "For Machiavelli, a world in flux allows men to become women and women to become men."[28] Whether people are born into the bodies of men or women, they can still exercise their virtue and secure their autonomy by acting like elites—or they can passively submit to fortune and take whatever comes their way. Biology is not destiny for anyone.

LIBERTY AND WAR

Liberty is an infinitely expandable goal even as its minimal presence is a necessary precondition for augmenting that or any other value. It is the ability to act freely, even to dominate if necessary. But Machiavelli believes only a "small part" of the people want to be free in order to rule over others. The rest, "who constitute an immense majority, desire liberty so as to be able to live in greater security."[29] Liberty and virtue are reciprocal. Not only do those with virtue seek liberty, but the ability to engage in virtuous relationships requires a government that enables liberty.

Liberty has two aspects: political and individual. Political liberty refers to the sort of twofold freedom that is possible with stable government. It includes domestic peace, or people's freedom from internal disorder as well as national independence, or a government's freedom to act as it wishes, independent of foreign control.

Maintaining political liberty may necessitate going to war to defend it. War can serve many purposes. Not only can it protect the state and reinforce citizen virtue, but it can also divert the population's attention from internal problems and conflicts, and benefit from the riches of the conquered. "A prince should therefore have no other aim or thought, nor take up any other thing for his study, but war and its organization and discipline, for that is the only art that is necessary. . . ." Warning against the use of hired soldiers (mercenaries) or troops supplied by another state (auxiliaries), Machiavelli concludes that a ruler "would prefer to lose with his own men than conquer with the forces of others, not deeming it a true victory which is gained by foreign arms."[30]

But Machiavelli recognizes that arms alone are inadequate to maintain political liberty: "The chief foundations of all states, whether new, old, or mixed, are good laws and good arms."[31] Throughout his writings, he points out that without law arms merely produce liberty for the few who command armies, not the many who serve in them. But he does think military service provides a sense of discipline, unity, and self-sacrifice essential to good citizenship.

Individual liberty requires, as a prior condition, political liberty. Once this is secured, individual liberty entails freedom from arbitrary actions by government, whether violent or not, that restrict personal independence of law-abiding citizens. While political liberty allows for the growth of a people's way of life, or culture, individual liberty is for self-governing, responsible citizens who both freely obey the law and constantly scrutinize it for needed change. The nature of individual liberty is related, in turn, to the form of government and its leadership.

FORMS OF GOVERNMENT

To Machiavelli, although many variations are possible, there are essentially two kinds of governments:

> All states and dominions which hold or have held sway over mankind are either republics or monarchies. . . . I will not here speak of republics, having already treated them fully in another place. I will deal only with monarchies, and will discuss how the various kinds . . . can be governed and maintained.[32]

Actually, those regimes Machiavelli terms *monarchies* are akin to forms of government Aristotle might have regarded as either monarchy, being based on "the favor of the inhabitants," or tyranny, where the ruler does "not mind incurring the charge of cruelty. . . ."[33] So classified, monarchies, or civic principalities, have more in common with republics than with tyrannies when the classification is based on Aristotle's distinction between good and bad forms of government. This is especially so when Machiavelli discusses the important value of liberty. It is present, but minimal, under tyranny, and maximized under a government that enjoys public support, whether its form is a republic or a monarchy. Machiavelli is a relativist when discussing forms of government. The fundamental need of people is for stability. But though liberty is a consequence of the intersect between stability and the nature of the populace, it may also be a contributor, since the most stable form of government, a republic, is the most free.[34]

Republics. A republic is founded by a strong, inspiring leader rallying a virtuous citizenry. It is constitutional, not necessarily in the strict sense of a written document, but because it fulfills the requirements Aristotle used to evaluate governments as good. First, it is based on law. Second, it is governed in the interest of most citizens, not just a few. And third, it is mixed, in that members of all classes have an opportunity to participate as citizens. Conflict between the classes can serve as a positive force, as long as such divisions are institutionalized and thus given a structure in which they can be resolved peacefully and according to law, as in ancient Rome. In this way, legitimate opposition serves to deflect ambition from corrupting the state.

Tyrannies. Machiavelli's relativism also extends to the other pole, tyranny. Where a people is less virtuous, all the laws and institutions cannot preserve liberty; and at the other end of the elite-mass continuum, only a cunning tyrant can secure stability.

> Therefore, a prudent ruler ought not to keep faith when by so doing it would be against his interest, and when the reasons which made him bind himself no longer exist.[35]

A ruler may be either a despotic tyrant or one or more citizens; the numerical ambiguity stems from the possibility that the ruler of a republic may be regarded as a single monarch or a large or small group of virtuous individuals.

Whatever the case, to Machiavelli a ruler's virtue is reflected in the ability to make the best use of human nature and establish a reputation for practical wisdom, that is, for skill, prudence, adaptability, single-mindedness, and firm leadership. Virtuous rulers have the judgment, energy, and charisma to unite others behind their government.

Under tyranny, the masses are subjects, much like the working class in Plato's *Republic*. They enjoy some political liberty in the form of independent, stable government. Individual liberty is greater for the ruling class than for the masses, however, since the interests of the former have priority, if not exclusive sway. The masses are content with this arrangement, perhaps recognizing that without the ruler they might be unable to maintain stability and could slip into total anarchy. More likely, they are so fearful and in awe of the ruling elites that they suffer from political paralysis. Lacking the virtue required of citizens, they both merit and need tyranny; for them, minimal liberty is better than none. In fact, the masses are probably so irrational, self-centered, awed, and frightened that they are largely blind to the unequal distribution of liberty between them and the elites. And when a tyrant is governing corrupt, vulgar masses who lack virtue (or when any official is engaged in international politics with other rulers), ordinary morality is not binding. Instead, a ruler's virtue consists of the ability to remain in power and maintain stability by always being prepared to use whatever means are necessary. This can range from generosity and kindness, through fraud, to use of physical force and the cover-up of cruelty and villainy. But "of all things that a prince must guard against, the most important are being despicable or hated," and "every prince must desire to be considered merciful and not cruel."[36] This requires effective use of available means, and Machiavelli recommends that rulers use the more extreme ones, such as violence, sparingly and at the minimum level needed to secure their ends. Fraud is ordinarily a better tool for everyday use; it is cheaper, more efficient, and more easily covered up than is force. Force is like dictatorship, a means for extraordinary times, and it is called for only when failure to use it can endanger major goals. Thus tyrants have a certain virtue of their own, expressed by arbitrary use of a double standard of morality.

Reminiscent of Aristotle's discussion of how a tyrant should act to preserve a bad polis, Machiavelli's suggestions for fraudulent behavior include such tactics as dazzling the public with conspicuous deeds and speeches, using persuasive talents to lull potential challengers to peaceful behavior without making any real concessions, and employing religion in a duplicitous way. Religion is simply one more potential instrument for secular ends. In a republic, it can help to reinforce positive citizen virtues. Under tyranny, a good religion is one that can help the state manipulate the masses, keeping them in line when the fear of secular punishment is not sufficient to secure obedience. Religious forms, ceremonies, and beliefs are, as pagan rulers concluded long before, just another way to control the populace. So the ruler should seem to be religious for appearance's sake because the masses like to see this in a prince. But in practice religious values should be disregarded. In fact, it can be dangerous for a prince to act on the moral precepts of traditional religion, because this may lead to defeat at the hands of enemies who do not do likewise. Nevertheless, even when he violates conventional morality, a ruler should try to seem moral.

The key to when to use force or fraud is reputation. Both means are especially useful to a new ruler, who has not yet had time to establish the habit of obedience. For example, Cesare Borgia dealt with a corrupt people by sending a cruel governor who secured order by force, making many enemies in the process. He then had this governor executed and the body displayed in public in a most barbarous manner. By first securing order through his governor's use of violence and then using violence and fraud to distance himself from the governor's cruelty, Borgia got the best of everything: order, public gratitude, and reputation.

An important aspect of fraud is that tyrants should do their best to impose on the masses the single standard they themselves reject. Subjects (and competing rulers) should be persuaded to obey a pious code of unselfish behavior, based on such traditional virtues as honesty, loyalty, obedience, peace, and trust. All the while, tyrants should use secrecy and deception to maintain the separation between the two moralities. Insofar as their goals allow, they should appear to follow a single standard, since "the vulgar is always taken in with appearances. . . ."[37] To act this way is virtuous because modern despots recognize no outside source for judging their actions, such as religion, and no legitimate superior power within their states, including law. As a student of Aristotle, Machiavelli holds with the view that the foundation of the most stable government must ultimately rest on the law. But he also recognizes, along with Aristotle, that in special circumstances the law may be set aside. In these cases, the ruler must use extralegal means, including force and fraud. These circumstances may be frequent, as in tyranny, or very rare or nonexistent, depending on the nature of the populace and any challenges to stability, internal or external.

The Prince appears to dwell on the extralegal, making it seem the preferred means for making everyday decisions, but a careful reading shows that the work moves between the two perspectives and makes a case for both sides.

Constitutional Rule: Monarchies and Republics. When Machiavelli says it is good if rulers can use law (and even love, generosity, and kindness) as the best means for everyday decision making, he is particularly addressing those who rule a monarchy or republic. "One . . . who becomes prince by favor of the populace, must maintain its friendship, which he will find easy, the people asking nothing but not to be oppressed."[38] Here, most people are citizens with a strong sense of civic virtue, rather than subjects ruled by fortune. They are honest, intelligent, law-abiding citizen-soldiers, who are courageous and devoted to duty. A ruler is strongest who rules with their consent and leads a citizen-army. Free from oppression, these citizens enjoy both political and individual liberty. Furthermore, ordinary citizens have as much liberty as those in government (though perhaps not as much public recognition or honor), because they have rulers who govern according to law and treat citizens as equals under that law. Ruling such citizens calls for a single standard of morality since the citizens are the ruler's moral as well as legal equals. The ruler should match their virtue in order to retain their support, both to remain in office and to secure their cooperation when defense of the republic is required. The popular militia, Machiavelli reiterates, is the only force that can be trusted. In this case, following conventional morality can contribute to political stability. Law, love, and generosity form a firm basis for long-term stability once a people has virtue. Machiavelli does not urge a constitutional ruler to be amoral, for in this type of regime, fraud does not fool the virtuous citizenry. In this case, the ruler must not only seem moral but actually be moral.

In effect, Machiavelli simultaneously describes the good or virtuous citizen who is qualified to rule and be ruled in turn, and recommends that people act accordingly if they aspire to the greatest liberty. This is possible, because human nature is not a property set in concrete but a variable quality open to individual choice or free will. Still, Machiavelli reaches conclusions that are as pessimistic as those of Plato and Aristotle. There are limits to how well any people can control fortune; and due to corruption, it is inevitable that even the best form of government will degenerate. Thus constitutional rule can deteriorate, as there is always the danger of citizens becoming apathetic and losing their special virtue. Then tyranny and loss of liberty follow, no matter what any laws or critics may proclaim.

Nation-States. In the final chapter of *The Prince,* Machiavelli reveals his ultimate political goal. He says,

> Having now considered all the things we have spoken of, and thought within myself whether at present the time was not propitious in Italy for a new prince, and if there was not a state of things which offered an opportunity to a prudent and capable man to introduce a new system that would do honour to himself and good to the mass of people, it seems to me that so many things concur to favour a new ruler that I do not know of any time more fitting for such an enterprise. . . . This opportunity must not, therefore, be allowed to pass, so that Italy may at length find her liberator.[39]

Such a prince would secure freedom for the people, and their emancipation would be on both levels, individual and political. Here Machiavelli links two concepts, since he finds greater liberty, whatever the virtue of the people or the kind of ruler they have, in the political framework of the nation-state. Smaller communities are too weak to resist invasion, especially by established nations. Thus Machiavelli sees the nation-state as the geographic framework appropriate to the most stable government possible. Machiavelli is concerned with not just getting power but keeping it, by building a strong, stable political system based on shared ideas and institutions. Noting that the most powerful models of his time were regimes like France and Spain, he concludes that the nation-state is more protective of both levels of liberty than a classical city-state or some medieval realm, whether a large empire or tiny duchy. The nation-state is the institutional context for modern political philosophy. On a pragmatic level, it refers to a people living in a defined geographic area who give their allegiance to a government. Its derivative, nationalism, is an emotional means for securing unity by emphasizing common characteristics and deemphasizing divisive ones.

People of a nation share an affection for objects of their cultural heritage such as a common history, values, language, literature, race, religion, even geography, and folk traditions. Myths, symbols, and heroes; customs and rituals; ideals, goals, and habits: all serve to bind individuals in a spirit of common identity that can transcend selfishness, ambition, and envy. Secular things take on a sort of religious quality, so that the secular and religious are fused in a civil religion that includes loyalty, patriotism, mission, and destiny. Even if national unity results in inequality, the "obscuring myth" of national loyalty serves as an emotional substitute. For "all men, regardless of wealth, station, and pedigree, share the common quality of a distinctive national identity and no one can claim or prove he has more of it than anyone else."[40]

Nation-states are the artificial creations of power-seeking individuals, or founders, and their supporters. A nation can be united by a founder, just as Florence and other cities were. A founder must be a charismatic leader who appeals to people's emotions, inspires them by providing the common goal to work for—a strong nation-state—and devises the necessary means by which the goal can be reached, including force and fraud when required. Neither purely inspirational nor purely rational, Machiavelli's founder uses a blend of both to achieve key objectives.

The use of various means is related to whether a founder becomes prince "through crime or intolerable violence, . . . by help of popular favour or by favour of the aristocracy."[41] In the second case (popular favor) a republic is the likely result, and the means relatively peaceable. But even if the founder comes to power by acts of cunning and force, in a setting where most people are vulgar masses, whether assisted by the aristocracy or not, the ruler's inspirational leadership can help raise the level and quality of virtue among the governed, bringing everyone closer to citizenship through patriotism. But so long as subjects lack adequate virtue, a ruler and his successors will govern as despots.

CONCLUSION

Machiavelli was an artist, painting a bold picture on a sweeping canvas. His political theory was based on the dynamic relationship between princes and peoples, fortune and virtue, force and fraud, elites and masses, stability and liberty, tyranny and republic, individual and collective. As the first political philosopher to recognize the importance and potential of the nation-state, he spoke not just to Italy, which did not unite until more than 300 years later, but to the world.

As advisor to virtuous citizens as well as governors, contemporary thinkers regard him as the first philosopher of modern citizenship, as Aristotle was the advocate of ancient citizens. He seeks to use the selfishness in human nature as a positive tool with which to build a stable, free nation-state. MacIntyre agrees, saying that Machiavelli exalts "civic virtue over both the Christian and pagan virtues"; and Wolin presents a strong case for considering him "the first truly modern political thinker," though he struggles "to express himself through the old [premodern] terminology."[42] Machiavelli discarded the medieval practice of writing in Latin in favor of vernacular Italian, and his inability to find a wholly new vocabulary to accompany his novel approach to politics may help explain some of the ambiguities in his thinking. So might his not infrequent suggestion of subtle satire.[43] As with most great political philosophers, thinkers today can never be sure how fully they understand Machiavelli. Certainly one cannot grasp his political thought whole. And given his life experiences, it is likely that is how he wished it.

But taken on his own terms, there is much about his philosophy that is clear. As the first of the early modern political philosophers, Machiavelli advances a hard, unified, but complex view of the world, based on an aggregate view of politics in which the virtuous individual has priority status. It is concerned only with "pure" power politics. Political considerations are supreme, and all else (including values such as morality, religion, ethics, justice), while important, is subordinate, instrumental, and dependent on the nature of the people. This separation of personal morality and necessary political practice contradicts the values of ancient and medieval political philosophers alike. But Machiavelli is not an immoral political philosopher, he is an amoral one. He states clear principles for the successful conduct of any state. First, people must take selfish human nature as it is found in living beings, some with virtue and some without, and act accordingly. Second, anyone who participates in politics must be virtuous, in the modern sense of imitating both a fox and a lion, and Machiavelli supports any means, including force and fraud, to secure the power that is the primary requisite for political stability. However, his personal preference, as exemplified by much of his life and his works, is for a republic, which permits the greatest degree of liberty.

To be a prince, one is required to work for greater liberty, both individual and political. A prince must be flexible and ready to use any means to secure this end, recognizing that regime stability and princely power are not only inextricably linked to each other but essential to liberty. When the state is secure, political action can be based on traditional values. But when stability is fragile and uncertain, ethics and morality must be set aside for "reasons of state." Consequently, the nature and purpose of his state differs radically from those who defined the ancient and medieval traditions. No longer is the state expected to help develop the soul or perfect people. Nor is it to teach anything like Aristotelian virtue. The direction of politics, and indeed political philosophy, is likewise transformed from a contemplative to an active mode. It is now about a new, modern idea of virtue, one that elevates appetite, power, liberty, and a kind of equality—in short, getting for self—over the communitarian values advocated by so many of his predecessors.

Machiavelli's prophetic vision has been transformed into reality. The nation-state (actual or aspired-to) is the almost universal basis for authoritative politics today, domestically and on the international stage. International politics takes place in a setting where individual states with shifting goals use ever-changing rules and any other means available to negotiate and bargain, unlimited by any external entity. Consequently, international relations is based on power politics; if there is no higher authority to enforce agreed-on behavior, national choice of means determines the outcome.

Machiavelli offers an explanation, if not absolution, for just about any form of government, ranging on a continuum from tyranny to republic. Although the relationship between the individual and the collective is dependent on the form of government, the nature of the people determines that form. In the end, virtuous individual wills imposing their desires on nature (i.e., on anarchy), not forms of government, are the paramount factor in the puzzle of politics for him. Political relations begin with individuals, not collectives.

Although Machiavelli rejects religion as anything but a tool to be used where it is most politically effective, in severing the medieval connection between religion and politics, he prepares the ground for the key political philosophers of the Protestant Reformation, Martin Luther and John Calvin. His devastating critique of the use of force and fraud by the medieval (and Renaissance) Catholic church helped sever the traditional link between politics and the papacy. He also set the stage for subsequent early moderns, such as Thomas Hobbes and John Locke, whose political orientation was, like his, primarily secular but who focused less on individual virtue than on such philosophical-legal fundamentals as contracts, law, and institutions.

When confronting Machiavelli's works, it is also important to evaluate his ideas both in light of past political philosophers and from the perspective of many of his severe critics over the centuries since he wrote. In terms of political progress, how is his philosophy an advance over the ancients? Despite his rejection of idealism, how does he build on the thought of Aristotle? Does he deserve the negative reputation that is synonymous with his name in many quarters? What in the style, method, and substance of his argument contributes to or refutes this reputation?

Notes

1. The Renaissance occurred from about the middle of the thirteenth century through the sixteenth century. For background on the Renaissance, see Jacob Burkhardt, *The Civilization of the Renaissance in Italy,* 2 vols. (New York: Harper & Row, 1958); Hans Baron, *The Crisis of the Early Italian Renaissance,* 2 vols. (Princeton, N.J.: Princeton University Press, 1955); and J. R. Hale, *Machiavelli and Renaissance Italy* (New York: Macmillan, 1961).

2. The Thomistic synthesis refers to the ideas of St. Thomas Aquinas, which are discussed in Chapter 7 of this book.

3. Copernicus is discussed in Chapter 11 of this book.

4. Neither work was published until a few years after Machiavelli's death. Quotations are from Niccolò Machiavelli, *The Prince,* trans. Luigi Ricci, rev. E. R. P. Vincent (New York: Mentor, 1952); for the *Discourses, The Prince and the Discourses,* trans. Christian Detmold (New York: Random House, 1950). References are to book and chapter numbers in the *Discourses* and chapter numbers from *The Prince* found in various editions. Among the other works of Machiavelli that treat political issues are *The Art of War* (1520), *The History of Florence* (1525), several satirical plays, and a large number of letters to his contemporaries. All of Machiavelli's works were placed on the Papal Index of books forbidden to Roman Catholics from 1559 until 1897.

5. It is "generally agreed that the same conception of political action and the same kinds of advice were consistently adhered to in both works." Sheldon S. Wolin, *Politics and Vision: Continuity and Innovation in Western Political Thought* (Boston: Little, Brown, 1960), 228–9.

6. Arlene Saxonhouse, *Women in the History of Political Thought: Ancient Greece to Machiavelli* (Princeton, N.J.: Princeton University Press, 1979), 173.

7. *The Prince,* ch. 15. To regard his views on method, human nature, power, and so on, as any more pessimistic than his most eminent predecessors would be to overlook both the optimistic potential he saw, which is noted throughout this chapter, as well as the pessimism imbedded in the views of the predecessors. Review, for example, Plato or Aristotle on political decay, or Augustine on the irrelevance of human effort for achieving the greatest end.

8. *Discourses,* intro.

9. *Discourses,* bk. 3, ch. 37; *The Prince,* ch. 21.

10. Leo Strauss, *Natural Right and History* (Chicago: Chicago University Press, 1953), 177–80.

11. *The Prince,* ch. 3; see also *Discourses,* bk. 1, ch. 37.

12. *The Prince,* ch. 15.

13. *The Prince,* chs. 7 and 8.

14. *The Prince,* ch. 6; *Discourses,* bk. 1, ch. 10.

15. *Politics and Vision,* 221.

16. *The Prince,* ch. 24.

17. *The Prince,* chs. 14 and 18.

18. *The Prince,* ch. 18.

19. *The Prince,* ch. 8.

20. *Discourses,* bk. 2, ch. 29 title.

21. *The Prince,* ch. 25.

22. Hannah Fenichel Pitkin, *Fortune Is a Woman: Gender and Politics in the Thought of Niccolò Machiavelli* (Berkeley: University of California Press, 1984), 7, 236.

23. Jean Bethke Elshtain, *Public Man, Private Woman: Women in Social and Political Thought* (Princeton, N.J.: Princeton University Press, 1981), 96, 99.

24. *Women in the History of Political Thought,* 151.

25. *The Prince,* ch. 25.

26. *Women in the History of Political Thought,* 157.

27. *Discourses,* bk. 3, ch. 26 title.

28. *Women in the History of Political Thought,* 165. Some examples of women who are fit to rule include Catharine Forli, whose exploits are noted both in *Discourses* and *The Prince,* and the fictional character Sofronia in one of Machiavelli's comedies, *Clizia.*

29. *Discourses,* bk. 1, ch. 16.

30. *The Prince,* chs. 12–14; see also Machiavelli's *The Art of War.*

31. *The Prince,* ch. 12.

32. *The Prince,* chs. 1 and 2. It is true that republics are more fully discussed in the *Discourses,* but despite this disclaimer, Machiavelli explicitly considers republics in ch. 5 of *The Prince,* and he says a good deal about them implicitly throughout this work.

33. *The Prince,* chs. 3 and 17. Machiavelli, like his intellectual mentor Aristotle, takes note of other forms as well and dutifully mentions Aristotle's six forms of government (*Discourses,* 111–2), although he chooses to focus on those of the one and the many, more than on those of the few.

34. Machiavelli's consistent republicanism runs through both *The Prince* and the *Discourses,* and has been discussed at length in such works as Mark Hulliung, *Citizen Machiavelli* (Princeton, N.J.: Princeton University Press, 1983); J. G. A. Pocock, *The Machiavellian Moment* (Princeton, N.J.: Princeton University Press, 1975); and Quentin Skinner, *Machiavelli* (New York: Oxford University Press, 1981).

35. *The Prince,* ch. 18.

36. *The Prince,* chs. 12 and 17.

37. *The Prince,* ch. 18.

38. *The Prince,* ch. 9.

39. *The Prince,* ch. 26.

40. *Politics and Vision,* 233. On pp. 204–6, Wolin discusses the passionate, religiouslike tone of the last ch. of *The Prince.*

41. *The Prince,* ch. 9.

42. Alasdair MacIntyre, *After Virtue: A Study in Moral Theory* (London: Duckworth, 1981), 220; *Politics and Vision,* 199, 214.

43. See, for example, Garrett Mattingly, "Machiavelli's Prince: Political Science or Political Satire," *The American Scholar* 27 (1955): 482–91.

Additional Readings

(* indicates alternative viewpoint)

DeGrazia, Sebastian. *Machiavelli in Hell.* New York: Vintage, 1993.

Hale, J. R. *Machiavelli and Renaissance Italy.* New York: Macmillan, 1961.

*Hulliung, Mark. *Citizen Machiavelli*. Princeton, N.J.: Princeton University Press, 1983.

*Pitkin, Hannah Fenichel. *Fortune Is a Woman: Gender and Politics in the Thought of Niccolò Machiavelli*. Berkeley: University of California Press, 1984.

Pocock, J. G. A. *The Machiavellian Moment: Florentine Political Thought and the Atlantic Republican Tradition*. Princeton, N.J.: Princeton University Press, 1975.

Skinner, Quentin. *Machiavelli*. New York: Oxford University Press, 1981.

*Strauss, Leo. *Thoughts on Machiavelli*. Glencoe, Ill.: Free Press, 1958.

Viroli, Maurizio. *Niccolo's Smile: A Biography of Machiavelli*. tr. Antony Shugaar. New York: Farrar, Straus & Giroux, 2000.

 Inventors of Ideas Online

Visit http://politicalscience.wadsworth.com/tannenbaum2 for links related to material in this chapter, including translations of a number of Machiavelli's major works.

10

LUTHER AND CALVIN: THE RELIGIOUS BASIS OF MODERN POLITICAL THOUGHT

INTRODUCTION

The Protestant Reformation was one of the first of several great modern revolutions in the sixteenth through the eighteenth centuries. The Copernican-scientific, industrial, French, and Kantian-philosophical revolutions that took place during the subsequent 200 to 300 years all had profound impacts on how people described and related to the world, how they viewed themselves, and how political society was organized and related to religion, science, and the economy.[1] Along with the upheaval in Europe already occurring because of the revival of Aristotle's writings, the adoption of Thomistic Christianity, and the growing conflict between princes and the pope, these revolutions would pave the way for the creation of many of the values and institutions important to modern notions of individualism and liberty.

Machiavelli's arguments and views defined politics in terms of self-interest and power. The scientific works of Bacon and Descartes would advance a belief in the ability of individual reason to apprehend the world. But the Protestant reformers provided the sense of religious individualism, stressing the ability of the individual to read biblical text without the need of an intermediary priest. Overall, politics, science, and religion contributed to redefinitions of the individual and society that would produce a major break between the ancient world of the Greeks, Romans, and the Christians, and the modern world that would begin to emerge in the sixteenth century.

Although the religious revolutions of the sixteenth century were significant in their defense of individual interpretations of the Scriptures, reformers placed limits on the new religious epistemology. Luther's and others' arguments were conservative reactions to Thomistic views of human nature and faith in reason, a backlash emphasizing the wretchedness of human existence as well as the limits of the humans' ability to know God. Much like St. Augustine, Protestant reformers emphasized faith over reason and the nonrational aspects of human cognition and religion.[2] This return to faith put Protestantism in conflict with both Thomistic Christianity and the emerging rationalism of science, producing a new battle of faith versus reason that would be played out during the Enlightenment, when religion and reason competed as rival means to support, know, and organize political and moral truths.[3]

Besides representing a doctrinal attack on Thomistic Christianity, the Protestant Reformation was also a revolution directed at the absolutism of the pope, including his control over the church; the meaning of Christian doctrine, and the sovereignty of secular rulers. Thus the Reformation was a continuation of attacks on the church started by Dante and Marsilius of Padua. But its roots also lay in other religious and political movements in Europe.

Prior to Luther and the Protestants, many religious movements and individuals had questioned the church's orthodoxy and control over doctrine. For example, St. Francis of Assisi (1181?–1226) had criticized the role of the church in the medieval world, and other groups, including women's religious orders, had challenged both Christian doctrine and social roles.[4] However, the popes had been able to control these movements enough to prevent them from posing a real challenge.

In addition to doctrinal attacks, there had been movements aimed at the structure of church hierarchy. For example, conciliarism, begun in the twelfth century, addressed the need to protect the church against papal heresy and misrule. The writings of some of the conciliarists argued that the pope needed to have his power limited by some types of general councils.[5] Conciliarism had an influence on writers such as Marsilius; and Luther's arguments against papal absolutism shared affinities with conciliar claims.

Other growing forces also challenged the monolithic Christian order. On the one hand, there was emerging nationalism and the strengthening of secular governments. People were beginning to think of themselves as loyal to a local monarch, not simply to the church and pope. Protestantism spoke to this new political sensibility in recognizing the importance of state institutions and loyalties. Protestantism and the civil rulers of Europe nurtured one another, as Protestant leaders turned to secular rulers for protection against the pope and secular leaders in turn used Protestantism to justify their political power.

Changes in the economy, creation of new trade routes, and emergence of a new merchant class as a result of both also contributed to a transformation of Christian Europe. Trade redefined the map of Europe, drawing people into contact with others and opening up cultures in ways that had not occurred before. Creation of new economies and classes meant development of new class interests which were often impatient and in conflict with religious values premised upon the old feudal structure. The new Protestant religious order anticipated and articulated these new class interests by making the pursuit of profit a more religiously acceptable and desirable pursuit than it had been previously.[6]

THE PROTESTANT REFORMATION

The Protestant Reformation grew out of and alongside these other changes. Luther, Calvin, the other Protestant reformers, and the Catholics who reacted to them, sought religious reforms to address the new reality of Europe. But religious changes could not occur without political revisions because the two were so closely intertwined that redefining one led to redefining the other.[7]

By attacking the pope and Thomistic doctrine, Protestant reformers broke up the unity and universalism of Catholic Europe. Questioning the hierarchy of the church led to new ways to define and organize religious structures, resulting in a movement that would eventually redefine civil institutions. The undermining of church authority led not only to the crumbling of the medieval political order but a loss of faith in civil institutions, which would later be addressed by Calvin and his followers. The ultimate result was a shift of religious authority to kings that thus bolstered their secular authority as well.

The political legacy of the Protestant Reformation was a new religious-political order in Europe. It redefined secular rule in terms of granting it divine authority, but also it paved the way for a set of constitutional values to limit it. Furthermore, it fostered a new relationship between the individual, the state, and God, clearly specifying that the individual and the state be connected to one another directly, rather than through God. However, the state would not have unlimited power over its citizens; rather, it would be subject to some constraints defined by Protestant individualism. Hence out of efforts to recognize the right of each person to read the Scriptures for him- or herself, the concept of religious individualism emerged. And with that individualism, concern with tolerating and protecting the rights of religious minorities became an issue. All of these changes would have important implications for subsequent modern political thought.

MARTIN LUTHER

Martin Luther (1483–1546) was first a monk and then a professor at the University of Wittenberg in Germany, a center of Protestant thought. The university was founded by Frederick of Saxony with funds collected by the church that were originally meant for a holy war against the Turks. When the war did not take place, Frederick refused to return the money. As for Luther, he was excommunicated by the pope in 1520, but he was protected from the church by Frederick and his heir.

Theology. Luther's disagreements with the church started early in his career when he attacked the sale of indulgences, or forgiveness for certain sins. But in addition, early on he came to the conclusion that human nature is wretched and sinful. In claiming this, Luther adopts Augustinian notions that saw humans as basically sinful. He states that the "soul is full of sin, death, and damnation," and contends that the body is contaminated by "evil lusts." Because of human sinfulness, individuals are powerless to know God, and because of this powerlessness, human reason is limited in its ability to understand God. Instead, one must rely upon faith for knowledge of God as well as for salvation. Relying on the performance of good deeds or other individual acts is insufficient to ensure salvation, again indicating the need to place full faith in God. Luther's adoption of Augustinian views placed him in direct conflict with Thomistic Christianity and the pope. He then began to criticize the pope's absolutism and the church hierarchy, and to shift toward the Bible as the revealed word of God.

The essence of Luther's refutation of the pope and the Catholic Church is found in his "Disputation on the Power and Efficacy of Indulgences," otherwise known as the Ninety-five Theses. He nailed this list to the church door in Wittenberg in 1517. Among the many disagreements, Luther states that the pope does not have the power to impose penalties beyond those imposed by church law (thesis 5); that people cannot always be certain of salvation (thesis 19); and that the pope's power over certain matters is no different than that of any other bishop (thesis 25).[8] Many of the other theses address the issue of the church selling indulgences.

The Ninety-five Theses and Luther's other writings make three main allegations against the church. He refers to these allegations as the "Three Walls" of the church in his 1520 "An Appeal to the Ruling Class." The first wall he attacks is the assertion that secular power has no control over the pope; that instead, the pope has control over civil authorities. Here, Luther argues that the distinction between secular and spiritual classes is a false one because all Christians are members of the religious class even though they perform different duties. Also, when a bishop acts, he does so for the congregation, all of whom have equal authority in the church. And those who exercise secular authority are equally members of the church, and perform duties that are different from but no less important than those of bishops. Whether secular or not, all are equally religious officers because they have been baptized.

For Luther, this means that secular governments, while exercising secular duties, are still spiritual in nature. Their duty, according to Luther, "is ordained by God to punish evil-doers and protect the law-abiding."[9] Since secular governments are granted their authority directly by God and not through the pope, they should be free to undertake their duties without interference from the church.

The second wall Luther confronts concerns the pope as the sole authority on the meaning of the Scriptures and papal infallibility. Luther disputes that the pope has a monopoly on the meaning of the Scriptures and is always correct, and that the church is identified with the pope. He argues that when St. Peter received the keys to the church, they "were not given to St. Peter only, but to the whole Christian community."[10] Hence the church is more than simply the pope; it is everyone who is a member of the faith. Also, if only the pope's word is final, why have Scriptures? The assertion by the pope that only his reading of the Bible is definitive seems to eliminate the need for anyone else to have or read them.

Luther's arguments against papal infallibility attack the special status of some individuals in the church. He says, "Everyone who has been baptized may claim that he has already been consecrated priest, bishop, or pope, even though it is not seemly for any particular person to exercise the office."[11] Thus, even though Luther describes all Christians as "priests of equal standing," this does not necessarily mean all should lead the church.

In "Freedom of a Christian," written in 1520, Luther addresses whether the pope, or any other religious person, is needed to interpret scriptures:

> If all who are in the church are priests, how do these whom we now call priests differ from layman? I answer: Injustice is done those words "priest," "cleric," "spiritual," "ecclesiastic," when they are transferred from all Christians to those few who are now by a mischievous usage called "ecclesiastics." Holy Scripture makes no distinction between them, although it gives the name "ministers," "servants," "stewards" to those who now are now proudly called popes, bishops, and lords. . . . Although we are all equally priests, we cannot all publicly minister and teach.[12]

According to Luther, each individual is capable of reading the Scriptures and rendering an interpretation. No reading, especially a pope's, is necessarily superior to any other's. This idea of a "priesthood of all believers" questions the role and need of the church in determining doctrine, and is a more individualistic view of religion than before.[13]

The third wall Luther attacks is the claim that only the pope can summon a council to resolve or address church issues, such as questions of doctrine. Luther argues that there is no scriptural basis for this claim. Rather, the Scriptures indicate that the church is more than one person, and that the pope is not the church; the people are. Thus all who are members of the church have the power, perhaps through a ruler, to call religious councils to vote on matters of doctrine. In other words, church membership is open to all who consent to it, the church is its members, and the membership has the authority to place limits on papal power by calling a council to resolve disputes.

Political Implications. Luther contends that his arguments are directed against certain church doctrines and claims, not the pope. Nonetheless, his views have important implications regarding the pope's power as well as the authority of civil rulers. By refuting papal infallibility, church structure, and control over civil rulers, Luther redefines the nature of Christianity. He envisions the church as composed of relatively equal members, the congregation as being the basis of the church, and the membership as granting its rulers the authority to act. All of these arguments imply political equality, constitutionalism, and the belief that political authority rests on the consent of the people. Eventually Luther's ideas would be applied to civil governments, restricting the way power and authority were allocated in their institutions.

More immediately, Luther's theology invests secular rulers with more authority than they had received before in Christian Europe. First, Luther indicates that civil authority receives its authority directly from God and not through the pope. This gives rulers a divine basis for power, but it also means that they are limited to serving God and not merely their own interests.

Second, Luther gives secular rulers an important task to perform. Given that humans are sinful and vice-ridden, the "state is God's servant and workman to punish the evil and protect the good."[14] Here, Luther returns to the Two Swords Doctrine, using it to support secular rule. He claims the pope has misinterpreted the doctrine, and that Jesus did not forbid or abolish secular authority by his statement on this point in Luke 22:7. More importantly, secular government does have important religious doctrines, and that instead of the two swords being divided, both are in control of the king.[15]

Third, even though he defends secular power, Luther does not advocate an absolutist and divine secular government. In a treatise of 1523, "Secular Authority: To What Extent It Should be Obeyed," he establishes limits for secular rule, first by discussing differences in types of rule and then asserting the need to limit rule through laws:

> It must be noted that the two classes of Adam's children, one in God's kingdom under Christ, the other in the kingdom of the world under the State, have two kinds of laws. . . . Every kingdom must have its own laws and regulations, and without law no kingdom or government can exist, as daily experience sufficiently proves. Worldly government has laws which extend no farther than to life and property and what is external upon earth.[16]

Christians have a duty to obey both rulers and secular laws:

> Because the sword is a very great benefit and necessary to the whole world, to preserve peace, to punish sin and to prevent evil, he submits most willingly to the rule of the sword, pays taxes, honors those in authority, serves, helps, and does all he can to further the government.[17]

Luther further states that only God can have control over souls, that secular governments have authority only over those who consent to their authority, and that no secular government can force people to believe.

What Luther creates is protection for individual conscience, a wall that defines limits over what a secular ruler can do. But what should one do if a prince exceeds his authority? Luther states that one should not resist government with force, but with truth and justice. One's duty as a Christian is to obey God first; and although one does not have to obey a tyrannical prince who acts in an un-Christian manner, one should only passively resist him.

Luther's political significance lies in his rethinking of the relationship between church and state authority vis-à-vis the individual as well as defining limits on both church and state power. In stressing these limits, Luther provided precedents for the later ideas of constitutionalism, tolerance, and separate roles for the church and state.

JOHN CALVIN

John Calvin (1509–1564) was the founder of one of the radical sects of Protestantism that developed after Luther in the sixteenth century. By showing that the church was a sick society, Luther had also thrown into question

the very order and fabric of the medieval world. And by attacking the authority of the pope, he had effectively contended that there was no single church
center. The result was political chaos that was partly addressed by turning to
rulers to fill the vacuum. Calvin continued this shift toward civil institutions
for the theological and institutional order that had been upset by the schism
between Protestants and the Catholic church. Calvin not only gave secular
institutions a moral authority they had hitherto lacked but paved the way for
divine absolutism in monarchical rule.

Political Theology. Calvin shares many arguments and assumptions with
Luther, including belief in the depravity of human nature, skepticism toward
reason and reliance on faith, and belief in the Scriptures as the revealed word
of God. In addition, he shares the belief that human deeds cannot ensure
salvation, insisting instead that individual souls are predestined, or not, for
salvation.

Calvin also agrees with claims by St. Augustine and Luther that government serves as a punishment and remedy for human sin. Following St. Augustine, Calvin adopts the notion of two churches, the visible and the invisible,
and he seeks a means to create unity in both of them. For Calvin, the invisible
church attains unity through Christian doctrine, while the visible church
achieves it through political institutions. Although the two churches have different ranges of application, they must work together to help promote Christian liberty. Thus legislative power is important to spreading and promoting
religion.

"On Christian Liberty" and "On Civil Government" are chapters in
Calvin's *Institutes of the Christian Religion* (1535) that deal with many of
these political themes. For Calvin,

> Christian liberty, according to my judgment, consists of three parts. The
> first part is that the consciences of believers, when seeking an assurance of
> their justification before God, should raise themselves above the law and
> forget all the righteousness of the law. . . . The second part of Christian lib-
> erty, which is dependent on the first, is that their consciences do not observe
> the law, as being under any legal obligation, but that, being liberty from the
> yoke of the law, they yield a voluntary obedience to the will of God. . . . The
> third part of Christian liberty teaches us that we are bound by no obligation
> before God respecting external things, which in themselves are indifferent,
> but that we may indifferently sometimes use and other times omit them.[18]

Christian liberty, then, is a spiritual thing that is directed toward God. It
does not involve material or sensual things; it involves moderation; and it
does not need to be witnessed by other people, only by God. Christian liberty
involves the conscience of believers; humans are free only when they direct all
their attention toward God. However, faith in God does not abrogate faith in
human institutions. These institutions are important to Christian liberty.
Government is necessary because humans are sinful and need it to ensure that
they live correctly and under the law of God.

Calvin distinguishes two types of government, the spiritual and the political, each with its own sphere of influence and duties:

> Man is under two kinds of government—one spiritual, by which the con-
> science is formed to piety and the service of God; the other political, by
> which a man is instructed in the duties of humanity and civility, which are
> to be observed in an intercourse with mankind. . . . The former species of
> government pertains to the life of the soul, and that the latter relates to the
> concerns of the present state, not only to the provision of food and clothing,
> but to the enactment of laws to regulate a man's life among his neighbors by
> rules of holiness, integrity, and sobriety. The former has its seat in the inte-
> rior of the mind, whilst the latter only directs the external conduct.[19]

Calvin states that these two governments, though examined separately, can
and should be considered together as fulfilling the same function—to help
humankind serve God.

In "On Civil Government," Calvin indicates how the two types of governments fit together. Disagreeing with Augustine, he does not see civil government as a "polluted thing." Instead, "This civil government is designed, as
long as we live in this world, to cherish and support the external worship of
God, to preserve the pure doctrine of God, to defend the constitution of the
church."[20]

Thus civil government has tremendous power to carry out its religious mis-
sions. There is almost no limit on its ability to enforce external behavior and
conformity. Among its powers, civil government can regulate luxuries and
human vices. For example, Calvin calls for a group of officials, whom he calls
ephors, to check and censor the magistrate to ensure that he uses his power
for Christian purposes. Calvin also distinguishes among three parts to the
civil administration of the polity; in addition to the magistrate are the law and
the people.

Like Luther, Calvin argues that the ruler's power is divine in origin:

> The authority possessed by kings and other governors over all things upon
> earth is not a consequence of the perverseness of men but of the Providence
> and holy ordinance of God, who has been pleased to regulate human affairs
> in this manner.[21]

Magistrates receive their commands from God, thus they are invested with
God's authority and serve as his agents. Calvin gives scriptural authority to
support this point, quoting the book of Romans: "By me kings reign, and
princes decree justice. By me princes rule, and nobles, even all the judges of
the earth."[22] Biblical support for princes gives them significant power, to the
point, in fact, that magistrates are not bound by temporal law. They are to act
to serve God's will and law.

As for the law, the second part of civil administration, Calvin appeals to
the natural law tradition. He contends that the law is the true and eternal rule
of righteousness prescribed to humans of all ages and nations who wish to
conform their lives to the will of God. He refers to the law of God, the moral
law, as natural law:

> Now, as it is certain that the law of God, which we call the moral law, is no
> other than a declaration of natural law, and of that conscience which has
> been engraved by God on the minds of men, the whole rule of this equity, of

which we now speak, is prescribed in it. This equity, therefore, must alone be the scope and rule and end of all laws.[23]

Moral law, which aims at equity, is the model of all human laws, which in turn should be framed toward it and supported by the people. Therefore, a true or well-regulated civil government respects God's law and directs individuals toward Christian liberty.

The people, the third part of civil administration, need external support from the government, the magistrate, and the laws to help them secure Christian liberty. The first duty of people is to obey the magistrate, willfully rather than out of fear. The second duty is to obey every command of the magistrate. Their allegiance is both political and religious; it requires people's active engagement. Individuals have a religious duty to the state, and that duty necessitates active participation. Because the state is a government of active believers, nonbelievers can be compelled to act according to certain laws or be exiled or branded heretics.

Like Luther, Calvin also addresses the issue of what to do with a magistrate who ignores the laws and goes against God. He argues that individuals must obey even those who abuse their authority because to disobey is to cross God:

> But, if we direct our attention to the word of God, it will carry us much farther; even to submit to the government, not only of those princes who discharge their duty to us with becoming integrity and fidelity, but of all who possess sovereignty, even though they perform none of the duties of their function.[24]

The people should obey the magistrate, even if unjust, because a magistrate may be willed by God to act unjustly in order "to punish the iniquity of the people." Moreover, Calvin asserts that it is not the task of the people to correct injustice; it is up to God to punish an unjust magistrate.

However, there is one exception to the obligation of the people to obey. That circumstance occurs when magistrates issue orders against the will of God. Here, Calvin states that "if they command anything against Him, it ought not to have the least attention."[25] In this case, the people have a duty to passively disobey the ruler.

Several implications flow from these arguments and the tripartite structure Calvin sets up for civil administration. One is the importance of checking arbitrary political power by use of law. In this case, it is not necessarily civil laws, but the law of God. More importantly, in describing the duties of the magistrate to God, the people to God, and the magistrate and the people to one another, Calvin sets up a civil government that invokes a series of covenants among the different parties. If the covenants are broken, some types of limited action may be taken to rectify the infractions. Yet passive resistance to the magistrate, even if he breaks with God and his duties, is the extent of the people's right to engage in civil disobedience.

Describing social relations in terms of covenants had political implications in itself. Such terminology formed the basis of early social-contract thinking, wherein the state is viewed, not as divinely ordained or natural, but as the

product of individual choice or will. Calvin does not argue that social contracts or covenants are the basis of political legitimacy or the reason for a
state to exist. States are necessary because of human sin and because God
wills them. However, other political thinkers in the sixteenth century, both
within the Protestant tradition and among Catholics reacting to it, developed
the social-contract argument further. And Hobbes, Locke, and Rousseau
would later employ this language in a way that would change how people
understood their political obligations and their society.

WOMEN AND THE PROTESTANT REFORMATION

The Protestant Reformation brought few long-term changes for women.
Much in the same way that earlier Christian movements initially encouraged
women to move beyond traditional roles, Protestant leaders enlisted women
to help in their battle against the pope. Yet once the main thrust of the Reformation was complete, leaders relegated women to their traditional roles as
mothers and wives. The only two permanent changes for Protestant women
were the creation of a special role for the parson's wife,[26] and strong encour-
agement to learn how to read, but only the Scriptures.[27] Beyond these
reforms, neither Luther nor Calvin advocate much change in the status of
women, in either the family or their relationship to their husbands.

Luther describes women and men in ways that are reminiscent of stereotypes held since the days of Plato and early Christianity:

> It is evident therefore that woman is a different animal to man, not only
> having different members, but also being far weaker in intellect. But
> although Eve was a most noble creation, like Adam, as regards the image of
> God, that is, in justice, wisdom, and salvation, she was none the less a
> woman . . . [and] not equal the dignity and glory of the male.[28]

He describes men in terms of their rational capacity and intellect, but he
again reduces women to their bodies, specifically, childbearing functions. He
says, "To me it is often a source of great pleasure and wonderment to see that
the entire female body was created for the purpose of nurturing children."[29]
Furthermore, because of women's function, they "should remain at home, sit
still, keep house, and bear and bring up children." Moreover, both divine
Providence and the biological differences between the sexes mean that
women are best suited to specific subordinate functions, in both the family
and the political community:

> The rule remains with the husband, and the wife is compelled to obey him
> by God's command. He rules the home and the state, wages war, defends his
> possessions, tills the soil, builds, plants, etc. The woman . . . should stay at
> home and look after the affairs of the household, as one who has been
> deprived of the ability of administering those affairs that are outside and
> the concern of the state.[30]

The ancient Greeks and earlier Christians had invoked God to justify the
respective roles of men and women, and Luther and Calvin do the same.

Luther's comments about men, women, the family, and the state indicate that the structure of the family is to provide the model and justification for the order of the state. In turn, the state uses its laws to enforce divine commands that define specific roles for women. As in *Antigone,* religion, politics, and the family mutually reinforce one another when it comes to defining gender roles. For Calvin, the subordination of women is justified because Eve tempted Adam and caused the Fall from Grace. This means it is God's will and punishment for women to be subordinate in both the family and politics.

CONCLUSION

The Protestant Reformation shattered the monolithic order of medieval Christianity, leaving in its place several new concepts in political thought. The theology of Protestant thinkers, such as Luther and Calvin, changed the relationship between church and state, which would eventually give the latter far more independent authority than it had had. Protestant thought, in its assault on the absolutism of the pope, also articulated ideas that would become increasingly important over the next few centuries. These ideas were related to constitutionalism, social-contract views of the state, the right to individual conscience, people as the source of power, and the right of individuals to act if their leaders failed to respect certain commands or boundaries. Finally, the shift away from the hierarchy of the church and the movement toward the right of each person to interpret the Bible for him- or herself provided the impetus for the emergence of a religious epistemology and individualism that would be supported by other forces transpiring in society. Together, they led to the creation of a new set of political assumptions and values regarding individual freedom and state authority that would depart dramatically from those that had existed for the past one thousand years.

But what type of individualism was created by the Protestant Reformation and for whom? Did or should the priesthood of all believers extend to women? Should they be viewed as equal both before God and on earth? Was the individualism created by the Protestants an open-ended freedom for individuals to do whatever they wanted, or were their limits to what freedom permitted? Moreover, at the same time that Protestantism seemed to be creating space for individuals, it also increased the power of secular rulers: Were these moves at cross-purposes to one another?

Notes

1. Franklin L. Baumer, *Modern European Thought: Continuity and Change in Ideas, 1600–1950* (New York: Macmillan, 1977), 26–34.

2. Duncan B. Forrester, "Martin Luther and John Calvin," in *History of Political Philosophy,* eds. L. Strauss and J. Cropsey (Chicago: University of Chicago Press, 1987), 319–21.

3. Alasdair MacIntyre, *After Virtue* (Notre Dame, Ind.: University of Notre Dame Press, 1984).

4. J. Leslie Dunstan, ed., *Protestantism* (New York: Braziller, 1962), 25; Bonnie S. Anderson and Judith P. Zinsser, *A History of Their Own: Women in Europe from Prehistory to the Present* (New York: Harper & Row, 1988).

5. Quentin Skinner, *The Foundations of Modern Political Thought*, vol. 2: *The Age of Reformation* (New York: Cambridge University Press, 1979), 114–15.

6. Max Weber, *The Protestant Ethic and the Spirit of Capitalism*, trans. T. Parsons (New York: Scribner's, 1976); R. H. Tawney, *Religion and the Rise of Capitalism* (New York: Pelican, 1966).

7. Sheldon S. Wolin, *Politics and Vision: Continuity and Innovation in Western Political Thought* (Boston: Little, Brown, 1960), 145.

8. Martin Luther, "The Ninety-five Theses," in *Martin Luther: Selections from His Writings*, ed. John Dillenberger (Garden City, N.Y.: Anchor, 1961), 489–500.

9. Martin Luther, "An Appeal to the Ruling Class," in *Martin Luther*, 410.

10. "An Appeal to the Ruling Class," 413.

11. "An Appeal to the Ruling Class," 409.

12. Martin Luther, "The Freedom of a Christian," in *Martin Luther*, 66.

13. Roland Bainton, *Here I Stand: A Life of Martin Luther* (New York: Abingdon-Cokesbury, 1950).

14. Martin Luther, "Secular Authority: To What Extent It Should Be Obeyed," in *Martin Luther*, 378.

15. "Secular Authority," 381.

16. "Secular Authority," 382–3.

17. "Secular Authority," 373.

18. John Calvin, *On God and Political Duty* (Indianapolis: Bobbs-Merrill, 1956), 27–31.

19. *On God*, 40–41.

20. *On God*, 46.

21. *On God*, 48.

22. Romans 12:8.

23. *On God*, 65.

24. *On God*, 74.

25. *On God*, 81.

26. Erik H. Erikson, *Young Man Luther: A Study in Psychoanalysis and History* (New York: Norton, 1962), 71.

27. Bonnie S. Anderson and Judith P. Zinsser, *A History of Their Own: Women in Europe from Prehistory to the Present*, vol. I (New York: Harper & Row, 1988), 264.

28. Luther, cited in *A History of Their Own*, 254.

29. Luther, cited in *A History of Their Own*, 261.

30. Luther, cited in *A History of Their Own*, 259.

Additional Readings

Skinner, Quentin. *The Foundations of Modern Political Thought*, vol. 2: *The Age of Reformation*. New York: Cambridge University Press, 1979.

Walzer, Michael. *The Revolution of the Saints: A Study of the Origins of Radical Politics*. Cambridge, Mass.: Harvard University Press, 1982.

Wolin, Sheldon. *Politics and Vision: Continuity and Innovation in Western Political Thought*. Boston: Little, Brown, 1960.

Inventors of Ideas Online

Visit http://politicalscience.wadsworth.com/tannenbaum2 for links related to material in this chapter, including the full texts of a number of Luther's and Calvin's major works.

11

COPERNICUS, BACON, DESCARTES, AND NEWTON: THE SCIENTIFIC BASIS OF MODERN POLITICS

INTRODUCTION

The politics of medieval Christianity rested on faith and ambivalence toward reason. It described a hierarchical view of the universe that defined a monolithic order of political values and power emanating from God to the pope and the church, down to inferior religious officials and eventually to secular rulers, men, and then women, and children.[1] Yet this political world rested not only on Christian theology but also on a set of scientific assumptions tracing back to Aristotle's writings, especially his *Metaphysics*. The Christian world was also understood through Plato's *Timaeus*, his account of the creation of the universe by some single demiurge called God, and the interpretations of Neoplatonists such as Plotinius (205–270) and Porphyry (232–?). The Neoplatonists took the ideas from the *Timaeus* and described the universe as emanating from a single Oneness or Being who served as the single cause or force creating and guiding the universe. Together, these scientific ideas formed a cosmology or theory of the universe that supported both the politics and religion of the Christian world.

But beginning in the sixteenth century, a new view of science emerged, questioning not only the old views of the universe held by the classics and the Christians, but ultimately uprooting the foundations of much of the religious and political order of the day.

THE ARISTOTELIAN-CHRISTIAN SCIENTIFIC WORLD

The universe of the Christians was one created and ruled by God, according to the features and traits described in Genesis, with the Earth at the center and man occupying the role as the master species and gender of the planet. To

145

St. Augustine, knowledge of how the world was constructed did not require an appeal to reason or science; faith alone was enough:

> When, then, the question is asked what we are to believe in regard to religion, it is not necessary to probe into the nature of things, as was done by those whom the Greeks call *physici;* nor need we be in alarm lest the Christian should be ignorant of the force and number of the elements—the motion, and order, and the eclipse of heavenly bodies. . . . It is enough for the Christian to believe that the only cause of all created things, whether heavenly or earthly, whether visible or invisible, is the goodness of the Creator, the one true God; and that nothing exists but himself that does not derive its existence from Him.[2]

The reemergence and incorporation of Aristotle's metaphysics altered the Christian political cosmology. If the political universe of the church consisted of the final and first causes initially described by Aristotle, Ptolemy, and other ancients, the writings of Aquinas, Dante, and other Christians created the theological hierarchy of the Christian cosmos.[3] It was the universe of Dante's *Divine Comedy,* with God, goodness, and paradise lying at one end, and the Devil, evil, and hell at the other.

Belief in this Christian cosmology had held sway for over a thousand years, but from the middle of the sixteenth century onward, modern science came to have an impact on Christianity and, with that, modern politics, political theory, and society. The development of modern science in the Enlightenment did so in several ways. First, it challenged the sovereignty of faith as the sole or primary way to understand and order the world. In its place, thinkers such as Bacon and Descartes argued that reason, especially scientific reason, guided by certain rules or methods, could check human errors and dogmas and result in greater understanding. Religion and religious superstition were often labeled as dogmas that limited the human mind.

A second challenge from science was how the universe came to be redefined. Christians described the universe as one created and actively governed by God, with all motion and activity within it striving toward the deity. For philosophers such as Nicolas de Malebranche (1638–1715), for example, the "Vision of God" is what accounts for motion in the universe, including how the mind and body interact. This Christian universe was not simply composed of things or matter, but was intertwined with moral properties of goodness because it was a creation of God. This meant that to describe the cosmos was also to ascribe moral goodness to it. These moral properties defined standards of conduct for man, through God's and natural law, and determined the best type of human laws and governments.

Scientific thinking, as it had developed to the sixteenth century, thus bore the characteristics of both Christianity and Aristotle. From Christianity, God was at the center of explanation of why the planets, the sun, moon, and stars rotate around the Earth and God provided the explanation of why there was something rather than nothing. From Aristotle and the Neoplatonists, the universe was described in terms of gradations of reality and the four causes. If the universe could be understood as movement from becoming to being, matter could be described both as being in motion from a lesser to a greater state of reality. The universe was also purposive, not mechanical, with all entities seeking their telos or final purposes. However, what if God did not exist or what if the universe was not purposive but instead operated like a machine? Could one envision a type of science that stripped God and final causes from it?

Scientists in the sixteenth through the eighteenth centuries challenged this vision of the universe, self-consciously seeking a break from the ways of the ancients and Christians. As early as the fifteenth century, Nicholas of Cusa had contended that the universe was different from what Christians thought. He had questioned whether the Earth was at the midpoint, and whether the universe had a center or finite boundaries at all. But it was in the sixteenth century that Nicholas Copernicus challenged the belief that the Earth was the center of the universe. Francis Bacon labeled religion as a superstition of the mind, challenged the relationship between faith and reason, and questioned the idea that the universe was governed by final causes. Descartes continued this line of attack by displacing God from the center of knowledge and turning toward man. And Newton completed the redefinition by recasting the universe in terms of mechanistic forces and laws of motion. By the middle of the eighteenth century, the old Christian cosmology was essentially moribund, and along with it the reign of Christianity as the main basis of political, social, and moral values. What occurred was either a secularization of the values of the Christian order, or a complete substitution of reason and the self for the church and the Bible as the grounds for human knowledge.[4]

Despite the eventual rejection of the Aristotelian-Christian cosmology by modern science, one should not assume that there was no learning or value associated with it. Efforts to chart the universe and map the stars became increasingly accurate and the models more complex. Mathematics, especially as it moved from the Arabic and Islamic worlds to Christian Europe, continued to develop, and efforts to understand medicine and anatomy, although crude by today's standards, kept alive the classical tradition and efforts to understand the world.

NICHOLAS COPERNICUS

Nicholas Copernicus (1473–1543) was a Polish astronomer who perhaps unwittingly destroyed the values of the ancient and Christian world and led a revolution that would help create the modern scientific one.[5] On one level, the aim of his book, *On the Revolutions of the Celestial Spheres* (1543), was quite modest; it merely seeks to make some minor adjustments in the Earth-centered, or geocentric, model of the universe. Ptolemy, in ancient Egypt, as well as the Greeks, Romans, and Christian Europeans, had assumed that the Earth was at the center of the universe. Yet to hold this belief, astronomers had had to make a series of assumptions about planetary movements, including that the planets occasionally move backwards or in small circles as they revolve around the Earth. As Copernicus puts it,

> The total world—with the exception of the Earth—is supposed to be carried from east to west by this movement. This movement is taken as the common measure of all movements. . . . Next, we perceive other as it were antagonistic movements, i.e., from west to east, of the sun, moon, and wandering stars.[6]

So what Copernicus initially attempts is to devise better mathematical equations to predict and explain the irregular motions of planets and other celestial bodies. But what he ends up with are doubts about contemporary assumptions:

> I think it necessary above all that we should note carefully what the relation of the heavens to the Earth is, so as not—when we wish to scrutinize the highest things—to be ignorant of those which are nearest to us and so as not—by the same error—to attribute to the celestial bodies what belongs to the earth.[7]

This rethinking leads Copernicus to further speculation on the place of the Earth in the universe:

> Although there are so many authorities for saying that the Earth rests in the center of the world that people think the contrary supposition is ridiculous and inopinable; if, however, we consider the thing attentively, we will see that the question has not yet been decided and is by no means to be scorned.[8]

Copernicus then explores the implications of assuming that the sun is the center of the universe and that the Earth is the third planet from the sun, orbiting around it along with other planets.

His aims may have been modest, but such speculation by Copernicus was not viewed that way by the religious community, and Protestant reformers condemned his book. Martin Luther, for example, stated, "This fool wishes to reverse the entire science of astronomy; but sacred Scripture tells us that Joshua commanded the sun to stand still, and not the Earth."[9] In 1616, the Pope declared the book heresy and forbade Catholics to read it.

Why was the book denounced? In many ways, a sun-centered model of the universe threatened the foundations of the Christian order:

> The drama of Christian life and the morality that had been made dependent upon it would not readily adapt to a universe in which the earth was just one of a number of planets. Cosmology, morality, and theology had long been interwoven in the traditional fabric of Christian thought described by Dante. . . . Copernicus's proposal raised many gigantic problems for the believing Christian. If, for example, the earth were merely one of six planets, how were the stories of the Fall and the salvation, with their immense bearing on Christian life, to be preserved? If there were other bodies essentially like the earth, God's goodness would surely necessitate that they, too, be inhabited. But if there were men and other planets, how could they be descendants of Adam and Eve, and how could they have inherited the

original sin, which explains man's otherwise incomprehensible travail on an earth made for him by a good and omnipotent deity? . . . Worst of all, if the universe is infinite, as many of the later Copernicans thought, where can God's throne be located? In an infinite universe, how is man to find God or God man?[10]

Medieval Christian theology had built its entire edifice on the assumption that the Earth was the center of the universe and not merely one of several planets. The geocentric model defined man's relationship to God and, in the process, defined who man was. What the church had done was to create a great theological chain of being, with the Earth lying in the central position;[11] the Catholic Church was at the center of the chain; and the pope, deriving his authority from God, able to claim he had a privileged position to lord over the earthly empire.

Thus to challenge the geocentric model was to displace the pope's and the church's central position, and to question Christian hierarchy, order, and status as dramatically as Luther and Calvin had done in regard to doctrine. Copernicus creates, in effect, a new center (of power), and the pope is not in it. Furthermore, in decentering the Earth, Copernicus moves away from a privileged position for both it and humankind. It was inevitable that his theory (as well as that of Galileo, a famous astronomer, who also supported a heliocentric model of the universe) would be condemned by the church.

Copernicus ultimately forced a rethinking of the universe, away from one that was God-directed to one run differently somehow. Perhaps the universe does not need constant divine guidance but instead, as some argue, it is like a watch. In this case, once the universe is built and wound up, it runs of its own accord. This changed who God is: no longer a father figure, but the great watchmaker.

Overall, one can describe the Copernican revolution as

a revolution in ideas, a transformation in man's conception of the universe and of his own relation to it. Again and again the history of Renaissance thought has been proclaimed an epochal turning point in the intellectual development of Western man. Yet the Revolution turned upon the most obscure and recondite minutiae of astronomical research.[12]

Although Copernicus started the revolution that destroyed the foundations of the medieval political order, neither he nor his immediate followers necessarily sought to destroy the truths of the Christian world. The problem was then how to find new foundations for old truths without destroying the old truths.

FRANCIS BACON

Francis Bacon (1561–1626) was an English philosopher and scientist as well as an important political official under King James I. He continued the rethinking of the assumptions of the Christian world started by Copernicus and others, proposing new methods to study the universe and redefining the interrelations among God, man, and the universe.

Bacon consciously seeks to rethink the assumptions of the ancients. In his book, *Novum Organum* (1620), he states that so far "no one has yet been found so firm of mind and purpose as resolutely to compel himself to sweep away all theories and common notions, and to apply the understanding . . . to a fresh examination of ideas."[13] Further, "We must begin anew from the very foundations, unless we would revolve forever in a circle with mean and contemptible progress."[14] And Bacon states that he seeks to do this because "My purpose, on the contrary, is to try whether I cannot in very fact lay more firmly the foundations, and extend more firmly the foundations, and extend more widely, the power and greatness of man."[15]

Bacon's arguments in *Novum Organum* are in part criticism of the deductive-reasoning methods of the ancient Greeks. Their methods, according to Bacon, are prone to all types of distortions and errors. In fact, much of *Novum Organum* criticizes the "four idols, of the mind," or mistakes that affect the human understanding. These are the idols of the tribe, the cave, the marketplace, and the theater.

The idols of the tribe are natural distortions arising from human nature. These are the tricks the senses can play, mistakes that result from the fact that human senses are like a distorted mirror. One is unable to perfectly grasp or understand the world because one is often tricked by experiences of the senses. The idols of the cave are the biases or distortions found within each individual. Each person has a unique perspective or limits, which lead to misperception of the world in various ways. The third idols are those of the marketplace. These are distortions that arise as a result of human interaction. Finally, there are the idols of the theater. These are the distortions that arise from biases in philosophical dogma. Since each of these idols contributes to limits on human understanding, Bacon advocates new foundations and methods of inquiry to address them.

For Bacon, the idols of the theater seem to be the most profound and damaging. He indicates that the logic and natural philosophy of the ancients, including Plato and Aristotle, are not pure but corrupted by the idols of the theater. Bacon criticizes respect for tradition as limiting to human knowledge and suggests that a clean break with the ancients is necessary if human understanding is to advance. He reserves his most biting criticism of idols of the theater, though, for religion. To him, religion and theology have perpetrated the "greatest harm" on human understanding, waging a war against science and knowledge. He contends that "neither is it to be forgotten that in every age natural philosophy has had a troublesome adversary and one hard to deal with; namely superstition, and the blind and immoderate zeal of religion."[16]

But it is not just religion in general that Bacon is concerned with. He states that it is Christianity, specifically its attempt to deduce a system of knowledge from the Bible, that is the real problem:

> For nothing is so mischievous as the apotheosis of error. . . . Yet in this vanity some moderns have with extreme levity indulged so far as to attempt to

found a system of natural philosophy on the first chapters of Genesis, on the Book of Job, and other parts of sacred writings; seeking for the dead among the living.[17]

The problem with using theology and God to explain the universe is that it assumes a purposive world, one wherein all phenomena that cannot be explained are simply attributed to some divine action. Thus Bacon's assault is on the Aristotelian notion of final causes, which had been adopted by Thomist Christianity and cosmology, to explain the structure and order of the universe:

> Nevertheless the human understanding being unable to rest still seeks something prior in order of nature. And then it is that in struggling towards that which is further off it falls back upon that which is more nigh at hand—namely, on final causes; which have relation clearly to the nature of man rather than to the nature of the universe.[18]

Bacon rejects appeals to final causes or telos for the universe as merely one example of a religious idol of the theater. The universe is not purposive in the way Christians think. It is completely without final causes, containing only mechanistic ones, which can be discovered, but not through the Scriptures or employment of deductive logic. Instead, Bacon argues for use of the senses, guided by scientific and experimental methods, to check the several idols and gain a real understanding of the universe.

The implication of Bacon's arguments is that God is unnecessary to explain nature or man; and that a natural philosophy dispensing with the dogma of theology is better able to explain the universe and develop human understanding. He thus offers the beginnings of the scientific method, a new way to gain and guarantee knowledge. Here, science begins to emerge as a tool for power and knowledge, and as a grounds for supporting certain propositions. Nature is something to be subdued, like a woman.[19] The new goals for science are also described by Bacon as where "human knowledge and power meet in one" in order to give man increased power. Thus power is the use of reason to subjugate nature; and reason is to be used for power and control, not for contemplative purposes.

Bacon's arguments depict theology in a new light. Instead of adopting the Christian or Augustinian perspective that faith and religion are needed to support reason, he charges faith and religion as enemies of understanding.

Aside from attacking religion directly, Bacon's arguments threatened the church in two ways. First, by criticizing faith and religion, Bacon undercut the basis of the legitimacy used to support the pope's power. That is, one could appeal to reason to question religious authority, including that of the pope. Second, by refuting the idea of final causes, Bacon destroyed the foundations of Christian cosmology, which supported the pope's claim of authority as coming directly from God. His arguments, in both cases, were even more of a threat to the universalism of the church than was Protestantism. He not only made religion an enemy but threatened to reverse the relationship between faith and reason that had sustained the church for 1,600 years.

RENÉ DESCARTES

René Descartes (1596–1650) was an important French philosopher who continued to develop many of the arguments about science Bacon had articulated. Like Bacon, Descartes consciously seeks to reconstruct or provide a new beginning for science and knowledge. In his first major philosophical work, *The Discourse on Method* (1637), Descartes notes that the human mind, being capable of errors, necessitates a method to check them. He argues that current knowledge is placed on "no better foundations than sand and soft shifting ground."[20] To correct the errors due to the poor foundations for human knowledge, Descartes states that he proceeded by

> emptying my mind of them one and all, with a view to replacing them by others more tenable, or it may be, to the readmitting of them, on their being shown to be in conformity with reason. I was firmly of the belief that by this means I should succeed much better in the conduct of my life than if, building on the old foundations, I relied on principles of which in my youth I had allowed myself to be persuaded.[21]

Thus the logic of reason was to be the means to decide what is true, or at least what is worth preserving. But, perceiving that his method might be destructive of political and moral values, Descartes argues for a "provisional code of morals" until such time as reason can support and maintain a new set of rules.

Doubt of the senses and the search for certainty started in the *Discourse* are further developed in Descartes's most famous work, *Meditations on First Philosophy* (1641). Here, he searches for the basic principles of all knowledge by finding something he cannot doubt. But the senses cannot be trusted because they can deceive. One can think one is perceiving the world truly but actually be dreaming; or, worse yet, God might be a great deceiver, or "malignant genius," constantly tricking men.[22]

Descartes continues to doubt all that can be doubted until he finds something that cannot be questioned, even if God is indeed an evil genius. That "something" is the processing of doubt and existence itself:

> If I am persuading myself of something, in so doing I assuredly do exist. But what if, unknown to me, there be some deceiver, very powerful and cunning, who is constantly employing his ingenuity in deceiving me? Again, as before, without doubt, if he is deceiving me, I exist. . . . And thus, having reflected well, and carefully examined all things, we have finally to conclude that this declaration, *Ego sum, ego existo,* is necessarily true every time I propound it or mentally apprehend it.[23]

Descartes's method arrives at certainty in the statement *"Cogito, ergo sum,"* or "I think, therefore I am." He concludes that he cannot doubt his own existence because thinking cannot be separated from existence.

Descartes's conclusion was significant in that the thinking self became the starting point for reconstructing human knowledge and foundations. It is an appeal to an epistemological basis, located in the self, to substantiate the world. This viewpoint is in clear contrast to St. Augustine and the Christians, who had started with God as the basis of knowledge. Descartes reverses the Christian order altogether. From the *cogito*, Descartes eventually deduces that God must exist, that He is not a deceiver, and that from God an entire world can be reconstructed through the use of reason. But all of his reconstruction is premised upon the certainty of one's own existence. God and religion are not primarily important to validation of the self or the world.

The goal of both of Descartes's books is to employ new rules to eliminate doubt, to protect against the deception of the senses, and to ensure that men are capable of overcoming the vices that distract the mind. In fact, according to Descartes, "good sense, or reason, is by nature equal in all men,"[24] so the rules of science he proposes can ensure that each person can reason equal to the level of any others. He sees scientific reason as a great leveler as it empowers every person to question and to doubt.

Despite the appeal to reason, Descartes is careful not to attack religion with the same boldness that Bacon did. Neither of his books attacks God; both appeal to God to help validate knowledge, and the *Meditations* is dedicated to theology faculty. Perhaps the reason for this avoidance of a direct attack on the church or God was fear arising from Galileo's condemnation by the church and forced recantation of his belief in Copernican theory in 1633. Descartes himself admits, in the *Discourse*, that the condemnation troubled him to the degree that he suppressed one of his own works.

Descartes's last book, *Rules for the Guidance of Our Native Powers*, was written in 1629, four years before Galileo was condemned, but was not published until 1701, after his death. It continues his search for truth and certainty through the use of doubt, reason, and attacks on false truths found in his other writings. But it contains no appeals to God or theology, making it perhaps Descartes's most radical and secular book.

In sum, although Descartes's philosophy does not attack final causes, it does relegate God to secondary status, behind the self. Scientific reasoning becomes the tool each person can use to question and explore the natural world. But this purpose of reason could also be used for other purposes, and it was a short step from examining the cosmos to questioning religion and the political world. Descartes's legacy, then, was to create a scientific epistemological individualism that supported the individualisms of Protestant theology and Machiavellian politics.

ISAAC NEWTON

Isaac Newton (1642–1727) was an English mathematician and physicist whose work altered seventeenth-century understanding of the world. In his *Principia Mathematica*, or *Mathematics Principles of Natural Philosophy* (1687), he reformulated explanations of how bodies in the universe interacted. Previous to Newton, gravity had been explained as a universal attraction of all objects to fall toward the center of the universe, that is, the center of the Earth. But when Copernicus displaced the Earth from the center, that explanation no longer sufficed.

Newton's three laws of motion helped provide an explanation of gravitational forces. He argues that nature "may all depend upon certain forces by which the particles of bodies, by some forces hitherto unknown, are either mutually impelled towards one another, and cohere in regular figures, or are repelled from one another."[25] These forces, for Newton, are part of nature itself.

Newton's universe, described in terms of physical forces and mathematical equations, however, means that religious final causes are not crucial to an understanding of everyday occurrences. Although Newton may still see God as the ultimate creator of the universe, his God and universe are much different from those of earlier Christians. God is an architect, a mathematician, or a great watchmaker, and the universe is like a great watch. Once God created or wound up the great watch of the universe, it started running on its own, according to laws, rules, and properties which man can ultimately understand and describe.[26] This is not a universe run by a great patriarch who maintains a watchful eye over the world and man. He, or it, is a God of a different character; and his presence and being are not part of the fabric of the world in the way they had been for Christian thinkers. Theological final causes were neither part of this universe nor necessary to explain it.

The implications of Newton's claims were that the natural laws of the universe are not moral, but mathematical. One could explain nature not by reference to God as the final cause, but through connections among force, mass, and acceleration.

This redefinition of the universe as something mechanical also meant a separation of factual descriptions and understandings of the world from moral claims. David Hume, an important eighteenth-century British philosopher, best captured the significance of this new universe when he argued that it is "almost inconceivable" how moral "oughts" could be derived from factual statements or states of affairs in the world.[27] His point was that the universe does not contain natural laws that have moral properties that are binding on individuals. Rather, the universe simply is, and everyone is part of it, but neither located at its center nor guided by any moral rules in it.

WOMEN AND THE SCIENTIFIC REVOLUTION

The shift toward reason and away from religion and faith as a way to understand the world also provided new ways to defend traditional family and gender roles. Scientific philosophers, such as Bacon and Newton, describe nature as a woman, or as female; and science and reason as male. This sets up opposition between the two, with masculine reason seeking to subdue the female world, much in the same way that Machiavelli had described a masculine virtue seeking to subdue a female fortune.

Reason, despite changing conceptions of the universe and political authority, remained a man's tool and would soon be employed to change all but the status of women. In fact, it would continue to support the subordination of women in the political process and the family throughout the seventeenth and eighteenth centuries.

CONCLUSION

According to Friedrich Nietzsche, a nineteenth-century German philosopher, "Since Copernicus, man seems to have gotten himself on an inclined plane—now he is slipping faster and faster into—what? Into nothingness?"[28] By displacing man from the center of the universe, Copernicus unleashed a rethinking of the Christian world that would have major repercussions for political theory and Western politics. It changed the way humanity viewed itself, and this change took on its own momentum, destroying the old world and creating a set of rational values that has come to be described as modern.

Copernicus's heliocentric model of the universe precipitated almost a second Fall from grace. Once humans were displaced from the center of the universe, the cosmology that supported Christianity was called into question, which placed in doubt the ability of God and religion to provide a foundation for moral and political authority. What political philosophy and humankind needed was a new "Archimedean point," or center on which old values could be rebuilt.[29] That Archimedean point and foundation was scientific reason.

The scientific thinkers posited that reason, when guided by the correct rules, had the capacity to cast away all false truths, dogmas, superstitions, and prejudices that stood in the way of human understanding. Reason was not meant to destroy either religion or the moral and political truths of the Christian order, but instead to place it upon more firmer foundations. But, as Nietzsche suggested, could reason turn upon itself, Christianity, and the reigning political order of the day? It eventually did just that.[30] Scientific thinkers looked for the rational basis of religion, questioned the existence of God, and ultimately asked for the rational basis behind moral truths and the political rule of faith, the church, and monarchies.

Scientific thinkers recast the structure of the universe by advocating reason as the basis of political authority. Could science be employed to liberate individuals? Could monarchs and rulers withstand rational examination of their power and privilege? And were there any issues that should be placed off limits from scientific examination? As Immanuel Kant would later ask, could God, freedom, and immortality be protected from rational and scientific analysis? If not, what would the implications be for humanity?

Notes

1. Alexandre Koyré, *From the Closed World to the Infinite Universe* (Baltimore: Johns Hopkins University Press, 1982), 2.

2. Thomas S. Kuhn, *The Copernican Revolution: Planetary Astronomy in the Development of Western Thought* (Cambridge, Mass.: Harvard University Press, 1985), 107.

3. *Copernican Revolution,* 109–11.

4. Hans Blumenberg, *The Legitimacy of the Modern Age* (Cambridge, Mass.: MIT Press, 1987).

5. Hans Blumenberg, *The Genesis of the Copernican World* (Cambridge, Mass.: MIT Press, 1987).

6. Nicholas Copernicus, "On the Revolution of the Celestial Spheres," in *Man and the Universe: The Philosophers of Science,* ed. Saxe Commins and Robert N. Linscott (New York: Random House, 1942), 49.

7. "Celestial Spheres," 51.

8. "Celestial Spheres," 51.

9. *Copernican Revolution,* 191.

10. *Copernican Revolution,* 192–93.

11. Arthur O. Lovejoy, *The Great Chain of Being* (Cambridge, Mass.: Harvard University Press, 1964).

12. *Copernican Revolution,* 1.

13. Francis Bacon, *Novum Organum,* in *Man and the Universe: The Philosophers of Science,* ed. Saxe Commins and Robert N. Linscott (New York: Random House, 1942), 129.

14. *Novum Organum,* 84.

15. *Novum Organum,* 141.

16. *Novum Organum,* 123.

17. *Novum Organum,* 99.

18. *Novum Organum,* 89.

19. Genevieve Lloyd, *The Man of Reason: "Male" and "Female" in Western Philosophy* (Minneapolis: University of Minnesota Press, 1984), 10–12.

20. René Descartes, *The Discourse on Method,* in *Descartes's Philosophical Writings,* trans. N. K. Smith (New York: Modern Library, 1958), 97.

21. *Discourse on Method,* 103.

22. *Discourse on Method,* 181.

23. *Discourse on Method,* 183.

24. *Discourse on Method,* 93.

25. Isaac Newton, *Mathematical Principles of Natural Philosophy,* ed. F. Cajori (Berkeley: University of California Press, 1946), xviii.

26. A. Robert Caponigri, *A History of Western Philosophy: Philosophy from the Renaissance to the Romantic Age* (Notre Dame, Ind.: University of Notre Dame Press, 1963), 295.

27. David Hume, *A Treatise of Human Nature,* ed. L. A. Selby-Bigge (Oxford: Oxford University Press, 1978), 469.

28. Friedrich Nietzsche, *On the Genealogy of Morals* (New York: Vintage, 1967), 155.

29. Hannah Arendt, *The Human Condition* (New York: Anchor, 1959), 234–36.

30. Reinhart Koselleck, *Critique and Crisis: Enlightenment and the Pathogenesis of Modern Society* (Cambridge, Mass.: MIT Press, 1988).

Additional Readings

Arendt, Hannah. *The Human Condition.* New York: Anchor, 1959.

Blumenberg, Hans. *The Legitimacy of the Modern Age.* Cambridge, Mass.: MIT Press, 1987.

Blumenberg, Hans. *The Genesis of the Copernican World.* Cambridge, Mass.: MIT Press, 1987.

Horkheimer, Max, and Adorno, Theodor W. *The Dialectic of the Enlightenment.* New York: Continuum, 1972.

Koyré, Alexandre. *From the Closed World to the Infinite Universe.* Baltimore: Johns Hopkins University Press, 1982.

Kuhn, Thomas S. *The Copernican Revolution: Planetary Astronomy in the Development of Western Thought.* Cambridge, Mass.: Harvard University Press, 1985.

Lindberg, David C. *The Beginnings of Western Science* (Chicago: University of Chicago Press, 1992).

Lloyd, Genevieve. *The Man of Reason: "Male" and "Female" in Western Philosophy.* Minneapolis: University of Minnesota Press, 1984.

Spragens, Thomas A. Jr. *The Irony of Liberal Reasoning.* Chicago: University of Chicago Press, 1981.

 Inventors of Ideas Online

Visit http://politicalscience.wadsworth.com/tannenbaum2 for links related to material in this chapter, including the full texts of *On the Revolution of the Celestial Spheres, Novum Organum, Discourse on Method,* and *Mathematical Principles of Natural Philosophy.*

12

HOBBES: SECURING PEACE

INTRODUCTION

When the great plague of 1665 was followed by the great fire of London in 1666, a committee of the English Parliament investigated whether Hobbes's "godless" book, *Leviathan,* might have been responsible for this sign of heavenly displeasure. He endured the inquiry, which ended without any charges being brought against him, but a frightened Hobbes never published again during his lifetime.

The English philosopher Thomas Hobbes (1588–1679) was a prudent man. The very opposite of a tough, rugged hero, Hobbes recognized his own sense of human frailty and insecurity and turned it into a virtue. He prided himself on his timidity as others did on their courage. The product of a premature birth, he came into the world during the threat of attack on England by the formidable Spanish Armada. He later wrote that "fear and I were born twins," and it is clear that fear of violent death dominated his life and work. The danger posed to England by the Spanish Armada was cancelled by an act of nature, when a violent storm wrecked a substantial part of the Spanish fleet. But there were other events in Hobbes's life that helped feed his sense of insecurity even while he coped by applying a brilliant intellect to the problems that faced him and his world.

His father, an incompetent minister, deserted the family when Hobbes was quite young. Hobbes showed an early talent for learning, which was recognized by an uncle. Able to read and write at age four, he entered Oxford University at fifteen, graduated five years later, and spent the rest of his life as a teacher and author. As tutor to the son of an aristocratic family, Hobbes traveled on the European continent and met some of the great scientists and philosophers of his age, including Galileo, Bacon, and Descartes.[1] Although best known today for works on politics and the law, Hobbes also wrote on science, mathematics, and religious topics.[2]

A quiet man, Hobbes lived a rather sheltered life. He had no wife, held no political office, occupied no academic position. He seemed only to want enough peace and security to pursue his scholarly interests. Yet those interests led him to take controversial positions on the great political issues of his time, and thus brought him to engage the world around him despite his efforts to be both scholarly and neutral.

Among the crises that provoked his interest (and, very likely, his fear) were two wars. One, on the European continent, was the devastating Thirty Years' War, fought over religious and territorial issues. England's entanglement in this conflict led to a second, civil war, the one with which *Leviathan* was most directly concerned. The issues involved were religious and political as well as social and economic. The major opposing political parties were the English Parliament (particularly its lower branch, the House of Commons) on one hand, and the monarch, King Charles I, on the other. They fought over three issues that ultimately could not be resolved peacefully.

The first issue, religious freedom, had, on one side, the Anglican Church of England and its head, King Charles I. On the other side were the independent Protestant sects, such as Congregationalists and Presbyterians, which were supported by a majority in the Commons. They criticized the Anglican Church, the state religion, for being too close in organization and liturgy to Roman Catholicism. They also rejected the claim of Charles I to rule by divine right, or direct authority from God. Divine right included the power to prescribe the official religion for all Englishmen and denied people's right to freely worship as they individually chose.

The second, political issue involved the unwritten English Constitution. Two major institutions of government had evolved out of the medieval experience, an executive, headed by the monarch, and a legislative body, Parliament. The issue was one of sovereignty: Where did the ultimate political authority for deciding critical questions such as religious freedom lie, with king or Parliament?

In the third problem area, social and economic issues were interrelated. A growing middle class was excluded from a government dominated by the feudal landowning aristocracy whose roots lay in medieval relationships between king and vassal. The middle class wanted greater political representation in Parliament, where such key issues as how taxes were apportioned between the classes were decided.

There was considerable overlap between those who were members of the middle class, the Protestant dissenters and the supporters of the Parliamentary (Commons) party. On the other side, the upper-class Anglican supporters of the monarchy tended to unite. When the opposing parties could not resolve their differences peaceably, civil war erupted.

The English Civil War was marked by the sort of violence and loss of life and property so vividly depicted in Hobbes's description of the state of nature in *Leviathan*. In the end, the Parliamentary side was victorious, and King Charles I was executed. The winning army established a religious, Puritan-dominated dictatorship under its general, Oliver Cromwell. However, this dictatorship did not last. Shortly after Cromwell died, the English restored the monarchy under King Charles II, son of the executed ruler. The timid Hobbes survived all this turmoil, and died peacefully in his bed at age ninety-one.

HOBBES'S METHOD

Hobbes's understanding of politics was influenced by the spirit of scientific investigation that prevailed during his lifetime. By the seventeenth century, this spirit had developed into a full-fledged revolution, due to discoveries by such scientists as Galileo and Bacon. There was a strong increase in the empirical study of physical bodies, earthly and heavenly. Scientists challenged ancient and widely accepted dogma about the universe. They rejected assertions by classical writers, particularly Aristotle's teleology, which was promoted by religious leaders and taught in the leading universities as scientific fact, and they favored knowledge that was discoverable without the aid of Aristotle, church, or Bible. Galileo's evidence, supporting the Copernican view, showed a universe with the sun at its center. Motion, not rest, was the natural state of heavenly and earthly bodies, which continued to move until blocked by some obstacle. The new scientific method proceeded by reducing each body investigated to its simplest elements, or motions, and examining the conditions under which certain consequences, or other motions, occurred. According to the scientists, combining these results could explain more complex motions.

Hobbes brought this new method to his discussions of politics, and *Leviathan* presents the scientific foundation for the best political organization he could conceive, based on his awareness of both the physics and political psychology of his time. It treats all life as matter in motion. Matter, or individual bodies, move about in a world where all things are equally regarded as physical objects that can be studied scientifically. Humans, goats, pocket watches, the heavens, and all else in creation can be explained by basic motions (or laws) from which other, more complex motions (or laws) stem. Hobbes's method thus reduces society to its elemental motions and then explains political behavior in terms of the motions that move those elements. Once the simple elements are known, complex political structures can be understood.

Correct terminology, the right definition of terms used for things being studied, was important to Hobbes. He believed that it duplicated the precision of geometry, which was key to the success of the natural scientists whose example he wanted to follow:

> Seeing that truth consists in the right ordering of names in our affirmations, a man that seeks precise truth had need to remember what every name he uses stands for and to place it accordingly, or else he will find himself entangled in words as a bird in lime twigs, the more he struggles the more belimed. And therefore in geometry, which is the only science it has pleased God hitherto to bestow on mankind, men begin at settling the significations of their word which settling of significations they call definitions and place them in the beginning of their reckoning.[3]

Hobbes is concerned about definitions because he thinks they are the route to scientific theory, or the words that correctly represent the physical world, and thus the soundest basis for political practice. Using accurate terms also helps people avoid "the errors which are brought into the Church from the entities and essences of Aristotle," which led people away from obedience to authority and into civil war.[4] This stance reflects Hobbes's nominalism. He holds that there are no essences, such as the soul, or pure truth, or virtue. The collective names given to objects such as tables, roses, and human beings are abstractions, arbitrary symbols for what individual things have in common. So references to such intangibles as souls, truths, or virtues are meaningless words, or what Machiavelli had called *phantoms of the mind*.[5]

HUMAN NATURE

Hobbes's scientific approach also influences his view of human nature. Human nature is, to him, simply a particular aspect of nature itself, and can thus be best understood by applying the same method as one would to the natural world.

Leviathan discusses human nature from the perspective of the individual, the basic building block of Hobbes's political universe. The individual is impelled by a singular motive force:

> I put for a general inclination of all mankind a perpetual and restless desire of power after power that ceases only in death. And the cause of this is not always that a man hopes for a more intensive delight than he has already attained to, or that he cannot be content with a moderate power, but because he cannot assure the power and means to live well which he has present without the acquisition of more.[6]

The individual, as the center of Hobbes's concern, is treated as an isolated being. This isolation has a clear psychological basis, rooted in three motives. First, all individuals are amorally selfish and controlled by their hedonistic desires and physical appetites. They are absorbed in their personal interests as they compete for scarce or limited goods such as wealth. Second, they seek power or domination of others to protect themselves and their goods. This is due to what Hobbes calls diffidence, or mistrust of others. Finally, they desire glory, the good opinion of others which makes them seem superior.

These passions direct the mind and spur voluntary actions. But before people act they first weigh pros and cons using reason. Reason, then, is passion's guide, enabling people to find pleasure, or what Hobbes calls felicity, and avoid pain by securing power. If passion tells individuals what they want, reason gives them practical advice on how to get it. Material appetites, therefore, are the simplest elements or motions that move us toward desires or away from aversions. The "restless desire" for power brings individuals into conflict with each other, while the hope to "assure the power to live well" and without constant fear leads them away from conflict and toward seeking peace.

Each individual is just a complex collection of these basic physical and psychological motions or motives. Larger entities, wholes, or collectives are merely the sum of their individual parts. Thus governments are aggregates of individual elements, and politics is the sum of these individuals' motives. Consequently, unlike most animals in nature, from ants to zebras, each human's private good differs from the common good. The common good is the sum total of many private motives, and it is to be achieved through mobilizing these individual motives.[7]

STATE OF NATURE

Hobbes's view of human nature is modern, materialistic, and individualistic. He was the first philosopher to relate these characteristics to an explicit state of nature. This state is "a time of war where every man is enemy to every man," and a "time wherein men live without other security than what their own strength and their own invention shall furnish them withal." The state of nature he depicts need not have ever existed; rather, it describes Hobbes's assumption of what life would be like without government. Hobbes's description is likely derived, at least in part, from his observations of England during the Civil Wars:

> In such condition there is no place for industry, because the fruit thereof is uncertain: and consequently no culture of the earth; no navigation nor use of the commodities that may be imported by the sea; no commodious building; no instruments of moving and removing such things as require much force; no knowledge of the face of the earth; no account of time; no arts; no letters; no society; and, which is worst of all, continual fear and danger of violent death; and the life of man solitary, poor, nasty, brutish, and short.[8]

The completely free reign of appetitive individuals leads to the most extreme results: friction between bodies that produces a state of violent anarchy, a war "of every man against every man." And "as the nature of foul weather lies not in a shower or two but in an inclination of many days together, so the nature of war consists not in actual fighting but in the known disposition thereto during all the time there is no assurance to the contrary."[9] In other words, potential violence can be as dangerous as actual war.

The state of nature is not only a condition of violence, but also one of "an anarchy of meanings," of many subjective understandings. Political terminology is in chaos, as there is no authority to pronounce correct definitions. A steady increase in disagreement over basic meanings led to the outbreak of civil war, with Protestant sects "creating a state of nature in religious affairs" and Parliament doing likewise in the secular arena by criticizing the sovereign.[10]

In this state of nature, each individual behaves like a solitary beast who feels no natural obligation to others and is guided by two basic urges, survival and self-satisfaction. Ungoverned by any higher moral law, there is no greatest good; good and evil are defined in relative terms through the two basic urges. Relative good is the name people give to pleasures and whatever strengthens their advantage over others. Relative evil is a name for weakness and pain. Thus relative good is found in the satisfaction of appetites and accumulation of power, relative evil in the constant possibility of violent death. In this amoral state of nature, each person has a natural right to self-preservation, "and consequently of doing anything which, in his own judgment and reason, he shall conceive to be the aptest means thereunto."[11] Any means used for self-defense is acceptable, and this same principle applies to satisfaction of appetites because each individual is the final authority or judge.

Natural right argues against inequality. All individuals are roughly equal by nature, both in their hope for satisfaction of appetites and in their ability to kill each other:

> Nature has made men so equal in the faculties of the body and the mind as that, though there be found one man sometimes manifestly stronger in body or of quicker mind than another, yet, when all is reckoned together the difference between man and man is not so considerable as that one man can thereupon claim to himself any benefit to which another may not pretend as well as he. For as to the strength of the body, the weakest has strength enough to kill the strongest, either by secret machination or by confederacy with others that are in the same danger as himself.[12]

As a result, everyone in the state of nature lives in equal fear of the relatively supreme evil: death at the hands of others. Everyone is insecure because there is no common power, no government. There is a certain irony in such a situation, where "having an unlimited right men enjoy nothing. Enjoyment presupposed security, yet security was incompatible with liberty."[13]

BASIS OF GOVERNMENT AND POLITICAL OBLIGATION

In the description of the terrible consequences of life in a state of nature, Hobbes shows his clear hostility to this condition. To enable people to secure their lives and possessions they must escape from this uncertain and fearful state. Hobbes asks what can bring isolated, independent, antisocial individuals together. What is the basic axiom of practical reason (or calculating prudence) on the basis of which individuals can be united?

Modern natural law holds the answer for Hobbes: reason applied to passion. One set of passions, self-defense and the quest for power, results in violence, but it is checked by another set, fear of death and the desire for safety, which prompts individuals to search for a way out of the impasse. It is reason that enables people to both restrain those passions that lead to violence, and recognize the underlying identity of interests that moves them to escape the chaotic state of nature.

Hobbes's version of natural law is modern in that it applies to selfish, amoral individuals who have no natural obligation to their fellow humans. The corollary to this is that it rejects any higher, objective moral law, such as the one that led to Plato's natural justice, or Aristotle's natural community, or Christian salvation. It is also modern in that it is power-oriented; following it maximizes one's power to satisfy appetites while minimizing the possibility of violent death. Therefore,

> the first and fundamental law of nature . . . is to seek peace and follow it. . . . From this fundamental law of nature, by which men are commanded to endeavor peace is derived this second law: that a man be willing, when others are so too, as far forth as for peace and defense of himself he shall think it necessary, to lay down this right to all things, and be contented with so much liberty against other men as he would allow other men against himself.[14]

To give up one's natural right to self-defense in exchange for peace is a rational exercise in securing power, since peace will ensure a future in which each is most able to pursue self-interest in a nonviolent environment. And the surest basis for peace, given Hobbes's view of human nature, is the "greatest of human powers": equal individuals united by voluntary consent. Through a covenant, or political contract, they must freely consent to surrender their natural right to self-defense. This right is transferred to a common power, to a sovereign authority that is placed in "one man" or "one assembly of men" empowered to act "in those things which concern the common peace and safety" in the name of the whole people.[15]

Thus the sovereign is at the heart of government. This sovereign must be able to use force because people do not change their natures when leaving the state of nature, so "covenants without the sword are but words, and of no strength to secure a man at all."[16] Also, the sovereign must be one. A problem during the Civil War was the multiplicity of those claiming to be sovereign. Furthermore, turning from history to logic, multiple powers are contrary to the basis of a valid contract, as they cannot provide one clear voice to settle disputes. When several claim authority to define the meaning of the law, confusion, instability, and violence, the very consequences the contract was instituted to prevent, are bound to occur. Multiple sovereigns are as bad as no sovereign at all.

The sovereign authority assumes what was, in nature, an individual right, namely, to determine the circumstances under which force is to be used, and all other means necessary for the pursuit of peace:

> A commonwealth is said to be instituted when a multitude of men do agree and covenant, every one with every one, that to whatsoever man or assembly of men shall be given by the major part the right to present the person of them all—that is to say, to be their representative—every one, as well he that voted for it as he that voted against it, shall authorize all the actions and judgments of that man or assembly of men in the same manner as if they were his own, to the end to live peaceably among themselves and be protected against other men.[17]

Thus once a commonwealth is instituted, the minority is obligated to follow the will of the majority in submitting to the sovereign. All must obey the law the sovereign commands, because without those commands life would be less tolerable, and resistance to the sovereign diminishes the level of peace in society. The safety of each is predicated on the obedience of all.

Hobbes clearly views government as an artificial creation with a practical purpose. It is a complex machine made up of similar machines, of individuals propelled by personal motives reacting to each other in a different manner than they would in a state of nature. It is a means, not an end. Its "good" is relative to how well it achieves its pragmatic purpose of civil peace. Yet, although its source is artificial and its ambition practical, its presence is essential. Government is a basic necessity and a symbol of our victory over nature.

SOVEREIGN AUTHORITY

When discussing the sovereign, Hobbes tends to use language that is ambiguous, often referring to the sovereign as "he," which reflects a personal preference for one individual, and a male. But the term can, for Hobbes, also indicate an assembly or body. Therefore, sovereign does not necessarily signify an individual who occupies an office, but it does mean the office or institution. In general, it denotes the government; in particular, the source of final decision-making authority in government.[18] The sovereign, as the title *Leviathan* tells us, is a mortal god: mortal because the office is the purely artificial creation of consenting individuals, godlike because the necessary powers conferred on it are absolute, indivisible, and perpetual.

All sovereigns, whether one, few, or many, are representatives "of all and every one of the multitude."[19] As representatives, they are agents of the populace. The people, in turn, are expected to identify with and agree to all the acts of the sovereign. At the same time, the sovereign is also the agent of the contract to which the people agree—all its power and its legitimate authority come from the political contract. Neither force alone nor any claim of a natural or divine source can be invoked to legitimize a sovereign. Without a contract, there is no sovereign. With a contract, no other justification is necessary, as consent gives the sovereign all the legitimacy required.

The sovereign, as a sovereign, is not a party to the contract. As the artificial creation of consenting individuals, a sovereign has no legitimate existence outside of or prior to its establishment. Therefore, the sovereign has no powers unless they are conveyed by the contract. And the chief power is to do all that is necessary to keep the peace.

A creature of the contract, the sovereign can make no promises to the individual contractors in advance of an agreement. Once a contract is created, the sovereign is the source of all guarantees, all law, and all rights. Sovereigns as sovereigns (i.e., in their official capacity) must be free to act as they see fit. No limit may be placed by others on this authority because "in those things which concern the common peace and safety" the sovereign must have all power needed to prevent breaches of that peace. They interpret the basic rules of governance that reside in the natural laws, even as they "are all subject to the laws of nature, because such laws be divine and cannot by any man or commonwealth be abrogated."[20] Practically speaking, the only limits that can be placed on the sovereign, beyond those specified in the contract, must be self-imposed.

Hobbes recognizes the risk in such a broad grant of sovereignty, as well as the peril in its absence. Whether sovereign power is given to one ruler, or to a few aristocrats, or to many in a popular assembly, it

> is as great as possibly men can be imagined to make it. And though of so unlimited a power men may fancy many evil consequences, yet the consequences of the want of it, which is perpetual war of every man against his neighbor, are much worse.[21]

Furthermore, if sovereigns have an interest equal to that of the people in preserving their power in order to keep the peace, they also have an official interest in limiting their power to the minimum needed to that end, since this is the ultimate source of their legitimacy.

Hobbes frequently uses religious references and arguments to bolster his political conclusions. He also grants the sovereign full authority over all religious teachings and forms of worship. The purpose of religion is fundamentally secular, to make people "more apt to obedience, laws, peace, charity, and civil society." Christian salvation comes from two simple virtues: religious faith and obedience to natural law. Beyond this, nothing is required of a people who would be good citizens of a "Christian Commonwealth." When power-seeking Catholic and Protestant sectarian clergy demand a "government of religion," they only serve to promote disunity, sedition, and civil war.[22]

NATURAL AND CIVIL LAW

To Hobbes, "the measure of good and evil actions is the civil law," not merely the momentary whims of the rulers. Furthermore, "The law of nature and the civil law contain each other and are of equal extent."[23] Although the former applies in the state of nature and government creates the latter, neither may legitimately violate the other. Without reference to natural law, civil law is incomplete; it needs natural law as a source of justification (or justice). However, natural law is inadequate to secure peace, as the state of nature amply demonstrates.

Under the contract, civil law is the command of the sovereign. Natural law is knowable, but unwritten, while civil (or positive) law must be framed in such a way that those commanded can know "what is contrary and what is not contrary to the rule." Although all law so commanded is by definition "just," this assumes that it falls within the legitimate contractual power of the government.

> A good law is that which is needful for the good of the people, and withal perspicuous. For the use of laws, which are but rules authorized, is not to

bind the people from all voluntary actions but to direct and keep them in such a motion as not to hurt themselves by their own impetuous desires, rashness, or indiscretion—as hedges are set, not to stop travellers, but to keep them in their way. And therefore a law that is not needful, having not the true end of a law, is not good. A law may be conceived to be good when it is for the benefit of the sovereign though it be not necessary for the people; but that is not so. For the good of the sovereign and people cannot be separated.[24]

Thus every civil law must have as its purpose the promotion of the public interest; that is, it must help secure the peace. The idea that law must be in the public interest is the corollary of Hobbes's stricture that through consent to the contract all members of the community become authors of the law, even if they do not personally consent to it.

The law must be framed so that it compels maximum peaceful obedience by frightening potential criminals who would breach the contract through illegal actions. At the same time, no one is to be punished for acts unrelated to known law, and the severity of punishment must always be equally administered so that it fits the magnitude of the crime.

Thus, although sovereign power is absolute, its purpose must always be to regulate all those parts of society necessary to secure peace. No act, and no law, may legitimately exceed the fundamental purpose of the political contract. Natural law and its derivative propositions, based on a clear understanding of human nature as it is, serve as guides to the scope and limits of sovereign command. Since the person or persons who exercise sovereignty are thus effectively limited if they would claim legitimacy, their power is in fact shared in a number of ways. What Hobbes argues for is clarity of authority, centralized in one source, not a grant of total authority or arbitrary power.

LIBERTY

As all consenting parties are by nature fundamentally equal, all legitimate acts of the sovereign must be applied equally to every member of the body politic. This includes liberty, which encompasses "all those things the right whereof cannot by covenant be transferred."[25] No contract, no sovereign, and no law can repeal the natural right of each individual to self-preservation, or life. This right is surrendered only conditionally, in exchange for a surer guarantee, when people consent to the contract; its ultimate protection still rests with each person.

The right to self-defense may be activated if a sovereign is no longer able to enforce the contract by maintaining the peace. If personal security is threatened, people are then, by definition, back in a state of nature with no other protection but their individual capacity for self-defense. Thus "no man is obliged, when the protection of the law fails, not to protect himself by the best means he can."[26] Self-defense may also be invoked by any individual whose life is threatened by sovereign action, such as a criminal who is condemned to death. When imperiled, all subjects are at liberty to defend themselves, even against the lawful authority. In this, Hobbes provides for an individual right of resistance to government.

Beyond resistance in the face of threat to life is the idea that sovereign authority is established to enable a number of opportunities to flourish. Among these are industry, agriculture, arts, letters, and society. Unlike natural right, these are absent in the state of nature, but securing them may be one of the reasons people seek peace and enter into the contract. Hobbes raises the question of whether sovereign action that neglects such opportunities, or is hostile to them, may also be regarded as a violation of the contract justifying resistance. His answer is that, as in the case of self-defense, each individual is the sole judge of whether to oppose the sovereign. The basis of such judgment is whether the state of nature seems preferable to an inadequate ruler. Although Hobbes appears to favor the latter, his political philosophy does not clearly preclude an individual from choosing the alternative. For Hobbes, then, government is the arena for the inevitable ongoing struggle between ruler and people. The sovereign can remain in power only as long as the populace thinks that resistance is a greater evil than obedience.

Beyond the right to resist, the liberty of each person is negative; it depends "on the silence of the law."[27] This residual liberty is found in all those circumstances for which the law neither commands nor prohibits action, including any economic, social, or cultural activities consistent with peace and security. In all such matters, individuals are free to act or not act as they see fit.

CITIZENSHIP, CLASS, AND GENDER

To anyone who focuses on the terrible majesty of Hobbes's sovereign, all who consent to the contract become subjects once government is in place. But those who point to limits on sovereign power and potential individual liberties that flow from those limits, particularly in the context of a government by the many, might find a role for active citizens. Hobbes's preference is for citizenship, but he is also a realist. Maxims like Machiavelli's apply here. If the populace that enters into a contract is thoughtless (i.e., behaves like Machiavelli's apathetic masses), then the sovereign, especially if one person, may act in an illegitimate way. This would, by definition, exceed the terms of the contract, but in this case the sovereign might well face little or no public opposition. However, the people might also be what Hobbes calls *reckoning*, that is, behaving like Machiavelli's virtuous elite.[28] Then the absolute sovereign must also be a limited ruler, having absolute control of decision-making authority within the scope of that limited power, but exercising no more power than is necessary to keep the peace. Reckoning citizens serve as checks on the illegitimate exercise of political power and are free to seek their own goals privately. Hobbes's point, like Machiavelli's, is that this outcome does not happen automatically, even though a legitimate political contract is in place. Only active, alert, informed, thoughtful citizenship can make it happen.

Who are these citizens? If all are fundamentally equal, then differences of gender or social rank cannot be translated into political subordination, so Hobbes seems to support class and gender equality. His position advances a radical outlook where such differences appear irrelevant to considerations of citizenship. On gender, Hobbes explicitly says,

> whereas some have attributed the dominion to the man only as being of the more excellent sex, they misreckon in it. For there is not always that difference of strength or prudence between the man and the woman as that right can be determined without war. . . . But the question lies now in the state of mere nature where there are supposed no laws of matrimony, no laws for the education of the children, but the law of nature and the natural inclination of the sexes, one to another and to their children. In this condition of mere nature, either the parents between themselves dispose of the dominion over the child by contract or do not dispose thereof at all.[29]

In other words, gender equality originates in nature, where there are at first parents but no marriage, just as there are no other long-term or legal arrangements. However, because "no man can obey two masters," only one parent can rule a child, and ordinarily this is the mother. It is for her to decide whether the child lives or dies, whether (as with the Amazons) it is turned over to males or kept by the female tribe, and how it shall be raised. In such a situation, we might assume that women, like all men, are free to consent to a contract and come under the sovereign as equals. To the contrary, though, Hobbes inserts an unwritten and unequal marriage contract, which precedes the political contract. Women are like servants, and both elect to subordinate themselves to men in the household; and this subservience continues under government.

To attempt to explain this, Hobbes says a family, like a people, can have but one sovereign. The ruler of the family is the male, the husband, the father. He is the master who rules his servants, including his wife. Indeed, it is men, not women—masters, not servants—who agree to leave the state of nature and establish the sovereign. Husbands and masters are authorized to consent in the name of their wives and domestics, who do not have an independent voice in the matter.[30] Thus, because of his position that all legitimate power rests on consent, Hobbes rejects any original argument supporting inferiority. But upon entering the family, women and servants are somehow to abandon their natural equality and accept an inferior position. If women and servants are equal to masterly men in the state of nature, are they not as rational or reckoning, as able to reflect on, reconsider, and renegotiate the agreement as fits their personal interest? Once the contract is operational, does the family replace the individual as the source of consent? If so, what does this say about Hobbes's vaunted individualism? Clearly, Hobbes fails to carry his egalitarian argument to its logical conclusion, and thus leaves women and servants subordinate, both in the family and under government. It is as if he suddenly abandons logical thought and unthinkingly accepts the typical prejudices of his time.[31]

FORMS OF GOVERNMENT

Hobbes's views on citizenship are related to the basic forms of government he treats. He distinguishes among three forms, each of which has a number of variations. Of the three basic forms, two are legitimate and the other illegitimate.

Commonwealth "by institution" is a legitimate form of government, initiated by consent of free and equal individuals to a political contract. Seeking to leave the state of nature, they agree to give up the natural right to self-defense and create a sovereign to govern them. "This done, the multitude so united in one person is called a COMMONWEALTH, in Latin CIVITAS."[32] It establishes rule by the sovereign through lawful institutions and procedures.

Altering Aristotle's terminology only slightly to fit modern tastes, Hobbes says that the legitimate sovereign of a commonwealth may be one (monarchy), few (aristocracy), or many (democracy). His personal preference is the rule of one because the authority of the monarch is the most unified and thus best able to keep the peace. But Hobbes is not a royalist who supports the authority of kings to rule by divine right. He favors a strong sovereign, but one who rules by consent, not fiat.

Hobbes also speaks of commonwealth by acquisition, or domain, "where the sovereign power is acquired by force," either through rebellion or war. This form of government is also legitimate so long as those conquered consent to it.[33] However, without consent to a valid contract, power acquired by force is not legitimate but a form of despotism.

Hobbes says that "slaves have no obligation at all" to obey a despot who comes to power by conquest and rules without, or contrary to, a contract.[34] Consent is always required, otherwise everyone is still in a state of nature. This position is merely an extension of the idea that people's obligation to a sovereign extends no further than the ruler's ability to protect them.

CONCLUSION

The central philosophical question for Hobbes is, "on what basis could the practice of government be conducted once society was no longer a community?"[35] In answering this question, he reinforces the foundation of modern politics, differentiating it from ancient and medieval philosophies by uniting absolutism and consent. Hobbes's early-modern perspective is evident at the outset in his method. Unlike such predecessors as the Protestant reformers, Hobbes takes his cues from the scientific revolution of his time. His advocacy of absolutism stems from the logic of his political reasoning but leads to conclusions in which consent limits absolute government.

Original consent activates the contract that creates the sovereign, and continuing consent sustains its legitimacy. Government need be only as strong as necessary to protect the law-abiding, its proper role being limited to providing a peaceful context in which citizens can seek whatever higher goods they define for themselves. Such private goals are not the business of government. Rather, they are the choice and concern of individuals exercising their equal natural rights, their liberty. Once the issue of peace is resolved, aggregate politics dominates as individuals take priority over any collective.

Hobbes was the first of the modern contract theorists. Prior to Hobbes, Protestant theologians and certain minor philosophers used the idea of the contract as a weapon to promote religious freedom. But with Hobbes, it becomes a tool for individuals seeking freedom in general, and freedom can be political and personal as well as religious. Thus any liberty not inconsistent with peace becomes permissible.

Leviathan is based on the prospect of the most extreme outcome. The sovereign exceeding (or breaking) the contract can only be stopped by individual resistance that, if it becomes widespread, plunges everyone back into the state of nature. Hobbes's contract is political, resting on a direct move to government from the natural state.

Hobbes insists on linking the possibility of a return to the state of nature to the necessity for servants to obey masters and wives their husbands. He thus advocates class and gender inequality in family and government, and his deficient logic in this case is evident. At the same time, his model has utility for understanding some perilous aspects of the current international scene. Nation-states today often relate to each other as Hobbes's individuals did in nature. As long as this situation continues, he warns, warfare will persist.

When he was almost halfway through his masterpiece, Hobbes wondered whether *Leviathan* might not be as useless as Plato's *Republic*. However, he quickly recovered, believing that the intellectual demands he would put on the sovereign were nothing like the burdens Plato placed on his philosopher-kings. Yet, just as he raised this issue, one might question whether he, like Plato, really meant all he said; or did his inconsistencies, contradictions, and ambiguities perhaps imply that he was less interested in setting forth a scientific blueprint for government than in raising questions about balancing individual liberty with social order?[36]

Notes

1. In addition to serving as secretary to Bacon for several years, Hobbes was part of a discussion group that included the scientific pioneers Galileo and Gassendi. Hobbes's life is treated in Richard Peters, *Hobbes* (Baltimore: Penguin, 1956), esp. 13–44; and more recently in Arnold Rogow, *Thomas Hobbes: Radical in the Service of Reaction* (New York: Norton, 1986).

2. Hobbes's English writings were collected in the nineteenth century in eleven volumes, his Latin works a few years later in five volumes. Chief among these was his most famous book, *Leviathan*, published in 1651. An earlier, longer work, *Elements of Law*, contained the basic ideas found in his later political philosophy and was completed in 1640. The political section of the *Elements* was published as *De Cive* (on citizenship), the more scientific part was called *De Corpore* (of matter), and the final part was titled *De Homine* (of man, a discussion of human nature). *Behemoth, or the Long Parliament*, a history of English politics and civil war, was written in 1668 but not printed until after his death.

3. Thomas Hobbes, *Leviathan,* ed. H. W. Schneider (New York: Bobbs-Merrill, 1958), ch. 4.

4. *Leviathan,* intro.

5. Note that Hobbes, despite such agreement, was opposed to Machiavelli's less scientific propositions, e.g., "that adequate generalizations could be constructed from experience" or "that political action would be more certain of success if it imitated the methods of ancient heroes." Sheldon S. Wolin, *Politics and Vision: Continuity and Innovation in Western Political Thought* (Boston: Little, Brown, 1960), 252.

6. *Leviathan,* ch. 11. For a thorough account of the subject, see Arnold W. Green, *Hobbes and Human Nature* (New Brunswick, N.J.: Transaction, 1993).

7. C. B. Macpherson, *The Political Theory of Possessive Individualism: Hobbes to Locke* (Oxford: Clarendon, 1962), thinks Hobbes's view of human nature was crafted for individuals entering a market economy: restless, acquisitive bodies engaged as equals and contracting with each other in the selfish pursuit of personal wealth.

8. *Leviathan,* ch. 13.

9. *Leviathan,* ch. 13.

10. *Politics and Vision,* 258.

11. *Leviathan,* ch. 14.

12. *Leviathan,* ch. 13.

13. *Politics and Vision,* 262.

14. *Leviathan,* ch. 14.

15. *Leviathan,* chs. 10, 17. A number of commentators call Hobbes's political contract a social contract, but as Hobbes is narrowly concerned with the creation of government the term *social contract* is best reserved for Locke and Rousseau. See http://politicalscience.wadsworth.com/tannenbaum2 for a link to an illustration of how Hobbes's political contract originates and the consequences of its termination. But also see Jean Hampton, *Hobbes and the Social Contract Tradition* (New York: Cambridge University Press, 1988).

16. *Leviathan,* ch. 17. Yet is it not curious, even paradoxical, that a law of nature results in an artificial sovereign? A further paradox is that the practical reason of Hobbes is rooted in irrationality, since what the sovereign declares is ultimately grounded on force, not persuasion.

17. *Leviathan,* ch. 18.

18. One way to know who the sovereign should be, Hobbes says, is that we can "see him absolutely able to govern his own family . . . "; *Leviathan,* ch. 30. However, not only does *Leviathan* speak of "him or them on whom the sovereign power is conferred" (ch. 18), but chapter 30 is titled "Of the Office of the Sovereign Representative," an institutional reference rather than a personal one.

19. *Leviathan,* ch. 19.

20. *Leviathan,* ch. 21.

21. *Leviathan,* ch. 20.

22. *Leviathan,* ch. 12. In his consideration of the role of religion, Hobbes discusses over 100 topics, including the Bible, blasphemy, baptism, excommunication, hell, Satan, and eternity. He finds authority in the Bible for the sovereign as head of church as well as state, and defends the Church of England against attacks by Roman Catholic and Protestant sectarian clergy; see esp. chs. 18, 22, 43.

23. *Leviathan,* chs. 26, 29.

24. *Leviathan,* chs. 26, 30.

25. *Leviathan,* ch. 21. A right is a moral claim on government, while liberty is the actual state of affairs that implements that claim.

26. *Leviathan,* ch. 27.

27. *Leviathan,* ch. 21.

28. *Leviathan,* ch. 2.

29. *Leviathan,* ch. 20.

30. Carole Pateman, *The Sexual Contract* (Stanford, Calif.: Stanford University Press, 1988).

31. One writer charges him with a "fatal inconsistency." Diana Coole, *Women in Political Theory: From Ancient Misogyny to Contemporary Feminism* (Boulder, Colo.: Lynne Rienner, 1988), 83.

32. *Leviathan,* ch. 17.
33. *Leviathan,* ch. 20.
34. *Leviathan,* ch. 20.
35. *Politics and Vision,* 241.
36. See Richard Flathman, *Thomas Hobbes: Skepticism, Individuality, and Chastened Politics* (Thousand Oaks, Calif.: Sage, 1993), which argues that Hobbes's purpose was to show how we could live with such tensions as authority and freedom, obligation, and individuality. For a different reading, see Leo Strauss, *The Political Philosophy of Hobbes: Its Basis and Its Genesis* (Chicago: University of Chicago Press, 1952). An interesting discussion of Hobbes's influence on the United States may be found in Frank M. Coleman, *Hobbes and America: Exploring the Constitutional Founding* (Toronto: University of Toronto Press, 1977).

Additional Readings

(* indicates alternative viewpoint)

Flathman, Richard. *Thomas Hobbes: Skepticism, Individuality, and Chastened Politics.* Thousand Oaks, Calif.: Sage, 1993.

Green, Arnold W. *Hobbes and Human Nature.* New Brunswick, N.J.: Transaction, 1993.

*Hampton, Jean. *Hobbes and the Social Contract Tradition.* New York: Cambridge University Press, 1988.

Macpherson, C. B. *The Political Theory of Possessive Individualism: Hobbes to Locke.* Oxford: Clarendon, 1962.

Rogow, Arnold. *Thomas Hobbes: Radical in the Service of Reaction.* New York: Norton, 1986.

Slomp, Gabriella. *Thomas Hobbes and the Political Philosophy of Glory.* New York: St. Martin's, 2000.

*Strauss, Leo. *The Political Philosophy of Hobbes: Its Basis and Its Genesis.* Chicago: University of Chicago Press, 1952.

 Inventors of Ideas Online

Visit http://politicalscience.wadsworth.com/tannenbaum2 for links related to material in this chapter, including an illustration of Hobbe's political contract and the complete texts of *Leviathan* and other major works.

13

LOCKE: PROTECTING PROPERTY

INTRODUCTION

In February 1689, John Locke sailed for England after a long exile in Holland. He had fled his home, fearing for his life after being implicated in a plot against the king. Locke's return to his native soil was as grand as the Glorious Revolution of 1688 that preceded it. William of Orange, the Protestant husband of deposed King James II's eldest daughter, Mary, had come to the throne in a relatively bloodless rebellion. Locke had served the new king as advisor in Holland, and was escorting the future Queen Mary back to England. In spite of these connections, which assured him a life free of political persecution, the perennially suspicious Locke refused to acknowledge authorship of his greatest political work as long as he lived.

Although he grew up in England during the same civil war that so frightened Hobbes, John Locke (1632–1704) drew less pessimistic conclusions from his life experiences. And his greater optimism was amply reinforced by the 1688 revolution, which helped resolve key issues that had provoked civil war and set England on a new course of stability. Professionally, Locke was a teacher of philosophy and a student of medicine, two occupations ideal for the individual of his day who would avoid political involvement. However, Locke greatly admired his father, a supporter of the cause against King Charles I and an officer in the Puritan/Parliament army. Later, friendship with a government official, Lord Shaftesbury, King Charles II's closest advisor, had directly involved Locke in English politics. He had served as Shaftesbury's secretary, physician, advisor, and family tutor. When Shaftesbury was dismissed for his efforts to keep Charles II's brother from the throne, Locke had followed him to exile in Holland.[1]

Charles's brother did succeed to the throne as King James II. The new monarch was a convert to Roman Catholicism, and he used his royal position to secure equal treatment for his coreligionists, who had been denied religious freedom and were discriminated against in appointment to political office. When Parliament objected to James favoring Catholics and using royal authority alone to justify his actions, he dismissed that body. His actions cost him much establishment political support, and he lost power altogether in the Glorious Revolution. Beyond the immediate exchange of kings, a long-range result was that England became a constitutional monarchy and was never again threatened by a ruler claiming divine right.[2]

The revolution, and the constitutional monarchy it established, were finalized in parliamentary legislation. The English Bill of Rights declared the supremacy of Parliament over king. It also declared the (lower) House of Commons a freely elected body, selected by the voters, which the king could not dissolve at his will. Responding to another grievance, the Bill of Rights stated that all English citizens accused of a crime had a right to trial by jury, conducted by judges who were independent of the monarch. To promote this independent judiciary, it granted judges fixed salaries and permanent tenure during good behavior. The law thus declared illegal the sort of actions that James II had asserted as his royal right. The English king became a limited ruler.

A separate law spoke to the religious issue. The Toleration Act granted religious toleration to all believers in England, except for Catholics and Unitarians, while retaining the primary position of the Church of England.

Locke's writings address a number of these historical issues from a philosophical perspective. In particular, his foremost political work, the two *Treatises of Government*, serves as a final rejection of rule by divine right of kings and it argues against the absolute sovereignty advocated by Hobbes.[3] It also addresses such issues as constitutionalism, limited government, and the right of revolution.

LOCKE'S METHOD

Locke's approach to political questions was influenced by his medical background as well as his membership in the Royal Society, an organization of scientists. He thought the world was governed by scientific laws, by order and uniformity. He sought a purely empirical basis for human knowledge, one that followed the approach of modern science by using observation and experience.

His method of thinking about politics begins with the human mind at birth. To use a Latin phrase often identified with Locke, the mind is a *tabula rasa*, a clean slate, a "white paper void of all characters, without any ideas." People are not born with any innate ideas, such as Plato's forms or Aristotle's telos. Rather than essences planted by a divine power, individuals have potential tendencies or capacities.[4] People's minds are shaped as they grow up, and training and experience develop their potential capacity for reasoning. Locke follows Hobbes in this, claiming that ideas stem from individual experiences acting on the senses, and that subsequent actions flow from those rational ideas.

Simple concepts such as "yellow, white, heat, cold" come to individuals through their senses and as a result of observations. As they mature, they are guided by desires and past experiences of pleasure and pain. It is pleasure that leads people to act, while pain alerts them to the potential danger of acting.[5]

Still, they not only have pleasurable and painful experiences but learn from them by reflecting on experience. Thus, a baby who experiences the pleasure of its mother's nursing associates her with the pleasurable ideas of food and warmth. Alternatively, a child burned by a hot stove learns to keep its distance from that object of its pain.

More complex ideas are created by uniting these simple ideas. In this way, a moral sense develops through experience and learning. As people grow in moral awareness, they come to prefer the directives of reason over those of immediate desire. That is, the individual quest for long-range moral happiness checks and limits the inferior search for short-range appetite satisfaction.[6]

HUMAN NATURE

Those who supported the divine right of kings argued that the monarch's authority over his subjects was based on the Scriptures. Divine right established a paternal or patriarchal relationship like that between a father and his children, which resulted in hereditary, total, and permanent dependency. No subject was born free, and none could outgrow the need for the royal father figure.

Locke, of course, disagrees. His two *Treatises* differentiate political authority from other forms of dominance. While paternal power may be appropriate when exercised over children whose reason has not fully developed, it is ill-suited to rational adults. Locke's account of human nature, and the state of nature and its law, are predicated on God as lawgiver who has no role as enforcer.[7] Thus

> To understand political power aright, and derive it from its original, we must consider, what state men are naturally in, and that is, a state of perfect freedom to order their actions, and dispose of their possessions and persons, as they think fit, within the bounds of the law of nature, without asking leave, or depending on the will of any other man. A state also of equality, wherein all the power is reciprocal, no one having more than another. . . .[8]

Individuals are all born free and equal. They are also part of the larger creation of God, who directs them to the good. And humans were given reason and a conscience, or moral sense, which distinguishes them from other animals. Consequently, human nature is a potentially virtuous mix of several elements: moral, rational, egoistic, and social.

Reason, developed through experience and acting in concert with awareness of good and bad, points toward nature's moral laws. These laws, established by God, direct people to act, freely and equally, as ethical beings. As such, individuals are basically trustworthy.

Even egoism is a positive feature of human nature for Locke. Although humans are appetitive individuals who seek to satisfy desires, the insatiable quest for pleasure is not necessarily selfish. As long as the purpose is to improve oneself rather than to hurt others, the search for happiness can be moral and rational, serving as the foundation of individual freedom.[9] Social by nature, individuals are inclined to trust their fellow human beings, who are also moral, rational, and egoistic. This enables everyone to act together for common goals. It also inclines people to goals that are beneficial to others at the same time as they benefit each individually.[10]

When Locke emphasizes these essentially positive aspects of human nature he seems more optimistic than Hobbes. It is easier to see such individuals entering into a contract to protect individual freedom than those living in Hobbes's state of nature, where the primary emphasis is on mistrust and conflict. But lurking in the shadows of Locke's philosophy is a traditionally dualist view of human nature. He writes as if life is a morality play in which good and evil struggle for domination. He mostly depicts the majority as moral, suggesting that his primary audience is a virtuous and rational people with a long-range outlook, capable of maintaining freedom. However, he also sees an irrational, antisocial, immoral side. Not all people are trustworthy; some, at least, are potentially inclined to undue selfishness and apt to harm others. Locke uses this other, darker side of human nature to show the dangers and pitfalls of life, especially life in the state of nature.

STATE OF NATURE

Locke's vision of the state of nature is like Hobbes's, but it develops aspects Hobbes omitted because they were less relevant to his crisis. Although both *Treatises* were likely drafted before the Glorious Revolution of 1688,[11] Locke's concern still may be related to its outcome. Why, when the sovereign authority (James II) was deposed, wasn't England plunged back into a state of nature, as Hobbes predicted should happen? Locke begins his inquiry into this critical question with an examination of the state of nature, that is, what life would be like without government.

Agreeing with Hobbes, Locke calls the state of nature a state of perfect freedom and equality. But it is also a moral state, because of the mutual trust and respect most people have for each other and for the rights and property of others. Thus Locke at first describes a rather benevolent state of nature. However, once his theories of property and natural law are fully examined one comes to see its less attractive side. Property includes three aspects: life, liberty, and estate.[12] Life, to Locke, doesn't mean just base existence, but a life used morally, in accord with God's aim. Liberty means freedom to act, but only within the limits of natural law.

Labor Theory of Estate. In nature, all have a collective right to estate, for in the beginning God gave the earth to everyone in common to provide for their lives. Since people all began on an equal level, nobody has a God-given right to any part of the earth. Here, Locke rejects the patriarchal property arguments supporting divine right monarchy. But where then does any individual's natural right to estate, to a part of the earth, come from? How does it become a part of one's property, which individuals are free to dispose of as they see fit? Locke says that human economic equality changed in the state of nature. The explanation for how this happened is found in Locke's labor theory of estate, which presents his theory of the origin of inequality and private property. "God, when he gave the world in common to all mankind, commanded man also to labor," expecting that individuals would make the best possible use of the earth by working it.[13] They are to do so by mixing labor with the natural resources of the earth to support themselves:

> Though the earth and all inferior creatures be common to all men, yet every man has a property in his own person. This nobody has any right to but himself. The labour of his body and the work of his hands, we may say, are properly his. Whatsoever, then, he removes out of the state that nature hath provided and left it in, he hath mixed his labour with it, and joined to it something that is his own, and thereby makes it his property.[14]

This suggests that humans are by nature hard workers who cannot be satisfied unless they are toiling to transform the earth for the satisfaction of their needs. Labor is both an expression and extension of each individual's nature or personality into objects. In other words, we are what we produce, and our product is both ours and what we are.[15] Each individual has a natural right to everything personally produced because individual labor is added to nature's product.[16] Furthermore, the hardest-working are those who more accurately reflect their God-given nature. Such people deserve more, and it is just that they receive more.

Locke's labor theory of estate has two qualifications, which were inserted by God to prevent excessive greed in the state of nature. The first is that no one individual is entitled to all the land; there must be "enough, and as good left in common for others." This limitation, in the context of seventeenth-century agricultural England, was primarily a statement in opposition to arguments favoring the divine right of kings. It meant that no one person could legitimately claim ownership of all land because it was given to him directly by God.[17] The second qualification is that no individual can take more of the land or its produce than can be used before it spoils. However, this limitation becomes irrelevant when people, in the state of nature, begin to value things that do not spoil, and which, by mutual consent, they take in exchange for the useful but perishable necessities of life. The most important of these nonperishable things is money, which is valued by common consent.

Locke thinks the spoilage qualification becomes irrelevant because, by consenting to value money, people agree to the consequences. These include unequal shares of land and money, with a few having a lot (though still not all for any one person) and many others having little or nothing. Thus the poor must sell their labor even if they receive only a bare subsistence wage, while all they produce becomes the property of their masters.[18] Locke assumes that those who end up richer are those who have worked harder for their wealth, or have the practical reason to get others to work for them. They naturally and rightfully get more, without any injury or injustice caused to others, who would be no better off if the wealthier were less acquisitive. Indeed, they are better off. The producers want more wealth, and so are spurred to improve productivity. Consequently, there will be more goods available for all than if resources remain undeveloped in the common pool. The total wealth of society is increased.

In sum, because of people's consent to the value of money, they agree to permit economic inequality. This action was originally taken in the state of nature, prior to the establishment of government. But when people come under political authority, individual rights and economic inequality are carried over into the new society.

Natural Law

The *State of Nature* has a Law of Nature to govern it, which obliges every one: and Reason, which is that Law, teaches all Mankind, who will but consult it, that being all equal and independent, no one ought to harm another in his Life, Health, Liberty, or Possessions.[19]

Natural law governs people in the state of nature. It is a set of principles that all rational people can know and agree on. Natural law defines natural rights, and it also serves to indicate the liberties those rights authorize.

The law of nature gives people a natural right to be free from the threat of violent death, enslavement, or theft of estate. Because there is no political authority in nature, everyone may exercise this natural right as they see fit and judge their own actions. The state of nature thus has a sort of natural justice. Although no one may violate natural law, it is just (and no violation) to enforce that law against those who have broken it by violating the property of others. However, punishment of violators must be calm and dispassionate, carried out in a way that is "proportionate to his transgression," and only for "so much as may serve for reparation and restraint: for these two are the only reasons why one man may lawfully do harm to another, which is what we call punishment."[20] The purpose of reparation is to right an injury by making it a bad bargain for the offender, following the dictum "an eye for an eye." Restraint prevents future injury by terrifying potential offenders. To Locke, these restrictions are part of natural justice, and those enforcing natural law must respect them or the enforcers themselves will have violated natural law and opened themselves to punishment. These limits on punishment apply to political authority as well as individuals, for what is unjust in the state of nature may not be done by government.

STATE OF WAR

In Locke's account, the state of nature seems to be a fine place. Most people follow their nature, acting daily in a moral, rational, and social manner. They work as hard as they can on what nature has provided for them, and are duly rewarded for that work. The resulting economic inequality is just and in accord with God's original purpose. The few who violate natural law are controlled by the many who dispense justice under a firm but fair system. What could possibly drive people, apparently living in a state of nature far distant from Hobbes's state of war, to want to leave this benign, even beneficial, environment? The answer lies in Locke's dualist view of human nature. Though he does not relate a tale as terrifying as Hobbes's account, the overall picture of the state of nature is not as rosy as a quick reading might suggest.

> And here we have the plain difference between the state of nature and the state of war, which however some men have confounded, are as far distant as a state of peace, goodwill, mutual assistance, and preservation; and a state of enmity, malice, violence and mutual destruction are one from another. Men living together according to reason without a common superior on earth, with authority to judge between them, are properly in the state of nature. But force, or a declared design of force upon the person of another, where there is no common superior on earth to appeal for relief, is the state of war. . . .[21]

So, although no one ought to harm another in the state of nature, it is force upon one's person that turns the state of nature into a state of war. Although most people are naturally law-abiding, it takes only a few lawbreakers to change a peaceful environment into a dangerous one. Such a change comes easily in the state of nature, where there is no known, unbiased judge acceptable to all who can deal with reported violations. Further, though all others are rationally obliged to help enforce natural law they might not, and those who want to enforce it are not always strong enough to punish the guilty.

The difference, then, between Locke and Hobbes turns on the extent to which the state of nature and the state of war occur at the same time. For Hobbes it always does; for Locke, just sometimes. But the result is the same for both. A benign state of nature can, suddenly and without warning, become a state of war, so people leave the state of nature to escape its uncertainty. The first step is to secure a government that can establish a more certain peace.

BASIS OF GOVERNMENT

People surrender their individual right to enforce natural law against offenders when they consent to a social contract. As all are free to leave a governed society at any time, those who stay and enjoy any of its benefits are assumed to give their unspoken consent.[22] The contract is originally instituted by unanimous consent, but once it is approved Locke rejects any further requirement of rule by unanimity, for that would perpetuate the state of nature. Instead, the majority has a right to act for everyone. Locke reasons that since every authoritative body must move in a single direction, and since all those who vote are politically equal, the numerical majority is legitimately the will to which all must submit as long as it acts justly. However, Locke assumes that only those with property are entitled to vote, so he gives effective power only to the majority of this group.

The social contract establishes a bi-level arrangement consisting of civil society and government.[23] Civil society is the people united. Its role is to delegate power to government, so it, not government, is the superior authority in Locke's scheme. All who consent to the contract are members of civil society. Lockean government is limited government, which means that not all aspects of life are subject to law. People surrender to government only as much of their natural rights as is needed for the ends for which it is made. These ends define the common good, or public interest, that government may institute and enforce. "The great and chief end . . . of men's uniting into commonwealths, and putting themselves under government, is the preservation of their property."[24] That is, governments are established to ensure people's freedom to lawfully use their property as they see fit. The role of government is not only to protect property, but also to secure the individual's right to almost limitless ownership.

For Locke, people's natural right to protect their property is delegated by civil society to government in order that it create a written rule of law to be executed by a known and impartial judge. It is the legislature that is charged with converting natural law into public law, and all are equally subject to that law. Once that is in place, a stable peace replaces the uncertain state of nature, giving everyone greater security to enjoy their property.

Thus citizens transfer natural legislative and executive powers to government. However, they do not surrender judicial power, the supreme authority to judge whether acts of lawmakers and executives are consistent with the public interest. If they conclude that the government has violated its trust, they may revoke their delegation of power and remove it. Authority then reverts temporarily to civil society until citizens establish a new government. As long as the social contract remains in force, civil society endures and can replace one government with another. However, both contract and civil society are destroyed by foreign conquest, which returns everyone back to the state of nature.

RELIGIOUS TOLERATION

Locke believes limited government should apply to the religious sphere. The divine right theory he opposed included an official religion, with the king as head of both state and church. The full power of government could be used against individuals who rejected any aspect of the official religion, whether dogma or ceremony. Those who professed or practiced "false" beliefs could be fined, imprisoned, even put to death. Locke argues instead for religious toleration and condemns persecution and the use of force. Political rulers have no special competence in religious matters. The business of government is not to judge the truth of opinions, religious or otherwise, but to provide for the safety and security of the commonwealth. Thus the ruler has no legitimate authority to enforce any religious edicts or views that do not obstruct the public order. Locke also thinks religious persecution and intolerance run counter to the spirit of the gospel of peace and the personality of Jesus.

Besides, Christianity is a rational religion, and "the same truths may be discovered and conveyed down from revelation, which are discoverable to us by reason, and by those ideas we may naturally have."[25] At the same time, no one, however inspired by God, can have revelation of any new ideas they cannot get from sensation or reflection. Here, Locke wants to undercut any special religious knowledge or authority that the clergy or their political superiors might claim. Instead, each rational individual is charged with personal salvation and has both the capacity to and responsibility for judging which religious propositions are to be accepted or denied. What the government might consider "false" belief is no barrier to a person's heavenly journey. On the other hand, obeying the demands of government contrary to one's own conscience may well interfere with salvation.

Locke believes that reason is simply natural revelation, while revelation is just natural reason enlarged by the Bible.[26] The central tenets of Christianity, particularly the existence of God and the role of Jesus, can be demonstrated by reason; the New Testament simply reveals the law of nature. There is nothing in Christianity that is contrary to reason, but revelation also has a role to play. The illiterate bulk of the population is not open to rational persuasion but would accept biblical instruction, so the advice of preachers is the best source of guidance for their moral behavior and personal salvation. However, even the masses are free to search for religious truth led only by individual conscience and unimpeded by government.

Locke distinguishes between the needs of body and soul, the secular and the spiritual, the public and the private, and the roles of state and church. The government is concerned with secular, physical demands, and religion with the spiritual needs of the soul. Thus the two types of needs are separate, and each can be consigned to a different authority. Government is to be limited to those matters concerning the public welfare, whereas religion, affecting the private good of individuals, is none of the government's business. In this way, Locke lays the philosophical foundation for the separation of church and state.[27]

Locke stops short of the logical consequences of his thinking, however. Like the Toleration Act approved by Parliament, Locke supports a revocable privilege for certain religious dissenters rather than a right to religious freedom for everyone. Atheists are not to be tolerated because they have no fear of God, so they cannot be trusted to make good citizens. Roman Catholics are also excluded from toleration because of their allegiance to the pope. In general, however, Locke believes that greater toleration promotes public order and the internal cohesiveness desirable in society, as well as supporting individual autonomy and freedom.[28]

GENDER, CLASS, AND CITIZENSHIP

When writing about women and class relationships, Locke rarely refers to them specifically in political situations. When he does mention them, he distinguishes between the rational and the irrational, much as he does when discussing economic success and religion. It is mostly from what he says about the private and the irrational that one can infer certain conclusions about their application to the political sphere. When it helps his case against divine right monarchy, Locke treats elites and masses, and husbands and wives, as equal; but when it does not help his position, he changes his tune and sanctions political, economic, and social inequality.[29] He is against patriarchalism, but Locke believes that public authority is not comparable to private forms of dominance such as those between master and servant or man and wife. Whatever their station, in a formal sense all humans are made in God's image and are born with an equal capacity to rationally contract and protect their natural rights by participating in the political process, but this equality does not extend to the private sector.

Consistent with his idea of justice, he says that a defeated aggressor who would use force to control others may be enslaved, and a criminal has renounced reason and can be imprisoned. With these exceptions, all people have a right to be free, and to freely contract for the use of their property. Thus

> a free man makes himself a servant to another by selling him for a certain time the service he undertakes to do in exchange for wages he is to receive; and though this commonly puts him into the family of his master, and under the ordinary discipline thereof, yet it gives the master but a temporary power over him, and no greater than what is contained in the contract between 'em.[30]

So, voluntary employment differs from slavery and penal servitude.

However, although servants have sufficient reason to enter into contracts of employment, their rationality is limited. As hired hands, they own no estates on which to develop their rational skills, as their landowning employers can do. As menial laborers, they have neither time nor inclination to focus on anything but daily existence. Just as they are incapable of knowing religious truth on their own, so they are excluded from active citizenship by their lack of reason. Employed as servants, many women fall into this category as well, and so do those married to workingmen. But what of those whose husbands have substantial property? It is precisely here that Locke's challenge to divine right theory should result in a recognition of full equality, but he again fails to overcome the prejudices of his time and develop his argument to its logical conclusion. He wants to undermine the divine right political argument, but not the patriarchal family.

This was not the case in the original state of nature, however. Parental power was given to neither the father nor the mother alone; each had equal title to authority over children. This demolishes the argument of patriarchalism that original authority was vested in the father alone. Yet, as sole administrator of family property, the father may set conditions for its inheritance. The acceptance of this legacy, presumably by the male heir if there is one, constitutes express consent to his authority. Thus the father has assumed the dominant role, and the mother, who formerly shared authority, has suddenly lost it. Locke has reintroduced the patriarchal family on the basis of children's consent. But consent of the wife is an additional contributor to this state of affairs. Women are human, and so not naturally irrational. They possess sufficient reason to voluntarily enter into a marriage contract. And the aim of marriage is the natural, God-given one of producing and rearing children, so once reproduction and education are attained and inheritance taken care of, the parties to the contract may consent to terminate it through divorce. However, Locke assumes that the wife has consented in the marriage contract to be ruled by the husband in all things, particularly decisions affecting family property. In case of disagreement over any issue, the husband has full authority as long as they are together. Despite possessing the reason to enter into marriage, the woman surrenders it to her husband and voluntarily removes herself from the ranks of the rational.[31]

Locke also finds a certain physical or natural basis for women's subordinate status. During their childbearing years they suffer continual infirmity as their bodies regularly either prepare for conception or are carrying children, all the while suffering considerable pain. This suggests that, in light of her regular disability, a wife's acceptance of the marriage contract and her consequent subordinate status in marriage is in her rational self-interest.

Even if science could alleviate her biological weakness, Locke offers additional reasons why the wife should submit to her husband. The woman who cares for a household is, in terms of her capacity for rational development, much like a servant, since all decision-making power rests with the husband. His reason is active, hers passive. Her family role interferes with the development of her reason, since she lacks the basic precondition for rationality: economic independence. Perhaps she could develop her reason through education, but if she marries she forfeits this opportunity. Unless she is independently wealthy, marriage keeps her in her place.

Subordination in the family most likely leads to political subjection for women. Although Locke is silent on this, most commentators believe that he justifies husbands speaking for the entire family in the political arena. By entering into the marital contract, then, women authorize men to represent them politically. When they consent to marriage, they also surrender their right to consent to government. Just as with laborers, children, criminals, and the irrational, Locke excludes women from citizenship.[32]

INSTITUTIONS AND FORMS OF GOVERNMENT

Locke favors any form of government that supports an individual's natural right to property, its acquisition, and its preservation in the hands of its rightful owner. For this reason, he automatically rejects two forms as illegitimate. They are the divine right of kings, which Hobbes also rejected, and absolute monarchy, which Hobbes advocated. To Locke, both forms give executive and legislative power to individuals, who lack an impartial judge. Such rulers favor their own private, selfish interests above the general good, and everyone is still effectively in the state of nature.

Locke spurns Hobbes's preference for executive supremacy. For him, the supreme power is the legislative, an institution established by contract with the limited power to turn natural law into civil law. Legislative supremacy takes place in two forms of government. Locke gives the name pure democracy to the form in which all citizens directly exercise lawmaking powers, as in ancient Athens. They do so by periodically assembling in one place and expressing their views on proposed laws. The vote of the majority of all citizens so assembled is binding on everyone. *Representative democracy* is the name he uses for a two-step process. First, the citizens, in an election, transfer legislative power to a small number of their body, who become their representatives. It is the votes of the majority of this elected legislature that determine the laws. Locke favors representative democracy as the more practical way of governing a large nation-state. Laws apply equally to all and set the standards of right and wrong that decide all controversies in society. Legislating should require only short meetings, after which members adjourn and are subject, along with everyone else, to the laws they have made. Legislative power also includes the authority to either exercise judicial power or appoint the "magistrates" or judges who exercise it.

The executive has the job of enforcing the laws, and this requires his constant presence. The executive is also the trustee of the legislature and has the power to support any sentence. All executive authority is delegated by the legislature, to which it is always accountable for its actions. Such accountability is essential to protecting individual rights, because executive authority is awesome and includes power over life and death. Like legislative power, executive power must be exercised justly and in accord with known law. Any assumption by the executive of absolute or arbitrary power is illegitimate. Executive power also extends to prerogative power, or the right to fix the details of legislation. It is neither practical nor possible, especially in short legislative sessions, for the law to spell out in advance all the circumstances under which it might apply. But prerogative power, like all executive power, is limited. It may not exceed the bounds of natural law, nor may it, except in an unforeseen crisis, go beyond the limits of written civil law. Executive authority also includes federative power, or the right to conduct foreign affairs.

DESPOTISM AND REVOLUTION

> ... where an appeal to the law and constituted judges lies open, but the remedy is denied by a manifest perverting of justice, and a barefaced wresting of the laws to protect and indemnify the violence or injuries of some men or party of men ... war is made upon the sufferers, who having no appeal on earth to right them, they are left to the only remedy in such cases, an appeal to Heaven.[33]

Although he prefers legislative democracy, Locke believes that this, like any other form of government, can become despotic. Despotism occurs when a government goes beyond its legitimate limits, which in turn activates the right of one or another body to change it. Locke gives a clearer idea than Hobbes of when this becomes necessary—of when government is not acting for the common good—and presents a wider menu of options for action, depending on the source of the despotism and its extent.

The executive might violate the law, for example, by ordering the unlawful use of force against innocent citizens. Exceeding the limited power granted under the contract may be opposed, the same as any other forcible invasion of the right of another. It is the obligation of the legislature in this instance to remove the executive from power.

The legislature itself might also exceed the limited power granted under the contract. For example, it might transfer its power to another source (only the contract can do this), or take the "property" of individuals in a way that violates natural law. But as legislative power is granted only conditionally, there always remains with the people the supreme power to remove or alter the legislature when they find that it has acted contrary to their trust. When this occurs, legitimate power temporarily reverts to civil society, and the majority of citizens can together exercise their right to change the government.

The legitimate change of government can come about peacefully or by force. When there are charges of lesser violations of the public interest by government, citizens may act through regular elections of legislators. Locke says that this power in the hands of the people is the best defense against rebellion or violent change. When the people are denied legal or electoral means to alter a government, particularly one that has perpetrated serious abuses of the contract, however, then their conditional obligation to obey the government is cancelled. Violence becomes their only recourse. Locke thus provides for a collective right to revolution, whereas Hobbes only allowed for an individual right to resist unjust authority.

Locke is conservative when he states the conditions under which this may become necessary. Violence should not be undertaken lightly, he insists. Only when there are a series of abuses, all pointing to a despotic aim, should citizens use force. However, under such circumstances, revolution by the people against their oppressors is preferable to continuing despotism. Despotism is worse than popular revolution because it effectively voids the contract, plunging everyone back into a state of nature. By contrast, legitimate collective violence temporarily substitutes the just authority of civil society for the unjust government until a new one can be established, but retains the original contract.[34]

CONCLUSION

Locke agrees in large measure with the views of his fellow early-moderns, Machiavelli and Hobbes, on the purpose of government and its organization, but his differences with these two predecessors often receive greater emphasis. Like them, Locke is a materialist. But he dilutes his materialism by introducing a divinity who encourages, in addition to individualism and acquisitiveness, rational social cooperation in state building.[35]

By modifying their strong skepticism and harsh depictions of human selfishness with a combination of scientific rationalism and biblical quotation, Locke's ideas became acceptable to those seeking a more hopeful approach to modern individualist politics than Machiavelli or Hobbes offered. Thus Locke portrays a more tranquil state of nature, one that is anarchistic but not always as savage and warlike as Hobbes's. His central question is, if all people are equal, egoistic individuals, and most are rational and social, what sort of government is best for them? He adds institutional details to Hobbes's ideas, and promises both greater political stability and individual liberty, including protection of individual property, through a contracted and limited government. So, like Hobbes, Locke is a contract theorist, or one who believes government is a human creation based on voluntary consent. However, Locke's social contract links government to a more complex artificial alliance than Hobbes conceived in his political contract. Does such complexity lead to a more stable government, resulting in greater individual liberty, or does it help to undermine stability and liberty, both of which Hobbes sought to protect with a simpler contract and a stronger sovereign authority?

His willingness to support a collective right to alter government, where Hobbes could not, may be related to how each one conceived of the original contract. Locke's is a dual, or two-stage, social contract. It establishes both a civil society and a government. Thus Locke can distinguish between the dissolution of the society and the dissolution of the government, while Hobbes could not. Locke insists on an aggregate view of politics which includes limited and representative government, separation of powers, legislative supremacy, and the collective right of citizens to change government. These constitute a series of checks Locke believes must be placed on Machiavelli's prince and Hobbes's sovereign for political authority to be both effective and just. In doing so, he further advises rational citizens on the differences between tyranny and liberty.

However, Locke bars the greater part of the population from citizenship, including women and common working folk. They are excluded from political participation on the grounds of an inadequately developed rationality, and their roles are restricted to family and economic relationships. This undercuts the radical universality of Locke's initial egalitarianism and serves as an example of the failure to carry his theory to its logical conclusions. Does this failure, which he shares with Hobbes, undercut the value of his overall political philosophy, or can such inconsistencies be dismissed when implementing his ideas without damage to that philosophy?

This bears on later implementation of his ideas, since as with all great political philosophers, the effect of Locke's thought was not confined to his own time. He has had a strong influence on such American political thinkers as Thomas Jefferson and his successors, and on the concept of property rights in the United States. He is also at the center of one of the leading political ideologies in the world today.[36]

Notes

1. Maurice Cranston, *John Locke, A Biography* (London: Longman, 1957) remains one of the best accounts of Locke's life.

2. A major proponent of divine right theory, Robert Filmer, wrote a work called *Patriarcha* to refute Hobbes's *Leviathan,* and Locke wrote the two *Treatises* to refute Filmer. Ch. 1 of Locke's *Second Treatise of Government* is a brief summary of the argument in the *First Treatise* against Filmer. On patriarchalism, see Gordon Schochet, *Patriarchalism and Political Thought* (New York: Basic Books, 1975). Comment on its relation to gender issues may be found in Arlene W. Saxonhouse, *Women in the History of Political Thought: Ancient Greece to Machiavelli* (New York: Praeger, 1985); Diana Coole, *Women in Political Theory: From Ancient Misogyny to Contemporary Feminism* (Boulder, Colo.: Lynne Rienner, 1988); and Jean Bethke Elshtain, *Public Man, Private Woman: Women in Social and Political Thought* (Princeton, N.J.: Princeton University Press, 1981).

3. John Locke, *Two Treatises of Government,* ed. Peter Laslett (New York: Cambridge University Press, 1988). The punctuation has been modernized and italics omitted in most quotations. Locke wrote on a wide variety of subjects, including economics, the acquisition of knowledge, education, religion, and tolerance. All were relevant to his political concerns. Locke's works on religious understanding include *A Letter Concerning Toleration,* published in 1689, and *The Reasonableness of Christianity,* 1695. The *Essay Concerning Human Understanding,* a theory of knowledge, appeared in 1690, and *Some Thoughts Concerning Education* in 1693.

4. John Locke, *Essay Concerning Human Understanding,* ed. Raymond Wilburn (London: J. M. Dent, 1947), bk. 1, ch. 1, sec. 1.

5. *Human Understanding,* bk. 2, ch. 1, sec. 3; bk. 2, ch. 20, sec. 1.

6. *Human Understanding,* bk. 2, ch. 12, sec. 1. Locke's methodological views are developed in Neal Wood, *The Politics of Locke's Philosophy: A Social Study of "An Essay Concerning Human Understanding"* (Berkeley: University of California Press, 1983); and John Yolton, *Locke and the Compass of Human Understanding* (New York: Cambridge University Press, 1970).

7. Richard Ashcraft, *Locke's Two Treatises of Government* (London: Allen & Unwin, 1987), presents an interpretation of the *Treatises* that links them to Locke's religious outlook.

8. *Second Treatise,* sec. 4.

9. Uday S. Mehta, *The Anxiety of Freedom: Imagination and Individuality in Locke's Political Thought* (Ithaca, N.Y.: Cornell University Press, 1992), finds that Locke's view of human reason actually endangers individuality.

10. On the social side of Locke's view of human nature, see Nathan Tarcov, *Locke's Education for Liberty* (Chicago: University of Chicago Press, 1984).

11. For a discussion of the dating of this work, see Peter Laslett, "Two Treatises of Government and the Revolution of 1688" in his intro. to the *Two Treatises,* 45–66.

12. For further discussion, see Alan Ryan, *Property and Political Theory* (New York: Oxford University Press, 1984); and James Tully, *A Discourse on Property: John Locke and His Adversaries* (New York: Cambridge University Press, 1980).

13. *Second Treatise,* sec. 32.

14. *Second Treatise,* sec. 27.

15. Sheldon S. Wolin, *Politics and Vision: Continuity and Innovation in Western Political Thought* (Boston: Little, Brown, 1960), 341. Also see Locke's comment that the food that "nourishes the wild Indian" is his, and "a part of him." *Second Treatise,* sec. 26.

16. See John Dunn, *The Political Thought of John Locke: An Historical Account of the Argument of the "Two Treatises of Government"* (New York: Cambridge University Press, 1969), 216, who notes that, to Locke, one who labors has "a right to the whole produce of his labor or to the price which it would bring on a market."

17. *Second Treatise,* sec. 28. Also see Neal Wood, *John Locke and Agrarian Capitalism* (Berkeley: University of California Press, 1984).

18. Some major consequences of Locke's justification of individual ownership are discussed in C. B. Macpherson, *The Political Theory of Possessive Individualism: Hobbes to Locke* (New York: Oxford University Press, 1962).

19. *Second Treatise,* sec. 6.
20. *Second Treatise,* sec. 8.
21. *Second Treatise,* sec. 19.
22. See Ruth Grant, *John Locke's Liberalism* (Chicago: University of Chicago Press, 1987).
23. See http://politicalscience.wadsworth.com/tannenbaum2 for a link to an illustrated comparison of Locke's social contract and Hobbes's political contract.
24. *Second Treatise,* sec. 124.
25. John Locke, *A Letter Concerning Toleration,* ed. Patrick Romanell (Indianapolis: Bobbs-Merrill, 1955), 28. This is the most important of Locke's four letters on toleration.
26. See Mario Montuori, *John Locke on Toleration and the Unity of God* (Amsterdam: Gieben, 1983).
27. On the interplay between religion and politics in Locke's writings, see Ian Harris, *The Mind of John Locke: A Study of Political Theory in Its Intellectual Setting* (New York: Cambridge University Press, 1994).
28. For a comparison between Locke and a French contemporary who advocated complete toleration for all groups, see Amie Godman Tannenbaum, *Pierre Bayle's "Philosophical Commentary": A Modern Translation and Critical Interpretation* (New York: Peter Lang, 1987); and Amie G. Tannenbaum and Donald G. Tannenbaum, "John Locke and Pierre Bayle on Religious Toleration: An Inquiry," in *Transactions of the Eighth International Congress on the Enlightenment* (Oxford: Voltaire Foundation, 1993).
29. For example, while "he wants to contest a husband's absolute (political) authority over his wife in order to eliminate this particular piece of ammunition from the patriarchalist arsenal," he also seeks to "maintain certain natural bonds there in order to demonstrate—again in opposition to patriarchalism—that since domestic and political relations are of a different ilk, the latter can never be derived from the former." *Women in Political Theory,* 87.
30. *Second Treatise,* sec. 85.
31. Daniela Gobetti, *Private and Public: Individuals, Households, and Body Politic* (New York: Routledge, 1992), discusses the relationship between Locke's assumptions of natural equality and its application in the family setting.
32. See, for example, Carole Pateman, *The Sexual Contract* (Stanford, Calif.: Stanford University Press, 1988). For a contrary view, see Melissa Butler, "Early Liberal Roots of Feminism: John Locke and the Attack on Patriarchy," *American Political Science Review* 72 (March 1978): 135–50.
33. *Second Treatise,* sec. 20. See also Julian Franklin, *John Locke and the Theory of Sovereignty: Mixed Monarchy and the Right of Resistance in the Political Thought of the English Revolution* (New York: Cambridge University Press, 1981).
34. A. John Simmons, *On the Edge of Anarchy: Locke, Consent, and the Limits of Society* (Princeton, N.J.: Princeton University Press, 1993), links Locke's theory of revolution to his views on consent and the state of nature.
35. For an understanding of Locke's social concerns and their welfare-state implications, see Martin Seliger, *The Liberal Politics of John Locke* (New York: Praeger, 1969).
36. That ideology is, of course, liberal democracy. On Locke's influence in the United States, see Louis Hartz, *The Liberal Tradition in America* (New York: Harcourt, Brace & World, 1955); H. Mark Roelofs, *The Poverty of American Politics.* 2d ed. (Philadelphia: Temple University Press, 1998); David Schultz, *Property, Power, and American Democracy* (New Brunswick, N.J.: Transaction, 1992). On ideology, see esp. G. de Ruggiero, *The History of European Liberalism* (Boston: Beacon, 1959).

Additional Readings

(* indicates alternative viewpoint)
Ashcraft, Richard. *Locke's Two Treatises of Government.* London: Allen & Unwin, 1987.
*Butler, Melissa. "Early Liberal Roots of Feminism: John Locke and the Attack on Patriarchy." *American Political Science Review* 72 (March 1978): 135–50.

Cranston, Maurice. *John Locke: A Biography*. London: Longman, 1957.

Gobetti, Daniela. *Private and Public: Individuals, Households, and Body Politic*. New York: Routledge, 1992.

*Mehta, Uday S. *The Anxiety of Freedom: Imagination and Individuality in Locke's Political Thought*. Ithaca, N.Y.: Cornell University Press, 1992.

Myers, Peter C. *Our Only Star and Compass: Locke and the Struggle for Political Rationality*. Savage, Md.: Rowman & Littlefield, 1998.

Ryan, Alan. *Property and Political Theory*. New York: Oxford University Press, 1984.

Tarcov, Nathan. *Locke's Education for Liberty*. Chicago: University of Chicago Press, 1984.

 Inventors of Ideas Online

Visit http://politicalscience.wadsworth.com/tannenbaum2 for links related to material in this chapter, including a visual comparison of Locke's social contract and comparison with Hobbes's political contract, and the full texts of Locke's major works.

14

Rousseau: Establishing Democracy

INTRODUCTION

While Jean-Jacques Rousseau (1712–1778) was traveling to visit his friend Diderot, who was in Vincennes prison for seditious writing, he read of a contest seeking the best paper on whether the arts and sciences had contributed to human morality. His autobiography tells of a sudden inspiration at that moment, a blazing vision that inspired the negative answer, and won him first prize in the contest.[1] This event led to a lifetime career as a creative thinker, during which he frequently challenged accepted wisdom. In the process, he managed to make enemies everywhere and to alienate almost every friend he had, even as he opened a window to a wholly new approach to political questions.[2]

Rousseau's political thought reflected the experiences of his confused life. In fact, the full force of his brilliant originality may have been blunted by his many emotional conflicts. Unlike the optimistic Locke, Rousseau was often dissatisfied with where he lived and what he had, and it is questionable whether he could ever have been happy in any one place or would even have found satisfaction living under the political system he created.

Rousseau was born in the city-state of Geneva, Switzerland, in a section where the poorer class lived. His mother died shortly after giving birth to him, and when he was ten years old his father fled the city to avoid prison. Instructed in the classics and philosophy, the precocious young man's education was cut short by financial need. Apprenticed in three different professions (notary, engineer, and engraver), he could not stick to any one. The unhappy Rousseau followed his father's example and ran away from Geneva when he was sixteen years old. He took up with a series of women, some of whom were of noble background and wealthy. But one who was a poor laundress became his long-term mistress. Rousseau returned to her sporadically over the years, and he claims that she bore five of his children, each abandoned at an orphanage at birth.

During a lifetime in which he was, at various times, a civil servant, music teacher, composer, and tutor, Rousseau enjoyed a successful literary career. He was part of the counter-Enlightenment, a romantic reaction against the reason and science represented by such Enlightenment thinkers as Hobbes and Locke. In contrast to them, Rousseau stressed the importance of passion and sentiment. He imagined himself placing his great intellect in the service of all humanity, championing the cause of the nonintellectual "common" people such as the honest peasants of old Geneva (from which, remember, he voluntarily fled).[3]

He did not hesitate to denounce the powerful, and one of his works, *Emile*, was condemned by the French authorities as an attack on the Catholic Church, the state religion of France. Threatened with arrest, Rousseau fled first to Switzerland, then to Prussia and England. After a time, no longer happy anywhere else, he returned to Paris to marry his laundress and live out his life. He died a decade before the outbreak of the French Revolution, to which his writings contributed a number of important ideas.

ROUSSEAU'S METHOD

In one telling passage, Rousseau reveals the core of his method of thinking about politics: "I hope that every-day readers will excuse my paradoxes; you cannot avoid paradox if you would think for yourself, and whatever you say I would rather fall into paradox than prejudice."[4] In his work, paradox takes center stage. Thus he does not complete his thoughts on some important ideas, or states that several strongly felt but logically contradictory propositions are all true, which leaves the solution to what he means for others.[5] One of the most famous examples of this is his claim that individuals are truly free when they are forced to do what they do not want to do. Another is that only if people surrender all their rights can they really enjoy them.

He rejects the materialist approach of modern thinkers and scientists such as Locke, Galileo, Diderot, and Newton. They used a rationalistic method to attack false beliefs and demolish the logic supporting tyrannical political systems so that individual liberty might emerge. Rousseau thinks their optimistic idea that reason results in progress and freedom is misplaced. Change in the human condition over time is not the same as progress or improvement. On the contrary, Rousseau thinks reason leads to human enslavement. One must substitute feeling for reason to truly understand human affairs and discover remedies for its deficiencies.

Rousseau admired the ancient political philosophers. He uses the ancients' values and institutions as a positive example for good citizens. However, he disagrees with writers like Machiavelli, who also admired the ancients but chose the individual as the building block of the legitimate political universe. To Rousseau, Machiavelli's elevation of the competitive, self-seeking individual over the harmonious collective can only lead to injustice. Instead, Rousseau uses Plato's organic perspective, but gives it a singularly egalitarian cast. The result is a brilliant, innovative work grounded in philosophical and political paradox.

STATE OF NATURE AND HUMAN NATURE

Rousseau does not describe a state of nature that validates the political behavior of his time, as Hobbes and Locke did, but one that explains the origins of human injustice and condemns existing conditions. In keeping with his method, his state of nature is a poetic model, mixing the traditional Christian themes of the fall of humanity in the Garden of Eden with an eighteenth-century secularism that rejects orthodox religion. The model tells of a paradise lost (the state of nature) and a paradise that can be regained in the future through a social contract. In contrast to the traditional Christian perspective, however, paradise is both lost and recovered on earth, not in heaven. And this will be accomplished through a change in human nature.

In contrast to Hobbes and Locke, who saw human nature as a constant with no likelihood of change, Rousseau presents several different and distinct phases of human nature. However, he thinks the changes so far have led to decline rather than progress in human affairs. Definable stages in the development of human nature are the primitive, aboriginal, transitional, and liberated. At each stage, there is a different human nature at work.

Of primitive, or original, human nature, he says,

> It is therefore no great misfortune for those primitive men, and certainly no great obstacle to their survival, that they go naked; have no houses, and lack all the useless things that we consider so necessary.
>
> On the first consideration it would seem that men in the state of nature, having no kind of moral relations or recognized duties among themselves, could not have been either good or evil, and had neither virtues or vices [except for] compassion . . . a virtue . . . so natural that even beasts sometimes show clear signs of it.[6]

The primitive or original human is found in the first state of nature. And when Rousseau says, "Man is born free," he means both men and women, who are born by nature into a primitive existence wherein they can do as they wish and live as they choose.[7]

This existence is situated in a not-unpleasant world, one that has no political or social institutions. Each inhabitant is an apelike noble savage, an innocent but lazy beast guided by two instinctive principles. The first is concern for one's own life and welfare.[8] (Self-preservation also governs those living in the state of nature of Hobbes and Locke.) The second is compassion or pity, the one natural virtue. It is reflected in concern for the suffering of others (not shown in Hobbes and Locke), and it prevents those with primitive natures from inflicting pain on others. It is natural freedom and compassion, not reason, that mark primitive humans as different from other animals.

In this state of nature, life is solitary, and individuals act out of simple, instinctive needs. Everyone is able to cope with life in a perfect, but unassociated, harmony. They only feel the need to care for their own requirements on a day-to-day basis. Each is self-sufficient, getting along without either a continuous need for others (in contrast to Plato and Aristotle, who see human nature as political) or any desire to harm others (contrary to Hobbes and Locke). Even the primitive act of sexual union which unites these isolated beings in a brief encounter is based on a spontaneous instinct to ensure that the species continues. The desire to be together quickly passes, leaving women to rear their offspring alone.

Individuals at this point have none of the features associated with civilization. They are without home, industry, or even speech. They know nothing of family life or friendship. They have a sense of neither progress nor vice. All are nomads, happy-go-lucky wanderers who roam the earth without any leaders to guide them. All are equal, without reasoning power but possessing a good nature. From this Rousseau concludes that no one has any natural authority to rule over others. Such people "are not bound to one another by any relationship sufficiently stable to produce a state either of war or of peace." The state of nature is neither a Hobbes-like state of war, nor is there a "generally accepted system of private property," or Lockean "estate," that government is created merely to preserve.[9] Thus avoiding violent death or the loss of property is not the motive that drove people out of this state of nature. All the same, it is a state to which humans can never hope to return because of the influences of civilization.

At some (unclear) point in time, primitive existence began its gradual transformation, moving toward what Rousseau calls civilization. The earliest indication of such change was that asocial beings began to draw together. For a number of reasons related to survival needs, isolated primitives left their solitary, wandering state, formed nuclear families, and settled into simple huts, thus inaugurating aboriginal society.

While Rousseau's transitions are the result of a complex process and he is not always precise or consistent about when one stage ends and another begins, the earliest intermediary point between asocial beings in the state of nature and the emergence of civilization is this aboriginal society. Relationships in this society are still regarded as "natural," and its inhabitants are still in a sort of state of nature; as Rousseau says, "The oldest form of society—and the only natural one—is the family."[10] The family is natural, even though people are no longer isolated but live in stable families, have developed speech, and own a "kind of property" in their simple wooden huts and a few vital tools. There is even a basic division of labor within the family, as men hunt for the family's daily needs, while women, who are no longer self-sufficient, tend to the home and children.[11]

How can this stage be considered natural when Rousseau originally considers the natural state as one of almost total isolation and independence of individuals, and when "regular contact between individuals," even in the family, contains the seeds of selfishness and begins the descent into civilization?[12] One explanation is that some "traits which have emerged in evolutionary history" are our "second nature." Even the casual encounters between primitives are "social in the sense that they are driven to express powerfully felt passions for one another." They are the earliest signs of "moral 'feelings'" in people.[13] In this sense, although nuclear families were not part of the primitive state of nature, they emerge naturally out of that state and maintain certain links with it.

To briefly summarize the rest of the transformation to civilization, after families were established they grouped into small tribal communities based on hunting and food gathering. This was followed by the first division of labor among men, between agriculture and metallurgy. Language, speech, and reason entered into the human equation. One by one, each of these developments struck another blow to natural freedom. The process accelerated, due to numerous developments in the sciences and the arts, and culminated in the institution of government. The move to civilization, and the emergence of the transitional stage of human nature, was thus complete.

The first part of the opening sentence of the *Social Contract,* which says that "Man is born free," refers to primitives in the natural state. The rest of the sentence reads, "and everywhere he is in chains." Here, Rousseau is speaking of the emergence of transitional human nature, and his central concern is with transitional people in the grasp of civilization, in other words, the egoistic individuals of Machiavelli, Hobbes, and Locke.

People in civilization are oppressed. They have been forced to stifle compassion, the one virtue they had in the state of nature and the source of the other virtues. Both society and the government that supports it are corrupt, and people are enslaved by tyrannical institutions. These institutions exist to promote an unnatural selfishness and inequality not found in the state of nature, and they do not shrink from intentionally harming people to secure obedience.

Rousseau says, "How did this change take place? I do not know."[14] His response is misleading; he thinks he does know. Civilization is the result of a conspiracy by a rational, calculating, selfish few against the many. It is based on the twin evils of private property and the division of labor. People moved from an economy of cooperative hunting to one of specialization, wherein some engaged in agriculture and others in crafting metal tools. As a result, a few accumulated considerable wealth, and inequality and a state of war between rich and poor were the consequences. Thus, "The first man who, having enclosed a piece of land, took it into his head to say, 'This is mine,' and found people simple enough to believe him, was the true founder of civil society."[15] Civilization was established then, as even Locke suggested, so that some people could secure long-term guarantees of unequal shares of private property for themselves. To do so, they created a lie (which echoed Locke), namely, that those who work the land, or get others to do it for them, own and have a natural right to that land and its product as an integral part of their property or estate. This lie was the basis of inequality, and people entered civil society and established government to perpetuate it.[16]

Rousseau goes on to say, "Thus we see how luxury, dissolution, and slavery have always been the punishment of our proud efforts to emerge from the happy ignorance in which eternal wisdom placed us."[17] The division of labor stemming from the origins of farming and metalwork led to the development of science, which was used to control nature. In its benevolent form,

Rousseau sees science as a practical device to improve the human condition. But he condemns it as the foundation of an immoral society that promotes luxury and dependence on other people and products. Such a society rewards people unequally, depending on their role in the economy. The results of civilization are both negative and positive for humans. On the negative side, civilization is the wellspring of human selfishness and exploitation, used by a small, elite minority to manipulate the masses by creating government and its laws. These laws, the rules of civilization, replace pity as the basis of morality. They promote the division of labor and private property and even empower the rich to send the poor to fight wars that only benefit themselves. Supported by such philosophers as Hobbes and Locke, laws also hide economic and social inequality behind a smoke screen of legal equality. For example, laws bar rich and poor alike from begging on the streets or engaging in armed robbery, but these are, of course, acts the rich have no need to commit. So, although the laws are written to apply equally to everyone, in practice it is the poor who are in fact most often subject to their penalties.

By such means civilization has shackled people in the chains of inequality. It has also fundamentally changed their original, primitive natures. Transitional people are mere slaves who are motivated by selfish appetites. Their humanity is diminished by a government that excludes them from real decision making, no matter how benign and apparently willing to discuss policies the few rulers may seem. Leisure and luxury dominate society, reinforced by vanity, competitiveness, and inequality.

Awful as this is, civilization does have another side, according to Rousseau. Some of the causes of their oppression can also serve as sources of liberation. Scientific discovery, artistic creation, and industrial progress, accompanied by the spread of useful information, can benefit all people by helping them improve their critical reasoning, their speech, and their sociability, perhaps leading them to consider abolishing the chains of civilization. And transitional people do have the potential for becoming fully social animals, a capacity their primitive ancestors lacked.

Commenting on the transition from the state of nature, Rousseau says, "but for the fact that misuse of the new conditions still, at times, degrades him to a point below that from which he has emerged, he would unceasingly bless the day which freed him forever from his ancient state, and turned him from a limited and stupid animal into an intelligent being and a Man."[18] Although the state of nature was not as bad as Hobbes pictured it, it was far from ideal. But once private property and the division of labor were established, human oppression was inevitable. Because human nature has fundamentally changed, from primitive to transitional, there is no possibility for people to return to the state of nature. Once hatched, the chicken cannot be returned to the egg. The solution is to change again, following the road to true freedom.

PATH TO LIBERATION

Compassion is the wellspring of the other virtues that could unite transitional people in just and harmonious community. They still have, deep down inside, natural feelings of pity that have been stifled by the oppressive chains of civilization. If these feelings were freed and combined with the sociable aspects of civilization, which emphasize human cooperation, change would be possible.

The first step is to recognize the injustice of remaining in slavery. People must strip off the layers of civilization to find their true selves. This will provide them with a philosophical basis for liberation. Rousseau also calls for a new form of civil society under a legitimate moral authority that ensures liberation by establishing a just legal and institutional basis. In pursuit of this goal,

> "Some form of association must be found as a result of which the whole strength of the community will be enlisted for the protection of the person and property of each constituent member, in such a way that each, when united to his fellows, renders obedience to his own will, and remains as free as he was before." That is the basic problem of which the Social Contract provides the solution.[19]

The problem goes beyond the mechanics of constructing a new government. To Rousseau, as long as people refuse to subordinate their private goals to the common good they cannot lead the best of lives. They must become part of a larger, unified society. Human association in this community should be based on the ancient philosophers' organic principle, as individuals will relate to the larger collective in complete interdependence. This resolves the twin problems of estrangement and domination found in civilization, since dependence would be equal for all. The line between self and other is wiped out, and the welfare of the individual merges and becomes one with the collective welfare.

Rousseau seeks a new form of community, one of both political and social democracy. He says people must find a form of association that provides all the material benefits of civilization, as well as stability and the protection of life, liberty, and estate for everyone, not just for a few. At the same time, it must allow all citizens to participate fully and obey only their real inner selves, not some external body. This will make them as free as they were in the state of nature while enjoying the benefits of the new community. In this more perfect constitution of society, the individual wills of transitional human nature will vanish.

THE SOCIAL CONTRACT

People enter the new community by agreeing to a new social contract. It is a dual, or two-stage, contract. Rousseau agrees with Hobbes and Locke that "Since no man has natural authority over his fellows, and since Might ʳ produce no Right, the only foundation left for legitimate authority in human societies is Agreement."[20] To Rousseau, the sovereign authority established by both Hobbes (government) and Locke (civil society) provides unjust controls on people in modern society (civilization). As a result, those authorities are no more valid than any other kind of despotism, such as one based on conquest or divine right.

Rousseau's scheme begins with people who revolt against despotism. This revolt need not be violent, and Rousseau does not think that just any violent revolution would lead to a moral community. But people must freely enter into a new basic agreement, a contract that creates a moral community for truly liberated people who are thereby removed from corrupt civilization. The sovereign authority rests in that community. And that sovereign community then establishes the government and names the officials who execute its will.[21] Legitimacy is ensured because the government is created solely to execute the will of this sovereign people.

A valid agreement is established through "the complete alienation by each associate member to the community of all his rights." When this is done, "it substitutes for the person of each of the contracting parties a moral and collective body" that has a united "will."[22] That is, by unanimous consent, equal individuals give up all the rights they have as transitional people living in civilization to the whole community. They do so without reservation, for otherwise tyranny remains in place. Each person gives up all rights, not to a body or government, but to the new sovereign authority that rests in the community that created it. This sovereign is a collective, organic public person with a will of its own.

Each member receives in return rights equal to all the others', but not the same rights that were surrendered. For example, members give up the absolute (Hobbesian) right to self-defense and the (Lockean) right to estate. The rights they receive in return are those the community then grants equally to all as it sees fit.

Rousseau says nobody truly loses in this exchange. Rather, everyone gains more power to keep what they rightfully have by "exchanging peril and uncertainty for security, natural independence for true liberty, the power of injuring others for . . . a right which corporate solidarity renders invincible."[23] This is because in place of many selfish individuals, the contract produces a moral body unified by a collective identity in a just society. In this community, each one is truly freer than under illegitimate government. Individuals carry with them all the positive benefits of civilization, such as learning, culture, industry, and even useful ideas of past political philosophers. One of these ideas is of true "Moral Freedom," which can only be realized through Rousseau's social contract.[24] Moral freedom is the quality that makes people virtuous masters of themselves. It is secured when people think of the good of all, the public interest, rather than submit to the slavery of private appetites. The contract is instituted to bring this about.

The contract does not require total equality. All are to be politically equal, subject to the same rights and responsibilities as everyone else. Economically, however, Rousseau is not a believer in identical shares. Some differences in wealth are acceptable as long as economic inequality does not interfere with political equality by allowing the wealthier to use their assets to gain political control. Nobody is to be rich enough to be able to buy another citizen's vote, or so poor as to be willing to sell it.

The General Will. The new form of association, the community, is the sovereign authority for everyone. It is a public "person," an organic body that has a will of its own, just as each individual has a life and will that constitute his or her identity. Rousseau's name for both the political process by which the sovereign authority is created and the goal of that process is the general will.[25] The general will is the only legitimate source of the decisions (laws) and governmental actions taken in the name of the community. It becomes the basis of legislative power once the contract is established.

The general will is founded on the natural primitive principles, that is, egoistic self-concern combined with compassion for others in a moral community. To Rousseau, it is the key requirement any society needs to be both stable and legitimate by having a social bond common to all members, or a public interest. In its absence people just have many different, private interests. The general will keeps liberated human nature morally free. It is a superior guide that expresses the values and laws that define justice, or the common good.

The set of shared values on which this will is based makes a community out of a collection of individuals. At root these values are primitive and sentimental, and thus beyond reason. However, people can rationally discuss their feelings about them when seeking the general will, because the result must be quite reasonable to ordinary people of common sense. The general will is also based on shared institutions and procedures which are rational, legal, and apply equally to all. The sum of these values, institutions, and procedures is a moral order that may not be legitimately contradicted by anyone.

As the only legitimate standard of justice, the general will ennobles people's feelings and elevates their souls. The general will tells people what they should do to make everyone happy, rather than simply supporting what they individually want, whatever the cost to others. The general will is always right. It is the common will or mind of the community which transcends all the individual minds involved in discovering it and unites them in complete harmony. It is at its peak when the individual is nothing without the collective.

The general will has three functions. It establishes the contract, it stands behind the contract, and it determines the laws that are enacted in "fixed and periodic" assemblies of all citizens.[26] These gatherings are called by officials, in accordance with law, to make legislative decisions. The agenda may include issues concerning any of three questions, which summarize the legislative power of the assembly:

1. whether the present form of government should be kept
2. whether the present officials should be retained in office, and
3. whether a proposed law conforms to the general will

This follows from the original agreement, for when people entered into the contract each agreed to obey only legitimate forms, officials, and laws defined by the periodic assemblies as necessary to the welfare of the community.

While the contracts of Hobbes and Locke called for public consent when they were instituted and at each election time, Rousseau's general will requires continuous public consent. All members of the community assemble to participate in making every law. Each member has a dual public role, as both citizen engaged in legislating the general will, and then as subject when obeying the law (another form of consent). When they obey legitimate law, people are following their higher interests and rejecting immediate, selfish concerns. When acting as a private person someone may express a selfish will, but in public everyone must participate in expressing the general will.

The general will is discovered in the assembly by complete consensus after a process of thorough discussion by completely informed citizens. The citizens are bound only by procedure. Like a jury, which decides its verdict only after a trial, they should be fully informed about the issues discussed but open-minded about solutions. They meet face to face, seeking consensus, not any compromise. The meeting continues until all are satisfied that the general will has been expressed. In the meeting, all must discuss the issues publicly. They can have no prior deals about how they intend to vote. To do so would be contrary to the general will, which can only emerge through spontaneous discussion and decision making.

Voting and Counting Votes. A unanimous vote is required to activate the original social contract, but on all subsequent matters the general will only requires a majority vote. This is not a simple Lockean (quantitative) majority, but one with a qualitative aspect that speaks to what everyone really wants, no matter how they vote. Thus "What makes the will general is not the number of citizens concerned, but the common interest by which they are united."[27] When they vote, they express their views about the public interest. But the general will refers only to those votes cast with that interest in mind, and excludes any votes reflecting private interests because the latter are simply wrong.

Rousseau distinguishes the general will (in the public interest) from the "will of all," or the vote of those following their private interests. If the majority vote reflects the will of all, "the prevailing opinion has no more validity than that of an individual man." For a vote to be valid, people must "take from the expression of these separate wills the pluses and minuses—which cancel out, the sum of the differences is left, and that is the general will."[28]

What Rousseau seems to say in this opaque phrase is that the citizens must first eliminate the votes of private wills. This immediately raises the question of how they can really know the difference (which Rousseau never addresses). Are those voting selfishly expected to freely admit it and even change their votes? It also implies that the majority of the remaining vote, even if a minority of the original total, represents the current general will. And if only one vote remains, all others having voted selfishly, this "majority" of one has discovered the general will.

Rights of Members. Discussing sovereign power, Rousseau says "that there is not, nor can be, any fundamental law which is obligatory for the whole body of the People, not even the social contract itself."[29] The sovereign general will is not limited by the social contract or by any law. The living sovereign citizens are the essence of the contract and make the law. This allows for great flexibility. As people's views of the public interest change, they must be completely free to alter the terms of the contract and the law to fit such change. Where Locke's contract was a restriction of the sovereign, Rousseau's is not.

Of course, "the Sovereign People, having no existence outside that of the individuals who compose it, has, and can have, no interest at variance with theirs." Since these individuals collectively are the general will, that will can have no real conflict of interest with theirs as individuals, or with that of the public interest as a whole. It cannot truly injure them in any way, since the two are actually one and indivisible. "Consequently, the sovereign power need give no guarantee to its subjects, since the body is incapable of injuring its members; nor . . . can it injure any single individual. The Sovereign, by merely existing, is always what it should be."[30] The sovereign need give no guarantee because it alone is the source of all rights. It grants or withdraws these rights at its will. No natural or private rights of individuals are exempt from this. Yet, as all grants and withdrawals are applied equally to all subjects, in accord with known procedures open to all, people are the masters of themselves, not slaves.

CITIZENSHIP, GENDER, AND EDUCATION

From the *First Discourse* on through the *Social Contract*, Rousseau makes clear that his models for the good citizen come from militarily strong and disciplined ancient city-states such as Sparta and Rome. There, men were both free citizens and patriots who loved their cities. Like them, Rousseau says that each citizen must be willing to declare his participation in the state as part of a unified citizen body where each and all of them will the general will. Every citizen must be ready and willing to act dutifully, doing what the general will commands, and fully identifying his personal will with these commands. There is no holding back. The citizen's commitment to the state and to his fellow citizens is total, and all are bound more by their moral feelings for each other and for the common good than by any formal legal stipulations. Laws exist to simply give outward form to what all good citizens accept.[31]

Rousseau agrees with most of his predecessors, from Aristotle to Locke, that the important business of government is to be handled exclusively by men. There are natural and irreversible gender differences that deny women any opportunity to participate as citizens. He even rejects the Lockean idea that women ever were or could be capable of entering into any sort of contract, even a marital one. Differences between men and women in Rousseau's account originate not in the first or primitive state of nature but in the second one, aboriginal society. At that time, people left their solitary, wandering condition of equality and total freedom:[32]

> The first developments of the heart were the result of a new situation in which husbands and wives, fathers and children, were united in a common dwelling. The habit of living together gave rise to the sweetest feeling known to man: conjugal love and paternal love. Each family became a small society, all the better united because mutual attachment and freedom were its only ties. This was the time when the first differences appeared in the two sexes' way of living, which had previously been the same. The women grew more sedentary and became accustomed to keeping the hut and the children while the men went off in search of food for all.[32]

In this "first revolutionary change," people joined in nuclear families based on strong feelings between couples and for their offspring. They instituted a simple division of labor, with women performing household and agricultural work, and men leaving home to hunt. A "kind of property" was introduced, and Rousseau awards title to it to the man as owner and master. Using a Lockean perspective, Rousseau asserts that man does the work that produces that property, so he owns it.

Thus the family is patriarchal, its operation based on the rule of man over woman and his offspring. Rousseau accepts this arrangement as natural, stating that "the law of nature bids the woman obey the man."[33] Relying on the arguments of Hobbes and Locke this time, he asserts that authority in the family must be indivisible. Only one parent can have the final, determining word, and the nature of the reproductive process requires that the authority be given to the man. He also justifies patriarchy by stating that woman is by nature the physically weaker sex. This weakness is compounded by the demands put on her body by the procreative process. An additional reason is that since he is the owner of the family property and therefore considered the provider to the children, who inherit any such property, he must know for certain they are his. Consequently, "the woman's conduct must be carefully supervised."[34]

Women's subordination in the family is mirrored by their disqualification for citizenship. This is because their thinking is of a practical sort, useful in domestic situations but lacking the kind of judgment necessary for public activity. Women's sexual function suffuses her "entire existence; it, rather than her humanity, defines her." They are physically oriented, "made for man's delight," born to "submit to man and even endure injustice at his hands." If women enter the public arena, trying to follow men's public example, they corrupt the political process as well as themselves and are no longer fit as wives or mothers. However, by raising their children with warmth and love, they provide a model that inspires men to display the civic virtues of generosity and friendship.[35]

Rousseau's observations on citizenship and gender are a mass of inconsistencies which "violate all the major principles of his ethics and social theory." Woman's nature restricts her to romance and domestic obligations, while man's horizons allow for limitless opportunities in public service. And although Rousseau freely condemns civilization because it turns men into unequal slaves, he not only accepts but endorses the economic and political inequality between the sexes throughout history. Indeed, he views its continuation once man is liberated as a positive outcome. He even suggests that the two sexes enjoy a sort of parity in this arrangement, that man's sexual and domestic dependence on one particular woman is equivalent to women's reliance on men for their economic and political sustenance.[36]

Rousseau's theory of education is closely linked to his ideas about gender and citizenship. In *Emile,* he tells how the teacher shapes the mind of his students, Emile and Sophie, by rejecting rote learning. They are to learn from nature, from experience, not by memorizing statements from lectures or books. They are to be taught only what they are ready to handle by virtue of their inner development. Such experiential education, a radical change from accepted practice in Rousseau's time, was promoted by him as a more natural approach, as was his proposal of a different kind of education for men and women based on the distinctive nature of each. Emile, the man, will be taught to be the breadwinner and prepared for citizenship. Sophie is to learn to be a good wife and mother.

Men and women are to be instructed according to their natural strengths. Men, who are strong, active, reasonable beings capable of patriotism, will learn how to be independent and earn their own living without relying on others. They will find out how to restrain their natural desires by taking a long-range perspective. Emile will learn a useful trade, such as carpenter or bricklayer, enabling him to live a simple but productive life.

Sophie, who is weak, docile, incapable of reason, and meant by nature to serve men, will learn the "feminine arts," such as sewing, needlework, and dressmaking. She will also be taught how to develop her instincts to arouse, tease, and satisfy men's sexual needs, while at the same time controlling their passions, thereby luring one of them into marriage. Women will also be taught to care for their homes and raise their children. Male children will be reared by both parents to have regard for their father and to develop the attitudes necessary for becoming good patriots.[37] Apart from the guidance of her husband and whatever she can pick up on her own, a woman's education will probably end with her marriage. A man's learning is never-ending if he lives in a just society. The *Social Contract* is a work to educate the citizen. His ongoing participation in the general will provides him with the perspectives and habits necessary to play his part in the community. Over time, his love for his fellow citizens and the city grows ever stronger, making him a better citizen, husband, and father.[38]

Freedom and Force. Once the general will is found, individual subjects who follow it simply obey their own real will because each of them has helped establish that will by acting as a citizen. By freely agreeing to be ruled by the general will, citizens agree to be ruled by its specific results. Thus everyone living under the general will is truly free. This freedom is moral, because it consists of obeying a just law that is self-imposed. All obey only the law they themselves have chosen, and obedience to self-prescribed laws "laid down by society" is Rousseau's definition of true freedom.[39]

Not everyone will be as obedient as they should be, however. Some may disobey the laws of the community. Seeking individual liberty the law forbids, they may reject the real freedom offered by the general will.

> In order, then, that the social compact may not be but a vain formula, it must contain, though unexpressed, the single undertaking which alone can give force to the whole, namely, that whoever shall refuse to obey the general will must be constrained by the whole body of his fellow citizens to do so: which is no more than to say that it may be necessary to compel a man to be free. . . .[40]

Coercion of the disobedient is justified because it reconciles freedom with authority. All citizens consented to obey the general will, both when they entered into the contract and after it is affirmed. This implies approval of the right of the body to use force on anyone who does not obey its commands, for otherwise law would be ineffective. The use of force helps the disobedient to obey their own true interests instead of their momentary desire to violate the law. It curbs individual interests, irrational passions, and immoral emotions, feelings, and appetites. Force is not used against their real will, which promised to obey, but their false will.

Because the general will is always right, and because obedience to it is the path to liberation, coercion is just; it helps lawbreakers to attain freedom. In other words, some people must be forced to be free. Subjects are never so free as when they are executed for crimes. Their real will is ardently cooperative, and only their false, selfish will is less than enthusiastic. Short of execution, the use of force is an educational and moral device. It teaches lawbreakers that they have been wrong and that true (moral) freedom lies in obedience to the general will. If they learn this lesson well, they can return to spiritual and political communion with their fellows as they participate once again in the general will.

NECESSARY CONDITIONS FOR SECURING A CONTRACT

Rousseau believes that freedom is not for everyone. There are few opportunities in human history for great change. Only when old traditions lose their grip and a small nudge to society would bring on the new can radical reformers plant the seeds from which the general will can grow.

Political considerations alone are insufficient when forming a community. Instituting the general will also requires a special set of social conditions. These include the presence of a legislator, a civil religion, certain geographic considerations, and various economic conditions that limit the role of wealth. Furthermore, the contract must establish a correct form of government containing several necessary executive institutions.

The Legislator. First "there is needed a superior intelligence which can survey all the passions of mankind, though itself exposed to none: an intelligence having no contact with our nature, yet knowing it to the full. . . ."[41]

This is the legislator. A divinely inspired person, the legislator has the wisdom to surmise the true public interest. Some historical and mythical examples Rousseau gives of exemplary legislators are Moses, in the Old Testament; Mohammed, in the Koran; Lycurgus, of ancient Sparta; and Romulus, of ancient Rome. Guide and teacher, devoid of any personal selfishness and devoted only to the public good, the legislator has a mission. He acts as the agent of the people and leads them to the community. The people seek this goal, but may not know how to reach it and may not recognize it unaided. The legislator enlightens them on what is really good for them by transforming each individual into a part of the collective whole. He thereby sets in motion the change in human nature from transitional to liberated.

The legislator is the giver of the contract, an expert who establishes the basic law and all necessary ideas and institutions to enable rule by the general will. The people indicate their approval by accepting the contract. Having created the community, the legislator then retires, for he has no place in the government. "Were it otherwise, the laws, mere ministers to his passions, would often do no more than perpetuate his acts of injustice, nor could he ever avoid the danger that his views as a man might detract from the sanctity of his work."[42] Even one as honest and wise and disinterested as he cannot be trusted to remain incorrupt.

The Civil Religion. In addition to the traditional divisions of the law into political (basic or constitutional), criminal, and civil, Rousseau adds another, which he considers "the most important of them all." This, the civil religion, includes the entire way of life of the people, their manners, customs, and opinions. The civil religion provides the emotional basis of unity in any regime.[43]

Rousseau has a religious sensibility but does not accept traditional religions because they can divide the community. "Everything that disrupts the social bond of unity is valueless. All institutions which set a man in contradiction with himself are of no worth."[44] He distinguishes among three kinds of religion. The first two work against community. One, the "religion of man," is based on a pure inner faith and takes no external form. A pure religion of the Bible, it directs people to otherworldly goals and is irrelevant to politics. A second is the religion of the priest, for example, Roman Catholicism. Treating people as individuals, as souls, rather than as patriots, it divides people between two authorities, church and state. Citizens are always in doubt about where their loyalties should lie in any conflict between the two. At root, it is "impossible for them to be at the same time devout individuals and good citizens."[45] Only the third, the religion of the citizen, is compatible with the general will. This civil religion sustains peace and guarantees true freedom. It unites in one set of shared values each person's civic and sacred duties. Though far from perfect, being founded on error and lies, it is essential to the just society as a religious and political force that promotes greater social unity. The task of the civil religion is to emotionally reinforce the general will. It requires three simple beliefs of all citizens: God, immortality of the soul, and the justice of the social contract and its laws. Those who die for the community, Rousseau proclaims, are martyrs in a just cause who will be rewarded in the life to come, while the wicked will be punished.

Geography and Wealth. When Rousseau considers the size of the territory and population needed to establish the general will, small is beautiful. The most desirable and natural geographic setting is a community of limited population, much like the ancient Athenian polis. Small size enables all citizens to know each other through face-to-face contact in legislative meetings. This strengthens the social bonds between them. And in a small community the diverse interests are not so many as to inhibit the development of the general will.[46]

Small size must be accompanied by a simple economy. Rousseau opposes large economic gaps between rich and poor not only for political reasons but because of their destructive social effects. Wealth encourages people to amass luxuries and produces class divisions that make society more complex and less open to consensus. Rich and poor alike accept false economic values. They focus on personal and class interests rather than the good of the whole. They allow no opportunity for genuine community.

Because the general will works best when people are not interested in great wealth, the economic distance between rich and poor must be limited, though not abolished altogether. Rousseau favors as homogeneous a populace as possible, living in a simple society, the best sort being an agricultural community. He rejects societies based on industry or commerce, arguing that it is attachment to the soil that infuses people with love of their community and true economic values.

EXECUTIVE INSTITUTIONS

The executive branch, or government, is needed by the community as an intermediary between the people acting as citizens and as subjects. It is the agent that administers the law, calling on people to follow the general will and serving as a buffer between it and individual wills, especially those of disobedient subjects.

Two permanent executive offices are critical. The chief executive, or magistrate, issues decrees that apply the law to particular individuals. To enforce the law he is assisted by an entire bureaucracy, including such officials as policemen and jailers. The censor is a second permanent position. This office enforces correct public opinion in conformity with the general will. It is the guardian of the community's shared values found in the civil religion. A combination of educator and indoctrinator, the censor is to be especially rigorous in monitoring the arts and sciences, as they can weaken the spirit of patriotism by overcritically examining the people's way of life, thus softening citizens' commitment to the community. They can also promote leisure activities that lure citizens away from public concerns, thus encouraging a greater regard for private interests.

Two temporary offices are held in reserve. The tribunate is created by the legislature, as needed, to serve as a check on any executive action contrary to the general will. The other temporary office, that of dictator, is empowered by the legislature as supreme commander in dire emergencies that the original legislator did not anticipate or provide for in the contract, such as war or natural disaster. The magistrate cannot fill this role, as he was chosen to act in normal times and not to deal with such emergencies.

FORMS OF GOVERNMENT

Rousseau prefers a republic, or government of laws guided by the general will, for without the general will no regime is legitimate. For this reason, he denounces representative democracy as an oligarchical grant of lawmaking power to a small body of individuals. Since sovereignty is unalienable, legislative power cannot be legitimately delegated to representatives. It must be exercised continuously by the entire body of citizens or there is no republic.

Rousseau supports the simplest mixed form of government possible. The mix is composed of direct democracy in the legislature and delegation of authority to the smaller executive branch to enforce the general will. The exact sort of executive he recommends depends on the size of the community and how the citizens choose the administrators.

Rousseau considers either of two kinds of executive both realistic and compatible with a republic. Monarchy is best suited to large, wealthy states because "the larger the population, the stronger, relatively, must the government be, if it is to function efficiently." Though inconsistent in its behavior, a monarch is the most vigorous of chief executives.[47] As for aristocracy, he regards the hereditary form as the worst and the elective form as the best, if conditions allow for its installation. It is a superior form in states of medium-sized population and wealth because of the honesty and wisdom of the elected magistrates.

Even though Rousseau advocates democracy as well suited to small states, even there he favors it only for the legislature, not for the executive. In other words, he is an opponent of pure democracy, wherein the entire population acts as both legislature and executive. Rousseau says this is unnatural, something that "has never existed, nor ever will." Agreeing with Hobbes and Locke (who termed this the *state of nature*) Rousseau says it cannot work because it requires a people of gods.[48]

Echoing Aristotle, Rousseau does not hold out hope that any form of government, even the most suitable and moral, can last forever. "From the moment of its birth" the community is threatened by decay. Individual selfishness lurks beneath the surface, even if seemingly eclipsed by the appearance of unity among citizens. Its submersion in the general will is, at best, only temporary. Rousseau thinks that "sooner or later the [executive] will oppress the Sovereign and break the social treaty." The best any combination of legitimate contract, good institutions, and the most suitable form of government can do is to postpone the inevitable.[49]

CONCLUSION

If I am part of the general will, a citizen free to vote my best judgment of the public interest, why am I wrong when in the minority? How can people surrender their freedom to the collective but retain it at the same time? Of what value is that freedom to me if accompanied by force used against my will? These are just a few of the questions raised by Rousseau's paradox-ridden thought.

Because of their ambiguities, his writings have meant different things to different people, and a number of politicians have espoused conflicting interpretations while claiming only to apply his ideas to their times. For example, *The Social Contract* represents some of the loftiest ideals any human has ever articulated, such as liberated man and the community based on people's higher nature. At the same time, its ideas have led to some of the lowest of human actions, such as the French Revolution's Reign of Terror.[50] The question of how responsible Rousseau is for encouraging the ruthless behavior of some of his self-styled followers revolves around an issue that he does not clearly address: How far does control of the general will extend—is it meant to be total, or are there limits to its authority? The same question may be asked of the civil religion and the censors, as well as the legislator, the tribunate, and the dictator.

Many ancient and medieval philosophers, from Plato to Aquinas, proposed uniting elitism and organicism in order to secure a stable justice. They were willing to reject popular government for moral order. Rousseau's early-modern predecessors, from Machiavelli to Locke, linked populist ideals with individualism to achieve personal freedom. Rousseau, a neomodern, argues for replacing a political system based on early-modern materialism with one based on the idealism and organicism of the ancients, but one that rejects their emphasis on abstract reason in favor of patriotic feelings to guide the masses to collective unity. In so doing, he joins populism with organic politics.

Rousseau advocates a popular sovereignty linked to moral obligation in a society that subordinates the individual to the collective and promises political liberty and equality for all. He gives the ordinary, nonintellectual human being who possesses little or no private property a new dignity. No matter how stupid or poor, each can make a valuable contribution to the collective, given the proper setting. As long as their potential is not frustrated by social, geographical, or institutional restraints, everyone can participate in willing the general will.[51]

In common with two earlier philosophers of contract theory, Hobbes and Locke, Rousseau shifts the burden of proof concerning who should rule. Because of what he wrote, those advocating political elitism today must show why it is in the public interest for the few to govern without being held to a reasonable standard of consent and oversight by the many. But in contrast to Hobbes and Locke, when it comes to men's political role Rousseau has no apparent middle-class bias. No man is excluded from participating; the general will is to stem from full participation by all citizens.

Only women are excluded, the one area wherein Rousseau is not radical but quite conventional. But because of Rousseau's failure to discuss the exclusion of women from citizenship in the *Social Contract,* can his support of this bias elsewhere in his writings be noted and then set aside without negating the balance of his ideas? Is there any philosophical reason why women cannot be citizens in his community? In fact, might women, with their greater capacity for compassion, arguably be at least equal to, and perhaps better than, men when serving as citizens?

Notes

1. The prize-winning essay was his *First Discourse (On the Sciences and the Arts).* It was followed over the next several decades by the *Second Discourse (On the Origin and Basis of Inequality),* a long article, "Political Economy," for Diderot's great *Encyclopedia,* two novels (*Emile* and *Julie*), and several autobiographical works, most notably *The Confessions.* Rousseau also wrote poetry, plays, an opera, a musical dictionary, and numerous letters, some of which were extended essays on politically relevant subjects. For a fine study of Rousseau's key political writings, see Roger D. Masters, *The Political Philosophy of Rousseau* (Princeton, N.J.: Princeton University Press, 1968); and for an in-depth analysis of his writings from 1737 to 1756, see Mario Einaudi, *The Early Rousseau* (Ithaca, N.Y.: Cornell University Press, 1967).

2. While criticized as factually inaccurate and self-serving in places, Rousseau's *Confessions* is a major biographical source. See also Christopher Kelly, *Rousseau's Exemplary Life: The Confessions as Political Philosophy* (Ithaca, N.Y.: Cornell University Press, 1987). An excellent three-volume biography is Maurice Cranston, *Jean-Jacques: The Early Life and Work of Jean-Jacques Rousseau, 1712–1754* (Chicago: University of Chicago Press, 1983); *The Noble Savage: Jean-Jacques Rousseau, 1754–1762* (Chicago: University of Chicago Press, 1991); and *The Solitary Self: Jean-Jacques Rousseau in Exile and Adversity* (Chicago: University of Chicago Press, 1997).

3. See "Dedication" to Jean-Jacques Rousseau, *Second Discourse,* in *The Essential Rousseau,* trans. Lowell Bair (New York: New American Library, 1974), 127–36, which is addressed "To the Republic of Geneva."

4. Jean-Jacques Rousseau, *Emile,* trans. Barbara Foxley (London: J. M. Dent, 1974), 57.

5. See Hilel Gilden, *Rousseau's Social Contract: The Design of the Argument* (Chicago: University of Chicago Press, 1983); but for a study that argues Rousseau's work is quite clear and consistent, see N. J. H. Dent, *Rousseau: An Introduction to His Psychological, Social, and Political Theory* (New York: Basil Blackwell, 1989).

6. *Second Discourse,* 151, 163, 164; see also Marc Plattner, *Rousseau's State of Nature: An Interpretation of the "Discourse on Inequality"* (De Kalb: Northern Illinois University Press, 1979).

7. Jean-Jacques Rousseau, *The Social Contract,* trans. Gerald Hopkins, in *Social Contract: Essays by Locke, Hume and Rousseau,* ed. Ernest Barker (London: Oxford University Press, 1960), bk. 1, ch. 1.

8. The term Rousseau uses for this self-concern is *amour de soi,* an innocent, "gentle" interest in oneself that neither challenges nor harms anybody. By contrast, *amour-propre* refers to an "avaricious and aggressive" urge linked to how society perceives us, and thus with such motives as vanity, power, status, envy, contempt, and control over others. Diana Coole, *Women in Political Theory: From Ancient Misogyny to Contemporary Feminism* (Boulder, Colo.: Lynne Rienner, 1988), 115; see also *The Political Philosophy,* 38–41.

9. *Social Contract*, bk. 1, ch. 4.
10. *Social Contract*, bk. 1, ch. 2.
11. *Second Discourse*, 176–77.
12. Susan Moller Okin, *Women in Western Political Thought* (Princeton, N.J.: Princeton University Press, 1979), 111.
13. Jean Bethke Elshtain, *Public Man, Private Woman: Women in Social and Political Thought* (Princeton, N.J.: Princeton University Press, 1981), 151–54.
14. *Social Contract*, bk. 1, ch. 1.
15. *Second Discourse*, 173.
16. Property transforms the "gentle self-regard" of *amour de soi* into *amour-propre; Women in Political Theory*, 115.
17. *First Discourse*, 215.
18. *Social Contract*, bk. 1, ch. 8.
19. *Social Contract*, bk. 1, ch. 6.
20. *Social Contract*, bk. 1, ch. 4.
21. See http://politicalscience.wadsworth.com/tannenbaum2 for a link to an illustrated comparison of Rousseau's social contract, Locke's social contract, and Hobbes's political contract.
22. *Social Contract*, bk. 1, ch. 6.
23. *Social Contract*, bk. 2, ch. 4.
24. *Social Contract*, bk. 1, ch. 8.
25. For an in-depth examination of the origins and development of this concept, one of the most powerful in the arsenal of political philosophy, see Patrick Riley, *The General Will Before Rousseau: The Transformation of the Divine into the Civic* (Princeton, N.J.: Princeton University Press, 1986).
26. *Social Contract*, bk. 3, ch. 13.
27. *Social Contract*, bk. 2, ch. 4.
28. *Social Contract*, bk. 2, ch. 3.
29. *Social Contract*, bk. 1, ch. 7.
30. *Social Contract*, bk. 1, ch. 7.
31. See Judith Shklar, *Men and Citizens: A Study of Rousseau's Social Theory* (New York: Cambridge University Press, 1969); and Zev Trachtenberg, *Making Citizens: Rousseau's Political Theory of Culture* (New York: Routledge, 1993).
32. *Second Discourse*, 176–77.
33. *Emile*, 370.
34. *Women in Political Theory*, 108.
35. *Emile*, 359; *Second Discourse*, 135.
36. *Women in Western Political Thought*, 99–100, 150.
37. For example, see *Emile*, 356–57.
38. For a discussion of the ultimate failure of some of these goals, see *Women in Western Political Thought*, 169–72.
39. *Social Contract*, bk. 1, ch. 8. Here Rousseau is concerned with "positive" freedom, or the liberty one has to do something good and moral. By contrast, Machiavelli, Hobbes, and Locke promoted "negative" freedom to do (or not do) whatever one wishes in the absence of any legal restraint. These terms originated in a discussion by Isaiah Berlin, "Two Concepts of Liberty," in *Four Essays on Liberty* (New York: Oxford University Press, 1969); see also Daniel Cullen, *Freedom in Rousseau's Political Philosophy* (De Kalb: Northern Illinois University Press), 1993.
40. *Social Contract*, bk. 1, ch. 7.
41. *Social Contract*, bk. 2, ch. 7.
42. *Social Contract*, bk. 2, ch. 7.
43. *Social Contract*, bk. 2, ch. 12.
44. *Social Contract*, bk. 4, ch. 8.
45. *Social Contract*, bk. 4, ch. 8.
46. Rousseau also suggested how his theories might be applied to geographic conditions in two places that were less than ideal: *Constitutional Project for Corsica* (1761–65) and *Considerations on the Government of Poland* (1771).

47. *Social Contract*, bk. 3, ch. 1.

48. *Social Contract*, bk. 3, ch. 4. Pure democracy is also called direct or "true" democracy, and even anarchy. To require the participation of everyone in deciding all actions of government, executive as well as legislative, is to promote either a utopia or a disorderly situation that results in total breakdown because of the inability to get total cooperation of every participant in each decision.

49. *Social Contract*, bk. 3, ch. 10.

50. Joan McDonald, *Rousseau and the French Revolution: 1762–1791* (New York: Athlone, 1968). That Rousseau's meaning is still contested is shown by conflicting interpretations of his work in recent books. Thus the question of Rousseau's contribution to ideology is presented as a one-sided issue by J. L. Talmon, *The Origins of Totalitarian Democracy* (New York: Praeger, 1960), and debated as a multisided one by several authors in Guy Dodge, ed., *Jean-Jacques Rousseau: Authoritarian or Liberal?* (Lexington, Mass.: D. C. Heath, 1971).

51. Note, however, that Rousseau's neomodernism is limited. His political idealism is not matched in his economic proposals, which accept some material inequality, albeit in a simple community where he expects this will have little effect on political relationships.

Additional Readings

(* indicates alternative viewpoint)

Cullen, Daniel. *Freedom in Rousseau's Political Philosophy*. De Kalb: Northern Illinois University Press, 1993.

*Dent, N. J. H. *Rousseau: An Introduction to His Psychological, Social, and Political Theory*. New York: Basil Blackwell, 1989.

Gilden, Hilel. *Rousseau's Social Contract: The Design of the Argument*. Chicago: University of Chicago Press, 1983.

Kelly, Christopher. *Rousseau's Exemplary Life: The Confessions as Political Philosophy*. Ithaca, N.Y.: Cornell University Press, 1987.

Masters, Roger D. *The Political Philosophy of Rousseau*. Princeton, N.J.: Princeton University Press, 1968.

Shklar, Judith. *Men and Citizens: A Study of Rousseau's Social Theory*. New York: Cambridge University Press, 1969.

Swenson, James. *On Jean-Jacques Rousseau: Considered as One of the First Authors of the Revolution*. Stanford, Calif.: Stanford University Press, 2000.

Trachtenberg, Zev. *Making Citizens: Rousseau's Political Theory of Culture*. New York: Routledge, 1993.

Inventors of Ideas Online

Visit http://politicalscience.wadsworth.com/tannenbaum2 for links related to material in this chapter, including an illustration of the differences between Rousseau's social contract, Locke's social contract, and Hobbes's political contract and the full text of a number of Rousseau's works.

15

MARY WOLLSTONECRAFT: ORIGINS OF MODERN FEMINISM

INTRODUCTION

Mary Wollstonecraft (1759–1797) is a Janus-faced figure in political theory. Writing in the midst of a tradition of political theory dominated by men, she employed many of their argumentative techniques, assumptions, and arguments regarding human nature and government, yet her conclusions defined a new role for women in society—that of equals to men. Thus her political philosophy both looks backward in its borrowing of traditional tools of analysis and looks forward in her innovative use of these tools to serve new ends that challenged the gender roles beliefs that were embedded in, and supported by the writings of Locke, Hobbes, and Rousseau.

Yet Mary Wollstonecraft was not alone. She was one of several female writers and political thinkers to take many of the arguments of modern politics, science, and liberalism and apply them to women. Her most famous book, *A Vindication of the Rights of Women* (1792), was widely read during her time and often commented upon, by both her contemporaries and later feminists, who described it as the origin and touchstone of modern feminism.

In addition to *A Vindication of the Rights of Women*, Mary Wollstonecraft wrote several other books, including *A Vindication of the Rights of Men* (1790). This book was written in response to Edmund Burke's attack on the French Revolution in his *Reflections on the Revolution in France*. In that book, Burke blamed the excesses of the revolution on the abandonment of tradition and the embrace of reason and abstract political rights. In denouncing the revolution and the government instituted afterward, Burke emotionally evoked female bodily and sexual metaphors, describing the revolution as "an orgy" and the new government as a "diseased prostitute."

Wollstonecraft attacks the use of sexual and bodily images in response to Burke. She crafts her own images, this time male, to indicate that virtue and gender are not connected, and to show that men were also responsible for the new order in France.[1] In contrast to Burke's emotional style and tone, Wollstonecraft employs the language of liberalism and reason, demonstrating that neither has a specific gender and that both can be invoked by women in defense of their interests. Thus Wollstonecraft's writings attack tradition, advocate reason and education, and offer arguments that draw connections between the irrational, the tyrannical, and the absence of learning. Making these connections leads Wollstonecraft to link the status of uneducated women to feudal aristocrats and lack of social progress. In the process, she appeals to liberal values to show how neither stands the test of rationality.

Reading *A Vindication of the Rights of Women* raises some questions about its context and audience and how these influences should be understood. Context and audience are issues with any work of political theory because personal interest or motivation in writing a book may influence how readers judge it. To read Machiavelli's *Prince* as a plea for a job rather than a political treatise may change its meaning. Similarly, if the primary audience of Descartes's books was a scientific community, this may influence how seriously one takes appeals to God in his methodology.

A Vindication of the Rights of Women can also be read somewhat autobiographically. Events in Wollstonecraft's life that factored into the book include her work in politics, especially her association with figures such as Thomas Paine, and her marriage to political activist William Godwin. Her familiarity with many of Britain's important male political writers likely also influenced *Vindication*'s arguments and language. Although the book is an appeal for the education and equal treatment of women, most likely the audience was mainly men who supported both the values of political liberalism and traditional roles for women. Wollstonecraft's argument for the education of women as necessary to make them better wives and mothers, then, can be seen as either a sincere claim on her part, or a rhetorical device meant to assure men that women's education would pose no threat to male dominance. Such assessments of the audience can throw light on how radical Wollstonecraft's arguments really are.

WOLLSTONECRAFT'S METHOD

Mary Wollstonecraft turned much of then contemporary political theory on its head. The tools of reason that the political writings of thinkers such as Machiavelli, Hobbes, Locke, and Rousseau had employed to challenge the authority of the church, faith, and the absolutism of monarchs were instead directed at the views they had on women. Wollstonecraft joined her male theorists in attacking the religious and familial metaphors that supported all three of these institutions, but she extended their arguments to question the conventional assumptions about the nature of men and women. Thus while Wollstonecraft shared much with these thinkers, she also broke new ground.

For philosophers such as Locke and Hobbes, in place of earlier appeals to God and the Bible to sustain authority, novel concepts articulated a new vision of politics. These concepts included appeals to social contracts, constructed by individuals, and contractual analogies as the basis of a political order that had to ultimately rest upon a rational foundation if it were to be considered legitimate. Hence ultimate political power resided in the individual who, outside of political society, created and defined the scope and authority of the polity.

But the development of modern political assumptions and ideas was primarily undertaken by men. Although the use of reason and the new assumptions challenged many traditional assertions about politics, views on the family and the role of women in both the family and politics were generally left undisturbed. Social contract logic redefined political society as a voluntary and artificial community constructed by humans, not by God. But it was a contract by and among men that appeared to exclude women from participation.[2] Thus women were still relegated to a secondary status.

The emergence of social contract thinking posed many challenges to the traditional role of women, however. First, modern social contract thinking assumed that the construction of political society was an act of reason or rationality. Hobbes, Locke, and Rousseau employed various conceptions of reason to challenge old political truths en route to showing how men, equipped with deliberative capacity, could create a new type of political order premised on consent. But the reason they defined, though seen by Bacon and Descartes as something universal, was really something found only among men, especially those who had been educated to control or eliminate the biases and passions that clouded the human understanding. Men had rational capacity, women a more emotional, passionate, or affective personality, meaning that there were contrasting roles for men and women due to their contrasting natures. Rousseau wrote in *Emile* that men and women have different capacities, and therefore Emile and Sophie should be educated differently in order to assume their respective roles as citizen-man and wife.

In emphasizing that political society was voluntary and premised on individual consent, writers such as Hobbes and Locke had to contend with defining how women consented to their roles. For premodern thinkers, justifying the subordination of women through consent had not been a problem because appeals to religion, tradition, and nature, not reason or personal consent, were invoked to defend it. But among the moderns, recasting society in terms of secular, rational, and consensual arguments meant that these same arguments could be applied to family and gender roles. Despite attempts to apply some of their political assumptions and tools of analysis to the family, for the most part philosophers exempted the private realm of women and family from the logic of their own arguments.

Hobbes, for example, assumed that in the state of nature men and women were equal, with children remaining the birthright of women. Upon the construction of political society and the family, though, women were excluded from politics, birthright switched to the husband, and wives were subordinated to their husbands.[3] Locke redefined political society as a voluntary association among equals. He redefines marriage similarly, holding out the promise of divorce as an option for women if the marriage threatens her rights. Yet, when it comes to determining the head of the household, Locke assumes that men naturally should rule over women, without invoking any good reason except nature or tradition.[4]

The problem for Hobbes and Locke, as well as for other political philosophers, was how to argue that women are free and rational enough to consent to a voluntary political order, and at the same time argue that women are not free or rational and are therefore properly subordinate to men.[5] These writers were trying to contend with a contradictory vision of human nature: That men, when educated or civilized, achieved their real rational nature; but that women were naturally passionate or irrational and that education would not change this.

One way out of these dilemmas was not to challenge the stereotypes at all, to just live with the contradictions. This meant the continued use of patriarchal and familial assumptions that had dated back to Aristotle, appropriated to serve new ends. As political society was redefined, so was the family. Yet the traditional-family model was never severed from the assumption that it was natural. It was redefined so that the patriarchal underpinnings continued to support it. Reason failed to challenge the structures of the family and women's roles; and a redefined political order continued to support them. And a social contract among men presupposed a sexual contract that subordinated women.

Not everyone remained content with one set of political rules and assumptions for men and another for women, however. Starting in the seventeenth and eighteenth centuries, women philosophers and thinkers challenged many of the assumptions about men, women, family, politics, and reason. They adopted "male" arguments and applied them to women. Some argued that the universalism of reason proclaimed by Descartes did in fact extend to women.[6] Mary Astell (1666–1731) argued in *A Serious Proposal to Ladies* that "all may think, may use their faculties rightly, and consult the master who is within them."[7] All that was required to perfect this thinking was an education for women comparable to that for men.

Others, such as Princess Elizabeth of Bohemia (1618–1680) and Margaret Cavendish (1623–1673), challenged Descartes and other male philosophers on a variety of points. If Descartes was correct that humans were above all thinking beings, his claim raised questions about how important the body, male or female, was to distinctions among the souls of individuals. If the body were unimportant to distinctions among men, why was it meaningful in differentiating men from women? Finally, Hannah More (1745–1833) questioned the minor role women were given in politics, contending that their efforts were as important as men's in the future happiness and progress of civilization.[8]

Although many political philosophers employed reason to challenge the traditions and assumptions that supported the church and the political authority of the monarchies, this same reason was not invoked by men to question how religion and tradition continued to support old assumptions governing women and the family. None of these thinkers even questioned how reason was being employed to provide new foundations for the old biases. Hence many male philosophers used reason to protect the traditional family, male authority, and female subordination. It was up to women philosophers of the seventeenth and eighteenth centuries, then, to examine the interconnections between reason, tradition, religion, and gender, and to extend the promise of science and reason to the defense of women. This is exactly what Mary Wollstonecraft did.

HUMAN NATURE

In *A Vindication of the Rights of Women*, Wollstonecraft argues against the proposition that women are naturally emotional or intellectually inferior. Her contention is that the lack of intellectual development in women is due to the differences in educational opportunities between the two sexes. While men receive an intellectual education, women are left to be educated by society, which results in cultivation of emotional and feminine traits. According to Wollstonecraft,

> It would be an endless task to trace the variety of meanness, cares, and sorrows, into which women are plunged by the prevailing opinion, that they were created rather to feel than reason, and that all the power they obtain must be obtained by their charms and weakness. . . .[9]

Wollstonecraft agrees in large part with Rousseau that manners are artificial, simply the product of society and education. But while Rousseau argued that the traits of men in society were artificial and those of women natural, Wollstonecraft extends Rousseau's arguments by asserting that feminine traits are the products of social convention and opinion as much as masculine ones are. *A Vindication of the Rights of Women* is in many ways as much a response to Rousseau as her first *Vindication* was to Burke. Yet, despite attacking Rousseau and his discussion of Emile, Sophie, and gender roles in *Emile*, Wollstonecraft appropriates many of Rousseau's assumptions regarding men in civilization and addresses them to the circumstances facing women. She thus questions the differences in social roles, education, and expectations between men and women in Rousseau's works, and argues for similar educational opportunities for both.

In her introduction to *Vindication*, as well as its dedication to the Bishop of Autun, Wollstonecraft argues that women have been rendered weak by a variety of causes, but that the current conduct of women's manners is produced by a false system of education more anxious to make them "alluring mistresses than affectionate wives and rational mothers."[10] The educational system, seeking to preserve women's innocence, does so by enforcing their ignorance. Any weaknesses displayed by women are thus the products of their lack of cultivation of understanding. This forces women to live according to the prejudices of society. The results represent not the true essence of women but the same corruptive influences of civilization as Rousseau described for men:

> In short, women, in general, as well as the rich of both sexes, have acquired all the follies and vices of civilization. . . . Civilized women are, therefore, so weakened by false refinement, that, respecting morals, their condition is much below what it would be were they left in the state of nature.[11]

For Wollstonecraft, the character of women is artificial, a consequence of the roles society defines for them. Women are fond of dress and gossip, are helpless, emotional, and weak, and act like children not because it is their nature but because they are educated or trained to be this way.[12]

Despite that men may be physically superior by nature, Wollstonecraft asserts that men are not content with this, instead seeking to make women inferior in other ways and to render them alluring objects who pay homage to men. Women have been placed so low in society that Wollstonecraft sees them as having sunk below the level of rational creatures. Out of ignorance, women are attracted to the attention of men and fall for it.

Consequently, society has adopted a mistaken notion of what female excellence is. In her dedication to the Bishop of Autun, she states the basic argument of *Vindication:* that women should be educated to be companions for men, because if not, no progress toward virtue and knowledge can be made. Women should have the same education because "truth is common to all," and all—including women—have the capacity to reason if given the proper education.

To support her claim that men and women are equal in their capacity to reason, Wollstonecraft poses and answers three questions that defend the universal role of reason, virtue, and education in human affairs:

> In what does man's preeminence over the brute creation consist? The answer is clearly as that a half is less than the whole, in Reason.
>
> What acquirement exalts one's being above another? Virtue, as we spontaneously reply.
>
> For what purpose were the passions implanted? That man by struggling with them might attain a degree of knowledge denied to the brutes, whispers Experience.
>
> Consequently, the perfection of our reason and capability of happiness must be estimated by the degree of reason, virtue, and knowledge, that distinguish the individual, and direct the laws which bind society; and that from the exercise of reason, knowledge, and virtue naturally flow, is equally undeniable, if mankind be viewed collectively.[13]

Much in the same way that Hobbes and Rousseau described humans in the state of nature as basically equal, Wollstonecraft asserts a fundamental commonality to human nature that transcends gender. All humans, not simply men, have the capacity for reason, virtue, and knowledge, yet not all are given the opportunity to display them. The education and other opportunities men and women are given produce the apparent differences between the two.

Wollstonecraft defines the "sensual error" as thinking that women's manners are naturally different from and inferior to those of men.[14] She contends that despite the many arguments given to account for the differences between the sexes, both have souls. Thus there is but one way to lead humankind to either virtue or happiness, and this is through the education all should receive. According to Wollstonecraft, women are taught inferiority, outward obedience, and to act as "ephemeron triflers."[15] Since by nature the virtue and knowledge of the sexes is the same, the only real difference between them comes from the superior advantage of liberty and education enabling men to see more of life.

Civilized women are therefore so weakened by false refinement that their condition is much lower than it would be were they left nearer to a state of nature.[16] Women act the way they do because emotionalism is promoted in them, which in turn leads to the dependency that makes it appear they cannot control themselves due to their ignorance.[17] According to Wollstonecraft, a "mistaken education, a narrow uncultivated mind, and many sexual prejudices tend to make women more constant than men,"[18] thus producing women's social personality.

The solution to these flaws is to extend the same educational opportunities to women as are given to men. Furthermore, instruction should be coeducational, and rich and poor educated together. For Wollstonecraft, to strengthen the female mind by enlarging it is to end women's blind obedience and living for pleasure. Yet she opposes private education for men and women, and wants neither educated simply in light of the opinions and manners of current society. Here, Wollstonecraft appeals to Rousseau, contending that the best education fosters understanding that strengthens the body and forms the heart.[19] Rousseau's goal of education, which he applied to men, Wollstonecraft extends to women.

WOMEN, THE FAMILY, AND GOVERNMENT

In attacking the lack of educational opportunities for women, Wollstonecraft draws a connection between the status of uneducated women, aristocrats, and the corrupting forces of civilization. She occasionally argues that women are enslaved by the family and political structure, and often contends that uneducated women are like nobles. They are not only undeserving of their position and power over men, but their ignorance corrupts men and society, much as Rousseau saw civilization corrupting and debasing men.

Wollstonecraft calls on the liberal values and arguments men used against the illegitimate power of the nobility and applies them to the status of women. She argues that it is cruel to subject a rational person of mature age to the mere will of another, including that of a king. Attacking the nobility, she declares,

> The preposterous distinctions of rank, which render civilization a curse, by dividing the world between voluptuous tyrants and cunning envious dependents, corrupt, almost equally, every class of people, because respectability is not attached to the discharge of the relative duties of life, but to the station. . . .[20]

In describing nobles as voluptuous and cunning, Wollstonecraft uses sexual language and stereotypes often applied to women. In the same way that nobles exercise excessive power, she describes women as tyrants who use power by unjust means and vice.[21] For Wollstonecraft, what is needed is a revolution in female manners in order to reform not only women but the world.[22]

> Women, as well as despots, have now perhaps more power than they would have if the world, divided and subdivided into kingdoms and families, were

governed by laws educed from the exercise of reason. . . . I, therefore, will venture to assert that till women are more rationally educated, the progress of human virtue and improvement in knowledge must receive continual checks.[23]

Here again, Wollstonecraft's comparison of families to kingdoms is important in that it connects the privileges of the *ancien régime* and the logic of paternal society. She contends that in both the monarchy and the family, pure authority, not reason, tends to rule. Wollstonecraft suggests that the justification of the one rests upon similar reasoning as that of the other. She offers that, "The divine right of husbands, like the divine right of kings, may, it is to be hoped, in this enlightened age, be contested without danger."[24] Wollstonecraft thus extends the arguments of John Locke and other liberals to the family sphere. If the tool of reason can be used to question and check excessive political power, the tool of reason, in the form of education for women, should similarly check women's excessive power over men.

Reexamination of familial authority leads Wollstonecraft to redefine family structure much as Locke sought to do. She contrasts the natural versus accidental duties of parents, the former being the duty to form the heart and enlarge the understanding of the child. The artificial duties of parents include control over whom a child shall marry once he or she is of age. For Wollstonecraft, such artificial duties are debasing and similar to a slavish respect for property. Furthermore, Wollstonecraft contends that the "father who is blindly obeyed is obeyed from sheer weaknesses, or from motives that degrade the human character."[25] The result is that women are under the dominion of parents too much and are denied their freedom. Only when the divine right of the parents is challenged, as it was in politics, and only when reason comes to prevail in parental authority, can the structure of the family change.

Similarly, Wollstonecraft argues that monarchical and aristocratic governments are incompatible with intellectual development. If flattery makes such kings useless, she says, is not the same true of women who are uneducated? She contends that it is impossible for any man to acquire knowledge when a king has unlimited power and when his pleasure shuts out learning.[26] Likewise uneducated women are oppressed and as useless as aristocrats.

Considering that the character of every man is formed by his occupation, Wollstonecraft indicates that women are like either slaves or despots as a result of their lack of reason. In addition to these parallels, Wollstonecraft invokes Rousseau's language regarding the corrupting effects of civilization to show how gender distinctions are artificial and damaging. She describes "wealth and female softness" as equally debasing to humankind. And she sees the origin of both in the same cause that produces other social distinctions: property. If it is from property that most of the societal diseases and vices flow, then property causes even more damage to women than to man or society as a whole because women are kept ignorant. But if women are educated, they become free, shed their excessive power over men, are better overall in the performance of their duties, and are less susceptible to the corruption of society.

THE LIBERATION OF WOMEN

Wollstonecraft recounts several benefits husbands and society can receive from having more enlightened women:

> Would men but generously snap [off] our chains, and be content with rational fellowship instead of slavish obedience, they would find us more observant daughters, more affectionate sisters, more faithful wives, more reasonable mothers—in a word, better citizens. We should then love them with true affection, because we should learn to respect ourselves; and the peace of mind of a worthy man would not be interrupted by the idle vanity of his wife. . . .[27]

She asserts that educating women refines their domestic taste and makes them better daughters, wives, and citizens. Indolent women do not make the best wives. And husbands and wives have little in common as a result of their different educations. Educating women would make them more loving and devoted wives.

Wollstonecraft also argues that running a family requires educated women. To be good mothers to their children, women must have good minds. The education of children is too important a task to be left to the ignorant. But when women are married off early, they never acquire a sense of identity, or knowledge of the world or the duties they should perform. Thus education benefits women, but it also benefits their husbands and their children.

Wollstonecraft invokes eighteenth-century language and faith in progress to show how the education of women benefits morality and society as a whole. She argues that the only solid foundation of morality comes from God, not man, and that this morality does not prescribe one set of virtues to one sex and a different set to the other. That is, she rejects gender-specific virtues, asserting, rather, that they are universal:

> I wish to sum up what I have said in a few words, for I here throw down my gauntlet, and deny the existence of sexual virtues, not excepting modesty. For man and woman, truth, if I understand the meaning of the word, must be the same. . . . Women, I allow, have different duties to fulfill; but they are human duties.[28]

Furthermore,

> To render mankind more virtuous, and happier of course, both sexes must act from the same principle; but how can that be expected when only one is allowed to see the reasonableness of it? To render also the social compact truly equitable, and in order to spread those enlightened principles, which alone can ameliorate the fate of man, women must be allowed to found their virtue on knowledge.[29]

For Wollstonecraft, prevailing notions of sexual character are subversive to morality and chastity. And such ideas must be universally applied for the betterment of society and the progress of civilization. Traditional sexual roles undermine morality by turning moral behavior into show rather than substance, more concerned with how men and women appear than with who they are. To Wollstonecraft, the separate roles for men and women mutually corrupt and debase both sexes.[30] Men fail to act modestly and chastely, while women, so long as they remain uneducated and treated like slaves, are incapable of virtue. Reason is necessary to modesty, so if women are to be modest, they must be educated so they will no longer hold back society.[31] Moreover, if girls and boys are educated together, society could promote good morals through early marriages. And if the two sexes are educated the same way, both are able to live according to the fundamental rule of social behavior, which is to "cherish such a habitual respect for mankind as may prevent us from disgusting a fellow-creature for the sake of a present indulgence."[32]

But despite the appeals made to social morality and the improvement of women as better wives and mothers, Wollstonecraft also provides other arguments for why education will benefit women themselves. On one level, Wollstonecraft contends that while women are presently considered voluptuous, "true voluptuousness must proceed from the mind," and that mutual respect will produce mutual affection. She also invokes religion and argues that for women to have an immortal soul they must be educated. An educated woman could develop a more comprehensive view of the world that would benefit her.

Perhaps more importantly, ignorant women are not good citizens. Lacking rational capacity, such women are unable to rise to the civic level that men achieve, thus remaining subordinate and virtueless until they are "in some degree independent of men."[33] Overall, for Wollstonecraft, women have three sets of duties: to the self, as a citizen, and as a mother. Education is necessary to all three.[34] Since women have some duties that are the same as those of men, they should similarly be educated to be good citizens and perform the duties that parallel those of men. In effect, women should stand in the same relation to the state that men occupy, subject to the same rights and limits. Hence the standards that Wollstonecraft adopts for women are the modesty and virtue of traditional women but otherwise the behavior and duties of men. Appealing for the universality of reason, she states, "Let woman share the rights, and she will emulate the virtues of man."[35]

WOMEN, MEN, AND CIVIL SOCIETY

The primary focus of Mary Wollstonecraft's arguments was directed toward the liberation of women from conventional societal views. Paralleling but diverging from Rousseau, her primary concern is reformation of the educational system. Change the way people are educated, and one will create a new and more equal society.

But much like Locke, reformation of the family appeared to be key to political reform. If John Locke rethought the relationship of the family to civil society in an effort to reject the patriarchialism of Filmer, Wollstonecraft took Locke's argument to their conclusion, making marriage a voluntary union of equals. A marriage of equals is the model for political society. Thus she does not advocate abandoning marriage as a cornerstone for civil society; instead Wollstonecraft reinvents it to serve her political vision.

Mary Wollstonecraft does not ignore the need for other political reforms, and she addresses them throughout her writings. Yet her political reforms are dual edged. On the one hand she calls for radical change—equal respect and treatment of men and women—but she seems to believe that this equalization of gender roles can occur within the institutions called for by many other of the reformers of the day. Like John Locke and Thomas Paine, she calls for the abolition of monarchy and aristocratic privilege, and she appears to endorse a republican form of government that protects both liberty and virtue. In fact, she endorses a vision of an ideal or good government very much in language reminiscent of Locke in that the "end of all political association is the preservation of the natural and imprescriptible rights of man which rights are—liberty, property, security, and the resistence of opposition."[36]

Wollstonecraft also attacked as corrupt both elections and parliamentary representation. Simultaneously, she advocated that women should have their own representatives while rejecting representation in general because it fostered despotism.[37] Moreover, in joining perhaps some of the more radical reformers of the day who saw society as pervaded by inequalities of all types, she contended that "the end of government ought to be, to destroy this inequality by protecting the weak."[38] Wollstonecraft's conception of the liberal state, then, was more activist or interventionist than might be expected, in that tending to the improvement of the virtue of the people ought to be a duty of the state. This, of course, would primarily be accomplished through her education reforms.

Finally, Wollstonecraft also demanded an end to primogeniture and reform of marriage property laws. She called for abolition of the death penalty, public executions, slavery, and the maintenance of standing armies. She also demanded religious toleration.[39] Other reformers of the day advocated similar positions. However, in her last book, *The Wrongs of Women*, she parted company from her male contemporaries and pressed the case for divorce.[40] While radical in its time, perhaps the right to divorce was a logical application of Locke's right to political revolution, only in this case applied to marriage. If both civil societies and marriages were the product of voluntary consent to secure certain ends, the parties to both should equally have the right to end both of these institutions.

CONCLUSION

Mary Wollstonecraft is a modern theorist sharing many ideas with other moderns such as Locke and Rousseau. She adopts the language of reason and the Enlightenment used by men to question political power and employs it to challenge parental authority and the structure of the family. By doing so, she seeks to extend the revolution of reason and liberalism to the status of women in the state as well as the family.

Wollstonecraft makes an appeal for equal educational opportunities for women. She claims that such equality would be good for women both because they could assume the same duties as men and because it would allow women to better perform their traditional roles. Wollstonecraft's arguments in *A Vindication of the Rights of Women* thus appear to have two contradictory goals: to question traditional gender, family, and political roles, while at the same time appealing to those values that supported patriarchalism. Her uniqueness as a political philosopher thus lies in questioning the private relations and roles of the family. In effect, she seems to open up the private lives of women to public inspection.[41] In doing that, she perhaps anticipates later twentieth century feminists who argued that the "private is political" as they too sought to question traditional family and gender relations.

Wollstonecraft's political legacy is significant yet ambiguous. Her writings influenced later feminists such as Susan B. Anthony and Elizabeth Cady Stanton. Emma Goldman and Suzanne LaFollette, both famous in the early twentieth century, described her as the first feminist and *A Vindication of the Rights of Women* a declaration of independence for women.[42] However, Harriet Martineau, an important nineteenth-century British writer, stated that Wollstonecraft was "not a successful champion of Woman and her Rights" because she was a "poor victim of passion, with no control over her own peace."[43] To Martineau, Wollstonecraft's personal life and unhappiness made the claims in her book too personal to address the broader needs and concerns of women. For others, depending on their viewpoint, Wollstonecraft's advocacy of universal morality and the same set of duties for men and women, and her appeal for women to be treated more like men, offer either the promise of equality or a denial of women's special insights, experiences, and feelings that distinguish them from men.[44]

Mary Wollstonecraft's assertions that men and women are alike in all essential characteristics, except for those produced as a result of education, anticipate later feminist arguments over the biological versus the social, that is, which factors account for differences in the natures of men and women. Some feminists have argued that there are essential, biological differences between the two, while others have contended that, except for the anatomical differences, the only important distinctions to emerge so far are those that are the result of education or political socialization.

Yet one wonders if the changes Wollstonecraft wanted could occur as she hoped. She seemed to believe that men and women could achieve equality within the existing political and familial institutions, yet could these institutions really permit the equality she wanted? Contemporary feminists, such as Catherine MacKinnon, argue that the law and society's political institutions are based on male assumptions such that women can never achieve equality within them.[45] Needed is a wholesale reform of society—perhaps from the social contract up—if women are to achieve parity. The debate over whether women can become equals within the existing institutions, or whether the emancipation of women could only take place within the context of more radical reform, remains a question to this day.

Vindication offers either the perfect prescription for women's emancipation by challenging family authority and contrasting gender roles, or it yet again limits women by preserving the family structure, maintaining traditional roles, and denying the distinct sphere of experience all women share. Whatever the final consensus on her legacy, Mary Wollstonecraft represents an important voice in the history of political thought. By extending the arguments of seventeenth- and eighteenth-century philosophers beyond religion and the political community to the family, she launched important challenges to the way tradition, politics, reason, and gender interacted. Wollstonecraft's writings raise important questions: Are men and women by nature the same or different? If different, in what respects, and do those differences mean anything politically in terms of what duties we assign to either? How do educational or socialization differences contribute to differences between men and women? Can women achieve equal rights to men by reforming contemporary society, or are more fundamental changes required?

Overall, Mary Wollstonecraft's significance, much like Antigone's, lies in her novel way to depict and organize the different spheres of life in a world that was changing. But whether her political theory and views on men and women provide an acceptable model for women's liberation remain a matter of debate to this day.

Notes

1. Virginia Sapiro, *A Vindication of Political Virtue: The Political Theory of Mary Wollstonecraft* (Chicago: University of Chicago Press, 1992), 203.
2. Carol E. Pateman, *The Sexual Contract* (Stanford, Calif.: Stanford University Press, 1988).
3. Thomas Hobbes, *Leviathan* (New York: Penguin, 1985), 254 (ch. 20).
4. John Locke, *Two Treatises of Government* (New York: Cambridge University Press, 1992), 321–22 (para. 82).
5. *Sexual Contract,* 231.
6. Margaret Atherton, *Women Philosophers of the Early Modern Period* (Indianapolis: Hackett, 1994), 3.
7. *Women Philosophers,* 4.
8. Bonnie S. Anderson and Judith P. Zinsser, *A History of Their Own: Women in Europe from Prehistory to the Present,* vol. 2 (New York: Harper & Row, 1988), 126.
9. Mary Wollstonecraft, *A Vindication of the Rights of Women* (Buffalo, N.Y.: Prometheus Books, 1989), 70.
10. *Vindication of Rights,* 9.
11. *Vindication of Rights,* 69.
12. *Vindication of Rights,* 124.
13. *Vindication of Rights,* 21.
14. *Vindication of Rights,* 62.
15. *Vindication of Rights,* 29.
16. *Vindication of Rights,* 69.
17. *Vindication of Rights,* 71.
18. *Vindication of Rights,* 40.
19. *Vindication of Rights,* 31.
20. *Vindication of Rights,* 153.
21. *Vindication of Rights,* 63.

22. *Vindication of Rights*, 54.

23. *Vindication of Rights*, 49.

24. *Vindication of Rights*, 50.

25. *Vindication of Rights*, 164.

26. *Vindication of Rights*, 25.

27. *Vindication of Rights*, 158.

28. *Vindication of Rights*, 59.

29. *Vindication of Rights*, 185.

30. *Vindication of Rights*, 147.

31. *Vindication of Rights*, 138.

32. *Vindication of Rights*, 145.

33. *Vindication of Rights*, 150.

34. *Vindication of Rights*, 150.

35. *Vindication of Rights*, 206.

36. Mary Wollstonecraft, as cited in *Vindication of Political Virtue*, p. 233.

37. Mary Wollstonecraft, *A Vindication of the Rights of Men*, in *The Works of Mary Wollstonecraft*, vol. 5, ed. Janet Todd and Marilyn Butler (New York: NYU Press, 1989), p. 9.

38. Mary Wollstonecraft, as cited in *Vindication of Political Virtue*, p. 233.

39. Susan Ferguson, "The Radical Ideas of Mary Wollstonecraft," *Canadian Journal of Political Science* 32 (September 1999): p. 427.

40. Mary Wollstonecraft, "The Wrongs of Woman," in *Mary, A Fiction, and The Wrongs of Woman*, ed. Gary Kelly (New York: Oxford University Press, 1976).

41. Wendy Gunther-Canada. *Rebel Writer: Mary Wollstonecraft and Enlightenment Politics* (DeKalb: Northern Illinois University Press, 2001) pp. 155-58.

42. *Vindication of Political Virtue*, 259–60.

43. Harriet Martineau, "The Woman Question," in *Harriet Martineau on Women*, ed. G. G. Yates (New Brunswick, N.J.: Rutgers University Press, 1985), 81–83.

44. Carol Gilligan, *In a Different Voice: Psychological Theory and Women's Development* (Cambridge, Mass.: Harvard University Press, 1982).

45. MacKinnon, Catherine A., *Towards a Feminist Theory of the State* (Cambridge, Mass.: Harvard University Press, 1989).

Additional Readings

Atherton, Margaret. *Women Philosophers of the Early Modern Period*. Indianapolis: Hackett, 1994.

Gunther-Canada, Wendy. *Rebel Writer: Mary Wollstonecraft and Enlightenment Politics*. DeKalb: Northern Illinois University Press, 2001.

Jacobs, Diane, *Her Own Woman: The Life of Mary Wollstonecraft*. New York: Simon & Schuster, 2001.

Kelly, Gary. *Revolutionary Feminism: The Mind and Career of Mary Wollstonecraft*. New York: St. Martin's, 1992.

Pateman, Carol. *The Sexual Contract*. Stanford, Calif.: Stanford University Press, 1988.

Sapiro, Virginia. *A Vindication of Political Virtue: The Political Theory of Mary Wollstonecraft*. Chicago: University of Chicago Press, 1992.

Wardle, Ralph Martin. *Mary Wollstonecraft: A Critical Biography*. Lincoln: University of Nebraska Press, 1966.

 Inventors of Ideas Online

Visit http://politicalscience.wadsworth.com/tannenbaum2 for links related to material in this chapter, including the Mary Wollstonecraft Shelley Chronology and Resource Site and the full text of *A Vindication of the Rights of Women*.

16

HUME, BURKE, AND KANT: CRITICS AND DEFENDERS OF THE ENLIGHTENMENT

INTRODUCTION

Theorists who were part of the Enlightenment shared many concerns and assumptions that defined modern political thought. During the period from approximately 1500 to 1800, many political thinkers and scientists shared the belief that religious values and the methods of the classical and Christian writers had failed to provide an exact and certain way for humans to know the world and to support their truths. Whether by Francis Bacon, René Descartes, Thomas Hobbes, or John Locke, appeals to science and reason were increasingly made in the hope that both could provide a better way to know the natural and political worlds. Employing reason, individuals could examine old assumptions and truths, ask if they were able to withstand rational scrutiny, and if not, create new political values and truths that would stand up to the demands of the increasingly scientific world.

One legacy of this attraction to science and reason was redefinition of how individuals saw the natural world and their role in and relationship to it. For example, by employing the scientific method, Nicholas Copernicus and Isaac Newton redefined how the universe looked and behaved. Similarly, numerous political thinkers used reason to question old political truths, the political order, and the boundary between religious and secular authority, producing new rational grounds for moral and political authority as well as a new role for individuals in a new type of political community.[1]

In regrounding politics in the logic of reason, many philosophers posited new ideas and assumptions to define their political world. For example, to justify political authority, Locke, Hobbes, and Rousseau employed the concept of the social contract and the idea of the voluntary will to obey as ways to explain the origins of civil society.[2] They meant that at some point in the distant past, individuals in the state of nature agreed to band together to form a civil society, to create a government, and to bind themselves to obey its laws, subject to certain specified conditions and limitations. Social contract theory justified a conception of political society premised on natural rights and the protection of individual liberty as the defining trait of politics.[3]

Hobbes, Locke, Rousseau, and other philosophers also shared the belief that political society is artificial, not natural; that there are limits and constraints on political authority; and that individuals have the right to create, and perhaps disband, political society if it fails to secure specific goals. All of these political truths could be verified by reason.

The implications of these new political ideas were not simply theoretical. In a number of cases, appeals to reason, social contracts, and individual rights led to revolution—in England in 1688, the American colonies in 1776, and in France in 1789. These were revolutions against monarchies, which produced political regimes vastly limiting or eliminating royal power in the name of individual freedom. They also yielded constitutional regimes that gave more protection and authority to people than had ever occurred before in history.

Although revolutions in the name of the universal rights for men took place, however, no such revolution for the rights of women followed. The many thinkers who redefined the family and its relationship to political society did not really change the lot of women in any practical way. As eighteenth-century British political philosopher Mary Wollstonecraft pointed out, the roles of women and the family were substantially exempt from the scrutiny of and liberation by reason that took place in other spheres of society. Though it opened many possibilities for men, the Enlightenment's emphasis on reason and order did continue to privilege the perspective and position of males.

But though modern thinkers turned away from religion and toward reason as the new tool of politics, several other philosophers of the eighteenth century started asking if reason alone could be the basis of politics and political understanding.[4] Rousseau, for example, is credited with being part of the counter-Enlightenment, or the Romantic reaction against science that stressed the importance of feeling, emotion, aesthetics, traditions, and conventions as important to politics.[5] Some political writers, often considered neomodern, argued that reason could not deliver all that it had promised, or that it would prove to be socially and politically destructive to many of the most important values modern politics had come to espouse. David Hume, Edmund Burke, and Immanuel Kant reexamine many of the assumptions of seventeenth-century politics and political thinking, producing a different set of values and concerns and questioning reason and its connection to politics.

DAVID HUME

David Hume (1711–1776) was a British philosopher, political thinker, and historian. His *Treatise of Human Nature*, published in 1739–40, he described as "dead-born from the press," although its long-term philosophical and political significance was greater. Other works, such as his *Political and Moral Essays* (1741–42), *Enquiry Concerning Human Understanding* (1748), and the multivolume *History of England* (1754–59) both provided Hume with much greater fame and helped spread his ideas far more successfully. Hume's writings question the role and importance of reason in human affairs. He is often described as an empiricist, or one who believes that all human knowledge comes from the senses. Yet his arguments question empiricism as well as the ability of reason to prove the existence of moral truths, natural laws and rights, and the intrinsic moral order of society.

According to Hume, all ideas stem from empirical impressions made upon the mind through sensation. By combining different mental impressions, they create new ideas. For example, people acquire an idea of a chair by perceiving the physical object, which leaves impressions of a chair on their minds. Thus human knowledge can be in part described as the development of relations or correspondences between ideas in the mind and physical objects in the world.

Individuals develop ideas and generalizations by empirically observing phenomena several times and then concluding that several events are related to one another or are causally connected in some way. For example, observing an explosion after two chemicals are mixed together several times leads individuals to conclude that one causes the other to change in some way to create an explosion.

Hume also argued that reasoning occurs by analogy. That is, people draw parallels between like causes and like effects so as to reach certain conclusions. For example, one of the most famous analogies of the seventeenth century was the belief that the universe was like a watch and God a watchmaker. Assuming that the universe was like a watch, and that every watch had to have a maker, people therefore concluded the universe had to have a maker who was like a great watchmaker.

In making these claims about how humans learn and know things, Hume was arguing for a way of acquiring knowledge and knowing that was characteristic of empirical science in the seventeenth century. However, such an empiricism could be proven neither empirically nor rationally. For example, regarding ideas as the result of some physical object causing impressions on the mind, Hume says,

> By what argument can it be proved, that the perceptions of the mind must be caused by external objects, entirely different from them, though resembling them (if that be possible) and could not arise from either the energy of the mind itself, or from the suggestion of some invisible and unknown spirit, or from some other cause still unknown to us?[6]

To be able to prove that ideas are the result of impressions on the mind, one would need to be in a position to observe these impressions occurring and to show that the impressions in one's mind conform to the external world. But one cannot escape the body to observe this, thus one cannot prove or substantiate that science and reason are accurate ways to describe the way people learn.

The implications of Hume's claims are many. For one thing, lacking the direct empirical evidence of seeing God create the universe, or any evidence to show that God and the universe are like a watchmaker and a watch, means there is no way to prove that God exists or that the universe has a maker. Neither empirical sensation nor reason based on ideas produced by impressions upon the mind can give us such proof.[7]

Second, Hume argues that there is no way to prove moral truths by appeals to reason.[8] In other words, ascertaining what is factually true cannot demonstrate what morally ought to occur:

> Nor does this reasoning only prove, that morality consists not in any relations, that are the objects of science; but if examin'd, will prove with equal certainty, that it consists not in any matter of fact, which can be discover'd by the understanding. This is the second part of our argument; and if it can be made evident, we may conclude, that morality is not an object of reason. . . . Take any action allow'd to be vicious: Willful murder, for instance. Examine it in all existence, which you call a vice. In what-ever way you take it, you find only passions, motives, volitions, and thoughts. There is no other matter of fact in the case. . . . Vice and virtue, therefore, may be compar'd to sounds, colors, heat, and cold, which, according to modern philosophy, are not qualities in objects, but perceptions in the mind.[9]

Thus some questions about objects are matters of empirical fact, but questions about morality and right and wrong are not; they are matters of obligation created in the mind. Questions of fact differ from those of moral value, and Hume asserts that it is "altogether inconceivable" to deduce a moral "ought" from an "is."[10] For example, just because one sees something happening, such as one person attacking another, one cannot rationally prove that the attack is wrong. Propriety and questions of moral right and wrong are not intrinsic properties of nature; morality is a question of feeling, not reason.

One example Hume uses to make this point is the issue of parricide. Many would claim that it is wrong for a child to kill a parent. Yet if the parent is an oak tree killed by one of its acorns that grew up and eventually supplanted it, one would not argue that it was parricide. Hume claims that factually the two situations are the same; the difference is that morality is ascribed to one but not the other by the human mind and feeling.

Hume's arguments suggest that reason cannot demonstrate the truth of morality, nor is there a way to show that there are natural laws prescribing a universal morality. Reason leads not to supporting certain claims but instead to questioning them. Rational inquiry cannot even prove the belief that reason itself is a true or an accurate way to understand the world. Other means would have to be developed to support the many claims being argued in the seventeenth century.

These philosophical views lead Hume to question numerous political ideas advanced in the sixteenth and seventeenth centuries. First, he argues that there is no way to prove that social contracts are the origin of political society, or that the duty to obey the law arises from a promise:[11]

> It is vain to say that all governments are or should be first founded on popular consent, as much as the necessity of human affairs will admit. This favors entirely my pretension. I maintain that human affairs will never

admit of this consent, seldom of the appearance of it; but that conquest or usurpation, that is, in plain terms, force, by dissolving the ancient governments, is the origin of almost all of the new ones which were ever established in the world.[12]

Hume contends that there is no empirical evidence to support the claim that a presocial state of nature or an original social contract ever occurred. Second, he charges that social contracts and the idea of promise making and keeping are conventional, not natural. How can individuals agree to keep their agreements unless there is some prior agreement that they should obey agreements? That agreement would in turn presuppose a previous agreement and so on, unless it can be proved that there is a natural moral basis compelling individuals to keep agreements. However, there is no such natural moral basis to support this contention.

Third, instead of viewing the origin of political society as a social contract, Hume sees its origins in the usurpation of power by one individual and the habit among others to obey that person. Fourth, Hume contends that the idea of justice arises out of selfishness, and "that those impressions, which give rise to a sense of justice, are not natural to the human mind, but arise from artificial and human conventions."[13] And not only justice, but political authority, law, morality, and obligation are the products of habits and conventions. Thus individuals do not obey rulers because they have willed or agreed to obey,[14] but because self-interest and artificial rules or social conventions create a sense of obligation in them.

Fifth, Hume's questioning of the ability of reason to answer some of the basic questions of philosophy have led some to argue that his writings have feminist aspects to them. In stepping outside of the then dominant rationalist philosophy of his day he viewed the world somewhat from the perspective of women who too were outsiders and forced to think about the world outside of the traditional male paradigm. Even more importantly, Hume's questioning of reason and his articulation of an important role for the passions in moral philosophy and ethics suggested that other ways of knowing, beyond the "male" use of reason, were valid and not necessarily inferior.[15] While equating maleness to reason and femaleness to the passions clearly stereotyped men and women, the implications of Hume's arguments were that differences between the sexes did not necessarily imply inferiority and superiority. Finally, by privileging experience as the source of knowledge, Hume's philosophy left open the possibility that the experiences of women could in their own right be a form of knowledge, equally valid to the knowledge and experiences of men. Hence, within David Hume's epistemology was an egalitarian strain, the implications of which would unfortunately not be felt by women for some time.

In sum, Hume's philosophical arguments led him to question the ability of science and reason to support the ideas of natural rules of justice, natural rights for individuals, or social contracts and promises as the basis of political authority and obligation. Political society and rules were conventions, premised on human habits; and moral truths were not self-evidently provable by demonstration or reason. Instead, they rested more upon nonrational factors. Hume's claims thus questioned the ability of philosophers of the Enlightenment to achieve the new rational foundations they desired.

EDMUND BURKE

Edmund Burke (1729–1797) was born in Dublin, Ireland, became an attorney, and served as a member of the British Parliament for six years during his political career. His most famous book, *Reflections on the Revolution in France,* was written in 1790. It criticizes the destructive excesses of the French Revolution, which were undertaken in the name of Rousseau, reason, and the "universal rights of man." But Burke does not attack all revolutions. He praises the Glorious Revolution in England in 1688, for example, because it was a defensive revolution[16] that sought to "preserve our ancient indisputable laws and liberties, and that ancient constitution of government which is our only security for law and liberty."[17] Likewise, concerning the dispute between the American colonies and Britain that would eventually lead to the American Revolution, Burke argued in Parliament that the colonies were defending the ancient rights of the English constitution.[18]

The heart of Burke's criticism of the French Revolution resides in how he sees society as constructed and how the actions of the revolutionaries went against the nature of social fabric. First, Burke rejects the idea that men can simply create a science of politics, or rationally create a political science, in the same way one can demonstrate or construct a mathematical proof. Thus,

> The science of constructing a commonwealth, or renovating it, is, like every other experimental science, not to be taught a priori. Nor is it a short experience that can instruct us in that practical science: because the real effects of moral causes are not always immediate; but that which in the first instance is presocial may be excellent in its remoter operation; and its excellence may arise even from the ill effects it produces in the beginning. The reverse also happens: and very plausible schemes, with very pleasing commencements; have often shameful and lamentable conclusions.[19]

According to Burke, many human actions have unintended or unanticipated effects. If one attempts to create a society through a social contract to achieve certain goals, it is uncertain if these goals can be met because of changes that occur over time. Hence large-scale social change is risky because it may produce undesirable results. So instead of radical modification, such as occurs in revolutions, social change should be more incremental and slower, seeking to connect the future with the certainty of social institutions that already exist and have proven successful and viable over time.

Burke's skepticism toward abrupt social change is premised on his view that society is a social contract, although a much different one than those offered by Hobbes, Locke, and Rousseau. First, he rejects many of the ideas of the other social contract theorists, such as the beliefs that a state of nature ever existed, that individuals were by nature equal in it, and that collective action in this situation could be morally binding. In "An Appeal from the New to the Old Whigs" (1791), Burke argues that there is a natural aristocracy among people rather than a basic equality among them.[20] Furthermore, concerning the idea of a state of nature, he says,

> In a state of rude nature there is no such thing as a people. A number of men in themselves have no collective capacity. The idea of a people is the idea of a corporation. It is wholly artificial, and made, like all other legal fictions, by common agreement.[21]

In other words, the social contracts of Hobbes, Locke, and Rousseau are fabrications, and people would have been incapable of creating morally binding rules by a simple compact or agreement if such a situation had existed.

Agreeing with Hume, Burke does not believe that ideas such as majority rule are natural; they too are a social convention. And it is unclear how a people could naturally agree to such a rule, or even agree that the promise to keep their word or obey a compact could be morally binding. The duties to obey the state and the laws come from sources other than the social contract, such as from God.

Although Burke rejects social contract thinking as it was understood at the time, he does not reject the idea of social contracts altogether. Rather,

> Society is indeed a contract . . . but the state ought not to be considered as nothing better than a partnership agreement in a trade of pepper and coffee, calico or tobacco, or some other lowly concern. . . . As the ends of such a partnership cannot be obtained in many generations, it becomes a partnership not only between those who are living, but between those who are living, those who are dead, and those who are to be born. Each contract of each particular state is but a clause in the great primeval contract of eternal society, linking the lower with the higher natures, connecting the visible and invisible world, according to a fixed compact sanctioned by the inviolable oath which holds all physical and all moral natures, each in their appointed place.[22]

The social contract, then, is produced over time and seeks to weave together the various events and traditions of a culture and its past, present, and future. This historical type of contract, for Burke, is the basis of civil society, which means that civil society is the product of historical human conventions, aimed at, not protecting natural rights, but serving human wants.[23]

Burke argues that change is required for a state to preserve itself. In the cases of the English and American revolutions, the aims were to preserve or restore the constitutional rights and liberties of men that had evolved in British society. To Burke, though, not all types of change aim toward the goal of preservation. In the case of France, the revolution was meant to break from the past. It was aimed at, not preserving the existing state and monarchy, but destroying it and creating a new civil society premised on new abstract rights derived from reason. To Burke, "the pretended rights" of theorists are certain to produce extreme, unanticipated, and undeserved behavior, as well as likely to upset "real" human liberties and rights, including rights to the "fruits of their industry," rights of inheritance, and the right to raise children.[24]

Burke's criticisms of the French Revolution parallel many of Hume's contentions. Burke agrees that social contracts and promises in the mold of Hobbes, Locke, and Rousseau fail to explain the nature of society and political obligation. Obligations arise over time, through social conventions, and appeals to reason cannot either discover these obligations or create new ones. Creating a society from scratch is difficult, if not impossible, because of the inability to foresee all the difficulties and situations that may upset the social order. Tradition can tell people more about social duties and society than can reason. In addition, any revolution appealing to abstract rights, or any assumption that civil societies are constructed on a promise to recognize certain natural and abstract rights, ignores the real rights of men that have been created in history. Only respect for tradition and conventions can protect these rights.

IMMANUEL KANT

Prussia-born Immanuel Kant (1724–1804) is often considered one of the most important philosophers in Western history. His *Critique of Pure Reason* (1787) changed almost all of the major assumptions about thinking up to that time. Some of his other works, such as the *Critique of Practical Reasoning* (1788), *Foundations of the Metaphysics of Morals* (1785), and his various political writings, similarly brought forth major changes in how people thought about morality, moral obligation, and even the relationship between politics and religion. Kant's other legacy was seeking to bridge the gap between the rational and empirical approaches to learning that had emerged during the Enlightenment. This was a problem Hume had addressed in his *Enquiry Concerning Human Understanding,* and Kant continued his examination to determine the limits of reason as it applied to human affairs.

Kant praises the role reason played in the Enlightenment. In his 1784 essay, "An Answer to the Question: What Is Enlightenment?" he says,

> *Enlightenment is man's emergence from his self-incurred immaturity. Immaturity* is the inability to use one's own understanding without the guidance of another. This immaturity is *self-incurred* if its cause is not lack of understanding, but lack of resolution and courage to use it without the guidance of another. The motto of enlightenment is therefore: *Sapere aude* (dare to know)![25]

Thus, to Kant, the Enlightenment represents use of one's own understanding for the purpose of questioning, making judgments, and reaching political conclusions. The Enlightenment also represents a public appeal to use reason to investigate and resolve disputes.[26] But to be able to undertake this sort of questioning individuals have to be free. So Kant's political message includes a defense of individual freedom and, along with it, an implicit challenge to political systems, in that it argues against individuals deferring to anyone else's authority as the final arbiter of truth and knowledge.

Although Kant advocates questioning and challenging, however, he draws a limit on freedom, contending that it does not include disobeying authority.

For example, Kant argues that a citizen cannot refuse to pay taxes if he or she disagrees with the political regime. Like Burke, Kant was affected by the French Revolution and concerned with what reason can and cannot achieve in human affairs. *The Critique of Pure Reason*, written before the revolution, and changes Kant made to the second edition, written after it, express those concerns.

In many ways, Hume's challenge, in the *Enquiry Concerning Human Understanding*, that reason could not prove the empirical basis of knowledge, is what prompted Kant to write the *Critique of Pure Reason*. The *Critique* attempts to draw connections between the empirical and rationalist methods of learning. Kant essentially agrees with Hume that one cannot prove that ideas in the mind correspond to external objects; there is no way to obtain either rational or empirical evidence to support this claim.

Kant also contends that neither reason alone nor empirical methods alone can give humans knowledge of the world. Rather, both are necessary to attain knowledge. But if human knowledge cannot be described as some correspondence between ideas in the mind and the world outside of it, then what is knowledge?

To answer this question, Kant appeals to Copernicus's switch from a geocentric to a heliocentric model of the universe:

> Hitherto it has been assumed that all our knowledge must conform to objects. But all attempts to extend our knowledge of objects by establishing something in regard to them a priori, by means of concepts, have, on this assumption, ended in failure. We must therefore make trial whether we may not have more success in the tasks of metaphysics, if we suppose that the objects must conform to our knowledge. . . . We should then be proceeding precisely on the lines of Copernicus' primary hypothesis.[27]

Using the Copernican analogy suggests that Kant is looking for a new perspective through which humans can view or think about human knowledge, much like Copernicus sought a new way to look at the universe in order to explain it.[28]

According to Kant, human cognition, or knowing, has its own basic patterns into which it organizes sense data, so individuals can understand the world only in terms of what human understanding permits. The limits on human understanding also mean that there are certain things humans cannot prove empirically or rationally. And this means one cannot know those things that lie beyond the capacity of either reason or sensation.

What is significant in Kant's argument is the claim that there are limits to what reason can achieve. The area of metaphysics is an example. For Kant, metaphysics is a purely speculative endeavor, seeking to understand the ultimate nature of things. Metaphysical claims had been important to philosophy since Plato, attempting to prove the existence of God, the truth of human knowledge, and the certainty of political prescriptions, among other things. Kant claims, however, that one cannot achieve either rational or empirical knowledge of the first principles of metaphysics. Appeals to either pure reason or empiricism lead to questioning all first principles, including and especially the existence of God, freedom, and immortality.[29] So to Kant, the certainty of first principles and foundations sought by Descartes and Bacon is impossible.

In place of reason and empiricism, Kant contends that it "may be necessary to deny *knowledge* in order to make room for *faith*."[30] By that, he means that some presuppositions must simply be accepted as true, and that these need to be protected from reason's assault if people are to preserve both knowledge and faith.

Kant's arguments in the *Critique of Pure Reason*, in destroying metaphysics, render assertions about natural law and an ultimate cosmology as grounds for politics impossible to defend. If people wish to preserve political and philosophical truths, they may have to assume they are true, or act "as if" they were true. That is, certain assumptions may have to be taken as rationally true, in order to make possible the creation of other values individuals wish to hold.

Politically, Kant's arguments have numerous implications. First, he rejects the ideas that a historical social contract ever existed and that it was the basis of political obligation. But like Burke, he redefines the idea of a social contract rather than throwing it out altogether:

> This, then, is an *original contract* by means of which a civil and thus completely lawful constitution and commonwealth can alone be established. But we need by no means assume that this contract, . . . based on a coalition of wills of all private individuals in a nation to form a common, public will for the purposes of rightful legislation, actually exists as a *fact*, for it cannot possibly be so. Such an assumption would mean that we would first have to prove from history that some nation, whose rights and obligations have been passed down to us, did in fact perform such an act. . . . It [the social contract] is in fact merely an idea of reason, which nonetheless has undoubted practical reality; for it can oblige every legislator to frame his laws in such a way that they could have been produced by the united will of a whole nation.[31]

For Kant, the idea of the social contract, while not a historical reality, serves as a "Platonic ideal" to regulate the commonwealth, an ideal to which the constitution and all laws must aspire.[32] It, along with human freedom, are ideas that act as both goals and assumptions defining human political society.[33] In fact, Kant argues that human freedom is the first principle of a constitution,[34] and that individual freedom, or autonomy, is a necessary presupposition of human morality. Unless humans are presupposed to have the capacity to be free and to make choices about right and wrong, it would be impossible to hold them morally responsible for anything.

Human freedom, then, is the basis of politics, morality, and metaphysics. The goals of politics and the constitution are to make it possible for individuals to be free.[35] But Kant's freedom is not of the type described by Hobbes and Locke, who saw it as some type of absence of external restraints. For Kant, freedom is a moral and rational freedom, a capacity to make moral choices;

and the political community is necessary to make this type of freedom possible. This suggests an intimate connection between morality, reason, and politics, with politics necessarily creating the conditions required for individuals to act as free and autonomous moral beings. Hence for Kant, the state and civil society may foster human freedom, while for Locke and Hobbes, the state may be an impediment to it.

CONCLUSION

Hume, Burke, and Kant were three neomoderns who developed philosophical and political views questioning the capacity of human reason to provide the first principles of political knowledge sought by other political thinkers during the Enlightenment. All three questioned the historical existence of social contracts as well as the capacity of such contracts, if they did exist, to provide for a morally satisfactory means of binding individual obedience to the state. All three offered alternative conceptions of the basis of political society, turning to social conventions, traditions, or a reformulation of social contract theory to support their views on what political society is and what it compels. And all three rethought what freedom and justice are, and how morality and politics interact.

In many ways, the arguments of Hume, Burke, and Kant attest to the limits of reason. If the task of the Enlightenment was to replace religion or religious faith with reason and science as the basis of political knowledge, by the beginning of the nineteenth century philosophers were raising serious questions regarding the viability of reason as the basis of knowledge and certainty. Reason had its limits; and unless it was contained, it could prove self-destructive by calling into question the very assumptions it had originally intended to protect.[36] Reason had the capacity to undermine itself. Hume, Burke, and Kant explored various ways to protect both reason and politics from reason itself.

As a consequence of this partial retreat from reason, many values that had been important to politics were called into question. Proof of human freedom, social contracts, and an intrinsic moral order were impossible, which necessitated other means to account for governmental authority and justice. If there was no such thing as a social contract created by individuals, what was left to define the relationship between individual and state in a way that would preserve freedom? The crisis of reason and the turn toward tradition and conventions opened up the possibility of a major rethinking of yet other ways to think about the relationship among politics, science, morality, and social conventions.

Despite the novelty of their thought, and the appeal to conventions, traditions, and the limits of reason, Hume, Burke, and Kant left a conservative legacy. If human society rested on traditions, how could social change occur, especially among cultures that historically denied some individuals freedom and rights? The crisis of reason and the appeal to tradition did little to change the status of women in marriage or society. For Hume, men and women retained the traditional roles and virtues that had always been ascribed to them. To Burke, since women had never enjoyed rights and liberties equal to those of men, appealing to history and tradition did not seem a viable way to develop political rights that would extend the privileges of men to women. And to Kant, women remained "passive citizens," relegated to second place behind men in the family and civil community.[37] Tradition and convention, much like reason, seemed to fall short in their capacity to provide a basis for the liberation of women, and of men. The question left from their works is whether the new ways of knowing they created really changed the political or social conditions of the average person, or whether, in fact, any philosophical ideas had any impact on the way the average person lived.

Notes

1. Alasdair MacIntyre, *After Virtue* (Notre Dame, Ind.: University of Notre Dame Press, 1984), 39; Hans Blumenberg, *The Legitimacy of the Modern Age* (Cambridge, Mass.: MIT Press, 1986), 3–13.

2. Patrick Riley, *Will and Political Legitimacy: A Critical Exposition of Social Contract Theory in Hobbes, Locke, Rousseau, Kant, and Hegel* (Cambridge, Mass.: Harvard University Press, 1982).

3. Leo Strauss, *Natural Right and History* (Chicago: University of Chicago Press, 1953).

4. Thomas Spraegens, *The Irony of Liberal Reasoning* (Chicago: University of Chicago Press, 1981).

5. Irving Babbitt, *Rousseau and Romanticism* (New York: Meridian, 1955).

6. David Hume, *An Enquiry Concerning Human Understanding* (Indianapolis: Hackett, 1984), 106.

7. David Hume, *Dialogues Concerning Natural Religion* (New York: Hafner, 1957).

8. David Hume, *A Treatise of Human Nature* (Oxford: Oxford University Press, 1980), 463.

9. *Treatise*, 468–69.

10. *Treatise*, 469.

11. *Treatise*, 547.

12. David Hume, "Of the Original Contract," in *Hume's Moral and Political Philosophy*, ed. H. D. Aiken (New York: Hafner, 1948), 362.

13. *Treatise*, 496.

14. *Treatise*, 542.

15. Annette C. Baier, "Hume: The Reflective Women's Epistemologist?" in *Feminist Interpretations of David Hume*, ed. Anne Jaap Jacobson (University Park: Pennsylvania State University Press, 2000), p. 22.

16 Edmund Burke, "An Appeal from the New to the Old Whigs, in Consequence of Some Late Discussions in Parliament Relative to the Reflections on the French Revolution," in *Edmund Burke: Selected Writings and Speeches*, ed. P. J. Stanlis (New York: Anchor, 1963), 522.

17. Edmund Burke, *Reflections on the Revolution in France* (New York: Pelican, 1969), 117.

18. Edmund Burke, *Speech on Conciliation with America*, ed. W. MacDonald (New York: American Book Company, 1904), 115, 125.

19. *Reflections*, 152.

20. "Appeal," 542.

21. "Appeal," 540.

22. *Reflections*, 194.

23. *Reflections*, 150–51.

24. *Reflections,* 149.

25. Immanuel Kant, "An Answer to the Question: What Is Enlightenment?" in *Kant's Political Writings,* ed. H. Reiss (Cambridge: Cambridge University Press, 1979), 54.

26. Hannah Arendt, *Lectures on Kant's Political Philosophy,* ed. R. Beiner (Chicago: University of Chicago Press, 1982), 18.

27. Immanuel Kant, *A Critique of Pure Reason,* trans. N. K. Smith (New York: St. Martin's, 1965), 22.

28. Hans Blumenberg, *The Genesis of the Copernican World* (Cambridge, Mass.: MIT Press, 1987), 595–614.

29. *Pure Reason,* 29; Immanuel Kant, *The Critique of Judgment,* trans. J. C. Meredith (Oxford: Oxford University Press, 1982), pt. 2, 148–49.

30. *Pure Reason,* 29.

31. Immanuel Kant, "On the Common Saying: 'This May Be True in Theory, But It Does Not Apply in Practice'," in *Kant's Political Writings,* 79.

32. *Will and Political Legitimacy,* 124–25, Immanuel Kant, "The Contest of Faculties," in *Kant's Political Writings,* 187.

33. Immanuel Kant, *The Philosophy of Law,* trans. W. Hastie (Clifton, N.J.: Augustus M. Kelley, 1974), 28.

34. Immanuel Kant, "Perpetual Peace: A Philosophical Sketch," in *Kant's Political Writings,* 99.

35. *Will and Political Legitimacy,* 130.

36. Richard Rorty, *Philosophy and the Mirror of Nature* (Princeton, N.J.: Princeton University Press, 1979).

37. Susan Mendus, "Kant: An Honest but Narrow-Minded Bourgeois?" in *Women in Western Political Philosophy,* eds. E. Kennedy and S. Kennedy (New York: St. Martin's, 1987), 33–34.

Additional Readings

Arendt, Hannah. *Lectures on Kant's Political Philosophy,* ed. Ronald Beiner. Chicago: University of Chicago Press, 1982.

Blumenberg, Hans. *The Legitimacy of the Modern Age.* Cambridge, Mass.: MIT Press, 1986.

Cassirer, Ernst. *Rousseau, Kant, Goethe: Two Essays.* Princeton, N.J.: Princeton University Press, 1963.

MacIntyre, Alasdair. *After Virtue.* Notre Dame, Ind.: University of Notre Dame Press, 1984.

Mendus, Susan. "Kant: An Honest but Narrow-Minded Bourgeois?" in *Women in Western Political Philosophy,* eds. E. Kennedy and S. Kennedy. New York: St. Martin's, 1987.

O'Gorman, Frank. *Edmund Burke: His Political Philosophy.* Bloomington: Indiana University Press, 1973.

Riley, Patrick. *Will and Political Legitimacy: A Critical Exposition of Social Contract Theory in Hobbes, Locke, Rousseau, Kant, and Hegel.* Cambridge, Mass.: Harvard University Press, 1982.

 Inventors of Ideas Online

Visit http://politicalscience.wadsworth.com/tannenbaum2 for links related to material in this chapter, including the full texts of some of Hume's, Burke's, and Kant's major works.

17

MILL: GROUNDING LIBERTY

INTRODUCTION

If the intensity of the early education of John Stuart Mill (1806–1873) brought on a nervous breakdown, the young Englishman was saved from its worst effects by the discovery of poetry and his introduction to the woman who would have a most singular effect on his life and thought. Mill met Mrs. Harriet Taylor, the wife of a wealthy merchant and mother of several children, when he was twenty-five. Over the next two decades their relationship deepened, as they were together constantly, discussing her work as well as his. One can picture cynical tongues wagging despite Mill's insistence that their relationship was purely platonic, and that he only wanted an innocent intellectual relationship with someone whose mind inspired his. It seems Mr. Taylor had no objections, dining at his club when the two friends met at his home. Mill and Harriet continued this relationship until three years after her husband's death, when they finally married. Sadly, she died only six years later, before Mill had written several of his major political works.[1]

Mill's *Autobiography* tells us he was the son of James Mill (1773–1836), a prolific writer on politics and related subjects whose work was devoted to cold, logical analysis. Young Mill had a rigorous education at home, supervised by his father and by family friends who were among the most prominent thinkers of their age. Beginning with the study of Greek, at age three, he was taught a range of other challenging subjects over the years, including Latin, algebra, logic, economics, and law. Any subject that might stir his emotions, such as religion or romantic poetry, was omitted. This education was guided by utilitarianism, the philosophical perspective his father had helped shape, and which young Mill accepted uncritically. In fact, he was so impressed by its teachings and extremely rational approach that by the age of fifteen, when his formal education was virtually complete, he fully subscribed to the utilitarian philosophy.[2]

UTILITARIANISM

> Utility, or the Greatest Happiness Principle, holds that actions are right in proportion as they tend to promote happiness, wrong as they tend to promote the reverse of happiness. By happiness is intended pleasure, and the absence of pain; by unhappiness, pain and the privation of pleasure.[3]

The philosophy called *utilitarianism* was the great contribution to political thought of Jeremy Bentham (1748–1832), assisted by Mill's father, James. It can be defined as a philosophy whose central concern is achieving the greatest good (or happiness) for the greatest number of individuals.[4]

Utilitarians base their rules for behavior on a few basic assumptions about human nature that parallel those of Hobbes and Locke. They assume that all human nature is pretty much the same, and that all of us are rationally calculating. Rational individuals are primarily motivated by personal self-interest, or selfishness. Utilitarian philosophy is appealing to such individuals, who seek to use selfishness in the search for self-realization. To utilitarians, pleasure is good, pain is bad, and all people are pleasure-seeking animals. Human action, then, is based on the individual desire to seek pleasure and avoid pain. They view society as no more than the sum of its quite diverse, separate parts, the atomistic individuals who compose it.

All people are regarded as equal when measuring social happiness, or the public interest. Each person, whatever his or her sensitivity, intelligence, or station in life, counts as one. The public interest is determined for any proposed law or other government action by calculating the net sum of all participants' individual interests, or happiness. Those who believe a particular act of government will bring greater happiness or pleasure are added together, as are those who believe it will cause increased pain. If the sum of pleasure is greater than the sum of pain, the public interest requires the government to act. If pain outweighs pleasure, the government is not to act. Social justice, or society's measure of right or wrong, is based on a series of such calculations; each separate law is subjected to it. The result is a society that brings the greatest happiness to the greatest number of people. Thus one duty of government is to conduct regular inquiries to discover what, on balance, its citizens want. This is the process referred to by Rousseau as discovering the will of all.

In utilitarian philosophy, the task of government is a limited one: to promote the public interest. It can do so in both negative and positive fashions. Negatively, the government acts to decrease pain in society. It applies penalties such as imprisonment, fines, even execution, to discourage antisocial behavior that causes pain to others. It is the job of government to define such behavior in the form of criminal laws, and to punish those who break them, but only to the extent that pain is caused. Law must be tailored so that punishment fits the crime. If public opinion shifts about whether a penalty is excessive, the law must be open to change. For example, in nineteenth-century England a child under the age of ten convicted of stealing an object worth two pence could be executed. This is no longer the case due to a shift in people's attitudes. On the positive side, government can increase the level of happiness in society by rewarding conduct it wants to encourage. This could take many forms, such as granting of tax deductions for individual contributions to non-profit, charitable organizations.

Apart from these rules, a limited government is to be neutral and uninvolved with law-abiding individuals. The law-abiding are free to act, or not act, as they wish. Their liberty, as Hobbes had said, is found in the silence of the law. Utilitarians assume that limited government is good government. But although earlier advocates of limited government, such as Locke, philosophically based it on a prior state of nature, natural law, natural rights, and a social contract, utilitarian philosophy relies on none of these features. They are all replaced by the principle of pain and pleasure.

Utilitarians were legal reformers who both reacted to and helped expand a shift in political power in Great Britain. At the beginning of the seventeenth century, England had been ruled by a monarch who claimed authority by divine right. As God's choice, the monarch was not answerable to any power on earth. The upshot was, first, civil war, and later the Glorious Revolution. In the process, the legitimate right to rule shifted from religious sanction to an unwritten contractual basis. The new constitutional monarch still gained office through heredity, but gradually had to share more power with the elected House of Commons. This meant the ruler had to accept restraints on what had once been a claim of unlimited authority.

Despite these changes, utilitarians saw the government as unwilling to frame laws to fit the sentiments of a growing urban middle class, which resulted from the Industrial Revolution. The House of Commons was controlled by an unrepresentative rural elite that favored the status quo. To advance toward a society reflecting the greatest good for the greatest number, utilitarians worked for laws to increase the size of the electorate that could vote for representatives to Commons. Over the course of the nineteenth century, the vote was secured first for the urban middle class, and then for the working class. The expansion of the vote shifted power further away from the monarch, to the executive (the prime minister) chosen by Commons, which is elected by, and thus represents, the voters. John Stuart Mill saw a danger in this extension of the vote.

MILL'S REVISION OF UTILITARIAN METHOD

[A] beast's pleasures do not satisfy a human being's conceptions of happiness. Human beings have faculties more elevated than the animal appetites, and when once made conscious of them, do not regard anything as happiness which does not include their gratification. . . . It is quite compatible with the principle of utility to recognise the fact, that some kinds of pleasure are more desirable and more valuable than others. It would be absurd that while, in estimating all other things, quality is considered as well as quantity, the estimation of pleasures should be supposed to depend on quantity alone.[5]

Mill suffered a nervous breakdown at the age of twenty because he lost his almost-religious faith in Benthamite utilitarianism. He decided that the happiness Bentham advocated must result from the pursuit of other, higher goals, not from seeking pleasure as an end in itself. As he later writes, "I regard utility as the ultimate appeal on all ethical issues; but it must be utility in the largest sense, grounded on the permanent interests of man as a progressive being."[6]

The Benthamite position might be paraphrased as, the quantity of pleasure being equal, golf is as good as political philosophy. In other words, the pleasure from the one has no greater status or priority than the pleasure from the other. All things that give people pleasure are equal.

Mill is unhappy with this rational but essentially cold calculation of early utilitarianism for three reasons. First, he sees it as too simplistic: it allows no place for the qualitative reckoning of pleasure based on a distinction between higher (human) and lower (more animal-like) pleasures. Mill's position is that "It is better to be a human being dissatisfied than a pig satisfied; better to be Socrates dissatisfied than a fool satisfied." An intellectual pleasure like philosophy is worth much more, qualitatively, than the joy of playing golf. "And if the fool, or the pig, are of different opinion, it is because they only know their own side of the question. The other party to the comparison knows both sides."[7]

Second, Mill thinks utilitarianism is too selfish. Intensely concerned with maximizing the pleasure of each individual, it allows no positive role to sacrifice for the benefit of others without some tangible reward, such as a tax write-off for a charitable contribution.

Third, Mill judges utilitarianism too asocial. It views society as nothing more than the sum of its individual parts. In contrast to such atomism, Mill wants to include a larger view of the public interest in his philosophy.

HUMAN NATURE

Mill presents his views on human nature without basing them on any state of nature, consistent with the utilitarian philosophy he learned as a youth. He also accepted its egalitarian position, believing that all humans are equal, rational beings. However, early utilitarianism had insisted that all individuals be treated alike, each counting as one in the utilitarian calculation. Mill is opposed to such uniformity. His more complex view of human nature sees equal individuals who nonetheless evolve at different rates. "Human nature is not a machine . . . but a tree which requires to grow and develop itself on all sides, according to the tendency of the inward forces which make it a living thing."[8]

Equality requires that all individuals be free to develop their personal, inner potential to the fullest, and at their own pace. The process should begin with the education of the young, to develop their faculties of reason, combined with training in the highest moral sensibilities possible. Participation and practice are the ways to a moral education, and such education begins at home, since the relationship a child "sees between its parents is an education—in justice or despotism." Family education is like political or economic training in that it enables the young to participate and practice social virtues. Mill sees the home as "the linchpin" of a moral society because it is there that the deepest human sentiments develop.[9]

Although he favors equality of opportunity for everyone to develop as individuals, Mill adds an elitist perspective. Personal development is uneven, and unique differences must be recognized. "The initiation of all wise and noble things comes and must come from individuals; generally at first from some one individual."[10] In fact, only a small minority can be called geniuses, only those truly willing and able to make unique contributions to human progress. These few learn to experience higher as well as lower pleasures, and so they have a basis for comparing the two, which most people lack. Knowing which pleasures are superior, they give up the lower pleasures of selfish appetite satisfaction, which motivate the many, to pursue qualitatively higher pleasures. They develop their character by applying inner originality and reasoned intelligence to solve pressing human problems.

Those who are not geniuses also have both an obligation and an opportunity. "The honor and glory of the average man is that he is capable of following that initiative; that he can respond internally to wise and noble things, and be led to them with his eyes open."[11] In this way the many, too, can lead qualitatively happy lives. If the large majority of people are at their best when they rationally choose to follow the lead of an original genius, they are at their worst when following selfish peers in apelike imitation. Especially when acting as a mob, the masses can be stupid and selfish. They act on impulse, not reason, substituting the lower, appetitive pleasure of being part of a crowd for the higher pleasures offered by the few original thinkers.

TYRANNY OF THE MAJORITY

In the past, tyranny had been viewed as stemming from the rule of one or a few, and democracy had opposed such despotism. Mill says it is wrong to think that because the government represents the people it will always rule in their interest. His views on human nature and its consequences lead him to point out a major danger of a purely utilitarian government, where all votes count as one and the majority rules. "The 'people' who exercise the power are not always the same people over whom it is exercised; and the 'self-government' spoken of is not the government of each by himself, but of each by all the rest."[12] Such government, acting as the agent of society, is especially vulnerable to the tyranny of public opinion, a despotism of an irrational majority that equates holding different ideas with being dangerous:

> The will of the people . . . means the will of the most numerous or the most active part of the people—the majority, or those who succeed in making themselves accepted as the majority; the people, consequently, may desire to oppress a part of their number. . . .[13]

The result is "tyranny of the majority,"[14] where the majority, conforming to public opinion, uses the power of society or government to silence the individual who is different. In early utilitarian terms, such individuals give the majority pain, not pleasure, by expressing views that displease the majority. Mill's concern is that conformity of the majority not be turned into a tyranny of uniformity, imposed on all by either society or government. Government can use force against dissent, society can use public opinion to suppress individuals, regardless of legal or constitutional safeguards. The unusual individual can be ground down as readily by the pressures of respectability as by the law. This problem is especially acute in large, industrial societies, which impose a "despotism of custom" antagonistic to eccentricity. Mill believes that "precautions are as much needed against this as against any other abuse of power."[15] The unique genius needs to be free from coercion to consider and discuss individual views of the truth in reasoned thought and debate.

In *On Liberty*, Mill stakes out "the nature and limits of the power which can be legitimately exercised by society over the individual."[16] This work is his considered defense of the lone dissident against forced conformity to a majority view in any aspect of life, religious, scientific, or personal. Reflecting his training in early utilitarianism and his revision of it, he defends freedom as an individual right without relying on "the fiction" of any original contract, natural law, or natural rights. In a moral system that judges actions by their consequences, all rights, including justice, equality, and impartial treatment, are based on their utility. Of course this means that these rights are conditional on their capacity to increase happiness, especially for the genius.

LIBERTY

[T]he individual is not accountable to society for his actions, in so far as these concern the interests of no person but himself [but] for such actions as are prejudicial to the interests of others, the individual is accountable and may be subjected either to social or legal punishment if society is of [the] opinion that the one or the other is requisite for its protection.[17]

Mill bases his defense of individual freedom on "one very simple principle, that the sole end for which mankind are warranted, individually or collectively, in interfering with the liberty of action of any of their number is self-protection." Liberty consists of doing what one reasonably desires without harming others. It concerns the part of one's personal life that should be beyond the control of others, especially the government. In other words, the job of government is limited to preventing "harm to others. . . . In the part which merely concerns himself, [the individual's] independence is, of right, absolute. Over himself, over his own body and mind, the individual is sovereign."[18]

The argument for liberty applies solely to adults in more advanced nations. Barbarians—people of backward countries—as well as children, are incapable of using freedom responsibly. They must be protected from themselves while they are educated to properly appreciate the benefits of free and equal discussion. The major aim of liberty is to enable people to develop their inner character, which results in personal and social benefits. Thus, if the grant of liberty might harm society, or if there is no social benefit, as in the case of children and savages, Mill opposes its introduction.

Mill distinguishes between two kinds of action: public and private. Public acts are those involving the rights of others, and it is the job of government to regulate such acts. Individuals have a right to "self-protection" and thus can be required by law not to physically harm others. They must also recognize their social responsibilities:

> Though society is not founded on a contract, and though no good purpose is answered by inventing a contract in order to deduce social obligations from it, everyone who receives the protection of society owes a return for benefit, and the fact of living in society renders it indispensable that each should be bound to observe a certain line of conduct toward the rest.[19]

Citizens are duty-bound to perform such obligations as paying taxes, giving evidence in court, and educating their children. Mill sees public education as a two-edged sword, however. It can lead to greater conformity, since everyone is exposed to the same views. But it can also promote liberty, diminishing the uncritical acceptance of custom among the majority by exposing them to higher intellectual and moral pleasures.

The state can also forbid marriage to those who might produce children they are unable to support. Such interference is justified to prevent lives of wretchedness and depravity for the children and the burden of overpopulation for society. Regulation of such public acts is always a rightful power of government.

Private actions are unrelated to public responsibilities. They are acts that cannot hurt others, and thus they affect nobody else's rights. Individuals are free to perform them as they choose.

Benefits of Liberty

> If all mankind minus one were of one opinion, and only one person were of a contrary opinion, mankind would be no more justified in silencing that one person, than he, if he had the power, would be justified in silencing mankind.[20]

Neither government nor society should interfere with any private actions because individual freedom to act has a double benefit. First, it leads to personal self-realization. If people are free to make their own choices in life, to practice diverse lifestyles based on what they consider best for themselves, they are able to seek self-fulfillment.

Second, society as a whole benefits from the liberty Mill advocates. Liberty promotes human social progress, which is the highest goal of social life. Social progress emerges through the introduction of new ideas, while their suppression damages society as a whole. In Mill's revised utilitarianism, silencing individuals by legally prohibiting the introduction of new ideas would in the end qualitatively cause more "utiles" of pain, to both the individuals silenced and social progress as a whole, than the pain suffered by majority public opinion in allowing full expression. Permitting rather than stifling free expression by individuals also has the utilitarian value of improving the quality of life for each individual who exercises this liberty, and thus for society as a whole.

Spheres of Liberty. Mill designates three areas of a person's life wherein exercising liberty harms nobody but the voluntary individual participants. These areas are to be completely free of public control, spheres in which liberty is an absolute right of every individual.

The first sphere, "liberty of conscience," extends to the expression and publication of personal opinion. It includes what people term freedom of speech, of the press, and of religion. The second, "liberty of tastes and pursuits," includes the selection of one's entertainments as well as career. The third, "liberty . . . of combination," refers to the free association of individuals who "unite for any purpose not involving harm to others," thus allowing for a multiplicity of independent groups in society. All three spheres are essential. "No society in which these liberties are not, on the whole, respected is free, whatever may be its form of government; and none is completely free in which they do not exist absolute and unqualified."[21]

But Mill imposes limits when opinion spills over into action:

> An opinion that corn-dealers are starvers of the poor, or that private property is robbery, ought to be unmolested when simply circulated through the press, but may justly incur punishment when delivered orally to an excited mob assembled before the house of a corn-dealer or when handed about among the same mob in the form of a placard.[22]

The immediacy of the potential harm and the appeal to the lower, impulsive nature of the mob are critical factors. Mill grants liberty only to secure the carefully considered expression of alternative views that promotes the two-fold benefit he so strongly defends.

TRUTH

Ultimately, the completely free expression of ideas leads toward the goal of truth, and "The truth of an opinion is part of its utility."[23] In other words, truth is not just an ideal that is valued for its own sake but because it is useful for achieving both individual and social progress. Individual liberty, constantly challenging accepted wisdom, enables truth to emerge. It is, to be sure, not a final truth, but a temporary and partial truth ever subject to revision and replacement.

Mill gives three main reasons why allowing free expression of opinions contrary to accepted beliefs fosters the continual discovery of truth. First, a new opinion might be true and supplant an old, false one. The belief that the

Earth was the center of the universe was replaced by the view that the sun is at the center, for example. Second, a new idea might be partially true. Exposing false ideas contained in part of the accepted view helps to correct old beliefs. The conclusions of Charles Darwin did not provide final answers about the origins of the species; rather, they served as a corrective, replacing one view with another. Finally, Mill makes the interesting point that even if a new idea is completely false, shielding an old, correct from attack would turn what is true into a mere prejudice. Allowing free expression of false views helps to strengthen the truth, for when the accepted view is challenged, people are forced to confront and demolish the new idea with evidence and reason. As a result of multiple challenges, correct ideas are prevented from losing vigor and simply lapsing into dogma. "Who can compute what the world loses in the multitude of promising intellects combined with timid characters, who dare not follow out any bold, vigorous, independent train of thought, lest it should land them in something which would admit of being considered irreligious or immoral?"[24]

Thus society benefits from individual liberty that enables free discussion, as it leads to the evolution of truth. Society loses out when liberty is denied. The greatest good for the greatest number ultimately lies in the long-range progress of society resulting from liberty. To follow the short-range appetites implicitly advocated by Mill's utilitarian predecessors is to impede progress.

LIMITED GOVERNMENT

Mill also believes that society benefits if government is prevented from interfering with acts of individuals beyond the three spheres already noted. The additional limits he imposes on government are not as absolute as are the rights of liberty of conscience, tastes and pursuits, and combination because they involve both individual and collective interests. The interests must be balanced, but the balance is to be tipped to favor individual choice whenever possible.

Mill's guiding principle is that so far as efficiency allows, power should be dispersed as widely as possible. On the other hand, government should serve as a central source of information so that individuals can make their own choices or decisions.

Mill describes three situations in which individual decision making is preferable to that of government. The first is when action can be done in a better way by individuals than by the government. If individuals can act more efficiently, as in the conduct of private economic enterprise, government should not intrude.

The second situation applies to an action that is not necessarily done better by individuals. But if their being allowed to do it helps to bring out hidden abilities that would otherwise be stifled, government may establish certain processes but should not interfere with outcomes. Examples of this are jury trials and elections.

Third, Mill opposes government action when it would add "unnecessarily" to its power. He fears big government, or a large bureaucracy, for they too pose a basic danger to individual liberty. As Mill says, "where everything is done through the bureaucracy, nothing to which the bureaucracy is really adverse can be done at all."[25]

These three situations (especially the third) may seem to offer strong support for a laissez-faire economy, one in which the role of government in economic affairs is minimal if not nil. Yet once again Mill recognizes complexities that restrain him from such a simple position. He advocates limited government, but the scheme he favors involves some political intervention in the economy. He prefers enlarging the scope of government to include economic measures designed, over the long term, to increase the size of the elite. As more people participate in a qualitatively better way of life, society as well as each individual benefits.

POLITICAL ECONOMY

Competition may not be the best conceivable stimulus, but it is at present a necessary one, and no one can foresee the time when it will not be indispensable to progress.

Most fitting, indeed, is it, that while riches are power, and to grow as rich as possible the universal object of ambition, the path to its attainment should be open to all, without favour or partiality.[26]

Mill's views on education and capitalist ownership underwent considerable change between the earliest and the last editions of his major economic work. Always concerned with the maximum improvement of individuals in society, his problem was to reconcile this goal with inequalities of birth and status that work against it. The question was how to unite maximum individual liberty and the benefits of economic competition with the equal opportunity of everyone to enjoy the results of social progress.

At first, he defended private property and sought to alleviate the injustices of birth through universal education. Early utilitarians and their Lockean predecessors had also thought that education could provide the key. Mill believed it could help, and supported laws to require compulsory education for all children. But he later rejected total reliance on education. He concluded that education cannot fully compensate for inequalities of birth such as poverty or illness. He also thought birth control and legislative reform might be useful devices, but he decided that these provisions, too, had only limited value. Therefore, even while expressing opposition to the tyranny of centralized socialism or economic equality for all, he supports economic and political arrangements that engage all workers in worthwhile labor and result in greater economic productivity while enabling laboring folk to participate in democratic decision making.

Mill asserts that under capitalism workers are passive wage earners who are not self-governing, and that the gap between them and owners is no basis for the development of individual self-reliance and democratic government. Since he regards all existing institutions and social arrangements as merely provisional, he encourages experiments in joint ownership through cooperatives that would actively involve workers in economic decisions. These cooperatives would be collectively owned by the workers and would compete with each other like capitalist firms. He envisions a large number of such small collectives nationwide, each one independently run by managers elected, and removable, by their worker-owners, and each one an experiment in workplace democracy.[27]

WOMEN, POLITICS, AND THE FAMILY

Mill holds strong egalitarian convictions concerning men and women, which were shaped by his utilitarian upbringing, early experiences, and contact with a number of independent, intelligent women. As a teenager, he spent a night in jail for illegally distributing birth control information. And he later had a long relationship with Harriet Taylor, who not only single-handedly gave lie to stereotypes of the time about women's place but wrote a book arguing for complete gender equality.

According to Mill,

> the principle which regulates the existing social relations between the two sexes—the legal subordination of one sex to the other—is wrong in itself, and now one of the chief hindrances to human improvement; and that it ought to be replaced by a principle of perfect equality, admitting no power or privilege on the one side, nor disability on the other.[28]

His ideas on gender relations mostly parallel those on liberty. The fullest development of people's capacities requires individual autonomy of men and women alike, so that everyone can contribute to social improvement. Absence of autonomy harms not only individuals but all of society. Women are deprived of opportunities, men of the intellectual stimulation from the competition and companionship of equal partners, and society of progress. The unjust political and legal subordination of one sex to another must be replaced by complete equality of opportunity.

He argues at length that gender differences are based on artificial and unnatural distinctions that are irrelevant to citizenship. He says that until equal opportunity is a fact there is no way to determine if there are any natural differences between men and women. Pointing to many women who had done important things despite legal and social prejudice, he explains that they would have done more had educational opportunities been open to them. That the elite must consist of both men and women is fundamental; and he further believes that once gender discrimination is subjected to rational examination and trial, discriminatory laws and practices will be abolished, and parity in politics and the workplace will be the order of the day.

Mill was a "brave and far-thinking feminist" who attacks various aspects of the patriarchal family and supports government intervention in domestic affairs. At the heart of women's unequal status is the institution of marriage. It makes women legal slaves, with no rights over their children, property, or their own bodies. To end the despotic control of husbands over wives, he thinks laws should protect women's rights, and marriage should be a freely contracted relationship that can be dissolved at any time, provided the children are cared for. The family is not only an institution for satisfying certain material needs but an educational forum as well. Both sons and daughters learn lessons about "the virtues of freedom" from the relationships they see between fathers and mothers.[29]

Despite his call for community ownership of property in the larger society, Mill exempts property arrangements and other domestic relations from such economic equality. He does say that as long as individual ownership is the law, husbands and wives should have control over what each brought to the marriage. But beyond this he rejects evenhandedness and maintains the traditional sexual division of labor within the household. "When the support of the family depends, not on property, but on earnings, the common arrangement, by which the man earns the income and the wife superintends the domestic expenditure, seems to me in general the most suitable division of labour between the two persons."[30] Mill thus assumes that in marriage women bear and raise children and tend the home while men go out and earn the family income. Women's domestic labor is unpaid, and there is no thought that wives might be paid a salary by husbands or that men might share in this work while their wives enter the labor force. Politics and home life, public and private, are strictly segregated, and only men are eligible to breach the barrier.

Outside of marriage, however, the full range of educational and career opportunities should be open to women on an equal footing with men. But disagreeing with his wife, Harriet, who favored allowing all women both work and marriage, Mill believes only a small number of single and divorced women, and perhaps some older married women without domestic responsibilities, should be allowed to join men at work and in politics. Most women are to be given the choice of career or marriage, but not both, a choice men need not make. Mill's opposition to overall gender justice stems from a refusal to question the conventional family arrangements of his time. And it is not consistent with his arguments for individual liberty.

REPRESENTATIVE GOVERNMENT

There is no difficulty in showing that the ideally best form of government is that in which the sovereignty, or supreme controlling power in the last resort, is vested in the entire aggregate of the community; every citizen not only having a voice in the exercise of that ultimate sovereignty, but being, at least occasionally, called on to take actual part in the government, by the personal discharge of some public function, local or general.[31]

Like his ideas on individual liberty, Mill's views on the political process stem from his conception of human nature. He favors a democracy, where "ultimate" power is in the hands of the people. But although it is, of course, a means of popular control, government is of greatest value as it improves the minds and characters of all its citizens, educating them about the public interest. "No government by a democracy or a numerous aristocracy . . . ever did or could rise above mediocrity except in so far as the sovereign Many have let themselves be guided . . . by the . . . more highly gifted and instructed One or Few."[32]

Government works best when all participate, but guided by an elite minority that includes all qualified men and women. They would populate the legislative and executive, educating the majority through wise laws and messages. In this way they could check the appetitive demands of the mediocre masses so that the majority do not lapse into tyrannical suppression of liberty. The best political system has a structure and a political process to allow for such guided participation. It is called representative government.

As with liberty, representative government is not for all peoples. Savages of backward nations can benefit more from an enlightened despotism designed to prepare them for self-government. Until they can cast aside their instinctive reliance on custom and learn from the free and equal debate that is part of liberty, they are incapable of managing their own affairs. However, the lower classes in advanced nations, such as Britain, are fully entitled to participate in government. The issue is how strong a voice they should have.

Mill recommends techniques to encourage better debate by strengthening the role of the elite minority. Even in the most civilized nations, some people should be prohibited from voting. Excluded are those unable to read or write, as well as people who do not pay taxes or who are criminals, bankrupt, or on public welfare. He also allows plural votes to the superior few, to prevent the ignorant masses from swamping them. Based on education, occupation, or ability to pass a general examination, each gifted adult would be able to cast two or more votes for their preferred candidates in any election.

To prevent majority tyranny and ensure the widest possible expression of minority (elite) opinion in the legislature, or lawmaking body, Mill advocates proportional representation. He assumes that there is great diversity of opinions in society, and that these would be organized for political purposes around a large number of political parties, each prepared to advance its views by reasoned discussion and legislative action. Proportional representation differs from single-member-district representation. The latter had been the practice in England from the origin of competitive elections to Mill's time (and indeed to the present). Under it, the legislative candidate in any district who receives the largest vote is declared the winner. There is no representation for those supporting other candidates, unless the person elected is willing to speak for them. As a result, the views of many minority groups are not represented at all in the legislature.

Proportional representation is an idea that emerged in the nineteenth century. It is designed to improve the chances for election of candidates representing many different parties, interests, or groups, based on the strength of each party in the voting public. There have been many schemes proposed for implementing proportional representation, some more complex than others, but the basic approach is fairly straightforward. Political parties receive a number of legislative seats in proportion to the number of votes each gets in an election. For example, in a 100-seat legislature, a party that received 54 percent of the total vote would get 54 seats; one with 21 percent of the vote, 21 seats; 14 percent, 14 seats; 6 percent, 6 seats; 3 percent, 3 seats; and 2 percent, 2 seats. In a single-member-district system, it is likely that such an electoral breakdown would result in two, or at the most three, parties dividing all the seats among them, depending on whether their supporters were concentrated in a few districts or widely dispersed. Under proportional representation, even a small party that would not be able to take a single district can secure a seat or two. In the example given, six parties (and thus six distinct views) are represented, and in a larger body even more views would be accommodated.[33]

Hypothetically, there is no limit to the number of parties that can secure representation under either system. In practice, however, Mill expects that proportional representation results in a voice for more parties and the participation of many able people of independent thought who would otherwise have no chance of being elected. That portion of the elite not serving in government is expected to promote liberty by expressing itself in public discussion and at the polls, where it is given more weight through plural voting and proportional representation.[34]

STRUCTURE AND ROLE OF GOVERNMENT

The voters' choices are channeled into a government organized to guide a nation-state. The legislative body, Parliament, is still sovereign and has two houses. The composition of the lower house, Commons, is determined by the results of elections based on proportional representation. Many more diverse opinions will be heard there following the introduction of the new proportional voting system.

The composition of the upper house is different than it actually was in Mill's time. No longer composed of a mostly hereditary nobility, it is made up of an expert intellectual and technical elite. Members are appointed based on their educational and job-related accomplishments.

Mill sees the legislature as a vast debating society for defining the public interest. In discussing proposed laws, each member presents personal, original views. The wishes of the citizens are filtered upward through this more representative, yet more elite, body and translated into wiser laws. Representatives also carry arguments for the long-term needs of society back to the ordinary citizens. Through regular communication, they serve as an educational force, teaching the public to distinguish between qualitatively better choices and merely short-term interests. In addition to enacting or rejecting proposed laws, the sovereign legislature has the job of criticizing, and ultimately controlling, the executive. The long-range goals of promoting individual liberty and social progress guide legislative oversight.

Under Mill's scheme, the executive continues to operate much as it did in his time. Made up of a small group of legislators who also have executive roles, when they act together as a committee, they comprise the cabinet. The cabinet as a body, and each of the members in it, are fully accountable to the legislature.

One of their tasks is to draft, following cabinet consideration, the laws that representatives in Parliament then discuss and either approve, amend, or reject. Individual members of the cabinet, as heads of government departments, are also expected to execute laws approved by Parliament with the assistance of a bureaucracy they supervise. They are responsible for defending the nation, securing internal order, and performing such necessary services as maintaining the public roads and delivering mail.

In effect, the executive is an elite within the larger legislative elite. Mill recognizes that the functioning of such a body, working under cabinet and individual responsibility, is a relationship that had been established in Britain by the middle of the nineteenth century. But his recommended changes in the electorate and the legislature ensure this tiny elite a larger role in advancing liberty and social progress than occurred in his time. As his elite is wise, it recognizes the value and necessity of not encroaching on individual freedom. Government (and its laws) are limited to keeping the peace, protecting the liberty of each individual, and providing for the welfare of the needy. A wise elite does not unnecessarily increase the power of government.

CONCLUSION

Mill draws on an idea common to other late-modern political philosophers, one that expresses the reason of the early-moderns but is sensitive to the criticisms of Hume, Burke, and Kant. To Mill, personal liberty is the motor that drives social progress. This establishes a new connection between the twin poles of the individual and the collective, one differing from that of the early-moderns while maintaining their emphasis on private freedom. Like the early moderns he distinguishes between public and private spheres of action, but unlike them he follows earlier utilitarian thinking and rejects any reliance on a state of nature, a political or social contract, natural law, or natural rights.

Limited government serves as a partner of the individual, protecting each person from threats to life and property, and especially from the danger that majority tyranny poses to liberty. Mill argues that, given human nature (as he sees it), only a moderately different political process, and the values of both liberty and equality, the two poles of individual and collective, as well as organic and aggregate politics, can be drawn closer together without sacrificing one for the other. This effort to balance these elements rather than reject one for the other differs from the perspective of ancient, medieval, and early modern thinkers. It also departs from the conclusions of neomodern thinkers, who insist the self cannot be separated from others, that by its *nature* the individual is part of the collective, and that the full development of both individual and collective depends on organic politics. To Mill, it is only as an individual, expressing personal qualities and unique perspectives and achieving self-realization, that anyone can contribute to social progress.

Mill's idea of social progress is no unified ideal stemming from any individual surrender of liberty, nor is the government or any other collective (such as the workplace) authorized to demand, or even request, such surrender. Mill remains very much an individualist, and his cooperative socialism clearly differs from total collectivism.

But how successful are his efforts to resolve fundamental dilemmas of political philosophy by trying to balance these several dualisms: individual and collective, governmental power and personal liberty, cooperative and individual ownership of production? Are there glaring inconsistencies that emerge from his efforts, and do they undermine his rather elegant resolution of these dilemmas, offending both committed individualists and resolute collectivists?

Notes

1. In addition to the *Autobiography,* published after his death, Mill's major works include the classic *On Liberty* (1859); his two important books on method, *System of Logic* (1843) and *Utilitarianism* (1863); *Principles of Political Economy* (1848), which fortified his position as the major English economist of his time; *Considerations on Representative Government* (1861); and his critique of Victorian gender relations, *The Subjection of Women* (1869), which is not as far-reaching as Harriet Taylor's earlier *Enfranchisement of Women* (1851).

2. For more on Mill's life and education, see Bruce Mazlish, *James and John Stuart Mill: Father and Son in the Nineteenth Century* (New Brunswick, N.J.: Transaction, 1975); and Joseph Hamburger, *Intellectuals in Politics: John Stuart Mill and the Philosophical Radicals* (New Haven, Conn.: Yale University Press, 1965).

3. John Stuart Mill, *Utilitarianism,* in *Utilitarianism, Liberty, and Representative Government* (London: J. M. Dent, 1910), ch. I.

4. For a fuller account, see John Plamenatz, *The English Utilitarians,* 2d ed. (New York: Oxford University Press, 1958).

5. *Utilitarianism,* ch. I.

6. Mill, *On Liberty,* in *Utilitarianism, Liberty and Representative Government,* ch. I. See also Jack Jackson, *A Guided Tour of John Stuart Mill's Utilitarianism* (Mountain View, Calif.: Mayfield, 1992); and John M. Robson, *The Improvement of Mankind: The Social and Political Thought of John Stuart Mill* (Toronto: University of Toronto Press, 1968).

7. *Utilitarianism,* ch. II.

8. *On Liberty,* ch. III.

9. Diana Coole, *Women in Political Theory: From Ancient Misogyny to Contemporary Feminism* (Boulder, Colo.: Lynne Rienner, 1988), 140–42.

10. *On Liberty,* ch. III.

11. *On Liberty,* ch. III.

12. *On Liberty,* ch. I.

13. *On Liberty,* ch. I.

14. *On Liberty*, ch. I. Mill got this term from Alexis de Tocqueville's *Democracy in America* (1835–40).

15. *On Liberty*, chs. I, III.

16. *On Liberty*, ch. I.

17. *On Liberty*, ch. V.

18. *On Liberty*, ch. I. See also John Gray, *Mill on Liberty: A Defence* (London: Routledge, 1983); and Gertrude Himmelfarb, *On Liberty and Liberalism: The Case of John Stuart Mill* (New York: Knopf, 1974).

19. *On Liberty*, ch. IV.

20. *On Liberty*, ch. II.

21. *On Liberty*, ch. I.

22. *On Liberty*, ch. III.

23. *On Liberty*, ch. II.

24. *On Liberty*, ch. II.

25. *On Liberty*, ch. V.

26. John Stuart Mill, *Principles of Political Economy*, ed. Donald Winch (New York: Penguin, 1985), bk. IV, chs. vii, sec. 7, and vi, sec. 2.

27. Samuel Hollander, *The Economics of John Stuart Mill* (Toronto: University of Toronto Press, 1985).

28. John Stuart Mill, *The Subjection of Women*, in *The Feminist Papers*, ed. Alice Rossi (New York: Columbia University Press, 1973), 196.

29. Susan Moller Okin, *Women in Western Political Thought* (Princeton, N.J.: Princeton University Press, 1979), 280; *Subjection*, 211, 212, 214.

30. *Subjection*, 213.

31. John Stuart Mill, *Representative Government*, in *Utilitarianism, Liberty and Representative Government*, ch. III.

32. *On Liberty*, ch. III.

33. See http://politicalscience.wadsworth.com/tannenbaum2 for a link to a table that illustrates the hypothetical results of two different voting schemes, single member district and proportional representation.

34. See Dennis Thompson, *John Stuart Mill and Representative Government* (Princeton, N.J.: Princeton University Press, 1976).

Additional Readings

Gray, John. *Mill on Liberty: A Defence*. London: Routledge, 1983.

Hollander, Samuel. *The Economics of John Stuart Mill*. Toronto: University of Toronto Press, 1985.

Jackson, Jack. *A Guided Tour of John Stuart Mill's Utilitarianism*. Mountain View, Calif.: Mayfield, 1992.

Kinzer, Bruce L. *England's Disgrace?: J. S. Mill and the Irish Question*. Toronto: University of Toronto Press, 2001.

Mazlish, Bruce. *James and John Stuart Mill: Father and Son in the Nineteenth Century*. New Brunswick, N.J.: Transaction, 1975.

Thompson, Dennis. *John Stuart Mill and Representative Government*. Princeton, N.J.: Princeton University Press, 1976.

 Inventors of Ideas Online

Visit http://politicalscience.wadsworth.com/tannenbaum2 for links related to material in this chapter, including an illustration of two voting schemes for legislative bodies and the texts of Mill's major works.

18

MARX: REVEALING HISTORY'S MEANING

INTRODUCTION

In the autumn of 1844, Karl Marx and Friedrich Engels met in Paris, and the world has not yet recovered. Despite great intellect and energy, Marx's writing style benefited from their collaboration. Engels, the less creative of the two, quickly grasped Marx's often obscure language and translated it into exciting prose that won popular approval. Beyond his literary skills, Marx relied on Engels for direction, loyalty, enthusiasm, and financial support. They were an unstoppable duo, contributing to many works published jointly and each having a hand in works published under the sole name of the other.[1]

For students, scholars, and the general public—that is to say, the world at large—Karl Marx (1818–1883) is arguably the most controversial figure in the long history of political philosophy.[2] Intellectual and activist, journalist, pamphleteer, revolutionary organizer and essayist, public figure and fugitive, he was author or coauthor of some fifty volumes of both scholarly and political writings. He was an opponent of much of the past, even while appreciating how that past served as a foundation of a more desirable future. Complex thinker, sharp-tempered, and an articulate speaker, debater, and critic of various contemporaries, he clashed with many people during his life.

In addition to the immeasurable effects of his work on world events, Marx profoundly affected a number of scholarly disciplines beyond political philosophy, most importantly economics and sociology but also art and literature.[3] Because of the wide reach of his theories and their many implications, it is hard to imagine an important aspect of study or life that has been immune to his influence. All this points to the multiple ways that thinking (and dogmatic) individuals have understood the tremendous output of this literary giant. Entering into the field of Marx studies is like embarking on an intellectual adventure relatively few other authors or books can offer. The questions he raised, the insights he had, and the solutions he proposed deal with the most significant issues facing humanity. Interpreters have found in Marx worthwhile ideas that they believe can be applied to such concerns as poverty, peace, feminism, discrimination, ecology and, ultimately, human survival. Given his vast output, and that of commentators on his work, there are many paths one can use to approach his writings. Any single route has its supporters and no one choice fully satisfies every critic.

Marx coauthored *The Communist Manifesto* with Engels (1820–1895), and it is their most influential work. A group called the Communist League, a semisecret workers' organization, commissioned them to draft a statement of purposes and this short pamphlet, written in the span of a few weeks, was the result. Engels produced the first draft and Marx the final one, but in a typically generous acknowledgement Engels says that "the fundamental proposition, which forms its nucleus, belongs to Marx."[4]

The program they outlined was forgotten for over twenty years, until a workers' uprising in Paris rescued it from obscurity. But if various details were "antiquated" within two decades, and if the relevance of its details depend on changing "historical conditions," at its heart it remains a potent summary of the key themes Marx and Engels treat in depth elsewhere.[5] Bold, direct, and confident, it presents the basic outline of a novel system in a straightforward, punchy prose style that is appropriate for the recruiting pamphlet it originally was. At its core is a radical analysis of the relationship of economics to politics throughout human history, and a profound critique of capitalism couched in the dramatic language of revolution.[6] In 1848, revolutions in France and Prussia enabled Marx to return to these countries, from which he had earlier been deported, to help and encourage the revolutionary forces. However, the revolutions were soon crushed, and Marx was forced to flee to London, his final home. The rest of his life was spent in research, writing, and political organizing.

MARX'S PROBLEM

The central problem the *Manifesto* addressed was human suffering, and its relationship to politics and economics. Over the preceding 160 years, Europe had experienced several major political revolutions, which were fought for two related objectives. One was national independence, and the other creation of democratic institutions or practices within existing nation-states. For the most part, these revolutions helped the bourgeoisie,[7] a growing capitalist class that sought freedom from control by monarchs and the upper-class nobility. The Glorious Revolution of 1688, for example, produced more representative institutions in the already independent nation-state of England, moving it from absolute to constitutional monarchy. Similarly, the American Revolution, fomented by the Declaration of Independence in 1776, led to both national independence through political separation from England and democratic institutions in the new nation-state. A third, the French Revolution of 1789, overthrew an absolute monarchy, replacing it with a more popular government.

To Marx, these political uprisings could be understood only when linked to economics. The growing Industrial Revolution flourished in many of the same nations that had undergone political revolution. It had emerged in eighteenth-century England and quickly spread to the independent United States and postrevolutionary France. The consequences of the Industrial Revolution were economic, political, and social.

Economically, major developments included large-scale production on assembly lines in manufacturing firms, whereas previously there had been only individual or small-scale production by a few workers. Manufactured goods were dispersed through large-scale distribution which expanded into international markets. A huge labor force, the proletariat or working class, performed the labor needed by the Industrial Revolution, extracting natural resources and producing finished products.

Politically, Marx detected close cooperation between business and government in these developments. A tiny part of the population, the capitalists, owned the means of production and acquired great wealth. Law and government-enforcement mechanisms protected both capitalist wealth and the means by which owners increased it.

To Marx, the social consequences were horrible. Oppression, exploitation, and injustice were widespread. Before the Industrial Revolution, most people had lived in rural villages or on landed estates and farms, where they had worked in agriculture or crafts. But as a result of the rise of large-scale manufacturing, job-seekers moved to crowded, ugly cities. A series of government reports, published in early-nineteenth-century England, detailed the consequences of this shift. Marx later used these reports as a research base for his writings. Describing the conditions of the working class, particularly those employed in mines and factories, the official accounts were shocking. Children as young as five years labored at dangerous machines in poorly lit and badly ventilated buildings and mines. Overworked and underfed, they toiled like slaves for up to eighteen hours daily. They were chained to their machines, exposed to murderous health conditions, beaten if they did not follow the overseer's orders, even locked up at night to prevent escape. Of course they received no education, and received a living wage at best. Treatment of adult workers paralleled that of their children. They too worked under dangerous, health-threatening conditions, putting in long hours at dull, repetitive jobs. The urban homes they returned to after their long workdays were overcrowded hovels in slums. Uneducated and underpaid, they faced the constant threat of unemployment.

In Marx's time, adults who were in the first generation to move from rural towns to the growing cities knew what their lives had been like before and could see what they had lost. Over many centuries, a traditional relationship had been established between upper-class lords, who were the landowners, and lower-class peasants, who worked the land. Although the two classes were unequal in treatment and reward, there was a sense that they were engaged in a joint enterprise. Traditional ties encouraged lords to a benevolent concern for "their" peasants, however minimal.

The Industrial Revolution shattered this customary relationship. Peasants who moved to cities faced a strictly businesslike connection with their bourgeois employers. Concerned only with maximum output for minimal investment, most bosses had no interest in the personal lives, abilities, or histories of their workers. All employees were interchangeable robots on an assembly line. Their value or monetary wage was determined by the owners, and supply and demand came first in this and all other considerations of production.

In their rural settings, both farmers and artisans worked through the entire process of producing foods or crafts. Independent artisans bought and owned their tools and raw materials, and were the owners as well as the producers of the finished goods. They could see the results of their labor and take pride in their work. By contrast, the industrial division of labor on the assembly line destroyed this connection between work and production. Each wage-earning worker made only a part of the finished product. None could claim ownership of any of it. Creative pride of workers was not an important element in the new industrial order.

The situation Marx faced, then, was one of great injustice that touched every aspect of industrial society. At the heart of his problem is the question, Why do some people lead a life of privilege while others are condemned to drudgery and abject poverty?

As discussed earlier, the issue of justice has been central to Western political philosophers since the origin of its culture. And several other explanations had been offered to account for the specific injustices facing the new industrial proletariat even before Marx wrote. Many workers believed their misery was caused by the machines they worked, and that if these were destroyed their old way of life would return. In a number of factory riots machines were wrecked. The workers judged responsible were imprisoned or deported for destroying private property, their fellow workers were (at least temporarily) unemployed, and overall conditions remained unchanged. Among the bourgeoisie, some saw no problem of injustice at all. They closed their eyes and minds to the way workers lived and labored. When they did notice some jarring example that caused them to reflect momentarily on the conditions of the working classes, they might blame it on "natural" causes that humans were powerless to remedy.

Thoughtful members of the middle class generally focused on one of two targets when trying to explain the plight of the proletariat. Some offered a religious explanation, others a political one. The religiously inclined saw original sin at the source of the problem. Remedies lay in moral reform; factory owners had to be shown the proper, "Christian" way to treat their workers. And workers had to be liberated from sin and drink by being taught the wisdom of the middle-class way of life. Politically motivated explanations focused on reform of secular institutions and practices. Workers had to be made part of the political process. If given the vote, they could elect politicians who would pass laws to protect them from the terrible conditions they faced.

Marx, however, uses a wider framework to understand proletarian misery. He puts the political and economic revolutions discussed earlier into unique historical perspective, concluding that the injustice is an aspect of bourgeois morality that justifies economic exploitation. This morality stems from the merger of representative democracy and capitalism, and has its roots in bourgeois values such as those of Hobbes and Locke, in which class interests are equated with the public interest.[8] Furthermore, he determines that "the modern bourgeoisie is itself the product of a long course of development, of a series of revolutions in the modes of production and of exchange."[9] As a result, the condition of society, even if unjust, is historically inevitable. Both the rise and the eventual fall of the bourgeoisie are part of destiny. It is a waste of time to try to reform those responsible, whether one works with individuals or through institutions. Bourgeois society is doomed to collapse.

METHOD: FROM HEGEL TO MARX

Marx reaches this overarching conclusion by using a new method of thinking about politics which he applies to analysis of the past in order to anticipate the future:

> Does it require deep intuition to comprehend that man's ideas, views and conceptions, in one word, man's consciousness, changes with every change in the conditions of his material existence, in his social relations and in his social life? What else does the history of ideas prove, than that intellectual production changes its character in proportion as material production is changed?[10]

Marx's method may be called *historical materialism,* or *dialectical materialism,* because it is both historical and dialectical in its approach to materialism. To develop the dialectical approach, Marx transformed ideas he found in the works of G. W. F. Hegel (1770–1831), a German philosopher.[11] Hegel's approach, much like Plato's, reveals what he considers the true reality that lies behind the everchanging appearances and contradictions individuals see in the world. To discover this reality, they must find a way to reconcile things that seem to be conflicting opposites, one the subject and the other the object, such as individual versus collective. The goal is to discover a new proposition, a synthesis, which unites the truth in each of the opposites. The process of reconciliation is repeated over and over through the long expanse of history until a final or highest synthesis is reached.

Hegel arrives at this rather abstract conclusion by judging that humans and nature were originally unified, and then divided by God to allow for human development and progress through conflict, but will be reunited at the end of history.[12] Human problems stem from looking at them from an individual point of view. People could see them for what they are, as being of no great importance, if they looked at them through the eyes of philosophers, who can transcend individualism and assume a comprehensive outlook. Just as the scientist seeks the universal and rational laws of nature, the job of the philosopher is to look for the larger reason behind history by using the dialectic process.

To guide individuals to this larger reason, Hegel focuses on three major social institutions, which are as important today as they were then: family, civil society, and the state. At its best, the family reflects a loving relationship, and its members act for the good of all family members, not just themselves. But this altruism is limited to only the few people who are members of any family. Facing the subjective family are the objective institutions of civil society. Here, people cooperate, at first, based on selfish motives. For example, they unite to keep the peace in order to stay alive and promote personal economic goals, as Locke argued. But to do so, they must also get involved as citizens, voting, paying taxes, and performing military service. These are activities of enlightened self-interest, which take people out of the narrow focus of the family to involve those not related by marriage.

The state is the synthesis that reconciles subject—the altruism of the family, limited to a few—with object—civil society expressing universal selfishness.[13] It reflects an altruism that is universal, because all people are members who have a personal stake in promoting its goals. Through the state, people find meaning in their lives. Without it, an individual would be diminished as a full and free person. Freedom here, as for Rousseau, is defined as liberty to obey as one knows one ought to, based on the belief that the goals of the state are superior to anything any individual might want.

Having crushed selfish individualism and upheld duty through obedience, Hegel then links state and history. There is a special reason behind every historical event that reveals itself gradually over time, ever in the direction of human progress. It works through a world spirit that has been ordained to ultimately free individuals from all dialectic divisions, such as humanity versus nature, or freedom versus duty, or individual versus collective. At any point in history the world spirit is located in the one particular nation-state with the spirit, or culture, that can contribute most to human progress. This spirit inspires the nation's people to world leadership. At any time in history, the nation that carries the world spirit is the *world-historical nation-state*. Whatever it does is just; it can do no wrong, as it acts to fulfill the reason or purpose given to it by history.

World-historical nations and their leaders (e.g., Alexander the Great, Julius Caesar, and Napoléon) are the unwitting tools of history, for it is the reason behind history, not their own free choice, that decides they shall be leaders and their nation's spirit shall be the dominant one. As a world-historical nation-state spreads its spirit to the world it enlarges the universal idea of true freedom. It defeats other, lesser nations in warfare, and then infuses them with a healthy dose of the world spirit from its national culture, which means that war is a primary means of progress. In this way, humanity evolves toward the ultimate goal of freedom, under which all contradictions will be reconciled. Freedom is to be found by obeying the reason of history, the march of justice in the world.

Marx accepts Hegel's argument that history is the march of rational justice in the world. Its goal is universal freedom, and the dialectical method is how people discover the path to that goal.

Materialism is Marx's key addition to Hegel's dialectical view of history. To Marx, people can have a truly scientific understanding of the reality that is human history only by applying Hegel's dialectic to material things. This is because the underlying driving force behind all of history is, in fact, material or economic.[14] In place of Hegel's spirit as the motor for progress, Marx substitutes material forces, and he replaces Hegel's nation-state as the vehicle for history with economic categories, or classes. Therefore, once people understand class motives and class relationships they can grasp the purpose and direction of a history that progresses by dialectical conflict and resolution. This in turn enables them to engage in *praxis*, or practice, by studying actual conditions and taking revolutionary action to achieve change. As Marx says, "The philosophers [such as Hegel] have only *interpreted* the world, in various ways; the point, however, is to *change* it."[15]

Note that Marx does not prove but simply assumes the priority of economics, specifically, that in every society in history so far politics is the result of economic forces and accompanying class struggles. Like Hegel, Marx also assumes that history is a series of necessary evils with a clear goal, which for him is a classless society that provides economic justice for all. As a result, he is certain that both the fall of the bourgeoisie "and the victory of the proletariat are equally inevitable."[16]

STAGES OF HISTORY

Marx's goal is worked out through history in definable stages or time periods, with the last stage yet to come. Writing of these stages, Engels says that in every one

> the prevailing mode of economic production and exchange, and the social organization necessarily following from it, form the basis on which is built up, and from which alone can be explained, the political and intellectual history of that epoch; that consequently the whole history of mankind (since the dissolution of primitive tribal society, holding land in common ownership) has been a history of class struggles, contests between exploiting and exploited, ruling and oppressed classes; that the history of these class struggles forms a series of evolutions in which, nowadays, a stage has been reached where the exploited and oppressed class—the proletariat—cannot obtain its emancipation from the sway of the exploiting and ruling class—the bourgeoisie—without at the same time, and once and for all, emancipating society at large from all exploitation, oppression, class distinctions and class struggles.[17]

The key to human history, then, is the epic of class struggles. Their origins, their development, and their promise of a better future form the substance of Marx's argument.[18]

Everyone has an inescapable physical need to sustain life. To fulfill this need people organize economic systems or modes of production, distribution, and consumption. At each stage of history, economic forces give rise to two major classes. Although the terms used for the two classes differ from one stage to another because the mode of production differs at each stage, these two classes are always enemies. Their class relations are grounded in oppression and injustice, since the ruling class (made up of the few) dominates and exploits the subject class (the many).

Classes originate in the division of labor. At first this division was sexual, based on bearing and raising children; then it divided those who hunted from those who raised crops. Over time, it evolved into a split between the intellectuals and those who did physical work. For example, when governments regulated economic output in ancient times, the ruling class included emperors and pharaohs as well as such specialists as scribes, bureaucrats, and priests. In each historical period, the authority of the ruling class stems from its economic role; it holds political power because it commands production. Social class and economics serve as the base, or substructure, on which a complex superstructure is founded. Superstructure includes politics, law, religion, the family, and ideas and institutions that are grounded in the economic base. People do not simply choose whatever ideas or form of government they like; rather, it is defined for them by their economic class system. Even human nature is shaped by economics, depending for its content on the class structure of society.[19] Substructure determines superstructure.

As part of its superstructure, every society has an ideology, or a set of values, beliefs, and attitudes that justify existing class relations. The ruling class always decrees an unequal division of property, compensating itself more highly from the common store and economically exploiting those who work with their hands. Religion serves rulers as a peaceful way to control any resulting lower-class protest, justifying exploitation by picturing a heavenly reward to make people indifferent to human suffering, and warding off the search for alternatives to earthly injustice. This is why Marx calls religion "the opium of the people."[20]

Class struggles in one stage are related to those in other stages, and every system produces the seeds of its own destruction. Every exploited class is driven to overthrow its rulers and install itself as the new ruling class. However, a ruling class can be displaced only when it becomes economically obsolete due to changes in technology. This becomes possible when new productive forces (e.g., new raw materials, tools, knowledge, sources of labor power) contradict existing productive and class relations. Over time, economic power shifts to the class that develops the new forces of production, the old ruling class is doomed, and no amount of force at its disposal can keep it in power.

But although each of the stages in the past ended with the fall of one ruling class and its replacement by another, this will not happen after capitalism is abolished. When the workers triumph, their victory will free everyone, and all class struggle will end.

Prehistory. The original human condition occurred at a time before there were written records. However, Marx's prehistory does not resemble the crude state of nature of Hobbes, Locke, or Rousseau. They all began with isolated individuals, while for Marx the earliest period centered on the tribe, which made all decisions collectively. There was no division between rulers and ruled. Everyone participated in a pure democracy.[21]

Economically, the system was a primitive communism. There was no private property, no possessions beyond those needed, and everyone shared from a common stock. However, in this primitive economy only very basic material needs were met, and sometimes not even those. If there was a simple division of labor it was not artificial, but was based on such natural biological differences as age and gender. Women tended the children, the stronger hunted, and the weaker gathered food.

There were no distinctions among tribal members, political, economic, or social. Only one class existed, and all were members of that class. Not only was there no private property, there was no slavery and no oppression, as these had no place in a subsistence economy.

Because private property, slavery, government, and class divisions were not present in prehistory, they are not rooted in human nature. These artificial traits and institutions were introduced at the onset of human history. Human nature, which is basically cooperative and unselfish, has no need of them, and they could be abolished in some future society without any real loss to humanity.

Precapitalism. At some point, the development of agriculture and tool making began. This led to a class-based division of labor and creation of a system of private property that produced an artificial poverty which was unjust, as some suffered while others flourished. The earliest governments were created to support the rights of the newly empowered class, by force if needed, and all the other elements of the superstructure followed.

In ancient times, the two major classes in dialectic opposition were master and slave. Masters included chiefs, warriors, landowners, and politicians. They were well-off, having possessions far beyond their basic needs. Most people were slaves, producing the goods for society but condemned to lives of artificial poverty, as they could only have what little their masters allowed. The oppressed slaves were kept in place by governments geographically situated in city-states, such as Athens and Rome, which controlled large empires.

A series of revolutions marked the shift from the ancient to the medieval, or feudal, stage which dominated the Middle Ages. The most important of these involved changes in economic modes of production; the political revolutions accompanying the barbarian invasions of the Roman Empire were merely the final blow to a decaying ancient stage and its economic relationships.

The two dialectically contending medieval classes were lord and serf. Like their predecessors, lords were the class of wealthy owners who enjoyed a relatively luxurious way of life, while impoverished serfs were the major producers of both necessities and luxuries. The term *lord* could refer to any noble, from king or emperor to minor baron. Feudal lords established governments geographically situated in realms. Depending on the locale, a realm could consist of anything from a small manor or castle to an empire. Whatever the setting, government was the means ruling lords used to control their subject serfs.

Due to changes in the modes of production, medieval laborers had greater practical and legal independence than at earlier times. As a result, serfs were somewhat freer than slaves had been. Although bound by custom to the land they lived and worked on, they were not legally the property of the lord. The two classes were related by an unwritten contract under which lords provided protection and administration, and serfs contributed their labor. Each side had obligations to the other.

If serfs were freer than slaves, then lords were relatively less powerful than masters. They had many means useful for oppressing their serfs, but they did not have the absolute power of life and death over all serfs that masters had maintained over slaves in ancient society.

Serfs could never have freed themselves from the lords. The spearhead of the end of feudalism were new urban merchants who transformed medieval economics, bankers who funded monarchs in wars against their nobles, and urban residents who secured royal charters giving them autonomy from local lords in return for their political support. By encouraging urban economic development and political influence, medieval rulers prepared their own graves. History could have it no other way.

Capitalism

Our epoch, the epoch of the bourgeoisie, possesses, however, this distinct feature: it has simplified the class antagonisms. Society as a whole is more and more splitting up into two great hostile camps, into two great classes facing each other.[22]

The Industrial Revolution brought yet another significant change in the economic mode of production, and marked the shift from the feudal to the capitalist stage of history. The two major classes in dialectic contention are, of course, bourgeoisie and proletariat. The former replaced lords as the dominant group in society, because in modern industrial economies capital is more important than land or hereditary titles.

Some medieval lords tried to cling to their privileged positions in the face of economic change by using all the political and other superstructural resources at their command. But they were ousted from power in a series of bourgeois political uprisings, especially the English, American, and French revolutions of 1688, 1776, and 1789, respectively. These uprisings marked a decisive shift of government control from realm to nation-state. Following the pattern of past stages, the bourgeoisie used government to rule and oppress the proletariat.

Capitalism is based on wage labor, and the worker is free to work for the employer offering the best pay. Workers are neither owned by capitalists nor are they considered bound to any employing individual or factory. They are therefore freer than serfs ever were. The obverse is, of course, that capitalists have less power than lords did. Their ability to oppress the subject class, though still very real, is diminished, particularly as far as the law is concerned. Under capitalism, everyone is formally equal under the law.

POVERTY AND ALIENATION

This relatively greater freedom does not satisfy Marx. If anything, the laws of economics under capitalism are even more oppressive than in earlier stages. As he says of the workers, "Not only are they slaves of the bourgeoisie class, and of the bourgeois State; they are daily and hourly enslaved by the machine, by the overlooker, and, above all, by the individual bourgeois manufacturer himself."[23] In addition to his well-known condemnation of the economic consequences of capitalism, Marx expresses a moral attitude. He was aware of the killing conditions under which vast numbers of poor children worked for twelve to sixteen hours a day for the barest minimum wage. Adults, he thinks, are little better off:

> Owing to the extensive use of machinery and to division of labour, the work of the proletarians has lost all individual character, and, consequently, all charm for the workman. He becomes an appendage of the machine, and it is only the most simple, most monotonous, and most easily acquired knack, that is required of him. Hence, the cost of production of a workman is restricted, almost entirely, to the means of subsistence that he requires for his maintenance, and for the propagation of his race.[24]

The heart of the problem, once again, is the institution of private property, which dates back to the beginning of history. The source of private property in the capitalist age is the profits capitalists make, or surplus value. Surplus value is the difference between the cost of raw materials and the selling price of any product. It is the value of the labor put in, or added to, the raw material. As Locke would concede, the addition of labor is what causes an increase in the value, and the selling price, of a product. Marx thinks that in any fair economic system labor should receive the economic rewards for its productivity—the surplus value. But under capitalism it does not. Instead it is paid the lowest possible wage needed to secure a continuing supply of workers. Laborers must work longer and produce more surplus product than they receive in order to provide for the luxurious lives of the bourgeoisie. This, Marx concludes, is economically unjust.

In addition, under capitalism there is, for the first time in history, overproduction. Seeking greater profits through increased sales, competing firms produce more than society can consume. In so doing, they show no regard for the common interest or good of society. They cannot do otherwise, because capitalists are forced by the economic system to compete or fail, and failure means falling into the proletariat. But markets become glutted with products that cannot be sold, profits drop, unsold goods rot in storage, prices and production are cut to get rid of the surplus, firms fail, and laborers are thrown out of work until the excess can be disposed of. Thus the crisis of overproduction gives way to one of underproduction, depression, and famine.

In a society in which there are more goods than are needed by those with property, the unemployed cannot even afford the basic necessities to keep themselves alive. This occurs even as capitalists block the most efficient use of social resources, which could provide sufficient goods and services for everyone. And like every past ruling class, the bourgeoisie employs all the institutions of the superstructure to maintain its hold on an unjust and increasingly inefficient system. In this way, capitalism creates the conditions for its own destruction.

Like its predecessors, capitalism sets up barriers against full development of human potential. It is a unified social environment that shapes and controls human nature, as the nature Darwin studied controls the lives of organisms. It selects or adapts some human talents, rejects others, encourages some capabilities, stunts the rest. As a result, everyone in capitalist society is alienated, bourgeois and proletarian alike. This is so because individuals exist for business and profits rather than the reverse. Everyone regards both people and products solely as things useful for profit. People are ensnared in the mad quest for surplus value.

No bourgeois institution escapes Marx's scathing denunciation, including government. It represents only the interests of the capitalists. No matter who is elected to office, preservation of the system is their first obligation. But Marx goes beyond politics and economics to denounce the entire superstructure of capitalism, including its law, philosophy, science, art, and religion. He says that in the end, "for exploitation, veiled by religious and political illusions, [capitalism] has substituted naked, shameless, direct, brutal exploitation."[25]

The capitalist system is bourgeois-oriented because it benefits the middle class economically. As for alienation, however, even the bourgeoisie suffers, for at root the system is unjust to all participants, whatever their economic status.

> The bourgeoisie, by the rapid improvement of all instruments of production, by the immensely facilitated means of communication, draws all, even the most barbarian, nations into civilization. . . . It compels all nations, on pain of extinction, to adopt the bourgeois mode of production; it compels them to introduce what it calls civilization into their midst, i.e., to become bourgeois themselves.[26]

Alienation at home is matched by that beyond national borders. To increase profits and get rid of surpluses, capitalists develop world markets. Similarly, an insatiable search for raw materials leads to colonies, established to secure continuing access to those resources. Bourgeois ideas of human rights for all, enshrined in such revolutionary documents as the English Bill of Rights, the American Declaration of Independence, and the French Declaration of the Rights of Man, accompany colonial expansion. The contradictions between these universal ideals of democracy and freedom and capitalist political control makes proletarians everywhere conscious of their real situation and prepares them for revolutionary action.

SCIENTIFIC SOCIALISM

Many others had voiced outrage against the capitalist system, including machine-wrecking workers and middle-class religious and political reformers who were shocked by reports of the conditions of the working class. But

Marx's moral indictment of capitalism has a special perspective that sets it apart from any of these. His views also set him apart from those discussed in the *Manifesto*, which were likewise socialist but not of his stripe. He agrees with the other socialists' opposition to the evils of capitalism, but he does not just condemn it. He believes he has identified the real, material, social change agent: the proletariat. The other socialists' understanding of root historical causes is limited, to him. They have no appreciation for the correct path of historical development, and so many of them oppose revolutionary action, favoring instead peaceful change through small-scale experimentation. To Marx, this is not only wrongheaded but counterproductive.[27]

Full understanding of what is really behind capitalism and what must be done stems from scientific socialism. It is scientific because it is based on the only correct method of analysis, historical or dialectical materialism. Use of this method distinguishes the Marxism of the *Manifesto*, communism, from other kinds of socialism. Marx believed this method makes people aware of a process that has been going on since the dawn of history. Before Marx, history accomplished its predetermined purpose without conscious human participation. People acted like other animals, based on a sense of necessity. History guided them to its ends through apparent accidents, such as scientific discoveries and the finding of uncharted lands:

> The discovery of America, the rounding of the Cape, opened up fresh ground for the rising bourgeoisie. The East-Indian and Chinese markets, the colonisation of America, trade with the colonies, the increase in the means of exchange and in commodities generally, gave to commerce, to navigation, to industry, an impulse never before known, and thereby, to the revolutionary element in the tottering feudal society, a rapid development.[28]

According to this interpretation, Columbus did not land in the Americas as an accidental by-product of his search for a new route to the Indies. Rather, his "discovery" was historically necessary because American natural resources were to become essential to destroy feudalism and help capitalist manufacturing. Even if Columbus did not know this, the hidden hand of history did, and it used him to further its goals. Since Marx wrote, however, people have the means to become conscious of the direction of history. They can now know the real causes and the inevitable outcome. They become aware, for example, that capitalist exploitation is based on class and gender. Liberation can never come from individual effort, or the goodwill of particular members of the bourgeoisie, however well-intentioned. Only united action to smash capitalism and rechannel its productive capacity into nonexploitative purposes will suffice.

GENDER AND THE FAMILY

> The bourgeois sees in his wife a mere instrument of production. He hears that the instruments of production are to be exploited in common, and, naturally can come to no other conclusion than that the lot of being common to all will likewise fall to the women.

He has not even a suspicion that the real point aimed at is to do away with the status of women as mere instruments of production.[29]

To Marx, the relationship between men and women is a most natural one and the source of the original, biological division of labor. Fundamentally, their natures are alike, both genders having similar potential in the bright future promised to them. Until then, gender relations will continue to be determined by economics.

Women were free, independent, and indeed rather powerful until late in the tribal era. Group marriage was the basic relationship between the sexes; and children were considered descendants of the female, a system called matriarchy, or mother-right. Then couples began to replace group marriages, and metal tools replaced stone implements. Women cared for the home while men cleared the forests, domesticated animals, and produced food and tools. This division of labor resulted in surplus production, and the men who raised the food and made the tools were considered the owners of this surplus of land, animal herds, and slaves. Seeking to pass on the new wealth to descendants, patriarchy, or father-right was instituted to replace mother-right. Insisting that they had to be sure who their offspring were, men established sexual fidelity as a key aspect of the patriarchal family.

The history of marital relationships has paralleled that of class relations since this *world-historic defeat of the female sex.*[30] All institutions, including the family, are part of the superstructure that exists to meet the demands of the economic system. They reflect the simultaneous conflict of class and sex from ancient times through the present capitalist system. Dominating marriage as they do class relations, ruling males get women to perform unpaid domestic work and serve as breeding instruments who are totally dependent on their husbands.

Under capitalism, contractual marriages replace the arranged unions of earlier eras. The principle of voluntary contracts between individuals in the capitalist economic market is extended to family formation. In principle, love becomes the basis of marriage, although it is the proletariat that can most afford such partnerships. The bourgeoisie is primarily motivated by economic considerations here, as in every other aspect of life. Women marry for wealth, men to enlarge the fortune they will pass on to their legitimate heirs. Such marriages of convenience turn into "the crassest prostitution" and lead to adultery. Where marriage is based on love, the result is "a wedded life of leaden boredom which is described as domestic bliss."[31]

Bourgeois women are better off than their proletarian counterparts, at least as far as social standing, promise for their children, and availability of creature comforts are concerned. This gives them a class interest in maintaining capitalism even as they have a gender interest in abolishing it, since private property is at the root of their oppression in the patriarchal family.

Proletarian women experience no such conflicting interests. Wherever they turn, capitalism enslaves them, as it does their husbands and children. Proletarian marriage can be based on love since there is no wealth or property to be gained or inherited. This circumstance deals working-class women a different sort of blow. They are oppressed as workers, performing productive as well as reproductive labor. They work outside the home at menial jobs to increase the pittance on which the family lives, even while bearing full responsibility for keeping house and raising children. The proletarian family thus produces the next generation of workers.

Capitalism, as part of the movement of history, is not an entirely negative situation. Along with ever-advancing levels of technology, its inclusion of women as workers establishes a new economic basis for the postrevolutionary future. The revolution will finally free all people, including women, and establish new social relationships. Once private property is abolished, nobody need be economically dependent on anyone else. The problem of legitimate heirs vanishes, as does the need for forced monogamy. The care and education of children becomes a public function, and the patriarchal family disappears. Women are free to enter sexual relationships, including marriage, because they choose them. The most natural bond, sex-love, is their motive, and gender relations are marked by equality and reciprocity.

THE FUTURE

In sketching out the account of the several stages that followed the prehistoric epoch, Marx champions dialectical progress. He traces increases in both economic capacity and freedom for the oppressed classes, indicating that in general things are getting better and better, even as conditions for the proletariat deteriorate. Marx's description ends with the account of capitalism, and then prediction begins.

When capitalist forces of production reach their point of greatest economic inefficiency and alienation and are ready to undergo change, the proletariat will rise up in a final revolution, overthrow the bourgeoisie, and establish a classless society. Although at first the proletariat "must constitute itself *the* nation," in the end it will "abolish countries and nationalism." This opposition to the nation-state suggests that Marx favors instead a small, polis-like political setting.[32]

Although Marx is sure that the proletarian victory is inevitable, how quickly this will happen is not predetermined. The end may be certain, but the means have to be worked out. Much depends on the level of awareness of the masses, which will move them to rise up at the proper time.

Whatever the timing, following the anticapitalist revolution society will undergo a transition to communism. During the transition, the means of production will be turned over to everyone to control in common. Furthermore, the separation of people into competing classes, and thus class struggle, will end.

Economically, the future will ultimately enjoy all of the benefits of prehistory with none of its problems. There will be a return to economic communism, which is the final goal of history. All the technological advantages of the past, which previously led to overproduction, will now become part of an industrial capacity allowing for economic abundance for everyone. This means a return to the prehistoric condition of social and economic equality for all, but under conditions of plenty that primitive peoples could never imagine. Because Communism will be a one-class (classless) society, differences will not be used to exploit people, nor will there be any private property, or property used for profit making. People will continue to have necessary personal possessions, such as clothing, but ownership beyond need will be abolished. Cooperation will replace competition, and shared abundance will replace artificial poverty. Moreover,

> When, in the course of development, class distinctions have disappeared, and all production has been concentrated in the whole nation, the public power will lose its political character. Political power, properly so-called, is merely the organized power of one class for oppressing another.[33]

The political future will also represent a return to prehistory, to a condition of anarchy.[34] There will be no more government, no political institutions, no coercion. The state will wither away because, like all other social institutions throughout history, bourgeois government is merely the tool of the ruling class used to maintain order and exploit the proletariat.

As with so much of the dialectical complexity of Marx's thought, the state in fact has dual functions. While historically inevitable, it is also a "Machiavellian" trick: It aids the proletariat even as it oppresses it. On the one hand, its more promising features, such as universal suffrage and individual rights, help to free proletarians from feudal ignorance, educating them to the prospective benefits of communal political activity. On the other hand, these advantages are not intended to help the workers attain greater freedom, but to delude them. Although bourgeois political practices supposedly compel governments to serve the will of the majority, they are in practice merely devices to fool the masses into believing they have power that in fact belongs to an elite minority. Even if capitalists do not personally run the government, their lackeys direct it in the interests of capitalism.

Since the state is only an instrument of the dominant class, it will disappear when the class struggle ends. When there is no class to oppress, the state has no purpose. "In place of the old bourgeois society, with its classes and class antagonisms, we shall have an association, in which the free development of each is the condition for the free development of all."[35] The future will be the beginning of a new, truly humane history of people whose material needs are fully met by a highly developed technology and for whom security needs are no longer an issue. Under communism, everyone will be fulfilled because each works for him- or herself as a part of the whole community. Women as well as men will be able to develop their unique talents in ways that contribute to the public good. Since everyone will be economically equal, they will be naturally cooperative. Living in a society where they see the benefits of cooperation, they will be aware of their obligations to the community, contributing according to ability and receiving according to need. To use Rousseau's terms, everyone shall be free to will the general will.

All that remains is the administration of things, such as the production and distribution of basic goods and services. This is what Marx referred to as the *realm of necessity*. Necessary work, such as street cleaning or road building, will be done, but the nature of the work will be completely changed. These are tasks a public educated to community obligations will do easily and willingly. People will assume temporary, rotating authority to direct this work, and they will not require coercion by anyone else to get the job done. State power will be "transformed into the simple administrative functions of watching over the true interests of society." To Marx, these are things that just about anyone can do without special training. Thus the division of labor will be no more. Even if a division of work tasks is required, it will not result in unequal distribution of the product of that work. Besides, since the final revolution will have occurred when the productive capacity of capitalism is at its peak, such tasks are not likely to demand as much of any individual's time in a cooperative society, where everyone pitches in.[36]

Cooperatively moving forward, everyone will enjoy the highest level of truly human civilization. Creativity, culture, intellectual life will flourish. There will be further advances in production and technology. However, these will be directed at human improvement, because the aim of their creators will be a higher level of civilization for all, not, as under capitalism, the satisfaction of individual greed and domination. Since there will be an end to history, at least as an arena for class struggle and alienation, there need be no further revolutions. The posthistoric epoch will mark the beginning of the truly humane history of unalienated humanity.

In the future Marx foresees, economics is no longer the most important element. It is subordinated to a vision of justice on earth: Marx returns to the theme of Plato. He offers the comforting assurance that the downtrodden proletariat will inherit the earth, for they are destined to win out. Marx's scientific understanding of history merely confirms the certainty of his conclusion.

CONCLUSION

The Communist Manifesto fires its opening words like a shot: "A spectre is haunting Europe—the spectre of Communism." These words are no longer adequate, for international communism no longer haunts. Claiming to be based on Marx's teachings, but disregarding, among other points, his insistence that capitalism must be fully developed before a final proletarian revolution can be successful, one wing of the Communist Party in Russia overthrew a royalist government and mostly feudal economy and renamed Russia the Soviet Union. The movement the party claimed to lead conquered and grew until one-third of the world's population lived in nation-states that officially revered Marxist views. But with the abolition of the Soviet Union, that movement has almost completely died out.

Today its future in Russia is uncertain, the orthodoxy of its adherents unclear. A few other places, such as North Korea and Cuba, still pay lip service to a more dogmatic version of Marxism. China appears to have moved away from Marxist economic ideas while maintaining a Soviet-like police state. The role of Marxism as a revolutionary call to arms has more recently been assumed by religious or ethnic nationalism.

Despite the fall of the old Soviet Union, the debates and writings on Marx's ideas show no sign of slowing down. The meaning of his work is still discussed and contested today in a continuing torrent of books, articles, and speeches by supporters and opponents throughout the world. It is safe to say this will continue as long as there are independent thinkers. Marx has been widely read, interpreted, denounced, and updated, and he has never lacked for advocates or foes.

Marx is clearly a neomodern who combined a passionate idealism and organic politics with a materialist analysis of history that pointed toward the end of that materialism in the future. If the alternatives he offers no longer seem as glowingly achievable as they once did to many of the world's peoples, he remains one of the most radical critics of Western capitalism.

His successors continued to analyze the evils of capitalism but disagreed on the best method for ridding the world of them. Some, like Eduard Bernstein, preferred a democratic solution, while others, like Lenin, were revolutionaries.[37] Both could find support for their positions in the works of Marx and Engels, and both addressed the question of whether Marx and Engels presented a common methodological approach, or whether they diverged. This chapter has suggested that the two converged, based in part on the third section of the *Manifesto* and its implications for scientific socialism. But those who point to the less dogmatic tone of Marx's writings before he worked with Engels note a strong concern for human dignity and choice in his *Economic and Philosophical Manuscripts*. They call him the author of a flexible historical materialism and claim that dogmatic or scientific Marxists are following the more rigid dialectical materialism of Engels. The latter is accused of misappropriating Marx's ideas, putting them in a historical straightjacket that excludes democratic choice or free will in favor of strict obedience to predetermined historical inevitability. This debate has more than scholarly importance, as it relates to Marx's responsibility for the ideas behind totalitarian communism.[38]

In either case, the ideas of Marx and Engels were an essential factor in the spread of communism, and their influence on world events is one reason to study early Marxism. Their resemblance to Socrates' questioning critique of selfish individualism and Plato's collectivist recommendations are further reasons.

Today people are aware of victimized people throughout the world, those facing poverty, high infant mortality, disease, slave labor, warfare, or imprisonment and death for speaking out against injustice. Would we care as much about these conditions, would we even know as much about them, without Marx's inspiration, without the moral passion expressed in his work?

Until reality merges with the ideal and the "ought" becomes the "is," thoughtful people will continue to ask with Marx why there is injustice in the world and what should be done about it. His political philosophy addresses these questions, even if it supplies no final answers. It gives direction and purpose to joint action, and we act politically today because of the issues raised by philosophers such as Marx.

Notes

1. Of the vast output from the pen of Marx and Engels, the core includes, in addition to the *Communist Manifesto* (1848), *Economic and Philosophical Manuscripts* (1844), *The German Ideology* (1846), *Das Kapital (Capital)* (vol. 1, 1867), and Engels's *The Origin of the Family, Private Property, and the State* (1884). *Capital*, vols. 2 and 3 (1885 and 1894) were edited by Engels after Marx died.

2. Of the many biographies of Marx, one that is both readable and scholarly is David McLellan, *Karl Marx: His Life and Thought* (New York: Viking, 1975).

3. For example, see Edward J. Ahearn, *Marx and Modern Fiction* (New Haven, Conn.: Yale University Press, 1991).

4. "Preface to the English Edition of 1888," in *Manifesto*. Quotations are from the trans. of Samuel Moore (London: Penguin, 1967). On Engels's career, see Terrell Carver, *Friedrich Engels: His Life and Thought* (New York: St. Martin's, 1990). On their collaboration, Carver has written *Marx and Engels: The Intellectual Relationship* (Bloomington: Indiana University Press, 1983).

5. *Manifesto*, "Preface to the German Edition of 1872" and "Preface to the English Edition of 1888." The uprising was the famous Paris Commune of 1871, which resulted in a workers' government lasting for only two months before it was crushed. Interestingly, the *Manifesto* called for centralization due to the failure of the bourgeoisie to unify Germany, while Marx's 1871 pamphlet about the Paris Commune, "The Civil War in France," lauded political decentralization in order to undermine the highly unified French state. "The Civil War in France" can be found in Robert C. Tucker, ed., *The Marx–Engels Reader*, 2d ed. (New York: Norton, 1978), 618–52.

6. See N. Scott Arnold, *Marx's Radical Critique of Capitalist Society: A Reconstruction and Critical Evaluation* (New York: Oxford University Press, 1990).

7. The French word for "middle class" is frequently used by Marx, often in a derogatory way. In Marx's writings, it refers to the capitalists who own the means of production and employ the members of the working class. The bourgeoisie has replaced the old aristocracy as the ruling class that wields both economic and political power, but is not the same as today's middle class. For further discussion, see Tom Bottomore, ed., "Bourgeoisie," in *A Dictionary of Marxist Thought* (Cambridge, Mass.: Harvard University Press, 1983).

8. In other words, Marx says the bourgeoisie acts like Aristotle's oligarchy, unjustly equating the interests of the few rich with the interests of all.

9. *Manifesto*, sec. 1.

10. *Manifesto*, sec. 2.

11. Hegel's major works that especially evoke this perspective are *The Science of Logic* (1812–16), *The Philosophy of Right and Law* (1821), and the posthumous *Lectures on the Philosophy of History*.

12. See Genesis. Hegel had been a student of theology, and the importance of religion is clear in his philosophy. However, the reconciliation between man and nature he foresees will come on earth, which sets him apart from religious writers such as Augustine.

13. For further discussion of some key features that help to unify Hegel's state, see David Schultz, "Hegel's Constitutionalism," *Commonwealth: A Journal of Political Science* 4 (1990): 26–46.

14. Marx's materialism originated in his relationship with a group of German philosophers known as the Young Hegelians, who used Hegel's method to criticize Prussian politics. One of them, Ludwig Feuerbach, wrote *The Essence of Christianity* (1841), which Marx particularly credits for his adopting a materialist stance. However, Marx's rejection of Feuerbach's individualism is clear from his "Theses on Feuerbach" (1845).

15. *Marx–Engels Reader*, 145. On what Marx used of Hegel's and what he added, see Sidney Hook, *From Hegel to Marx: Studies in the Intellectual Development of Karl Marx* (Ann Arbor: University of Michigan Press, 1962).

16. *Manifesto*, sec. 1.

17. "Preface to the English Edition." See also Joseph Ferraro, *Freedom and Determination in History According to Marx and Engels* (New York: Monthly Review, 1992). There is a difference between what Engels calls the mode of production and its close relative, the means of production. The means include workers, machinery, and tools that produce goods. Owning or controlling the means of production gives the capitalists their economic and political power. The mode refers to how the means of production are organized—e.g., by individual craftsmen working alone (as in medieval times) or by collaborative labor in a factory (as in capitalism); or, perhaps most importantly, by capital vs. labor, (as in capitalism) or collectively, with common ownership and operation of the means of production (as in communism).

18. See http://politicalscience.wadsworth.com/tannenbaum2 for a link to a chart illustrating Marx's stages of history.

19. W. Peter Archibald, *Marx and the Missing Link: Human Nature* (Atlantic Highlands, N.J.: Humanities, 1992).

20. *Marx–Engels Reader*, 54. For a discussion of Marxism as a secular theology, see Neil Reimer, *Karl Marx and Prophetic Politics* (New York: Praeger, 1987).

21. One scholarly source for Marx's account of primitive society was Lewis Morgan, *Ancient Society, or Researches in the Lines of Human Progress from Savagery Through Barbarism to Civilization* (New York: Holt, 1974), originally published in 1877.

22. *Manifesto*, sec. 1. See also Anthony Brewer, *A Guide to Marx's Capital* (New York: Cambridge University Press, 1984). *Capital*, Marx's most sustained scholarly piece, was based on his study of the capitalist mode of production. Aspects of this study are found as early as the 1844 *Economic and Philosophical Manuscripts*, heavily augmented by Marx's later analysis of the evolution of capitalism in England.

23. *Manifesto*, sec. 1.

24. *Manifesto*, sec. 1. See also Bertell Ollman, *Alienation: Marx's Conception of Man in Capitalist Society*, 2d ed. (New York: Cambridge University Press, 1976).

25. *Manifesto*, sec. 1.

26. *Manifesto*, sec. 1.

27. *Manifesto*, sec. 3. Elsewhere, Marx did allow for the possibility of peaceful transition to socialism in some countries; See *Marx–Engels Reader*, 523.

28. *Manifesto*, sec. 1.

29. *Manifesto*, sec. 2. Marx's comments about sexual relationships are scattered throughout a number of his works, beginning with the early *Economic and Philosophical Manuscripts*. The most sustained examination of this issue by the partners is *Origin of the Family*.

30. *Marx–Engels Reader*, 736.

31. *Marx–Engels Reader*, 742.

32. *Manifesto*, sec. 2.

33. *Manifesto*, sec. 2. From his earliest writings, Marx suggested that the transition to communism might come in stages, including "a revolutionary dictatorship of the proletariat." *Marx–Engels Reader*, 220, 538. However, he did not say much about specifics. See also Hal Draper, *Karl Marx's Theory of Revolution*, vol. 3: *The Dictatorship of the Proletariat* (New York: Monthly Review Press, 1986).

34. Marx is one of the few major political philosophers to advocate anarchism as a primary requirement for dealing with the problems he identified. Most philosophers advocate a legitimate role for government, either to help make people better, or at least as a means of protection from the dangers of unregulated freedom.

35. *Manifesto,* sec. 2; see also Ian Forbes, *Marx and the New Individual* (New York: Routledge, 1990).

36. *Marx–Engels Reader,* 441, 732.

37. Eduard Bernstein, *Evolutionary Socialism* (New York: Schocken, 1961); V. I. Lenin, *State and Revolution* (New York: Vanguard, 1929).

38. See, for example, Erich Fromm, "Foreword," in *Karl Marx: Early Writings,* ed. T. B. Bottomore (New York: McGraw-Hill, 1964); Norman Levine, *The Tragic Deception: Marx Contra Engels* (Oxford: Clio, 1975); and Alvin Gouldner, *The Two Marxisms: Contradictions and Anomalies in the Development of Theory* (New York: Oxford University Press, 1980).

Additional Readings

(* indicates alternative viewpoint)

Archibald, W. Peter. *Marx and the Missing Link: Human Nature.* Atlantic Highlands, N.J.: Humanities Press, 1992.

Arnold, N. Scott. *Marx's Radical Critique of Capitalist Society: A Reconstruction and Critical Evaluation.* New York: Oxford University Press, 1990.

Carver, Terrell. *Friedrich Engels: His Life and Thought.* New York: St. Martin's, 1990.

Ferraro, Joseph. *Freedom and Determination in History According to Marx and Engels.* New York: Monthly Review Press, 1992.

Forbes, Ian. *Marx and the New Individual.* New York: Routledge, 1990.

*Gouldner, Alvin. *The Two Marxisms: Contradictions and Anomalies in the Development of Theory.* New York: Oxford University Press, 1980.

Hook, Sidney. *From Hegel to Marx: Studies in the Intellectual Development of Karl Marx.* Ann Arbor: University of Michigan Press, 1962.

*Levine, Norman. *The Tragic Deception: Marx Contra Engels.* Oxford: Clio, 1975.

McLellan, David. *Karl Marx: His Life and Thought.* New York: Viking, 1975.

Megill, Allan. *Karl Marx: The Burden of Reason.* Lanham, Md.: Rowman & Littlefield, 2002.

Ollman, Bertell. *Alienation: Marx's Conception of Man in Capitalist Society.* 2d ed. New York: Cambridge University Press, 1976.

 Inventors of Ideas Online

Visit http://politicalscience.wadsworth.com/tannenbaum2 for links related to material in this chapter, including an illustration of Marx's stages of history and the full texts of the *Communist Manifesto* and other Marxist works.

19

POSTMODERN POLITICAL THOUGHT: FREUD, NIETZSCHE, AND THE END OF REASON

INTRODUCTION

By the onset of the twentieth century the values of early-modern political thought had come to be seen in a new light. These were the values that had helped destroy the medieval era and then had become the foundation for political thought in Europe. Yet social changes, and philosophers' reactions to those changes, led many people to conclude that modern values were exhausted, and that the modern era based on those values was drawing to a close.

Political thinkers focused on the social and political conditions produced by the Industrial Revolution, including rapid urbanization and population increases as well as the upheaval and misery accompanying numerous wars and revolutions. Vast numbers of people suffered, while a few lived well. The wealthy sent the children of the masses to their deaths in wars that seemed to benefit only themselves. Observing this history, numerous political thinkers described the values of the West as basically decadent, debased, materialistic, hollow, even nihilistic.

At one point, early-modern political thinkers, such as Locke, Hobbes, Bacon, and Descartes, had expressed faith in reason and science, foundations upon which the moderns had built firm political truths yet that faith had turned to skepticism. It had begun when Hume and Kant criticized the conclusions of the early moderns, pointing out the limits of establishing any pure basis for political authority or justice. Philosophers Edmund Husserl (1859–1938) and Martin Heidegger (1889–1976) argued that science, reason, and technology had reached their limits and were now obstructing solutions to many important problems.[1]

Rousseau, Hegel, and Marx had questioned the basis of the early-modern glorification of individual selfishness and the resulting alienation of people from their true, natural roots. They had claimed that nothing but a radical change could bring about justice in the world.

By the turn of the twentieth century, another complementary, but in some ways a more devastating, challenge was coming from those who questioned a fundamental perspective that had united all moderns, early, neo, and late: the idea of progress. The critique of reason and the modern values it encouraged, expressed in the works of the psychologist Sigmund Freud, and the philosopher Friedrich Nietzsche, was perhaps the final breach of the intellectual defenses of the modern era.

SIGMUND FREUD

Sigmund Freud (1856–1939) is considered the father of modern psychoanalysis. He spent most of his adult life in Vienna, but as he was Jewish he fled for England in 1938 after the Nazi invasion of Austria. Perhaps his main contribution to politics was his theory that human psychology and nature are repressed by cultural forces and institutions, and that such repression influences individuals' political actions.[2]

Freud emphasizes the importance of sexuality and sexual development to human nature. He asserts that human sexual drives influence morality, laws, and cultural values. Although earlier thinkers had addressed sex roles and perhaps sexuality as one aspect of politics, they had subordinated sexual drives to reason and concluded that reason was the preferred basis of politics. But to Freud, human instincts, including the sexual drive, develop through childhood and are critical to defining personality and motivating behavior. The sex drive, and related human passions, clash with other urges in the human psyche, which leads to a politics based on individuals with conflicting internal pressures. More specifically, the human drives are essential to defining the cultures people develop, but at the same time create uneasiness at living in those cultures because of the conflicts at the core of the human condition.[3]

Freud describes the human psyche as partly governed or trapped by basic human drives, such as sex and aggression, which need to be satisfied.[4] In his books *The Ego and the Id* and *The Complete Introductory Lectures on Psychoanalysis*, he describes childhood conflicts with parents as eventually producing three components in the adult psyche: the id, ego, and the superego. Put simply, the id represents basic passions and impulses, such as the sexual drive, or eros. The ego represents the rational aspect of humans; and the superego represents the social pressures of family, church, government, and the like, which seek to subdue human behavior, or control the id. The id is in constant struggle with the ego and the superego. That is, basic human drives of the id, such as sex and aggression, need to be curbed by the ego or superego, or else they could lead to self-destructive and dangerous outcomes.

Endless Human Misery. In Freud's most somber and pessimistic book, *Civilization and Its Discontents*, which sums up many of the ideas he had been exploring throughout his life, he applies his theory of psychoanalysis to social and political (or at least cultural) analysis. He wrote the book in 1930 in Germany, between the two world wars. Hitler was coming to power over the dead body of German democracy, and it appeared that liberal values and society were collapsing in Europe and North America. The book provides a theory of human nature, a vision of the state and society, and a description of how humans are at war with civilization, the human condition, and the psyche itself.

All individuals seek happiness, Freud says, and "What decides the program of life is the pleasure principle. This principle dominates the operation of the mental apparatus from the start."[5] But the desire for happiness is thwarted by three forces: the human body, the external world, and relationships with other individuals. Of the three factors contributing to human misery—preventing happiness—he concludes that

> What we call our civilization is largely responsible for our misery, and that we should be much happier if we gave it up and returned to primitive conditions. I call this contention astonishing because, in whatever way we may define the concept of civilization, it is a certain fact that all things with which we seek to protect ourselves against the threats that emanate from the sources of suffering are part of that very civilization.[6]

Thus the chief cause of human misery is the culture people have created for themselves. But however uncomfortable they are with civilization, Freud argues that humans in the primitive or presocial era were probably no happier or more secure.

He defines civilization as the "whole sum of achievements and the regulations which distinguish our lives from those of our animal ancestors and which serves two purposes—namely to protect men against nature and to adjust their mutual relations."[7] Much in the same way that Hobbes saw the creation of civil society as a way out of the anarchy and war in the state of nature, Freud sees the rules and institutions of civilization as a means of protecting individuals against the external threats that nature and others pose. These threats exist in part because humans are not by nature cooperative:

> Men are not gentle creatures who want to be loved, and who at the most can defend themselves if attacked; they are, on the contrary, creatures among whose instinctual endowments is to be reckoned a powerful share of aggressiveness. As a result, their neighbor is for them not only a potential helper or sexual object, but also someone who tempts them to satisfy their aggressiveness on him, to exploit his capacity for work without compensation, to use him sexually without his consent, to seize his possessions, to humiliate him, to cause him pain, to torture and to kill him.[8]

Not subject just to rational impulses, humans are driven by the need to satisfy their basic desires, including their sexual and aggressive impulses. Without some restraints, individuals would kill one another. Thus civilization, including the creation of the state, is an important advance for humans in that it creates rules and institutions that restrain the id, making it possible for individuals to live together.

Costs of Civilization. The creation of civilization and social order does not come without a price. To Freud, all humans are motivated by the twin goals of utility and pleasure. On the one hand people seek pleasure, but on the other they require rules and institutions that serve to restrain their aggressive impulses, and these two often conflict. Put another way, on some occasions the id (human desires) comes into conflict with the ego, the superego, and the rules of society. This necessitates some mechanism to regulate human behavior, and that mechanism is the state:

> Human life in common is only made possible when a majority comes together which is stronger than any separate individual, and which remains united against separate individuals. . . . The replacement of the power of the individual by the power of the community constitutes the decisive step of civilization.[9]

That is, when the rules of politics become the force that regulates human behavior, people are able to live together and enter civilization.

But although the need to preserve oneself is a driving force to create civilization and the state, eros serves as the glue that holds society together:[10]

> Love relationships . . . constitute the essence of the group mind. . . . Our hypothesis finds support in the first instance from two passing thoughts. First, that the group is clearly held together by a power of some kind: and to what power could this feat be better ascribed than to Eros, which holds together everything in the world?[11]

Thus the basic drives for life, love, sex, and survival propel people toward civilization.

Yet, according to Freud, entering civil society is sort of a social contract, which originates

> with a renunciation of instinct, a recognition of mutual obligations, the introduction of definitions, pronounced inviolable (holy)—that is to say, the beginnings of morality and justice. Each individual renounced his ideal of acquiring his father's position for himself and of possessing his mother and sisters.[12]

The origin of the political community, then, has a conflicting character. It is a consequence of following the demands of one's survival instinct and erotic drive, yet it is also born out of fear of patricide, or what Freud calls the *Oedipus complex*, and the need to regulate social taboos, such as incest.[13] The state originates to regulate familial and sexual forces that threaten to destroy individuals.

At the same time, though, eros also drives humans toward freedom and against the demands of civilization. Social controls themselves create this desire for freedom by proscribing aggressive and sexual behavior. Civilization and political society are made possible only by the sublimation of human instincts and drives. Yet civilization is built upon the renunciation of what is still an instinct, and culture upon the frustration of what are still basic drives.

Thus eros is set against civilization, driving individuals to rebel against the very institutions that make survival possible.[14]

It is not easy for people to prevent hostile or other instinctive behaviors, despite social repression, because to do so represses their nature. For Freud, "if civilization imposes great sacrifices not only on man's sexuality but on his aggressivity, we can understand better why it is hard for him to be happy in that civilization."[15] Civilization and social rules are produced by the need of individuals to preserve themselves from death, yet civilization also frustrates the id and the satisfaction of other human desires. Ultimately, it frustrates human nature, presenting "a struggle between *eros* and *thanatos*, between the instinct of life and the instinct of destruction, as it works itself out in the human species."[16] Although civilization is a product of instincts, it frustrates basic drives, which in turn leads to drives to attack it due to another instinct. Social behavior, as well as individual behavior, then, is composed of numerous drives which humans seek to control and repress, but which at any minute might break out and destroy them and civilization.

Consequently, people seek civilization and society to be happy, yet both are the cause of misery. Individuals are at war with civilization, but more importantly, they are at war with their own souls, seeking to subdue the non-rational and unconscious, and bring them under control of the rational. Human nature requires expression and satisfaction of the impulses, yet satisfaction of those same desires may lead to death. The goal of civilization is to control this human tendency toward self-destruction while at the same time regulating eros. In the end, Freud doubts whether civilization can control humans' self-destructive nature without perpetually frustrating and suppressing freedom and human nature, thus destroying humanity in another way, by preventing happiness.[17] He sees the arational, conflicting human needs perpetually challenging the rational order of society, threatening wars and anarchy, forever.

FRIEDRICH NIETZSCHE

Friedrich Nietzsche (1844–1900), a German philosopher and classical scholar, spent most of his life in Switzerland, where he taught at the university in Bern. He is a very important writer in the history of Western thought, but also very misunderstood. Although he has been described as the inspiration for Nazi Germany, careful reading of his works shows that his ideas are not the basis of fascist thought; the Nazis used his writings to suit their own purposes.[18] In addition, he has been described as a nihilist and relativist, but Nietzsche himself dismissed such labels.

Nietzsche, like Freud, is very pessimistic about his culture. He agrees with Freud that bourgeois civilization and culture frustrate true human nature. But unlike Freud, who viewed all forms of culture as inhibiting,[19] Nietzsche sees Christianity and early-modern values as the triumph of social decadence over human nature and a slave morality over a master morality. Following Kant's skepticism about the possibility of reason to resolve certain philosophical issues and provide a foundation for moral and political values, Nietzsche sees clear limits to the ability of reason and modern philosophy and politics to secure firm foundations for its truths. Modernity, if anything, undermines itself, producing nihilism, or belief in nothing, and the urge to destroy.

Human Nature and the Transvaluation of Values. Nietzsche's criticism of nineteenth-century politics derives from a distinction he makes between master and slave moralities. Describing the master morality, he says,

> When the ruling group determines what is "good," the exalted, proud states of the soul are experienced as conferring distinction and determining the order or rank. . . . It should be noted immediately that in this first type of morality the opposition of "good" and "bad" means approximately the same as "noble" and "contemptible." . . . According to master morality it is precisely those who are "good" that inspire, and wish to inspire, fear, while the "bad" are felt to be contemptible.[20]

The master morality is the product of a strong, free, life-affirming ruling class. It is a morality of those in power, those who wish to honor human nature, and represents the values of the warrior.[21]

By contrast, the slave morality has its origin in the values of the weak and the oppressed, who create a morality that attacks the judgments proclaimed by the master morality. According to Nietzsche,

> Here is the place for the famous opposition of "good" and "evil": into evil one's feelings project power and dangerousness, a certain terribleness, subtlety, and strength that does not permit contempt to develop. According to slave morality, those who are "evil" thus inspire fear. . . .[22]

The juxtaposition of master and slave moralities is important to Nietzsche, because it is the historical act of replacing master with slave that has led to a critical decline in human affairs. This *transvaluation of values,* as he calls it, started when Socrates, the Jews, and the Christians replaced the noble morality of the ancients with a morality of slaves and weaklings.[23] Slave morality is the product of resentment and labels as good all that denies the strength and vitality of human nature. Religion, especially Christianity, is included in the ethos of slave morality because it praises a set of otherworldly values that deny noble human existence and individual power, which Nietzsche sees as the true expression and greatness of man.

For Nietzsche, modernity and its ideological offshoots, liberalism, democracy, and socialism, are symptomatic of slave morality. All endorse the position of the weak and deny the life-affirming values of human nature the master morality once endorsed. Modern politics is the victory of the slaves over the masters, the rabble over the leaders, and the triumph of a set of dehumanizing values over human nature, resulting in the denial of freedom and the production of weak and resentful individuals.

Crisis of Modernity. The transvaluation of values is the origin of what Nietzsche describes as the crisis of modernity.[24] This is a crisis of nihilism, of denying the reality of human existence, and wrongly seeking to provide a rational foundation for morality.

According to Nietzsche, the project of the Enlightenment and modernity

> has not been so modest. With a stiff seriousness that inspires laughter, all our philosophers demanded something far more exalted, presumptuous, and solemn for themselves as soon as they approached the study of morality: they wanted to supply a rational foundation for morality—and every philosopher so far has believed that he has provided such a foundation.[25]

Seeking to construct this rational foundation for morality, philosophers have used science and reason in place of religion. Yet science has been incapable of being such a foundation: "Science is not nearly self-reliant enough to be that; it first requires in every respect an ideal of value, a value-creating power, in the service of which it could believe in itself—it never creates values. . . ."[26]

One flaw in grounding morality in science is that by itself science is unable to distinguish right from wrong in an objective fashion. A second flaw in science as a basis of morality lies in the belief, espoused by religious thinkers, that there is such a thing as immutable truth. To Nietzsche, there is no such unchanging truth,[27] "only a perspective seeing, only a perspective 'knowing'."[28]

Because he denies any absolute truth and the ability of reason to provide uncontestable foundations for knowledge, Nietzsche argues that the attempt to replace religion with scientific reason as the basis of knowledge has produced, not certainty of knowledge, but a continual "tyranny of reason" that started with Socrates and was greased by Copernicus. This tyranny has denied human freedom,[29] and put humankind on a self-destructive path toward nihilism, a denial of all truths, including the legitimacy of reason itself.[30] It did all this, first, by subjecting all other values and systems of knowledge to the test of reason, rejecting those that could not be rationally demonstrated or supported. Reason then turned on itself and questioned its own presuppositions, which revealed that its own claims could not be rationally defended either. Reason in search of truth wound up destroying truth.

Nietzsche's discussion of modernity builds on Kant's criticisms of reason.[31] In his *Critique of Pure Reason*, Kant sought to place limits on reason in order to protect religious faith and God from rational scrutiny. But modernity could not provide such limits. In *Thus Spoke Zarathustra*, Nietzsche's hero, the philosopher-warrior Zarathustra, proclaims that God is dead. But Nietzsche claims that he did not kill God; it was the decadent culture produced by slave morality and the tyranny of reason that did so.

To Nietzsche, bourgeois culture demonstrates that there are no transcendent values, no eternal truths, no natural laws, and no firm or everlasting foundation for knowledge. All knowledge is created by people in a specific historical situation, and there are no moral truths independent of people creating them. Bourgeois culture has broken down and is self-destructing. Nietzsche's self-appointed task is to announce the need for creation of a new philosophy, one that creates new values. Yet it cannot be the traditional philosopher who fashions these values. It must be commanders and legislators who formulate truth, by proclaiming it through their "will to power."[32] The new philosophy and new politics must reject slave morality, nihilism, and the tyranny of reason, and impose on the world a new set of values that affirm the underlying noble traits of human nature, thus creating a new history and era for humanity that radically breaks with contemporary culture.

NIETZSCHE, FREUD, AND THE ORIGINS OF POSTMODERN POLITICS

One legacy of both Freud and Nietzsche was their belief that modernity was flawed and that efforts to use science and reason to guide human affairs had reached their limits and were bankrupt. There was a nonrational aspect to human affairs that demonstrated the limits of science and reason, because reason conflicted with many other human impulses and drives, denying or frustrating human self-realization, satisfaction, and freedom. The goal for both philosophers was to recover these drives, understand how they operate, and determine how they can serve our true needs.

A second legacy of both Freud and Nietzsche was in the influence they have had on twentieth-century political thought, especially after World War II.[33] For example, Freud's views on human sexuality and its relationship to freedom and liberation had a significant impact on many writers, such as Herbert Marcuse in *Eros and Civilization*, William Reich in the *Mass Psychology of Fascism*, and Theodore Adorno in the *Authoritarian Personality*. These authors use Freudian concepts to explain political repression, paths for securing political freedom by liberating human sexuality from taboos and social constraints, and the rise and psychology of fascism and authoritarian personalities.

As for Nietzsche, his influence is much more ambiguous and complex. His efforts to create new meanings in a world that had been rendered meaningless, due to the absence of absolute truths, had a significant influence on the creation of a philosophy known as existentialism.[34] According to French existentialists as diverse as Jean Paul Sartre (1905–1980) and Maurice Merleau-Ponty (1908–1961), as well as non-French existentialists, such as Martin Heidegger, there is no inherent rational order in the universe; individuals must make choices that create order and meaning. Politically, existentialism has followed many paths, with the views of adherents supporting different ideological positions ranging from liberal democracy to communism and even fascism.[35]

Three of Nietzsche's themes, the tyranny and limits of reason, the belief that modernity failed in its project, and the need for a new set of values for a new era of history just beginning, have also influenced other postmodern thinkers. Postmodernism started as a populist criticism of art and architectural styles of the twentieth century as elitist and authoritarian. It spread to the humanities, which developed techniques of literary criticism stressing the importance of language and the role of the reader in giving meaning to a book. At the same time, changing conditions in many of the technologically advanced nations of Western Europe and North America were leading to postindustrial societies in which traditional manufacturing as the main form of economic activity was disappearing. These countries are now engaged more in services, including the application of computer knowledge, than was characteristic of previous eras. The outcome of this economic transformation has been change in social organization, including new definitions of the ways people come together to work, play, and otherwise occupy their time. Postmoderns say that the result is a new economic and political reality rendering old political concepts meaningless and requiring a new way to think about society.

The writings of Thomas Kuhn and Paul Feyerabend reinforce postmodern assertions that science is not a progressive body of knowledge. Kuhn, in *The Structure of Scientific Revolutions,* and Feyerabend, in *Science in a Free Society,* argue that many people view science as simply the accumulation of new data to build better theories and explanations of the world. Both contend that science is not simply a set of abstract rules that cumulatively builds knowledge. Rather, it is characterized by numerous revolutions, or what Kuhn calls *shifts in paradigms,* wherein new cultural values and assumptions in fact determine what are considered valid scientific theories, what shall be called facts, and what shall be counted as knowledge.[36] For example, Kuhn argues that the shift from a geocentric to a heliocentric vision of the universe, sparked by Copernicus, carried with it a new way of thinking about the world, as well as a new way to organize knowledge and undertake scientific activity.[37] The point for both Kuhn and Feyerabend is that science is not the rational foundation its supporters claim, and in many cases a scientific way of knowing may actually be a barrier both to other ways of knowing and to political action in that it impedes alternative methods of tackling issues.[38]

Drawing on Nietzsche and philosophers of science like Kuhn and Feyerabend, such postmoderns as Richard Rorty, Jean-François Lyotard, and Michel Foucault criticize the moderns' attempts to use reason as a foundation for ethics, politics, and philosophy. According to Rorty, reason cannot supply verification for its own truths. He contends that scientific rationality is unable to prove that it is the absolute and only true basis for knowledge.[39] Politics and philosophy must reject belief in this universal foundationalism, and instead seek to base ethics and politics on local traditions and customs and what he calls a conversational model of politics, which takes into account a pluralistic vision of society accepting many different types of knowing and ways of thinking about the world. Rorty sees scientific reason as only one of several ways of knowing, and no one system of knowledge as necessarily superior to another.

Similarly, Lyotard contends that one characteristic of modern philosophy was to link together the languages of justice, politics, and science.[40] What this resulted in was the reduction of politics and ethics to science, meaning that moderns believed political and moral questions could be resolved through proofs and appeals to reason. Lyotard argues, however, that since the 1960s or so, the notion of what knowledge is has changed. With the advent of computers, it has become clear that knowledge and reason are not foundations but commodities that are bought and sold. This change in the conception of knowledge, as well as the movement of society away from a basically industrial culture to a postindustrial one, means that the role of reason and knowledge must be reexamined. Alteration of this role entails the disconnection of politics from science, and recognition that science and reason cannot be the "grand narrative" or foundation for all of politics and society. Like Rorty, Lyotard believes that there are many ways of knowing and of thinking about politics, and that postmodern society should recognize the inability of science and reason to resolve all political questions or provide a comprehensive foundation for politics and society.

Foucault says that modern political philosophy saw reason as the unifying force of modern knowledge and politics.[41] But this human-centered view is now giving way to a language-centered reality, one that sees human language as important to defining and uniting knowledge with politics. Foucault is also concerned with the importance of the role of power. Modern political power assumes a head (king) or identifiable agent in man who is in control.[42] It also assumes that there is a unique power center in society which determines what is socially acceptable and prohibited. Foucault asserts that such power threatens individual freedom to act or choose.

Collectively, postmoderns claim that modernity, including its claims that truth is grounded in scientific rationality, is dead, and that a new, third political epoch is upon us.[43] The rejection of the universality of scientific reasoning is giving way to the articulation of a pluralist theory of politics and justice that turns to local traditions, or mininarratives, to form the basis of political and ethical values for each community. The focus on local customs and values is intended to respect diversity as both a form of social organization and a means to realize the emancipation of groups traditionally excluded from modern discourse. Postmodern politics turns away from viewing reason as the single force to define political truths, and it denies the capacity of reason to continue to serve as the liberating force it once was. The hope of the postmodern philosophers is to break the links between science, reason, and politics that placed in the hands of a few the ability to define and control political power. If the reign of scientific reason can be broken, there will emerge a more diverse and pluralistic vision of society, which will produce a more open and democratic social order. This will liberate the individual from the tyranny of reason, much in the same way that reason liberated the modern from the tyranny of religion.

FEMINISM AND POSTMODERN POLITICS

Although Freud and Nietzsche have had important influences on many political movements in the twentieth century, including postmodernism, their views on women and the family stand in sharp contrast to the origins of feminism and the women's liberation movements since World War II. Both Freud and Nietzsche remain wedded to traditional roles for women, and the two genders in general, that had persisted since the time of the ancient Greeks. Like those of their predecessors, however, their arguments provide new twists on or justifications for the old stereotypes.

Freud argues that the distinction between masculine and feminine is not simply psychological or social, but has biological roots traceable back to the male and female sex-cells. He asserts that during conception the male cell is "actively mobile and searches out the female one, and the latter, the ovum, is immobile and waits passively. This behavior of the elementary sexual organisms is indeed a model for the conduct of sexual individuals during intercourse."[44]

Thus for Freud, masculine means "active" while feminine means "passive," and this male/female and active/passive distinction carries with it important implications. For one thing, it suggests unique sex roles for men and women. Freud says there is no feminine libido, or sex drive, only a masculine one, which pursues its goals independent of women's consent. Second, the distinctions reveal contrasting social roles for the two, with men and women destined to assume the traditional roles of head of the family and wife and mother respectively. To Freud, these roles are rooted in a biological or natural basis.

In its conclusions about women, the legacy of Freudian psychology also downplays the importance of female sexuality, and indicates that women appear to be psychologically affected or inferior because they are not men.[45] For example, Freud describes the sexual development of boys and girls.[46] Freud asks why the strong attachment of girls for their mothers comes to an end while boys' attachment to their mothers persists, becoming an important variable influencing politics and the origins of the state. After offering answers related to nursing in infancy, Freud concludes that girls' hostility toward their mothers develops when they hold the mother responsible for their lack of a penis and do not forgive her for being put at a disadvantage. Blaming the mother in this way is what Freud calls the castration complex, and it consists of what Freud calls penis envy, wherein girls desire to have a penis and be like men because without the male sexual organ they feel inferior. Penis envy affects many aspects of a girl's, and then a woman's, psychological character, including being responsible for, among other things, sexual passivity, frigidity, vanity, and lack of sense of justice. Overall, Freud invokes biology, female psychology, and penis envy rather than Victorian social customs or prejudices to explain and justify the secondary, passive, and otherwise traditional roles of women in society.

Nietzsche argues against nineteenth-century efforts to provide equal education for, and otherwise recognize and create more rights for women. He claims that belief in equality between the sexes is a result of the triumph of slave morality and that making women more self-reliant is one of the "worst developments of the general uglification of Europe."[47] Women have steadily lost influence since the French Revolution because they have retreated from their proper roles and functions in society.

For Nietzsche, men should be trained to be warriors, while women should be trained to be "playthings" and "recreation" for the warrior. He says,

"Man's happiness is, I will. Woman's happiness is, He will,"[48] suggesting that a woman's desires and interests should be satisfied through those of her man. Her highest concern should be her appearance, she should be silent when it comes to politics, and she should be regarded as man's property. Overall, Nietzsche rails against the emancipation and education of women as contrary to their nature, contending that they should not try to be like men because men themselves are merely corrupted versions of what real "supermen" would be if it were not for the slave morality that has infected modernity. Hence, despite the trends in nineteenth-century Europe toward more equality and expanded roles for women, Nietzsche protests against both, urging continuation of their traditional position.

In spite of the influence of Nietzsche and, to a lesser extent, Freud, on postmodernism, contemporary feminists have adopted many postmodern perspectives.[49] They have done so because postmodernism and feminism share many views and concerns, among them that postmodernism offers room for traditionally oppressed groups to express themselves without fear of being silenced by a tyranny of reason.[50] Feminists such as Sandra Harding also reject the tyranny of reason and science, viewing it as a masculine tool of oppression.[51] Feminists see in the pluralistic ideas of postmodernism a vision of emancipatory politics that defines a new role and respect for the voices and perspectives of women. Instead of seeking to create a politics like Mary Wollstonecraft's or John Stuart Mill's, which sought to give women the same rights as men and make them become more like men, postmodern feminist thought depicts many possible roles for women, premising the judgment and definition of gender roles not on a "male" model of politics but upon the distinct experiences of women.

One of the hopes of postmodern feminism is that a break with reason and the assumption of "male" as the model for both sexes will finally produce a real emancipatory politics for women. Since the days of Sophocles' *Antigone* in ancient Greece and on through the Christian and Modern eras, philosophers have offered numerous religious, familial, and political arguments to define and defend the traditional roles of women as simply wives and mothers. By employing a vision that challenges the male norm for politics, postmodern feminists see a way out of the limitations imposed on them when they adopted political arguments and tactics that grew out of an essentially male-dominated political world. Thus psychologists such as Carol Gilligan, responding to Freudian assertions, contend that women have their own unique experiences, or "voice," which deserves respect for how it differs from that of men.[52] Women's perspective is neither better nor worse than that of men; it is simply different. And postmodern feminism, unlike the politics of feminist movements growing out of the logic of modernity, is able to respect this difference.

POLITICAL PHILOSOPHY AT THE DAWN
OF THE TWENTY-FIRST CENTURY

Do Freud and Nietzsche mark the end of one era and the beginning of a new one? In many ways, they provide a break with the past, but in others, they set the tone for a twentieth-century marked by severe questioning of many of the assumptions that had organized political thinking in modernity, if not for the last 2,500 years.

Modern philosophers attempted to create a new "Archimedian point," or foundation upon which to build a political order and set of values.[53] That pivot point was reason and science, replacing religion and the religious values that had held the Christian world together. But Copernican appeals to science first displaced humans from the center of the universe and then set off centuries of struggle to use reason to find a new location in the cosmos for them. Ultimately the pursuit of truth through reason served only to undermine its very enterprise.[54]

Freud and Nietzsche severely criticized modernity. Freud's argument was that culture, as a mirror of the struggles within the human soul, was the source of human misery. The battle between eros and thanatos meant that human nature was at war with itself, a war played out in the cultural institutions people had created for themselves. To Nietzsche, the values of modernity were self-destructive and in need of replacement; they were destroying human nature altogether. The conclusion for both thinkers was that reason had limited capacity to control human nature, define social rules, and regulate political behavior. Their legacy was to inspire political movements in the twentieth century that turned away from science and reason, seeking instead recognition and creation of a postmodern politics to address the crisis of modernity.

The twentieth century was one unlike any other in human history. By far it was the bloodiest, with millions of people dying in two world wars and numerous revolutions over ideas. Nazism, fascism, communism, and liberalism were the reigning ideologies over which people clashed. President Woodrow Wilson once stated that nationalism would be a moving force in the century, and millions more died in its name, whether in gas chambers in Auschwitz or death camps in Bosnia. Proof that ideas matter may reside in the amount of violence and carnage they produce.

The century also saw the development and use of the first atomic bombs, and debates raged over whether justice demanded "from each according to his abilities to each according to his needs";[55] or that inequalities were arbitrary unless they worked first to the advantage of the least representative person in society;[56] or that individuals were entitled to all of the fruits of their labors so long as no force or fraud was involved.[57] The first quote represents the sentiments of Marxism, the second the ideology of welfare state liberalism and a commitment to political and economic equality, while the third is a reference to conservative defenses of a free market society committed to political and economic liberty. In many ways, all three of these political philosophies represented different strains or aspects of modernity, appealing to political liberty or equality as basic goals, sustained by the logic of reason to defend their claims as truths.

By the latter part of the twentieth century, many wondered if political philosophy had meaning any more, or whether one could speak of political truths. Perhaps Thrasymachus and the Sophists were right in the enunciation of relativism. Enter postmodernism.

There are several ways in which postmodernism has challenged the assumptions of modernity. First, postmodern critics have questioned the way moderns depicted nature and the relationship of humans to it. Since at least the time of Francis Bacon, in the seventeenth century, moderns, with the possible exception of Rousseau, have viewed humans as separate from nature and the natural world, and movement out of a state of nature into society as positive progress.[58] In addition, moderns have generally seen nature as something to serve human needs, something to exploit. One goal of science, then, has been to help humans control and exploit nature to serve their needs. And moderns have linked freedom to rationality, seeing in reason the capacity to choose ends and make choices.

Postmodern challenges to modern values have recently attacked this vision of humans' relationship to nature, contending that they are not distinct from, but part of it. This means that modern industrial civilization is not the virtue it has been assumed to be; perhaps nature deserves more respect than it has received. Postmodern challenges to modernity thus give environmental movements significant theoretical and intellectual support. Environmentalists' demands to stop polluting and to refrain from cutting down trees in the tropical rain forests, for example, address some basic questions about how humans live and interact with one another and the physical world. Although environmental demands are political, at their core they also challenge broader and deeper cultural assumptions of modernity.[59]

A second way in which postmodernism has challenged modernism is by legitimizing the demands of oppressed political groups. If reasoned discourse is not the only judge of truth, arguments of other types, previously considered irrational, have a better chance of being heard without suppression. Hence postmodern challenges by Richard Rorty and Jean-François Lyotard claim that there are no grand narratives or values; instead local communities and traditions, or mininarratives, each determine their own values and truths.

This suggests a third legacy of postmodernism, justification of a new community-based, or communitarian, politics wherein each local community, however it is defined, is the judge of its own truth and behavior.[60] Communitarianism directly challenges modernity, shifting the focus of politics away from emphasis on autonomy and freedom of the individual and toward that of the collective, the community. Such a shift places individual freedom at the mercy of community sentiment, in the process questioning the priority on individual freedom that was important to moderns such as Hobbes and Locke when they attacked the power of divine right monarchy. Postmodern attempts to free oppressed voices may be undermining one of the core values of modernity, the linkage of freedom to reason. Thus postmodernism's communitarian values have mixed results for the causes of liberation and freedom.

Yet the lessons of postmodernism are profound in light of events at the end of the twentieth and the beginning of the twenty-first centuries. On the one hand, the fall of the Berlin Wall, the collapse of European Communism, and the apparent triumph of capitalism led some to conclude that the West had won, Liberalism had vanquished all its foes, and the end of history had arrived.[61] Yet the tragic events of September 11, 2001, a subsequent declaration of war against global terrorism by President George Bush, and his labeling of North Korea, Iran, and Iraq as part of an "axis of evil" raise the specter that ideas still matter and that western values have not necessarily won. As one political theorist describes it, the battle is perhaps now Jihad versus McWorld—a reference to a clash between western economic and political globalism and Islamic cultures.[62] Finally, even within the West debate rages over ideas and ideologies, evidenced by street protests in Seattle, Washington, and around the world, over the power of the World Trade Organization.

Have postmodern challenges to date altered twentieth- and twenty-first century political theory? In many instances, political theory remains trapped within the cosmological and metaphysical issues that have been problems since the days of the ancient Greeks. Then, philosophers such as Plato constructed a political theory in terms of how it modeled the unchanging truths and reality of the universe. Plato defended the idea of absolute truths against the Sophists, who believed that there were no such truths and that political relativism was the only option. Medieval thinkers adopted the absolutist position on religious grounds, placing belief in God at the center of the universe.

Moderns sought a rational edifice upon which to model knowledge and politics. Science changed how people perceived reality and the role of individuals and God in the universe. Copernicus displaced humans from the center of the cosmos, and then Newton redefined it as operating much like a clock or machine, without God's day-to-day involvement. Charles Darwin, by developing the theory of evolution, brought into question the origins of the human species and how different from other animals humans actually are. Freud then questioned how much control individuals even have over their own minds. Finally, Albert Einstein and other physicists developed theories of the universe questioning not only its origin but also whether it even has a center at all. The result of these repeated challenges was first to pit science against religion, leading to doubt of some of the most fundamental assumptions about the existence of God and human mortality. From there, reason turned on itself, asking if it could ever be certain of either the truth of its assertions or even its own method. As a result, by the end of the twentieth century, it no longer looked like there was a viable cosmology to anchor political theory as it had in the past.

CONCLUSION

After all the centuries of questioning, is it possible any longer to make assertions about politics and justice that can be considered and defended as true and final? Are there any new questions to ask or, more importantly, are there any new answers that really depart from the past? Is the lesson of philosophy one of moral and political relativism? And what role do humans have in a universe that perhaps lacks a center or definition? Does this lead philosophers to question human goals, purposes, identities, and even the basic possibility of truth? These are but some of the questions that remain at the beginning of a new millennium.

Notes

1. Edmund Husserl, *The Crisis of European Sciences and The Transcendental Phenomenology,* trans. David Carr (Evanston: Northwestern University Press, 1990); and Martin Heidegger, *Being and Time,* trans. J. Macquannie and E. Robinson (New York: Harper & Row, 1962).

2. Peter Gay, *Freud: A Life for Our Time* (New York: Norton, 1988), 547.

3. Bruno Bettelheim, *Freud and Man's Soul* (New York: Vantage, 1984), 101, 107.

4. Charles Brenner, *An Elementary Textbook on Psychoanalysis* (New York: Doubleday, 1957), 18.

5. Sigmund Freud, *Civilization and Its Discontents* (New York: Norton, 1989), 25.

6. *Civilization,* 38.

7. *Civilization,* 42.

8. *Civilization,* 69.

9. *Civilization,* 42, 49.

10. *Civilization,* 108–9.

11. Sigmund Freud, *Group Psychology and the Analysis of the Ego* (New York: Norton, 1959), 23–24.

12. Sigmund Freud, *Moses and Monotheism,* trans. K. Jones (New York: Knopf, 1939).

13. *Civilization,* 51–52.

14. Jeffrey B. Abramson, *Liberation and Its Limits: The Moral and Political Thought of Freud* (New York: Free Press, 1984), 8–9.

15. *Civilization,* 73.

16. *Civilization,* 81–82.

17. *Civilization,* 112.

18. Walter Kaufmann, *Nietzsche: Philosopher, Psychologist, Antichrist* (Princeton, N.J.: Princeton University Press, 1968); Steven E. Aschheim, *The Nietzsche Legacy in Germany: 1890–1990* (Berkeley: University of California Press, 1992), 233.

19. *Freud: A Life for Our Time,* 547; *Freud and Man's Soul,* 101.

20. Friedrich Nietzsche, *Beyond Good and Evil* (New York: Vintage, 1966), 204, 207.

21. Friedrich Nietzsche, *Twilight of the Idols,* in *Twilight of the Idols and the Antichrist* (New York: Penguin, 1968), 92.

22. *Beyond Good,* 207.

23. Friedrich Nietzsche, *On the Genealogy of Morals,* in *On the Genealogy of Morals and Ecce Homo* (New York: Vintage, 1967), 34; *The Antichrist,* in *Twilight,* 117; *Beyond Good,* 108; *Twilight,* 29–30.

24. Nietzsche, *Ecce Homo,* in *On Genealogy,* 310, where Nietzsche describes *Beyond Good and Evil* as "in all essentials a critique of modernity, not excluding the modern sciences, modern arts, and even modern politics."

25. *Beyond Good,* 97.

26. *On Genealogy,* 153.

27. *On Genealogy,* 150.

28. *On Genealogy,* 119.

29. *Twilight,* 33.

30. *On Genealogy,* 155.

31. Tracy Strong, *Friedrich Nietzsche and the Politics of Transfiguration* (Berkeley: University of California Press, 1988), 37.

32. *Beyond Good,* 136.

33. In fact, in *Ecce Homo,* 326, Nietzsche predicted that someday his name would be associated with reevaluation of all morality and questioning of the belief in a "moral world order."

34. Vincent Descombes, *Modern French Philosophy* (New York: Cambridge University Press, 1979); *Politics of Transfiguration,* 9.

35. Sonia Kruks, *Situation and Human Existence: Freedom, Subjectivity, and Society* (Boston: Unwin Hyman, 1990).

36. Thomas S. Kuhn, *The Structure of Scientific Revolutions* (Chicago: University of Chicago Press, 1970).

37. See ch. 11 in this book.

38. Paul Feyerabend, *Farewell to Reason* (London: Verso, 1987), 106–7.

39. Richard Rorty, *Philosophy and the Mirror of Nature* (Princeton, N.J.: Princeton University Press, 1980), 316–20.

40. Jean-François Lyotard, *Just Gaming* (Minneapolis: University of Minnesota Press, 1985), 22–23.

41. Michel Foucault, *The Order of Things* (New York: Vintage, 1973), 384–86.

42. Michel Foucault, *Power and Knowledge* (New York: Pantheon, 1980), 82–96; "Truth and Power" and "Panopticism," in *The Foucault Reader,* ed. P. Rabinow (New York: Pantheon, 1984), 56–60, 206–14.

43. David Harvey, *The Condition of Postmodernity* (New York: Basil Blackwell, 1989), 113–21, 327–29.

44. Sigmund Freud, "Femininity," in *Freud on Women: A Reader,* ed. Elisabeth Young-Bruehl (New York: Norton, 1990), 344.

45. *Freud on Women,* 20, 41.

46. Sigmund Freud, "Some Psychical Consequences of the Anatomical Distinction Between the Sexes," in *Freud on Women,* 304.

47. *Beyond Good,* 162.

48. Friedrich Nietzsche, *Thus Spoke Zarathustra,* trans. W. Kaufmann (New York: Viking, 1966), 67.

49. Linda J. Nicholson, "Introduction," in *Feminism/Postmodernism,* ed. L. J. Nicholson (New York: Routledge, 1990), 1–16, provides a good overview of the connections between feminism and postmodernism.

50. Sondra Farganis, "Postmodernism and Feminism," in *Postmodernism and Social Inquiry,* ed. D. R. Dickens and A. Fontana (New York: Guilford, 1994), 101–26.

51. Sandra Harding, *The Science Question in Feminism* (Ithaca, N.Y.: Cornell University Press, 1986); *Whose Science? Whose Knowledge? Thinking from Women's Lives* (Ithaca, N.Y.: Cornell University Press, 1991).

52. Carol Gilligan, *In a Different Voice: Psychological Theory and Women's Development* (Cambridge, Mass.: Harvard University Press, 1982).

53. Hannah Arendt, *The Human Condition* (New York: Anchor Books, 1959), 234–36.

54. *Politics of Transfiguration,* 76; Alasdair MacIntyre, *After Virtue* (Notre Dame, Ind.: University of Notre Dame Press, 1984), 38.

55. Karl Marx, "The Critique of the Gotha Program," in *The Marx–Engels Reader,* ed. Robert C. Tucker (New York: Norton, 1978).

56. John Rawls, *A Theory of Justice* (Cambridge, Mass.: Harvard University Press, 1971).

57. Robert Nozick, *Anarchy, State and Utopia* (New York: Basic Books, 1974).

58. Shane Phelan, "Intimate Distance: The Dislocation of Nature in Modernity," in *In the Nature of Things: Language, Politics, and the Environment,* ed. J. Bennett and W. Chaloupla, (Minneapolis: University of Minnesota Press, 1993), 44–64.

59. See Jane Bennett, *Thoreau's Nature: Ethics, Politics and the Wild* (Thousand Oaks, Calif.: Sage, 1994).

60. Michael Sandel, ed., *Liberalism and Its Critics* (New York: New York University Press, 1984), provides a good collection of essays by communitarians who question many modernist assumptions.

61. Francis Fukuyama, *The End of History and the Last Man* (New York: Avon Books, 1993).

62. Benjamin R. Barber, *Jihad v. McWorld* (New York: Times Books, 1995).

Additional Readings

Abramson, Jeffrey B. *Liberation and Its Limits: The Moral and Political Thought of Freud.* New York: Free Press, 1984.

Arac, Jonathan. *After Foucault.* New Brunswick, N.J.: Rutgers University Press, 1988.

Arac, Jonathan, ed. *Postmodernism and Politics.* Minneapolis: University of Minnesota Press, 1986.

Bettelheim Bruno. *Freud and Man's Soul.* New York: Vantage, 1984.

Connolly, William. *Political Theory and Modernity.* New York: Basil Blackwell, 1988.

Feyerabend, Paul. *Farewell to Reason.* London: Verso, 1987.

Feyerabend, Paul. *Science in a Free Society.* New York: Schocken, 1978.

Foster, Hal, ed. *The Anti-Aesthetic: Essays on Postmodern Culture.* Seattle: Bay Press, 1983.

Foucault, Michel. *The History of Sexuality,* vol. 1. New York: Vintage, 1980.

Foucault, Michel. *The Order of Things: An Archaeology of the Human Sciences.* New York: Vintage, 1973.

Gay, Peter. *Freud: A Life for Our Time.* New York: Norton, 1988.

Harvey, David. *The Condition of Postmodernity.* Cambridge: Basil Blackwell, 1989.

Kaufmann, Walter. *Nietzsche: Philosopher, Psychologist, Antichrist.* Princeton, N.J.: Princeton University Press, 1968.

Lyotard, Jean-François. *The Postmodern Condition: A Report on Knowledge.* Minneapolis: University of Minnesota Press, 1984.

Rorty, Richard. *Philosophy and the Mirror of Nature.* Princeton, N.J.: Princeton University Press, 1980.

Strong, Tracy. *Friedrich Nietzsche and the Politics of Transfiguration.* Berkeley: University of California Press, 1988.

Young-Bruehl, Elisabeth, ed. *Freud on Women: A Reader.* New York: Norton, 1990.

 Inventors of Ideas Online

Visit http://politicalscience.wadsworth.com/tannenbaum2 for links related to material in this chapter, including the full texts of some of Freud's and Nietzsche's major works.

20

INVENTORS OF IDEAS
AND THEIR INVENTIONS:
THE CONTINUING
CHALLENGE

THE IMPORTANCE OF IDEAS

Do ideas matter?[1] Or are all the writings of political philosophers mere words signifying nothing when compared to, say, economics?[2]

As far as we can tell, governments originated from the human need for physical security and to minimize economic scarcity. These were the earliest conceptions of the public interest or general welfare. Before there was any philosophy or political philosophy, the available political choices were either to live in a tribal setting[3] or under a monarch who ruled an army-empire.[4] In each form of government, violence was the primary means to effect political change, since the decision makers in both forms typically opposed change. Tribes expected conformity with ancient traditions that were not to be altered. The rulers of army-empires were usually dictators who governed the population as they did their armies, expecting total obedience to their commands, which were based on pure self-interest and determined after minimal consultation with other elites. It was the invention of ideas that led to the creation of additional political options. Ideas can still perform this function for us, for we all are born into a culture which, much like those tribal and imperial regimes, indoctrinates us in our early years that it is the greatest, indeed the only choice we should consider, and that the public interest demands our complete loyalty. The study of political philosophy is designed, at its best, to present alternative visions of the public interest.

Political actions and institutions are based on political ideas that political philosophers invent, or the absence of such ideas. Over time, great thinkers have responded to crises in their communities by voicing new ideas that respond to social problems. They were, and are, brilliant human beings who (like all of us) had flaws and limitations. But no matter which of their views you support, all their ideas are of great value, for they sought to offer novel ways to tackle problems by constructing new visions of politics that would bring order to the confusion they perceived. And, since they were philosophers, they gave *reasons* to support their claims about who should rule, how, and for whose benefit. As a result, they enable us to examine the values of our culture in comparative perspective, and give us an understanding of ideas that might not be part of the orthodox culture.

Be it Aristotle's thoughts on human nature and the universe, St. Augustine's vision of the two cities, Machiavelli's elites and masses, Hobbes's and Locke's images of the state of nature, Mary Wollstonecraft's criticism of gender roles, Mill's concept of liberty, Marx's critique of capitalism, or Freud's depiction of the human psyche, their ideas have produced change. They have done so as weapons of the weak raised against other ideas that served as tools of repressive regimes. They have been banners around which political movements and revolutions have rallied, helping to topple monarchies and create parliaments, replacing czars and emperors by republics and dictatorships of the proletariat, and dismantling iron curtains and walls in Berlin. Their ideas can be a force for uniting peoples, but they can also be used to divide, because nations and cultures may be moved to war against their national or cultural opponents who hold contrary ideas.

The study of political philosophy shows us patterns in the past that we can examine through artificial, abstract, but ultimately meaningful terms such as *ancient, medieval,* and *modern.* These terms, and related ideas, offer new perspectives for evaluating, even changing, current government structure, organization, and behavior in ways that might be useful in working toward the goal of expanding political progress.[5] Thus they increase our ability to act as free, responsible citizens by helping to liberate us from slavery to the few—or the many.[6] We are dependent on them because the great thinkers provide values that the rest of us could not have invented, even after decades of continual discussion with friends and other citizens. Without them, therefore, where else could we turn for these special insights?

CONTINUITY AND CHANGE

Political philosophers from Plato to the postmoderns have used terms such as *justice, authority, law,* and *government.* Does this validate the view of philosopher Alfred North Whitehead that Western thought "consists of a series of footnotes to Plato"? In a sense there is some continuity in the enterprise of political philosophy, since it has often consisted of the effort to understand the role of humans within the cosmos. More recently, the noted astronomer, Stephen Hawking, said of efforts to understand the origins of the universe:

> if we do discover a complete theory, it should in time be understandable in broad principles by everyone, not just a few scientists. Then we shall all, philosophers, scientists, and just plain ordinary people, be able to take part in the discussion of the question of why it is that we and the universe exist. If we find the answer to that, it would be the ultimate triumph of human reason—for then we would know the mind of God.[7]

But has the use of common terms varied so much over time that they meant different things to different thinkers? That would confirm the statement attributed to Heraclitus, an ancient Greek philosopher, that all is in flux, as demonstrated by the fact that "It is not possible to step twice into the same river."

Given an awareness of the past, we see that both are in a sense correct: Continual change is a constant fact of life. That change may be slower (as during the Middle Ages) or faster (as in the modern and postmodern eras). There may be those who seek to slow the pace of change (called "conservatives") or even reverse it by rejecting new ideas ("reactionaries"), as well as those who would gradually advance change ("liberals") or seek swifter transformation ("radicals") by accepting new ideas.

Understanding and reflecting on the development, change, and renewal of key ideas—the inventions of political philosophers—keeps alive the possibilities for both greater political progress and human freedom in a world where Thrasymachus and his successors, in common with the old tribal and imperial regimes, would rather we focus on the here and now and stop trying to invent and learn new ideas and practices. They would have us halt our questioning and even forget the inventors of ideas, thus yielding to the power of their tyranny as the only option for the future.

New political ideas can thus provide a perspective that tells us much about the meaning of life and the role politics and related thought play in helping establish a more meaningful life, as each of us understands it. In this way they not only help us make sense of a changing world; they also give a sense of direction for identifying where change is called for. However, they cannot show us the actual future; that is something we have to build, day by day.[8] At one time monarchy was the preferred choice for governments, while now various democratic forms typically linked to freedom and equality are the most desired. Who knows what new ideas will emerge and gain acceptance in the future? The ability to invent is limited by history or, as Karl Marx put it, individuals "make their own history, but they do not make it just as they please; they do not make it under circumstances chosen by themselves, but under circumstances directly found, given and transmitted from the past."[9] In other words the invention of ideas falls within a tradition and a history dating back over 2,500 years.

CONCLUSION

This book has provided a comparative framework for understanding and evaluating the ideas that comprise Western political philosophy by noting the major categories its contributors consider. These include methodology, a view of human nature, and the relationships between the individual and the collective, science and faith, reason and emotion, and gender and citizenship, among others. This work has also addressed the content of a number of new ideas created by their inventors.

The ancient philosopher Plato raised some hard questions about justice and order, and demonstrated how consideration of such questions can lead to standards for judging actual governments. Aristotle considered the role of balanced government, traditional community, and the hierarchical relationship between different kinds of communities in defining the public interest.

While most medieval thinkers focused on the religious community as the center of political thought and action, the early moderns deemphasized the role of community in favor of the individual. Machiavelli advocated individual liberty in a new setting called the nation-state, composed of virtuous citizens and officials, which would promote private freedom. Hobbes stressed the need of a clearly defined sovereign authority to minimize criminal violence and a political contract to define government's powers and limits. Locke underscored the importance of "property," a civil society that required a social contract, and a responsible legislature.

The neomoderns argued that the early modern focus on the individual did not provide "real" freedom, but actually corrupted individuals by removing them from their "natural" social context. Their inventions focused on identifying a new form of community that would overcome poverty and alienation. Thus Rousseau stressed political equality and the need for a general will as the basis for a new, smaller political community, one in which wealth would play no part in governmental policy making. Marx pointed to the role of economics throughout history as the fundamental precondition for a community that would realize history's goal of economic justice for all. Finally, the late modern John Stuart Mill sought to reconcile the emphasis of early and neomodern thinkers by considering the social value *as well as* the personal significance of individual liberty.

The enterprise of political philosophy over time emerges from a very human need: to reconcile the tension each of us feels in choosing between several perhaps incompatible politically relevant ideals. A central tension this book has focused on is the proper balance between the roles of the individual and the collective. It would seem that, by nature, we need both to be fully human. This observation leads to several questions worth considering in our ongoing quest to at least narrow the gap between these ideals while promoting political progress:

- Which of the philosophers came closest to reconciling individual and collective?
- How important were the inventions of each of the others in contributing to this reconciliation?
- How can we apply this reconciliation to some practical problems we face today, both in the domestic and international spheres?[10]
- What are some practical problems that do not seem amenable to political progress using the ideas of our inventors, and what does this say about the continuing challenge both to future inventors of ideas and to us as their potential implementers?[11]

Understanding the views of all the thinkers we have considered enables us to evaluate proposed "new" ideas, and to grasp how really "new" (or how recycled) they are. We should also realize that any idea, philosophy, or thinker is open to criticism, particularly from those who support a different general outlook, such as ancient, medieval, modern, or postmodern.

Consequently, one can react to opposing values like a strict Sophist who criticizes the contradictions in the values of others, but refuses to acknowledge one's own. Or, after concluding that no philosophy can ever lead in practice to an ideal world, one can develop an irony-laden, cool cynicism that gives up the attempt to work for change. Finally, we can become engaged in the effort to reconcile tensions and promote political progress by using honest criticism based on the views of philosophers with whom we do not agree while always being open to additional criticism, newer ideas, and further discourse.

If you would follow the last of these approaches, you might well begin by considering the following questions:

- What are some political ideas we all should—or should not—value?
- How highly would you value each of the following as best for all individuals and/or societies:

> Specific rights granted the individual against the government—especially not to be harmed or made worse off, physically, politically, economically, or socially. Included are the right to life and security of all people, particularly the innocent; just or fair treatment by government officials in cases of arrest, trial, or imprisonment, including due process of law and the presumption of innocence; freedom of speech, religion, and press; and freedom to join groups that pursue any goals in a nonviolent manner without being subject to discrimination or persecution.

> The right to be a productive member of society. Included are the right to not be enslaved, and the equal opportunity to work and to freely change one's occupation.

> Access for all to basic needs. Included are a minimum wage or standard of living that provides for a decent diet and housing; universal education, health care, old age insurance; and a clean environment.

Even though we might not ourselves be inventors of ideas, considering these and like issues will enable us to contribute in our own way to the enterprise of political philosophy. Then we might say, following Descartes,[12] "I think, therefore I am *free.*"

Notes

1. Recall Plato, Chapter 3, for a discussion of the reality of ideas.
2. See Marx, Chapter 18, for further discussion.
3. Examples include groupings such as the Hebrews of the Old Testament, Athens before Solon, Huns, Goths, and ever-diminishing numbers of indigenous peoples in the modern world who are mostly found in less-developed parts of the world.
4. For example, ancient Assyria, Babylonia, or Egypt.
5. For an earlier definition of political progress, see Chapter 1. It may be worthwhile to consider with which political thinkers and ideas you most agree; which ideas are most useful for political progress (note that the two are not necessarily the same); how much better you are able

to defend your own political ideals against challenge from the alternatives presented by various philosophers; and how much less (or more?) confused you are now about the significance of the inventors of ideas and their recommendations.

6. Indeed, without political philosophy what would freedom, or any other political idea, signify? See the warped misuse of ideas by Orwellian propagandists for some clues to the answer to this question.

7. Stephen Hawking, *A Brief History of Time: From the Big Bang to Blackholes* (New York: Bantam, 1990), p. 175.

8. A late modern philosopher not discussed in this book, Albert Camus, in *The Myth of Sisyphus and Other Essays* (New York: Random House, 1955) would say we are *condemned* to build our own futures. In *The Rebel: An Essay on Man in Revolt* (New York: Random House, 1956), Camus offers his thoughts about how we can do so.

9. Karl Marx, "The Eighteenth Brumaire of Louis Bonaparte," in *The Marx–Engels Reader*, ed. Robert C. Tucker (New York: Norton, 1978), p. 595.

10. Imagine, for example, that you are a citizen of nation X (not unlike the Soviet Union in 1991, or a newly created nation), one that is bankrupt: politically, economically, and morally. The leader has resigned, and you have to participate in the selection of a successor. There are two candidates for the job, each of whom will present a plan for reviving the nation. Each represents a different leadership style and different values, plans, and ideas. Your job: follow their campaigns and choose one for the job. The applicants: Socrates and Thrasymachus.

11. Consider, for example, the ongoing question of whether it is possible to reconcile traditional and modern doctrines and governments in a humane way without doing damage to either perspective. This challenge was brought home to Americans in the tragedy of 9/11/01. Or consider the problem of controlling nuclear, biological, and other weapons of mass destruction. Do the ideas of the thinkers point in fruitful directions, or are new ideas needed?

12. See Chapter 11, p. 214.

Additional Readings

Anastaplo, George. *But Not Philosophy: Seven Introductions to Non-Western Thought*. Lanham, Md.: Lexington Books, 2002.

Barber, Benjamin. *Jihad vs. McWorld*. New York: Times Books, 1995.

Friedman, Thomas. *The Lexus and the Olive Tree*. New York: Farrar Straus Giroux, 1999.

Honig, Bonnie. *Political Theory and the Displacement of Politics*. Ithaca, N.Y.: Cornell University Press, 1993.

Putnam, Robert. *Bowling Alone: The Collapse and Revival of American Community*. New York: Simon & Schuster, 2000.

Sterba, James. *Social and Political Philosophy: Classical Western Texts in Feminist and Multicultural Perspective*. 2d ed. Belmont, Calif.: Wadsworth, 1998.

INDEX

Charles I, King, 159, 174
Charles II, King, 159, 174
Christianity, 64, 74–88, 89. *See also*
    Roman Catholic Church
    and faith vs. reason, 82–83, 146,
        151
    Augustine and transformation of
        politics of, 77–82
    Bacon's attack on, 150–151
    cosmology of, 91, 145, 146, 147
    equality, human nature and, 75–76
    messages of, 74–76
    Rome and, 76–77
    science, impact of, 146–147
    Thomistic, 133, 134, 135, 136,
        151
    women, role of, 91
Cicero, Marcus Tullius, 6, 64, 66–71,
    74, 75, 93–94, 99, 107, 108
    and Aquinas, 96, 97
    and Aristotle, 67
    and Augustine, 66, 69, 77, 78,
        81, 82
    and Plato, 65–66, 67, 70
    On Duties, 67, 70, 71
    on family, 70
    on justice and law, 68–69
    on leaders, 70–71
    On the Commonwealth, 66, 67–68,
        69–70, 78
    On the Laws, 66–67, 68, 69–70
    On the Orator, 67, 71
    on virtue, 69–70
    women, role of, 70
Citizens/Citizenship
    Aristotle on, 54, 56, 57
    Hobbes on, 168–169
    Locke on, 182–184
    Machiavelli on, 123, 124, 126,
        128
    Mill on, 245
    Rousseau on, 201–204
City-states, 114
    polis *See* Polis
Civil disobedience, question of, in
    Antigone, 23, 24
Civilization, Freud on, 279, 280–281
Civil law, Hobbes on, 166–167
Civil religion, Rousseau on, 205–206

Civil society
    Hegel on, 261
    Locke on, 181, 186
    Wollstonecraft on, 221–222
Class
    Hobbes on, 168–169
    in Aristotle's polis, 54
    in Plato, 40–42
    Locke on, 182–184
    Marx on, 262–265
    structure and functions, Plato on,
        40–42
Collective vs. individual, 8, 50, 58
Columbus, Christopher, 268
Commonwealth
    Augustine on, 78, 81
    Cicero on, 67–69, 70, 93–94
    Hobbes on, 170
    John of Salisbury on, 93–94
    of Christians, 75
Communism, 270, 271, 272, 273, 289,
    291
    in Plato, 42
Communist League, 257
Communist Party, 272
Communitarianism, 290–291
Community
    Aristotle on, 51–54
    Christian, 75
    sense of, in Stoicism, 63, 64
Concept clarification, 13–14
Conciliarism, 134
Congregationalists, 159
Conscience, question of, in *Antigone*,
    23, 24–25
Conservatism, 289–290
Constantine, Emperor, 76, 77, 90, 106,
    109
Constitutional rule, Machiavelli on,
    126–127
Constitutions, Aristotle on, 49, 55
Contract, 171
    Rousseau on necessary conditions
        for, 204–206
    social contract *See* Social contract
Copernicus, Nicholas, 112, 147–149,
    155, 226
    heliocentric model of universe,
        147–149, 154, 155, 285, 291